The Stature of Theodore Dreiser

THE STATURE OF

a critical survey of the man and his work

edited by ALFRED KAZIN and CHARLES SHAPIRO

with an introduction by ALFRED KAZIN

Indiana University Press, Bloomington

THEODORE DREISER

Copyright © 1955 by the Indiana University Press
Library of Congress Catalog Card Number: 55–8446
Manufactured in the United States of America
by H. Wolff, New York
Designed by Marshall Lee

Acknowledgments

The staffs of the Indiana University and the University of Pennsylvania libraries were particularly generous with their kind help. This work is especially indebted to: Mr. Neil Boardman, Mr. Fred Hanes, Miss Geneva Warner, Mrs. Alice Crippen, Mrs. Margory Jewell, and Mrs. Barbara Warren of Indiana University; and Mrs. Neda Westlake and Mr. Adams of the Special Collection Division of the University of Pennsylvania Library (which houses the invaluable Dreiser collection); Mr. G. William Hume of Occidental College and Miss Ann Harris of Los Angeles aided in bibliographical research.

Special thanks are owing to Lawrence Janofsky for his patient and unusually understanding editing of the manuscript.

Contents

3 INTRODUCTION : *Alfred Kazin*

I Reminiscences : 13

15 THEODORE DREISER : *Edgar Lee Masters*
17 AN AMERICAN MEMORY : *Ludwig Lewisohn*
21 PORTRAIT OF DREISER : *Ford Madox Ford*
36 SOME CORRESPONDENCE WITH THEODORE DREISER :
   James T. Farrell

II Early Newspaper Reviews : 51

III The Critical Battle : 69

71 THE BARBARIC NATURALISM OF MR. DREISER :
   Stuart P. Sherman
81 AN APOLOGY FOR CRUDITY : *Sherwood Anderson*
84 THE DREISER BUGABOO : *H. L. Mencken*
92 THE ART OF THEODORE DREISER : *Randolph Bourne*
96 ASPECTS OF A PATHFINDER : *Thomas K. Whipple*
111 OUR FORMULA FOR FICTION : *Sinclair Lewis*
113 "AN AMERICAN TRAGEDY" : A HUMANISTIC
    DEMURRER : *Robert Shafer*
127 THEODORE DREISER REMEMBERED : *John Chamberlain*

132 REALITY IN AMERICA : *Lionel Trilling*

146 DREISER AND THE TRIUMPH OF ART : *Saul Bellow*

149 DREISER'S IMAGINATION : *John Berryman*

154 THEODORE DREISER : HIS EDUCATION AND OURS :
Alfred Kazin

161 DREISER'S DIFFICULT BEAUTY : *Alexander Kern*

IV Studies : 169

171 SISTER CARRIE : HER FALL AND RISE : *Malcolm Cowley*

182 DREISER'S "SISTER CARRIE" : *James T. Farrell*

188 THE SURVIVAL OF THE FITTEST : *Robert H. Elias*

204 OF CRIME AND PUNISHMENT : *F. O. Matthiessen*

219 THEODORE DREISER AND "THE BULWARK" :
Granville Hicks

225 DREISER AND NATURALISM REVISITED :
David Brion Davi

237 DREISER, AN INCONSISTENT MECHANIST : *Eliseo Vivas*

246 THEODORE DREISER AND THE DIVIDED STREAM :
Charles Child Walcutt

271 BIBLIOGRAPHY

The Stature of Theodore Dreiser

INTRODUCTION

"The impression is simply one of truth, and
therein lies at once the strength and the horror of it."

> —The Newark *Sunday News* on
> *Sister Carrie*, September 1, 1901.

At a time when the one quality which so many American writers have in
common is their utter harmlessness, Dreiser makes painful reading. The
others you can take up without being involved in the least. They are "literature"—beautiful, stylish literature. You are left free to think not of the
book you are reading but of the author, and not even of the whole man
behind the author, but just of his cleverness, his sensibility, his style.
Dreiser gets under your skin and you can't wait to get him out again: he
stupefies with reality:

> *Carrie looked about her, very much disturbed and quite sure that
> she did not want to work here. Aside from making her uncom-
> fortable by sidelong glances, no one paid her the least attention. She
> waited until the whole department was aware of her presence. Then
> some word was sent around, and a foreman, in an apron and shirt
> sleeves, the latter rolled up to his shoulders, approached.*
>
> *"Do you want to see me?" he asked.*
>
> *"Do you need any help?" said Carrie, already learning directness
> of address.*
>
> *"Do you know how to stitch caps?" he returned.*
>
> *"No, sir," she replied.*
>
> *"Have you had any experience at this kind of work?" he inquired.
> She answered that she had not.*
>
> *"Well," said the foreman, scratching his ear meditatively, "we do
> need a stitcher. We like experienced help, though. We've hardly got
> time to break people in." He paused and looked away out of the*

*window. "We might, though, put you at finishing," he concluded
reflectively.*

*"How much do you pay a week?" ventured Carrie, emboldened by
a certain softness in the man's manner and his simplicity of address.*

"Three and a half," he answered.

*"Oh," she was about to exclaim, but she checked herself and allowed
her thoughts to die without expression.*

*"We're not exactly in need of anybody," he went on vaguely, look-
ing her over as one would a package.*

*The city had laid miles and miles of streets and sewers through
regions where, perhaps, one solitary house stood out alone—a pioneer
of the populous ways to be. There were regions open to the sweeping
winds and rain, which were as yet lighted throughout the night with
long, blinking lines of gas-lamps, fluttering in the wind. Narrow
board walks extended out, passing here a house, and there a store, at
far intervals, eventually ending on the open prairie.*

*"He said that if you married me you would only get ten thousand
a year. That if you didn't and still lived with me you would get nothing at all. If you would leave me, or if I would leave you, you would
get all of a million and a half. Don't you think you had better leave
me now?"*

These are isolated passages—the first two from *Sister Carrie*, the third
from *Jennie Gerhardt*—and normally it would be as unkind to pick passages from Dreiser as it would be to quote for themselves those frustrated
mental exchanges that Henry James's characters hold with each other.
For Dreiser works in such detail that you never really feel the force of any
until you see the whole structure, while James is preoccupied with an
inner meditation that his own characters always seem to be interrupting.
But even in these bits from Dreiser there is an overwhelming impression
that puzzles and troubles us because we cannot trace it to its source. "One
doesn't see how it's made," a French critic once complained about some
book he was reviewing. That is the trouble we always have with Dreiser.
Carrie measuring herself against the immensity of Chicago, that wonderful night scene in which we see a generation just off the farms and out
of the small towns confronting the modern city for the first time; the
scene in which Hurstwood comes on Carrie sitting in the dark; Jennie
Gerhardt's growing solitude even after the birth of her child; Clyde
Griffiths and Roberta Alden walking around the haunted lakes when he
is searching for one where he can kill her—one doesn't see the man

writing this. We are too absorbed. Something is happening that tastes of fear, of the bottom loneliness of human existence, that just barely breaks into speech from the depths of our own souls; the planet itself seems to creak under our feet, and there are long lines of people bitterly walking to work in the morning dark, thinking only of how they can break through the iron circle of their frustration. Every line hurts. It hurts because you never get free enough of anything to ask what a character or a situation "really" means; it hurts because Dreiser is not trying to prove anything by it or to change what he sees; it hurts even when you are trying to tell yourself that all this happened in another time, that we are cleverer about life than Dreiser was. It hurts because it is all too much like reality to be "art."

It is because we have all identified Dreiser's work with reality that, for more than half a century now, he has been for us not a writer like other writers, but a whole chapter of American life. From the very beginning, as one can see in reading over the reviews of *Sister Carrie,* Dreiser was accepted as a whole new class, a tendency, a disturbing movement in American life, an eruption from below. The very words he used, the dreaminess of his prose, the stilted but grim matter-of-fact of his method, which betrayed all the envy and wonder with which he looked at the great world outside—all this seemed to say that it was not art he worked with but *knowledge,* some new and secret knowledge. It was this that the reviewers instantly felt, that shocked the Doubledays so deeply, that explains the extraordinary bitterness toward Dreiser from the first—and that excited Frank Norris, the publisher's reader (Dreiser looked amazingly like the new, "primitive" types that Norris was getting into his own fiction). Dreiser was the man from outside, the man from below, who wrote with the terrible literalness of a child. It is this that is so clearly expressed in Frank Doubleday's efforts to kill the book, in the fact that most literary and general magazines in the country did not review the book at all, that even some newspapers reviewed the book a year late, and that the tone of these early reviews is plainly that of people trying to accustom themselves to an unpleasant shock.

Sister Carrie did not have a bad press; it had a frightened press, with many of the reviewers plainly impressed, but startled by the concentrated truthfulness of the book. The St. Louis *Mirror* complained that "the author writes with a startling directness. At times this directness seems to be the frankness of a vast unsophistication. *** The scenes of the book are laid always among a sort of people that is numerous but seldom treated in a serious novel." The general reaction was that of the Newark *Sunday News,* almost a year after the book had been published. "Told with an unsparing realism and detail, it has all the interest of fact. . . .

The possibility of it all is horrible: an appalling arraignment of human society. And there is here no word of preachment; there are scarcely any philosophic reflections or deductions expressed. The impression is simply one of truth, and therein lies at once the strength and the horror of it."

This was the new note of the book, the unrelieved seriousness of it—but a seriousness so native, so unself-conscious, that Dreiser undoubtedly saw nothing odd about his vaguely "poetic" and questioning chapter titles, which were his efforts to frame his own knowledge, to fit it into a traditional system of thought, though he could not question any of his knowledge itself. Writing *Sister Carrie,* David Brion Davis comments, "was something like translating the Golden Plates." For Carrie was Dreiser's own sister, and he wrote without any desire to shock, without any knowledge that he could. Compare this with so "naturalistic" a book as Hardy's *Tess of the d'Urbervilles,* where the style is itself constantly commenting on the characters, and where the very old-fashioned turn of the prose, in all its complex urbanity, is an effort to interpret the story, to accommodate it to the author's own tradition of thought. Dreiser *could* not comment; so deeply had he identified himself with the story that there was no place left in it for him to comment *from*. And such efforts as he made to comment, in the oddly invertebrate chapter titles, were like gasps in the face of a reality from which he could not turn away. The book was exactly like a dream that Dreiser had lived through and which, in fact, after the failure of *Sister Carrie,* he was to live again, up to the very brink of Hurstwood's suicide.

It was this knowledge, this exclusive knowledge, this *kann nicht anders,* this absence of alternatives, that led people to resent Dreiser, and at the same time stunned the young writers of the period into instant recognition of his symbolic value to them. We never know how much has been missing from our lives until a true writer comes along. Everything which had been waiting for them in the gap between the generations, everything which Henry James said would belong to an "American Balzac"—that world of industrial capitalism which, James confessed, had been a "closed book" to him from his youth—everything free of "literature" and so free to become literature, now became identified with this "clumsy" and "stupid" ex-newspaperman whose book moved the new writers all the more deeply because they could not see where Dreiser's genius came from. To the young writers of the early twentieth century, Dreiser became, in Mencken's phrase, the Hindenburg of the novel—the great beast who pushed American life forward for them, who went on, blindly, unchangeably, trampling down the lies of gentility and Victorianism, of Puritanism and academicism. Dreiser was the primitive, the man from the abyss, the stranger who had grown up outside the Anglo-Saxon middle-class

Protestant morality and so had no need to accept its sanctions. In Sherwood Anderson's phrase, he could be honored with "an apology for crudity"; and in fact the legend that *Sister Carrie* had been suppressed by the publisher's wife was now so dear to the hearts of the rising generation that Mrs. Doubleday became a classic character, the Carrie Nation of the American liberal epos, her ax forever lifted against "the truth of American life." So even writers like Van Wyck Brooks, who had not shared in the bitterness of Dreiser's early years, and who as socialists disapproved of his despair, now defended him as a matter of course—he cleared the way; in the phrase that was to be repeated with increasing meaninglessness through the years, he "liberated the American novel."

Dreiser now embodied the whole struggle of the new American literature. The "elderly virgins of the newspapers," as Mencken called them, never ceased to point out his deficiencies; the conservative academicians and New Humanists, the old fogeys and the young fogeys—all found in Dreiser everything new, brutal and alien they feared in American life. Gertrude Atherton was to say during the first World War that Dreiser represented the "Alpine School of Literature"—"Not a real American could be found among them with a magnifying glass"; Mary Austin was to notice that "our Baltic and Slavic stock will have another way than the English of experiencing love, and possibly a more limited way. . . . All of Theodore Dreiser's people love like the peasants in a novel by Bojer or Knut Hamsun. His women have a cowlike complaisance such as can be found only in people who have lived for generations close to the soil"; Stuart Sherman, in his famous article of 1915 on "The Barbaric Naturalism of Theodore Dreiser," made it clear that Dreiser, "coming from that 'ethnic' element of our mixed population," was thus unable to understand the higher beauty of the American spirit.

So Dreiser stood in no-man's-land, pushed ahead like a dumb ox by one camp, attacked by the other. Everything about him made him a polemical figure; his scandals, miseries, and confusions were as well-known as his books. The "liberals," the "modernists," defended books like *The "Genius"* because "it told the truth"—and how delighted they must have been when John S. Sumner tried to get the book banned in 1915 and anybody who *was* anybody (including Ezra Pound, John Reed and David Belasco) rushed to its defense. To the English novelists of the period (and *Sister Carrie* owed its sudden fame to the edition Heinemann brought out in London) he was like a powerhouse they envied amid the Georgian doldrums of literary London. How much of that fighting period comes back to you now when you discover Arnold Bennett on his feverish trips to America identifying all the raw, rich, teeming opportunities of American life with Dreiser, or listen to Ford Madox Ford—"Damn it all, it *is* fun to see that poor old language, that vehicle for conveying moderated thoughts, having the guts kicked out of it, like a deflated football, over all the fields of the boundless Middle West." While Mencken, in Dreiser's name, slew William Lyon Phelps in his thousands, the young English discovered that Dreiser was the friend of art. Each side in the controversy used Dreiser, and each, in its own way, was embarrassed. How many times did the young Turks have to swallow Dreiser's bad books, to explain away his faults, and how clear it is from reading Paul Elmer More (who was a deeper critic than his opponents and would have been almost a great one if he had not always tried to arm himself against American life) that he was always more moved by Dreiser's cosmic doubts than he could confess. More settled the problem, as he settled every writer he feared, by studying the man's "philosophy"—where he could show up Dreiser to his heart's content, and, in a prose that could not have been more removed from the actualities of the subject, prove that he had disposed forever of this intellectual upstart.

This pattern remained to the end—Dreiser was the great personifier. When he went to Russia, even the title of the book he wrote had to begin with Dreiser rather than with Russia; when Sinclair Lewis praised Dreiser in his Nobel Prize speech, he did so with all the enthusiasm of a Congressman trying for the farm vote; when Dreiser delivered himself of some remarks about Jews, the *Nation* was not so much indignant as bewildered that this son of the common people could express such illiberal sentiments; when he spoke against England at the beginning of the Second World War, there was a similar outcry that Dreiser was letting the masses down. It is typical of Dreiser's symbolic importance that a writer now so isolated as James T. Farrell has been able to find support for his own work only in Dreiser's example; that the word *plebeian* has always been used either to blacken Dreiser or to favor him; that Eisenstein suffered so long to make a film of *An American Tragedy* that would be the ultimate exposure of American capitalism. When Dreiser joined the Communists, his act was greeted as everything but what it really was—the lonely and confused effort of an individual to identify himself with a group that had taken him up in his decline; when he died in 1945, in the heyday of American-Soviet friendship, one left-wing poet announced that Dreiser's faults had always been those of America anyway, that he was simply America writ large—"Much as we wish he had been surer, wiser, we cannot change the fact. The man was great in a way Americans uniquely understand who know the uneven contours of their land, its storms, its droughts, its huge and turbulent Mississippi, where his youth was spent." Even Dreiser's sad posthumous novels, *The Bulwark,* and *The Stoic,* each of which centers around a dying old man, were written about with forced enthusiasm, as if the people attacking them were afraid of being called reactionary, while those who honestly liked them reported that they were *surprisingly* good. And how F. O. Matthiessen suffered all through the last year of his life to do justice to Dreiser as if that would fulfill an *obligation* to the cause of "progressivism" in America.

But soon after the war all this changed—Dreiser was now simply an embarrassment. The reaction against him was only partly literary, for much of it was founded on an understandable horror of the fraudulent "radicals" who had been exploiting Dreiser before his death. And thanks not a little to the cozy prosperity of a permanent war economy, America, it seemed, no longer required the spirit of protest with which Dreiser had been identified. The writers were now in the universities, and they all wrote about writing. No longer hoary sons of toil, a whole intelligentsia, post-Communist, post-Marxist, which could not look at Alger Hiss in the dock without shuddering at how near they had come to his fate, now tended to find their new ideology in the good old middle-class virtues. A new genteel tradition had come in. Writing in America had suddenly become very conscious that literature is made with words, and that these words should look nice on the page. It became a period when fine writing was everything, when every anonymous smoothie on *Time* could write cleaner prose about God's alliance with America than poor old Dreiser could find for anything, when even the *Senior Scholastic,* a magazine intended for high-school students, complained of Dreiser that "some of the writing would shock an English class." It is of this period, in which we live, that Saul Bellow has noted in his tribute to Dreiser: "I think that the insistence on neatness and correctness is one of the signs of a modern nervousness and irritability. When has clumsiness in composition been felt as so annoying, so enraging? The 'good' writing of the *New Yorker* is such that one experiences a furious anxiety, in reading it, about errors and lapses from taste; finally what emerges is a terrible hunger for conformity and uniformity. The smoothness of the surface and its high polish must not be marred. One has a similar anxiety in reading a novelist like Hemingway and comes to feel that in the end Hemingway wants to be praised for the offenses he does not commit. He is dependable; he never names certain emotions or ideas, and he takes pride in that—it is a form of honor. In it, really, there is submissiveness, acceptance of restriction."

The most important expression of the reaction against Dreiser is Lionel Trilling's "Reality in America." This essay expresses for a great many people in America just now their impatience with the insurgency that dominated our famously realistic fiction up to the war, and not since Paul Elmer More's essay of 1920 has anyone with so much critical insight made out so brilliant a case against Dreiser; not since William Dean Howells supported Stephen Crane's *Maggie* and not *Sister Carrie* has anyone contrasted so sharply those notorious faults of style and slovenly habits of thought which our liberal criticism has always treated as "essentially social and political virtues" with the wonderful play of mind and fertility of resource one finds in Henry James. Never has the case against the persistent identification of Dreiser with "reality" in America—coarse, heavy, external reality—been put with so much intellectual passion. For Mr. Trilling is writing against the decay of a liberal movement ruined largely by its flirtation with totalitarianism, by its disregard of human complexity and its fear of intellect. No one who has followed the extent to which our liberal critics have always acknowledged that Dreiser *is* a bad thinker—and have excused it on the grounds that the poor man at least "told the truth about American life"—can help but share Mr. Trilling's impatience with what has recently passed in this country for liberal "imagination."

But may it not be suggested that Henry James as a cultural hero serves us as badly as Dreiser once did? What happens whenever we convert a writer into a symbol is that we lose the writer himself in all his indefeasible singularity, his particular inimitable genius. A literature that modeled itself on Dreiser would be unbearable; a literature that saw all its virtues of literature in Henry James would be preposterous. If one thing is clear about our addiction to Henry James just now, it is that most of our new writing has nothing in common with James whatever. For James's essential quality is his intellectual appetite—"all life belongs to you"—his unending inner meditation, and not the air of detachment which so misleads us whenever we encounter it on the surface of the society James wrote about—the only society he knew, and one he despaired of precisely because it was never what it seemed. Just now, however, a certain genteel uninvolvement is dear to us, while Dreiser's bread lines and street-car strikes, his suffering inarticulate characters, his Chicago, his "commonness"—are that bad dream from which we have all awakened. As Dreiser's faults were once acclaimed as the virtues of the common man, so now we are ashamed of him because he brings up everything we should like to leave behind us.

There is no "common man"—though behind the stereotype (how *this* executioner waits!) stand those who may yet prepare all too common a fate for us all. Literary people, as a class, can get so far away from the experience of other classes that they tend to see them only symbolically. Dreiser as "common man" once served a purpose; now he serves another. The basic mistake of all the liberal critics was to think that he could ever see this world as something to be ameliorated. They misjudged the source of Dreiser's strength. This is the point that David Brion Davis documents so well in his study of what Dreiser and the early naturalists really believed. For as Mr. Davis shows, these writers and painters were "naturalists" only in the stark sense that the world had suddenly come down to them divested of its supernatural sanctions. They were actually obsessed with the transcendental possibilities of this "real" world; like Whitman, they gloried in the beauty of the iron city. In their contemplative acceptance of this world, in their indifference to social reform, in their awe before life itself, they were actually not in the tradition of political "liberalism" but in that deeper American strain of metaphysical wonder which leads from the early pietists through Whitman to the first painters of the modern city.

This gift of contemplativeness, of wonder, of reverence, even, is at the center of Dreiser's world—who can forget the image of the rocking chair in *Sister Carrie,* where from *this* cradle endlessly rocking man stares forever at a world he is not too weak but too bemused to change? And it is this lack of smartness, this puzzled lovingness for the substance of all our mystery, that explains why we do not know what to *do* with Dreiser today. For Dreiser is in a very old, a very difficult, a very lonely American tradition. It is no longer "transcendentalist," but always it seeks to transcend. This does not mean that Dreiser's philosophy is valuable in itself, or that his excursions into philosophy and science—fields for which he was certainly not well equipped—have to be excused. It does mean that the vision is always in Dreiser's work, and makes it possible. Just as the strength of his work is that he got into it those large rhythms of wonder, of curiosity, of amazement before the power of the universe that give such largeness to his characters and such unconscious majesty to life itself, so the weakness and instability of his work is that he could become almost too passive before the great thing he saw out there, always larger than man himself. The truth is, as Eliseo Vivas says in his essay, that Dreiser is "not only an American novelist but a universal novelist, in the very literal sense of the word. The mystery of the universe, the puzzle of destiny, haunts him; and he, more than any other of his contemporaries, has responded to the need to relate the haunting sense of puzzlement and mystery to the human drama. No other American novelist of his generation has so persistently endeavored to look at men under the aspect of eternity. It is no . . . paradox, therefore, that . . . while Dreiser tries to demonstrate that man's efforts are vain and empty, by responding to the need to face the problem of destiny, he draws our attention to dimensions of human existence, awareness of which is not encouraged by current philosophical fashions. . . ." To understand how this gets into Dreiser's work one must look not back of it but into it for that sense of "reality" which he thirsted for—that whole reality, up to the very shores of light, that made him cry out in *Jennie Gerhardt:* "We turn our faces away from the creation of life as if that were the last thing that man should dare to interest himself in, openly."

This is what makes Dreiser so painful—in his "atheism," his cosmology; this is what dismays us in our sensible culture, just as it bothered a generation that could never understand Dreiser's special bitterness against orthodox religion, against the churches; this is what drove Dreiser to look for God in the laboratories, to write essays on "My Creator." He may have been a "naturalist," but he was certainly not a materialist. What sticks in our throats is that Dreiser is outside the agreed boundaries of our concern, that he does not accept our "society" as the whole of reality, that he may crave after its fleshpots, but does not believe that getting along is the ultimate reach of man's effort. For we live in a time when traditionalists and "progressives" and ex-progressives alike are agreed that the man not to be trusted is the man who does not fit in, who has no "position," who dares to be distracted—when this great going machine, this prig's paradise in which we live just now, is the best of all possible worlds.

Dreiser committed the one sin that a writer can commit in our society —he would not accept this society itself as wholly real. And it is here, I think, that we can get perspective on his famous awkwardness. For what counts most with a writer is that his reach should be felt as well as his grasp, that words should be his means, not his ends. It is this that Malcolm Cowley noticed when he wrote that "there are moments when Dreiser's awkwardness in handling words contributes to the force of his novels, since he seems to be groping in them for something on a deeper level than language." This is what finally disturbs us about Dreiser in a period when fine writing is like a mirror that gives back our superficiality. Dreiser hurts because he is always looking to the source; to that which broke off into the mysterious halves of man's existence; to that which is behind language and sustains it; to that which is not ourselves but gives life to our words.

Alfred Kazin

Reminiscences

Edgar Lee Masters

THEODORE DREISER

Jack o' Lantern tall shouldered,
One eye set higher than the other,
Mouth cut like a scallop in a pie,
Aslant showing powerful teeth.
Swaying above the heads of others.
Jubilant with fixed eyes, scarcely sparkling.
Moving about rhythmically, exploding in laughter.
Touching fingers together back and forth,
Or toying with a handkerchief.
And the eyes burn like a flame at the end of a funnel.
And the ruddy face glows like a pumpkin
On Halloween!

Or else a gargoyle of bronze
Turning suddenly to life
And slipping suddenly down corners of stone
To eat you:
Full of questions, objections,
Distinctions, instances.
Contemptuous, ironical, remote,
Cloudy, irreverent, ferocious,
Fearless, grim, compassionate, yet hateful,
Old, yet young, wise but virginal.
To whom everything is new and strange:
Whence he stares and wonders,
Laughs, mocks, curses.
Disordered, yet with a passion for order
And classification—hence the habitual
Folding into squares of a handkerchief.

From *The Great Valley,* The Macmillan Co., 1916.

Or else a well cultivated and fruitful valley,
But behind it unexplored fastnesses,
Gorges, precipices, and heights
Over which thunder clouds hang,
From which lightning falls,
Stirring up terrible shapes of prey
That slink about in the blackness.
The silence of him is terrifying
As if you sat before the sphinx.
The look of his eyes makes tubes of the air
Through which you are magnified and analyzed.
He needs nothing of you and wants nothing.
He is alone, but content,
Self-mastered and beyond friendship,
You could not hurt him.
If he would allow himself to have a friend
He would part from that friend forever
And in a moment be lost in wonder
Staring at a carved rooster on a doorstep,
Or at an Italian woman
Giving suck to a child
On a seat in Washington Square.

Soul enwrapped demi-urge
Walking the earth,
Stalking Life!

Ludwig Lewisohn

AN AMERICAN MEMORY

Prose and veracity came stalking in; they came, very properly, from the
Middle West. The East was hopelessly cultured and colonial. Rude men,
men lacking in the traditional polish of the Anglo-American gentleman,
made their appearance. Their rudeness, their un-English names, the very
solecisms and barbarisms of their style, were like rain on parched earth.
All was dust. Youths like myself who adored style and finish and form,
and understood them too, were willing, for the hour, the day, the year, to
have them forgotten, to have them trampled on. The time would come
when form could be again married to vigor and beauty need no longer
be estranged from veracity. And quietly I hoped that this reunion would
be in the days of my maturity my special contribution to the literature of
my country and my period. . . . But in 1907 anything that was not rose-
water tasted sweet upon the tongue. . . .

It was in the offices of B. W. Dodge & Company that, like a symbol of
the life and literature to come, Dreiser first appeared on my horizon. He
had on an elegant overcoat with a curved-in waist line. It didn't suit him
at all and represented his romantic yearning for brownstone fronts and
plush furniture and chandeliers full of prisms. The great rude man who
was to renew American literature had romanticized the trimmings of the
'nineties. It was from his own depths that he had written those words in
Sister Carrie that sounded so amusingly like a line of Pope, "Who would
not dream upon a gilded chair?" Not only did he wear that preposterous
overcoat; he still went out on Sunday mornings in a Prince Albert and
a silk hat. He had an apartment somewhere near Morningside Park. In
this matter of the apartment uptown and the Sunday-morning walks an
alien influence may have wrought upon him. Considerations of business
may also have entered at this particular period. But that chapter in his
life was even then running down. Ben Dodge, an intelligent, hearty, generous, bearded fellow, with a slightly rowdy flavor of an older America
about him, was fast drinking himself to death. Another partner of the
firm—canny, suburban, church-going—was transferring his interests. The

From *Cities and Men,* Harper & Brothers, 1927.

last act of the Stuyvesant Press (founded in connection with B. W. Dodge) was to print Harris Merton Lyon's *Sardonics*. The whole undertaking collapsed. Dreiser turned elsewhither. I believe that he bought an interest in the *Bohemian Magazine*. Then, except for occasional letters, we lost sight of each other.

We foregathered again several years later. He had assumed his right and permanent character and attitude. He loomed in a Greenwich Village apartment. Gone were the trappings of the last pangs of youthful yearning. He drank little and did not smoke at all. He spoke with a somber, ironic joy of his now thoroughly established reactions to literature and civilization. His explanation of all the phenomena of life in crude biochemical terms had, philosophically considered, something childlike about it. What impressed one was the vast, brooding, sorrowful, compassionate vision of life that chose to express itself thus. From this jeering and sometimes ribald talk there came to me the pity in his large heart out of which he had created his incomparable old men: Gerhardt, the old Irish politician in *The Financier,* the tragic Jewish father in *The Hand of the Potter*. Paintings in the latest grotesque fashion hung on his wall on Tenth Street. These paintings may have been a substitute for the gilded chair of other years. Out of his starved youth there remained a longing which had once been fixed upon "mansions"; now it was fixed on sophistication. It did not, luckily, soften his tread or alter his direction. He crashed on. . . .

Nothing could alter him, nothing affect him. That was his great strength. I cared more for the rhetorical properties of letters then than I do now. Dreiser knew how much I admired him. And so he took it very kindly, though a little wonderingly, when I pointed out to him that "betimes" doesn't mean sometimes, that it was ghastly to sprinkle a page with such phrases as "no less" or "of sorts," ghastly to call anything from a building to an orchard an "affair" and that "amble" and several other favorite words of his didn't mean what he thought they did.

We used to meet at the Kloster Glocke (later to be called the Convent Bell) on Fourth Avenue. Dreiser ate a certain fish food there with unvarying relish. The beer was memorable and one of the waiters a chap who affected an acquaintance with arts and served us with gusto. To our favorite table Dreiser brought a story he had just finished. I went over it with him, confining my criticisms and corrections to purely formal matters. He was extremely good-humored and really docile about it all. When the story appeared, I found all my corrections embodied in the text. But Dreiser had been busy making corrections, too. For every barbarism I had eliminated, two had slipped in. I knew then that it mattered little. Now I know that, in the deeper sense, it matters not at all. Nor has it, I think, been sufficiently emphasized in all the public twaddling about Dreiser's bad writing that he does not always write badly even on the purely formal side. He is simply insensitive and uncritical on that side. Yet in the very story we discussed at the Kloster Glocke there appears suddenly amid masses of particularly awkward prose this: "Simple natures that fasten themselves like lichens on the stones of circumstance and weather their days to a crumbling conclusion." Dreiser probably doesn't see the difference between that and certain other sentences on the same page. But I single it out, amid many others, as a warning to the glib elegants who declare unqualifiedly that Dreiser cannot write.

The result of these various talks and conferences was that Dreiser asked me to write a little book about him. *The Genius* had been withdrawn from circulation. His fundamental work was in hand. I do not know whether the late Stuart Sherman had already formulated his theory of the "animal behavior" of Dreiser's characters. But the time was ripe for a biographical and critical interpretation. In any continental country this would have been seen. But in America there still prevailed the silly notion that only the dead are worth discussing. Publishers looked coldly upon our plan, which was consequently abandoned.

Of many subsequent meetings two stand out in my memory as significant of the new world that was being built up within America by a group of curious, fearless and impassioned spirits. Dreiser asked a number of men to come to his apartment to discuss the publication of an annual which was to illustrate the new literature as well as the new art. His place was lit by candles and the shadows were heavy. Detaching themselves from them, I remember especially the forms of Robert Henri and George Bellows. Henri was rather elegiac about the project; Bellows was blasphemously enthusiastic. He had both head and light. Literature cannot have been very heavily represented. Mencken was absent and I remember being irritated by George Nathan's glossy and purring detachment. The powerful natures in literature are always propagandists on one side. Dreiser really wanted the plan to come to something. He was really more concerned over the new art than over his special contribution to it. But the meeting scattered without coming to any practical conclusions and of the whole project no more was heard.

The second meeting took place during the most depressing period of the war. Dreiser and I had had luncheon alone together in a little Italian restaurant downtown. We walked toward his house in a flurry of early snow. He lifted his cane toward the sky with an unusual passion and denounced the blood and hypocrisy and tyranny of the war and derived these things rightly from certain ethical concepts which he declared to be the historic flails and scourges of the race. His grim and reasoned denunciation heartened me. His agreement with my sentiments and opinions gave me an assurance of the hope that it might be possible to build a decenter world than the old world of patriotism and repression and conformity to powers that might at any moment give the command of murder of both the body and the soul. Standing there in the snow with Dreiser, I remembered Charleston and the smiling sentiments of its gentry and its literature. We were seeing what such sentiments and such writing come to. We were seeing that the new literature was more than a matter of form or fashion or technique. It was the most vital of the forces that could save an otherwise ruined world. I left Dreiser still heavily gesticulating in his condemnation of the evil that was darkening the sun. I was more than ever convinced that he was not only a great writer, but a good man and a lover of his kind.

Ford Madox Ford

PORTRAIT OF DREISER

When I converse with Mr. Dreiser, he converts me, according to the temporary set of the tide of his passions, into a simulacrum of something that for the moment he abhors. I become for him a Nazi Jew-baiter; a perfidious Briton; an American financier; the proprietor of brothels in Paris; an unpractical poet; a mere unit floating in and indistinguishable from eleven hundred million similar units; a Jewish proprietor of chain-goods stores; a hereditary aristocrat; an incapable and reactionary small farmer; a contemptible member of the official American Communist Party; a Washington hanger-on. . . . At all these simulacra of myself for hours and hours Mr. Dreiser hurls gigantic trains of polyphonic, linked insults. . . .

I have the sensation that I am walking in the dark along a railway line whilst Mr. Dreiser hurls at me immense handfuls of Pullman cars that go hurtling away over my head, invisible, resonant, innocuous. . . . There is a war time psycho-mnemonic reason for this image which I will later explain. . . . In the meantime, at odd moments, I say in a still, small, yet penetrating treble:

"Don't be so angry, Dreiser . . . *I* don't care." Because, whatever simulacrum of myself he may be in the mood to rid the earth of, it is certain not to be the *persona* of the mood I am in for the moment.

Immediately silence falls. Then Mr. Dreiser says quickly and with almost feminine solicitude:

"What? What? . . . No, I'm not angry. . . . You mustn't mind me. . . . I'm emphatic by nature. . . . It doesn't mean anything. . . . All the same there *are* sixteen and a half million Knights of Columbus like you in this country. . . . That's a problem, isn't it? . . . You'll admit that it's a problem. We've got to get rid of all you lecherous and insupportable swine. . . . To Hell with you all. You're turning this country into the Pope's stamping ground. . . . You're . . ."

I am for the moment, say, in the mood to be a French Royalist. I advance along the rails that are darkly gleaming in the light of the star-shells over Albert behind me. I advance cautiously but with valour, in my

From *Portraits From Life*, Houghton Mifflin Co., 1937.

mind whiffling before me a light rapier with which immediately or sooner or later I shall destroy the Titan who, couched in the dark valley behind Martinpuich, is hurling all those too elevated railway trains over my head. . . . It is in fact exactly the mood of the last duty I performed in 1916 before I lost my memory. The railway trains then overhead were our own naval howitzer shells which made exactly the noise of weary trains. . . . That mood always falls upon me when I confront the belli-cosities of this giant of wrath and war who on occasion, with the swiftness of light, will become a prodigy of almost feminine solicitude . . . and then will go on all over again. Until he is exhausted.

It is with me conversational technique. I represent, as the reader will by this time no doubt have observed, the novelists who believe that there is a way of doing things as opposed to the novelists of genius. These last set vine-leaves in their hairs, grasp pens as large as weavers' beams, and with enormous strokes pen polyphonic rhapsodies, accusing us meanwhile of carving ingenious patterns with tooth picks on peachstones. . . . or of being poets. . . . For when Mr. Dreiser wishes finally to indicate that I am a sort of fusionless village imbecile he says:

"You're a poet. . . . That's what you are. A regular poet."

Naturally I retort:

"It's you who are the poet," and so get under way.

He, at the end of his voice's tether, sits himself down at his long, Esherick-made table and lays out the cards for a Miss Milligan. . . . In a voice so low as to be irritatingly half-inaudible I take up the discussion where he has left it. . . . I don't know if I am as large as Mr. Dreiser. If he has the advantage in height I take it out in girth; or, if I am a little taller, he is larger-boned. At any rate we are both big and tempestuous. But when it comes to voice in argument his is that of several town bulls, mine is as small and persistent as that of the cricket in a stone wall. I have too the advantage that my accent is unusual for Mr. Dreiser. . . .

I say . . . half-whispering:

"Obviously the first duty of Christendom . . . if we can be called Christendom any more. . . ."

Mr. Dreiser says:

"What? . . . What's that? I can't hear you . . ."

I repeat, only a quarter-whispering:

"The first duty of Christendom is to succour and comfort the brothers and collateral descendants of Our Lord . . ."

A look of horrified bewilderment comes over Mr. Dreiser's face. He slams the ten of diamonds on the nine of hearts when it should have been clubs. He is speechless in his incredulity.

I continue:

"I suppose our comity of nations . . ."

And I go on and on, digressing, speaking almost inaudibly, starting one hare and chasing another . . . I continue to suppose we are a comity of nations in the Western Hemisphere; that we can call that comity Christendom . . . Well, but even Mahometans still reserve special honours for the descendants of their Prophet; the Chinese for those of Konfutsze. . . . Occasionally Mr. Dreiser dashes out, like a bull at a picador. But he is exhausted by having shouted at me for four hours and I avoid his charge by making another digression of subject.

As a rule he gets the last blow in and when I talk I am usually wondering how he will do it. . . . The last time it went like this. It was past two in the morning after a Christmas dinner. He stood up violently; cast his cards all over the long table and exclaimed:

"You hell of a fellow. You're keeping the whole house up with your mumbling. . . . You'd go on . . . till the conversion of the Jews."

There is of course no answer to that. You can't keep whole households up and it is not really proper to oppose anyone who can suddenly drag in for your confusion a line from the finest poem in the English language. So we stagger off to our couches.

From all which it will be perceived that as the poet says;

I've a friend across the sea; I love him and he likes me.
I'll murder you with savage looks if you don't admire his books.

And I will, too.

I first came in contact with Dreiser in, I think, late 1914 . . . and the event, as all the major events of an existence are apt to be, was for me rather symbolical. I was Battalion Orderly Officer in Cardiff Castle at the time and part of that humble job being the disposal of hundreds of character sheets, a task taking hours and calling for no attention, I sent my bâtman from the guardroom into the castle to fetch me a book that the *Outlook* of London had asked me to review as a farewell to their public.

I had for years been writing for that journal a weekly article about anything that came into my head . . . mostly about books, but quite frequently about any passing event that amused me. And it was a symptom of the naïveté not merely of myself but of the ordinary public school Englishman of my day that I should be shocked by the howls about German atrocities that were going up from the more lively and excitable press. I wrote therefore a pained editorial in the *Outlook* suggesting that it would be a good thing if the Press in commenting on the proceedings of the Enemy Country should do so in terms of the 'gallant Enemy' as had been the case in the Napoleonic Wars and the Middle Ages. I disliked thinking that civilization should in these matters have receded six or seven hundred years. War, I thought . . . and a good many of my compatriots then thought too . . . should be conducted along the lines of some sort of polite Queensberry rules before a well-conducted audience such as you see every fourth of July in the grandstands at Lords for the Eton and Harrow match that closes the London season.

And it was symptomatic of the rather languidly Tory audience of the *Outlook* of those days that my article evoked no protest from my readers, save for one letter written by a very old lady who said that, if I wanted the Enemy forces to win I was at liberty to do so, but that it was rude to say so in public. . . . Nevertheless it had become obvious to me that for my sort of philosophy the times were quite out of joint, and I signified to the editor that I should probably do his paper harm and I would prefer to give up writing for a London audience. He asked me to go on writing for him, but I was rather out of tune with writing at all in those days, and finally he sent me the *Titan,* asking me to review it for him as a farewell pledge of friendship.

If you could turn up that review you would be—I hope kindly—amazed at the unsophisticated pain of the little, young, naïf, correct soldier man who, standing on his feet before a guardroom window, had written it, almost in tears. . . . Because, whatever you may say for or against it, the *Titan* is a milestone on the long road of our civilization.

Reading again today that cool projection of the career of Mr. Yerkes who was later to cause no end of a storm in the teacup of London transport finance I am amazed to find that it is really not such hot stuff after all. I don't see why, things being as they are, he shouldn't collar the tramway system of his adopted city. Everybody does—or tries to. I don't see why he shouldn't be promiscuous. Everybody is today—or is said to try to be. Obviously his earlier speculation with the city funds of Philadelphia was questionable. . . . But that had occurred in the *Financier,* an earlier book of the unfinished triptych. . . . And Cowperwood had paid for his being insufficiently dishonest to get away with it by spending some months in Clink where, amongst his meditations he had learned sophistication.

No, the *Titan* does not shock me today. It is just a rendering of normal life a few years ago when life was simpler and less corrupt. Reading it now I find myself unconsciously regretting that Cowperwood didn't bring off his final trolley coup and have a more agreeable time with women. If you sell your soul to the devil, I mean, you ought to see that you get a good price.

But, back in the second decade of this century while the Big Words were still alive, the *Titan* very naturally made one's gorge rise. The Big Words . . . Loyalty, Heroism, Chivalry, Conscience, Self-Sacrifice, Probity, Patriotism, Soldierly Piety, Democracy even, and even Charity which some translate as Love . . . those big words and the golden naïvetés that they stood for were probably in that year going stronger than they ever before had gone . . . certainly in officers' messes and guardrooms and no doubt outside, for all I know. The War had given them an extraordinary life with which to give their last kick. We were going—all volunteers at that date—to damn well *make* the world fit for Heroes and Democrats and Patriots! . . . Christendom, that was what it was going to be. . . . And absolutely safe for the Taxpayer too. Because for us the lowest and most repulsive of all vices was malversation of public funds. . . . That really was so . . . Well, there was probably a time when you too thought like that. . . . Unless you are very young!

Anyhow there I stood before the guardroom window, looking out on the battalion prisoners crouched at the feet of the high elms munching hunks of bread . . . and wrote with my fountain pen, about the *Titan* and the life that it revealed, what was really an unconscious keening for a world that was to pass away.

As in the case of Thomas Hardy I am pretty sure that the *Titan* was not the first book of Dreiser's that I had read. I know I had even then in the back of my head some idea of *Sister Carrie* as an agreeable fairy tale of an entirely cheerful kind. . . . A sort of glowing, goldenish spot, as for me it remains. I must have read it in one of the first years of the century when, after it had been murdered in New York by Mrs. Frank Doubleday, the London reviewers received it with spring torrents of praise. It must have struck me with pleasure as the story of a nice, pretty little, industrious and careful girl having a real good time . . . but real, you understand. That meant that Dreiser, at least in the girl's story, must have employed a pretty good technique. Otherwise my mind would have rejected the book altogether . . . as being false. The Hurstwood side of the story simply did not remain in my mind. I daresay the idea of an employed man, sinking amidst desperate expedients lower and lower, was in the early years of this century, so unfamiliar to me that it did not seem real. . . . Alas, alas! . . . Or perhaps the very nature of the catastrophe of that unfortunate individual seemed rather what the French call *voulu* . . . Arbitrary. I can't have believed that a smart man would have grabbed a handful of banknotes just because he found his employer's safe open. It must have seemed to me that the writer had not employed in inventing his catastrophe as much of the iron determination to make it not merely plausible but an act of the blind force called Destiny that is behind all human tragedy . . . as much as in those days I exacted of the novelist.

At any rate, for many many years I went about with, in my mind, the idea of *Sister Carrie* as a goldenish spot in the weariness of the world. . . . And I don't know that now, when I have re-read the book a couple of times, I don't feel much the same . . . and I shall probably this afternoon take another read in it just for my own pleasure. There can no higher compliment be paid by one novelist to another. At any rate when ten or a dozen years ago I had my first eccentric meeting with Mr. Dreiser and when Mr. Dreiser said hurriedly that he had read all my books and liked them very much and I had replied just as hurriedly that I had read all his and liked them very much too, I was not lying as hard as he . . . for if I said that I liked *Sister Carrie* very much it was the exactly right phrase. And by that time enough water of horrors had flowed under the bridges of the world to make me regard the *Titan* as merely a record of normal life. As for the *Financier,* when I had read it in, say, 1919 it had struck me as another pleasant fairy tale in which a mildly amoral and not unpleasant character had found his sufficiently agreeable happy ending with promise of wedding bells complete. . . . And at that date, as far as I knew, *Sister Carrie,* the *Financier,* and the *Titan* were all the books that Dreiser had written . . . I had forgotten *Jennie Gerhardt* which I had not liked . . . and which I went on and go on not liking. I can't help it if, as I suspect, it is Mr. Dreiser's ewe lamb. At any rate it is the only one of his books which I ever heard Mr. Dreiser mention—several times and as if with regretful affection. . . . But indeed it is the only one of his books which I ever heard Mr. Dreiser mention.

I am not, at any rate for the moment, criticizing Dreiser—the spirit, the method, the impulse, the whatever it is that has hurled his books at us. And of course I am not criticizing the Mr. Dreiser who hurls those railway trains of imprecations over my head whenever he meets me. I am merely stating likes and dislikes—which is a very difficult thing. Let us be explicit. . . . There is Stendhal for whose methods I have the very greatest admiration. He is perhaps the writer type as conscious artist and his French is impeccable, flawless, like Toledo steel . . . Toledo, Sp. . . . But I don't like him and except for the *Rouge et le Noir* I can't read him . . . not the *Chartreuse de Parme,* not his writings on Love. But poor dear old Flaubert, who was another shouting Berserker, I like and can read all the time, though today he is much out of fashion in the country of the Lilies.

So I like and can read Dreiser except for Jennie Gerhardt—and she depresses me.

I hear you say:

"How is this? . . . This man is denying his gods."

But it is not so. . . . It is only that this man is like other men who after half a century, or a quarter, or a decade or a lustre or a year or a month or a week of sedulous bus-driving takes a busman's holiday . . . according to his necessities. I don't know why busmen in especial should be taken as given to resting their minds by riding on other drivers' buses, but so it is said to be. When they have had a hard week they spend their day off being driven in blissful idleness from Putney to the Strand or from Washington Square to Grant's Monument and back. They say they feel like gentlemen!

So during fifty years or so of sedulous bus-driving . . . or no, it is rather more like the occupation of the ringmaster. When you are a conscious writer you watch your subjects, your characters, your words, in particular, as you put them down . . . as if they were lions, wolves or plaguy little cats performing on the sawdust of the ring. And 'Crack!' goes your long whip and they skip into their places and Columbine goes slick through the paper hoop and lands beyond on the white horse's back like a gull on the wave-crest. . . . And at the end of fifty years or so—if you are any good—you can make the beastly little things called words do what you want even when your back is turned or your eyes closed. . . .

Only . . . at times, you know, it is wearisome, that job. You get so that you want to write like a drunken Irish carter galloping a waggonload of split infinitives down a blind alley on a Glasgow Saturday night. And then, afraid of yourself; afraid that if you go on in that mood you'll really get yourself into trouble with the critical Police and lose your job and see your children starve and your name dishonoured, you throw your inkstand, like St. Dunstan, at the wall and say—or at least I do—"Damn it all. Let's go and ride with Dreiser and see how he gets his old bus along."

Did I ever tell the story of Mrs. Elliot of Old Elvit, Durham? She had gone to see a man hanged, up by the Castle, and had had a seat in the front row; coming home in the crowd an old gentleman in front of her had dropped dead in a fit; just as she was entering her door a coal-lorry ran away beside her and ran over two children who had been playing in the street. So she fell into her room; pulled off her bonnet by the strings; collapsed into a chair and exclaimed:

"Losh, mahn, will this day be *nowt* but pleasure!"

That's what riding with Dreiser is like . . . for me.

And I guess—and I am not using the word *vulgariter,* I am really hazarding the conjecture—that that's what reading Dreiser is for everyone and that is why, for his country and for the world outside Dreiser is a Doctor Johnson, or a Flaubert-plus-Balzac, or a Wagner or a Tolstoi or a Michelangelo or . . . I can't think of any others for the moment, but there are two or three more. . . . Men who outpass nationality as now

and then peaks from the sea bottom transcend their fellows and emerge
beneath the skies. . . . I am not of course appraising. Dreiser may be as
great as Michelangelo, or Tolstoi or Wagner, or less great or more. When
you are beside a mountain you can't see its relative importance . . . but
you can judge the nature of its stone. And Dreiser has the gift of univer-
sality. . . . If you like to call it American–ness you can—in the sense that
a sort of uniform spirit has overrun the Western world so that they are
eating nearly as many and nearly as filthily indigestible canned products
in Paris and London today as they are in Chicago. In that sense Dreiser
is even hyper-American, for London devoured his products with avidity
thirty years before there was any Dreiser-consumption at all anywhere between Terre Haute and Sandy Hook. . . . And that was not merely generosity in the London critics. . . . It was because the London critic saw
himself as he would like to be if he could be it without being discovered
—in the figures of Cowperwood or Sister Carrie or the Genius. . . . As
later the American *homme moyen sensuel* saw, but for the grace of God,
himself in the hero of the *American Tragedy*.

To me it is magnificently symbolical that Dreiser should have been born
in Terre Haute since that town has the aspect of being the very navel of
the country. And it is French in name and Papist in origin and very
largely German-speaking . . . or Irish or Swedish or any old language
but English. And in Terre Haute two queer, nationalist-internationalist
spiritual adventures happened to me before ever I knew that Mr. Dreiser
had there been born . . . typically enough in a German, Catholic, lower
middle class family. In, that is to say, a stratum of society that developed
itself in the early decades of the nineteenth century between those of the
least wealthy tradesmen and the cream of the mechanics—the children,
let us say of upper servants, sewing-machine drummers, non-articled lawyers' clerks. It was a very definite new stratum that arrived all over the
world at about the date of Mr. Dreiser's birth and that under the stimu-
lus of a compulsory education very superior to that paid for by the upper
and middle classes was beginning to see the expediency at once of getting
rid of the Big Words for which they had no especial use and of getting a
grasp on all sorts of reins of power. . . . For it was not for nothing that
there arrived almost simultaneously not only, in America, Mr. Dreiser
and, in England, Mr. Wells and the late Arnold Bennett . . . but amongst
Teutons, Latins, and Orientals, Mr. Hitler, Mr. Mussolini, and Kemal
Pasha and Sun Yat Sen, all of them set on reducing the whole world
to a sort of common denominator and all born to that stratum of
society. . . .

Most of all it symbolizes for me the eclipse of the proud, real Middle-
Class, Anglo-Saxon domination of the world . . . an image that came to

me in Terre Haute itself . . . I was sitting, that is to say, some years ago, at two in the morning, with the window open and the door ajar in the guest house of the convent of the Holy Child near that city. I was playing solitaire—which is also one of the occupations of Mr. Dreiser—because the intolerable efficient central heating of the hospitable spot made it impossible to sleep. The door pushed itself open before the form of the local policeman. He said:

"Ye're English, ain't yez? . . . I've come to tell ye I hate yez because of the sorrows of the Dark Rosaleen."

His father had been born in County Sligo, but he himself had never been outside Hoozier land.

. . . And next morning, waiting for an automobile to take me away, I was looking listlessly at the programme and accounts of a local Americanization Society. A thrill went slowly through me. I had observed that all the Americanizers had names like Elstheimer, Nielsen, Lobkowitz, Guertli, Wellenhausen . . . and those they were working to Americanize were called Drake, Hopkinson, Marsh, Masters. . . . And I heard myself say *Fuit Albion et magna gloria Victoriae.*

I am not making a song and dance about that. It is merely one of those coincidental phenomena that are apt to assume too great proportions for the observer far from his usual Paris, London or New York and in Indiana it is not so astonishing as all that. But if it is a small fact it is none the less a fact and when a day or so later I heard that Mr. Dreiser had been born in that place it gave me a mental shock that crystallized a great many images for me. I don't know why, but somewhere in the corner of the mind where inaccuracies are stored, I had hitherto thought that Mr. Dreiser was a born Philadelphian who had passed most of his years editing a newspaper in Baltimore. It was before the period when he had had the opportunity to use me as a mental punching ball for five hour periods and I had found him to be usually gently and almost wistfully speculative, inclined rather to listen to me than to indulge in tirades. . . . Indeed on the occasion of my first meeting with the author of the *Titan* we had for a period of three or four hours talked of nothing but words and styles and Mr. Dreiser had been so completely in agreement with me that I had taken him to be a larger and gentler Conrad. He had disliked assonances quite as much as I did . . . and the writing of Mérimée, Balzac, and of all other writers whom it is proper to contemn. . . . And we had agreed completely as to the main stream in the history of the novel . . . as to its passing from Lope de Vega and the Spanish picaresques, by way of Defoe and Richardson, to Diderot, Stendhal and Flaubert and so to Conrad and James and the writers of the then just awakening Middle West. . . . Indeed Mr. Dreiser, even on the surface, seemed to know quite as much of the technique of writing as I did . . . and I gave him mental credit for knowing a little more. So that, in that perverse corner of my mind I had summed him up as any other Anglo-Saxon *generosus, filius generosi* who had got his learning at one or other of the older universities of Penn's state and had pursued his studies of Latin civilization and letters in the otiose editorial chair of one of the more august Baltimore instructors of the public. I *knew*, you understand, that that could not be the fact. . . . But one's instincts nourished by inflections of the voice and mildnesses of the mind are so much stronger than mere knowledge. . . . Indeed, I don't know that to this day I don't go on somewhere at the back of my mind believing that Mr. Dreiser is a gentle, highly cultured being, of an immense erudition and a wistful desire to penetrate always deeper into the interstices of pure learning . . . that that is what you would find him to be if you scratched beneath the surface.

But on the Chicago day, after I had left Terre Haute, when someone brutally and with official print, in *Who's Who* or something of the sort, convinced me that Mr. Dreiser had been born in Terre Haute in such and such a *milieu* and such and such circumstances, it was as if an immense new pattern of the world revealed itself to me. And I am glad that the revelation came in that way—after I had satisfied myself by personal observation that Mr. Dreiser was something quite different. Had I, I mean, been convinced before I met him that Mr. Dreiser was some sort of literary hobo I might well have taken on myself some such attitude as that of Mrs. Frank Doubleday and have gone on with averted nostrils calling for musk whenever his printed page swam before my eyes. . . . As it was, when I came upon some of his words that are no words, queer grammatical solecisms and the other harsh oddnesses that at times affected me as if someone were thrusting a sharp needle upwards through the seat of the chair I was occupying, I thought according to my mood that they must be due to indifferent proof-reading, haste, or the ignorance of English compositors setting up Middle Western expressions—or merely to the fact that Dreiser knew what he was about and was trying after effects hitherto unessayed. And I had had the extraordinary readableness of his books to confirm me in that last view. You have to remember that the English literary scene with which I was till then most familiar is one of a uniform sedateness that resembles the surface of a duck pond completely covered by a North American water weed whose name I cannot for the moment remember—something like Ina Canadensis. So that when anything really exciting came along the English critic was apt to be far more enthusiastic than his transatlantic confrère . . . that is why so many of the really American writers from Whitman and Crane to Ezra Pound and Dreiser received their accolades in London whilst their home critics and public

and publishers and their female relatives were still delicately fainting at
the thought of them. And by reversing the orientation you see explained
why a number of British authors who cut no ice in their own countries
find their niches between Sandy Hook and the Golden Gate.

And then . . . nothing was ever more true than that *mal d'artrui n'est
que songe*. To Mrs. Frank Doubleday and the typesetters of Messrs. Har-
pers and to Colonel Harvey and all the rest of those who blocked Dreiser's career, Dreiser was an immense big black wolf who would make the
world unfit for their delicate susceptibilities, corrupt their young children,
block their ambassadorial careers at the court of Saint James's where Cowperwood's final female companion was *persona grata*. . . . There were in
short, for them, a hundred reasons—But a hundred thousand!—why the
writings of Dreiser should be a pain in the neck . . . and an immense
one that they all sensed without putting it to themselves in words. . . .
They felt in their bones that Dreiser was not merely a big bad wolf but
a mastodon-symptom of an ice-age, an immense, slow-moving convulsion
of a continent that when it should have passed would leave neither them
nor their houses nor their names, their accents, their syntaxes, their baby-
talk nor their world any more observable beneath the indifferent skies
that spread from Maine to the meridian and the Occident.

To the English critic all these pains were not even dreams. They were
unaware that they had any Terre Haute, any Middle West; they were
certain that they had no Dreiser to disturb the Ina Canadensis. And it *is*
fun, when you spend your life aping sedulously the language of the front
page of the *Times Literary Supplement* so as eventually to ensure your
own appearance in that House of Lords of Reviewers. . . . And mind
you, that is not an easy job. It calls for years and years of real good be-
haviour. . . . Damn it all, it *is* fun to see that poor old language, that
vehicle for conveying moderated thoughts, having the guts kicked out of
it, like a deflated football, over all the fields of the boundless Middle West.
. . . Don't believe that it was only Taine who felt an irresistible urge to
shout at afternoon teas in Oxford drawing-rooms the word of Cambronne.
. . . So the poor tired London critic had his hours in the realm of transatlantic, underworld faëry and expressed in his journals his gratitude in
a foam of praise.

Dreiser obviously is untidy . . . but he has to be untidy in order to be
big. He wants you to read immense wads of pages; you could not do it
if they were my peach-stone carvings. I know that he cherishes wistfully
the idea that one day in a great good time and a great good place he will
go through all his books, smoothing out excrescences, restoring neolo-
gisms like 'objectional' to their original form of 'objectionable,' introduc-
ing *charpente* into his frameworks and giving to all novels *progressions*

d'effet framed in words of an impeccable justness. Because Mr. Dreiser knows all about all those things. An immense, omnivorous reader with one of the most tenacious memories that the world can ever have seen, he knows as much about literary technique as about brokerage operations. . . .

There was a German philosopher called, I think, Weininger whose landlady's daughter would not let him seduce her. So he wrote an immense—I believe that it is in Germany a standard—book to prove that all women were rachitic nitwits. In the course of that work he had to prove that no woman had ever possessed genius. So he said that genius was made up of immense memory; no women ever had good memories; therefore no woman could ever be a genius. . . .

I think that, in his discovery that genius and vast memory were commensurable, that blind hen, as the Germans say, had found a pea. The writer of vast memory has an ease of production and in consequence a sureness that can never be aspired to by a writer who must document himself as he goes along. He can produce his instances without delay and, most important of all, he never has to force his subject around so as to bring in a second-rate instance. The difference between a supremely unreadable writer like Zola and a completely readable one like Dreiser is simply that if Zola had to write about a ride on a railway locomotive's tender or a night in a brothel Zola had to get it all out of a book. Dreiser has only to call on his undimmed memories and the episode will be there in all freshness and valour.

If you want an image of him at his writing you have to imagine him like a compositor before the formes of his mind. He stands at a considerable height, back on his heels, passes his fingers through the forelock of his silver hair, pauses for an instant and then like lightning his hands dart in and out over the types. He has instance A, a reporter at a lynching; instance X, a farmer seeking his lost Phoebe; instance L, a man realizing that though he is free by the death of his wife, his hands must fall powerless at his side, for the only freedom for him is that of death . . . And so on through instances ", #, $, %, & Z . . . each instance a memory out of years back or yesterday, of points here and there and anywhere on the span of a continent or so. And each memory becomes as it were a letter, a colour, an illumination and so, with immense speed, the pages build themselves up and become books. Of course he will make slips.

In the revolution of the resounding ages Dreiser stands for the emergence of the Teuton-Slav over the surface of a world till yesterday given over to Latin and then Anglo-Saxon cultural dominance. . . .

It is that aspect of world change that he voices as Defoe voiced London of the Plague, Lope de Vega, Spain, and Petronius Arbiter, Rome . . . or

Homer, the Age of Bronze . . . I am again not making appraisals. When
you read him the North American Republic has lost its Anglo-Saxon,
Victorian aspect to such an extent that you might say it has become an
appanage of the German one. . . . Or still more, that it is undergoing an
evolution that is part of a world-convulsion. For, as I have already adum-
brated the same is true of almost every unit of the Western world and of
many Oriental congeries. We are all of us going finally away from handi-
crafts toward a life characterized above all things by an eschewing of all
sedulousnesses. We all wear shop clothes because the solitary tailor cross-
legged on his bench is a distasteful image to our mass-production minds;
we all—in whatever nation—use words in which Bowery suffixes of Oriental origin are tacked onto Hellenic, Teutonic, or Latin roots. . . . And
with that wordological time-saving we have leisure to lounge from cafe-
teria to movie in long afternoons of untroubled bliss. . . . I read this
morning in my Paris paper that the French premier had *knockouté* with
non-Aryan thoroughness of rejoinder a Basque-Celtiberian lower middle
class deputy who posed as the champion of the son of St. Louis, and I am
going to lunch on *cornid bif* canned in Madagascar because, here in Paris,
we are in the middle of a very unspectacular revolution and the butchers
are all asleep beside their chopping blocks.

It is because he renders for us this world of fantastic incertitude that
Dreiser's work is of such importance. . . . The note above all being that
of incertitude.

. . . And most important of all, neither Mr. Dreiser the private gentleman, nor Dreiser, the personality that emerges from his books, has any
settled panacea for world improvement or even for world enlightenment.
They have between them one settled passion—but neither has any more
pattern than has a chart of the Milky Way. They will, passionately, like
you and me, see one aspect of life one day and another the next—and if
either of them is in the mood for curing the ills of the world he may passionately at one moment proclaim some panacea and very shortly after
may declare with almost equal passion that the very ill itself will in the
end save humanity. That is today inevitable for any man who is a thinker
as opposed to the protagonists of one Interest or another . . . If it were
my business to cure the ills of France this morning I should be sure—but
absolutely certain that the only thing that could do the trick would be the
restoration of the Monarchy. But I should go to sleep, probably, with a
last thought to the effect that very likely Mr. Blum will do a lot of good.

For it is characteristic of a confused world dominated by a hybrid social stratum that of necessity never had any use for the Big Words . . .
that along with the disappearance of Continence, Probity, and the belief
in revealed religion, Truth should have developed the bewildering faculty

of the chameleon and have taken on like Janus, two faces . . . There is no longer any one Faith, no longer any one Cause, no longer any one anything for the reasoning man. So the novelist—the authentic and valid novelist whose duty it is to record his world in crystallized form so that it may be of advantage to posterity—the novelist seeing both sides of Truth can do no more than take one side at one moment and the other immediately afterwards. . . .

But you might as well add the corollary that no poet or novelist can stay in one road for long . . . and if, like Mr. Dreiser, he is a very passionate poet and filled with red blood, his course, viewed from the air, will appear a bewildering zig-zag; he will have his reactionary half-miles, dash passionately forward for some furlongs, progress horizontally, and finally ascend to the empyrean exclaiming, "A curse on all your houses!" And at that Dreiser and Mr. Dreiser so rarely synchronize! . . .

Mrs. Dudley in her admirable book on Dreiser and his times—which is even more about the times than about Dreiser—recounts how Dreiser once declared that from now on Science should be his only guide to the problems of the dreary empty spaces that surround humanity. But before the pronouncement could appear in print he was already writing that Science was all blah and scientists pompous misleaders of the body politic. . . . And indeed, one day here in Paris, I had been reading one of Dreiser's wistful tributes to Latin-derived civilization and arts. But going out to have tea with Mr. Dreiser I found him cursing the French and all their Latin-derived and petrified characteristics . . . and cutting short his stay and taking the next boat to Germanic Gotham. . . .

And the one passionate belief, doctrine, rule of life, and morality that unites both gentleman and writer is this . . . that humanity has a right to happiness. . . . It is astonishing how the idea of happiness pervades his printed work and his conversation. It pervades them wistfully . . . "I don't know whether this man was happy or not," he will write . . . and it pervades them with a passion of rebellion, of hope or despair. There are times when you will see Dreiser—and imagine that you see Mr. Dreiser—shake fists at Heaven, Hell, Purgatory, the Earth, the Sea, Morality, Ethics, Laws, and Local Regulations and swear:

"By God, men *shall* be happy in spite of all your foul, unspeakable practices. . . ." In which, if you come to think of it, he unites the doctrines of Nietzsche and Christ.

Yet the last thing I heard him say, to remember, was as it were out of the blue, because we had been talking of a way of cooking bananas and he was just getting into his car:

"Ah, you think you will one day reach a stage when everything will be all right . . . a long period of quiet happiness. . . ." But—and he shook his heavy head mournfully: "You never will. Never. Never. One never does."

It was queer to hear him echoing in that *obiter dicta* the last words—"Never the time and the place and the loved one all together" of the octogenarian optimo-pessimist of the Victorians. . . . But I daresay, if you could pursue the train of thought, you might find a good many parallels between Browning and Dreiser.

At the same time I wouldn't mind betting, if not my hat then at least my second-best shoes, that, in this time of cherries—*Oh, connaissez vous le temps des cérises!*—with the gay sunlight pouring all across the Western Hemisphere, recumbent somewhere in California or Westchester County, Dreiser is declaring—with emphasis—that this is a gay old world with infinite, great, good places in which, for periods extending into eternities, one may have the best of all good times. . . . And I'm sure I don't know whether I do or don't agree with him. ,

James T. Farrell

SOME CORRESPONDENCE WITH

THEODORE DREISER

I met Theodore Dreiser only twice, once at the time of the Democratic National Convention in Philadelphia in 1936, and again, in the summer of 1944, when he paid his last visit to New York. One morning in Philadelphia, during the time of the Convention, I ran into H. L. Mencken, who mentioned that Dreiser was in town and gave me the name of the hotel at which he was staying. I went there, phoned his room, and identified myself. He asked me to come up.

Dreiser was quite like his pictures. He greeted me with cordiality, but at the same time, he was, apparently, absorbed in thoughts or interests of his own. We talked casually, and mainly about literature. Dreiser made no attempt to direct the subject of our conversation, so our talk flowed along the lines set by my own remarks and observations. Though he was seemingly preoccupied, he was at the same time listening to me. Thus, when I spoke of Dos Passos, his response was quick. He said he thought "that fellow Dos Passos" had done something good. He praised Dos Passos' work.

My impression then was of a big bulk of a man, self-centered, not too graceful; but also of a man who was kind and even soft. It was clear to me that he did not know my own writing, and at the time he may or may not have even associated my name with anything he may have heard about my work. As I dimly suspected, he invited me to his room largely because when I spoke to him on the house phone of the hotel, I mentioned that Mencken had told me of his presence in Philadelphia. Also, I assume that he thought I was a young writer coming to see him for something, and that because of this, there was a certain wariness in the way that he spoke with me.

It was pleasant talking to him. I was not too observant. I felt quite at

From *The General Magazine and Historical Chronicle,* University of Pennsylvania, Summer, 1951. And also *Reflections at Fifty,* Vanguard Press, 1954.

my ease, and made observations about political affairs, about the convention which I was attending, and, as I have already indicated, about books and literature. As I recall, I spoke most spiritedly when I alluded to propaganda and literature. In the spring of 1936, my polemical book, *A Note on Literary Criticism,* had been published, and I expressed to Dreiser some of the ideas that I had defended in that work. But I sensed by the changing expressions on his face that he must have felt that I was overreacting on critical questions.

The visit must have lasted about forty-five minutes. A secretary came in as I was leaving, and Dreiser, wanting to introduce her, turned to me and asked me to tell him my name again.

In the summer of 1944 I went to see him at the Hotel Commodore, where he was staying. He had had some correspondence about this visit, and I believe that he looked forward to it. The year previously, I had written an article on *Sister Carrie* in *The New York Times Book Review.* Shortly after the appearance of this article, he had written me:

> *My Dear Farrell:*
> *I was pleased to read your revaluation of* Sister Carrie *in the* New York Times, *as much pleased as I was interested by the anti-reactions of a number of literary critics reaching from the Atlantic to this coast. At least you are safe in insisting that it has endured, critics or no.*
> *Whether you recall it or not I enjoyed our brief contact in Philadelphia in July 1940. (Dreiser misremembered the year: it was, as I have mentioned above, 1936.)*
> *Thanks, and all my best wishes.*
> *Theodore Dreiser*

Also, as a consequence of this article, I had received a letter from Mrs. Dreiser (Helen Richardson), stating that Dreiser wished her to ask me if I would agree to "serve as Co-Executor with Alfred Kazin, Robert Elias and the University of Pennsylvania in the event of" her death. And also, "before that event, to advise from time to time on literary matters of importance in connection with his estate." I accepted this as an honor.

I corresponded with Dreiser from that time on until his death. His letters, which I shall quote and refer to below, had been very warm and friendly.

On shaking hands with Dreiser in his hotel room, I immediately saw that he had aged since 1936. Now he was an old man. His face was thinner, and it was quite wrinkled. His neck was wrinkled. He wore gray trousers and a white shirt, and stood a great deal of the time while we talked. He was talkative; in fact, outgoing. We chatted for about two hours or more.

Mentioning New York, he said that it wasn't the same as it had been. He said that he no longer liked it. He preferred California and Hollywood to New York, but only in a comparative sense. There was no satisfactory place in which to live in America. And he asked me what was happening among younger writers? What were they producing? Did I know of any good and promising new books which were appearing? At the time I was so busy with other work that I didn't have the chance to read many new books. Those which I had read or looked at were quite mediocre. I mentioned this, and added that many young writers seemed to be seeking security in ways which I regarded as escapist. Dreiser spoke of one book which he had looked at, *The Lost Weekend*. He was, as he talked of it, both spirited and even a little cantankerous, but gently and warmly cantankerous. And, at the same time, he was puzzled and bewildered. His comments ran something as follows:

"Farrell, why do people write books like that? Why do they write about drinking? What kind of a subject is that? That's not new. There's nothing new in that for me. For years, I've been burying relatives who drank themselves to death."

And then, he reeled off some names. This one, gone to a drunkard's grave. That one, the same.

He shook his head, and spoke with insistence and puzzlement. All of his life, he had seen this, drinking, and alcoholics, and people going to drunkard's graves. In the light of all the drunks he had known and seen, and apparently in the light of the fact that he had buried some himself, he wanted to know why in the name of God a young man wanted to write a book about a drunk.

"Farrell, that's not something to write about. I know all about drinking and drunks."

Mostly, our talk was of writing, of literature and of the literary scene. He kept asking me questions about these matters. And now and then he would make some remarks of the past, and of how New York was different, and no longer of interest to him. In the course of our conversation, I asked him if he would finish the Cowperwood trilogy. He said yes, and told me that he was working on it. I remarked that I would very much like to read it. And then, at moments, he would become preoccupied. He was attending to various business affairs, apparently relating to the sale of his house in Mount Kisco. I was living in Pleasantville for the summer, and invited him out to see us. He said he would very much like to come, but did not know whether or not he could, because of his business affairs. His trip East had been a business trip.

As I recall this, it seems to me that on this trip Dreiser was closing out the accounts of an entire past. And as we talked, and I watched him and listened, I became more aware of the fact that he had aged. Now and then, he would cough rather dryly, and he took several drinks of water. Remembering his photographs, and recalling him in the Philadelphia hotel room, almost eight years previously, I became even more struck with the way in which he had aged. There was a certain sadness in this realization. I had admired his books ever since I had first read them. Despite the statements of many critics, however, I had never regarded myself as his disciple. His example, his strength and persistence in the face of opposition, the sympathy and depth of feeling in his writing—all this had encouraged me. When I was a young man, the realization that Dreiser had persisted in fighting the good fight for literary integrity, and the knowledge that he was alive and had won his battle had been something to hearten me. At the same time, I had never, except in moody moments, and perhaps for a short period, agreed with his general ideas. However, Dreiser had been an influence in my life: his example had been an inspiration. For a young writer, the accomplishments of an older writer often shine as great deeds. There is magic in the name of that older writer. Time was when there was magic in the very name, Theodore Dreiser. Some sense of that old magic remains today with me. Names have such an effect on us in our boyhood and in our youth. I recall how in my boyhood, the names of some baseball players exerted this same magical effect on me: Eddie Collins, Joe Jackson, Ty Cobb. Today, if I go through an old box score in a faded newspaper and see these names, old boyhood emotions of wonder come back to me. The name, Theodore Dreiser, was the first literary name to penetrate my consciousness in this way.

There was, then, a certain sadness for me, sitting in that room in the Hotel Commodore on that day in June, 1944, talking with him, and realizing that here was Theodore Dreiser, and that he had become an old man.

There had been a period late in the 1930's when I had come to think that Dreiser would write no more novels, and that the Cowperwood trilogy would never be completed. But before I went to see him for this second and last time, I had started to reread some of his writings. I became convinced that he would write more. Now and then, if the question of Dreiser came up in conversation, I would remark that Dreiser was far from written out. Talking to him, I also thought of this, and told myself that he had not written his last.

I first heard the name Dreiser late in 1924. I was then a clerk, working in an express office in Chicago, and had begun to attend De Paul University in the evening. I was tremendously eager and ambitious; also, I was naive. I was struggling to win confidence in myself, and to equip myself so that I would have a future. In the book of readings, assigned in my

English course, his essay, *Hey-Rub-a-Dub-Dub,* was reprinted. I read it as an assignment. There was an instantaneous feeling of recognition on my part. I saw this as a sad essay, and yet it seemed to me to register a sadness that was in life, in people. While I was naive and almost wholly unread, I had, in my twenty years, had much experience with human beings. In fact, I had already gotten an education in human nature; I had absorbed this as part of the process of my growing up. I had come in contact with sufficient sadness in the lives of others to know that life was both sad and serious as well as rich in possibilities. Around this same time, I had read the last chapter of Walter Pater's *The Renaissance.* It begins:

> *To regard all things and principles of things as inconstant modes or fashions has more and more become the tendency of modern thought. Let us begin with that which is without—our physical life. Fix upon it in one of its more exquisite intervals, the moment for instance, of delicious recoil from the flood of water in summer heat. What is the whole physical life in that moment but a combination of natural elements to which science gives their names? But these elements, phosphorous and lime and delicate fibres, are present not in the human body alone: we detect them in places most remote from it. Our physical life is a perpetual motion of them—the passage of the blood, the waste and repairing of the lenses of the eye, the modification of the tissues of the brain under every ray of light and sound— processes which science reduces to simpler and more elementary forces. Like the elements of which we are composed, the action of these forces extends beyond us: it rusts iron and ripens corn. Far out on every side of us those elements are broadcast, driven in many currents; and birth and gesture and death and the springing of violets from the grave are but a few out of ten thousand resultant combinations. That clear, perpetual outline of face and limb is but an image of ours, under which we group them—a design in a web, the actual threads of which pass out beyond it. This at least of flame-like our life has, that it is but the concurrence, renewed from moment to moment, of forces parting sooner or later on their ways.*

And referring to our impressions of the world, Pater wrote that every one of these "is the impression of an individual in his isolation, each mind keeping as a solitary prisoner its own dream of a world." For "Not the fruit of experience, but experience itself is the end. A counted number of pulses only is given to us of a variegated, dramatic life. How may we see in them all that is to be seen in them by the finest senses?" I believed all of this with my whole being. And then these famous sentences of Pater's:

"To burn always with this hard, gemlike flame, to maintain this ecstasy, is success in life." And then, the concluding sentence of this chapter: "For art comes to you proposing frankly to give nothing but the highest quality to your moments as they pass, and simply for those moments' sake." I was profoundly stirred by these words. They stimulated in me feelings both of sadness and ambition—ambition to live, to feel and to experience.

To associate this essay of Pater with Dreiser's *Hey-Rub-A-Dub-Dub* may seem far-fetched. But this association exists in my memory. The impression which Dreiser's essay left on me was one of tragedy and truth. Life was confusing. I was only twenty. What was success? What did it all mean? I wanted many things. I wanted to burn with a "hard, gem-like flame." And here was this man named Theodore Dreiser, looking out at life, and life was so confusing. Chicago was as confusing. Sitting in the class room on Randolph Street, with the night dark through the windows; tired, hearing the noise of nervous motor horns on Michigan Boulevard below, recalling a noisy day of nervous work in the express office, knowing that lads and their girls were passing on Randolph Street below to see shows, to dance, to enjoy themselves and kiss and pet on dates, I felt as though I were like the man who had written *Hey-Rub-A-Dub-Dub*. And at forty, I might be like he was. I might look out on the world as he did, poor and wondering. "History teaches me little," Dreiser wrote in one part of this essay, "save that nothing is really dependable or assured, but all inexplicable and all shot through with a great desire on the part of many to do or say something by which they may escape the unutterable confusion of time and the feebleness of earthly memory." And then, a few lines below, Dreiser wrote:

> *I look out at the river flowing by now, after hundreds of millions of years of loneliness where there was nothing but silence and waste (past so much that is vivid, colorful, human) and say to myself: Well, where there is much order and love of order in every one and everywhere, there must be some elemental spirit holding for order of sorts, at any rate. Stars do not swing in orbits for nothing surely, or at least I might have faith to that extent. But when I step out and encounter, as I daily do, lust and greed, plotting and trapping, and envy and all uncharitableness, including murder—all severely condemned by the social code, the Bible, and a thousand wise saws and laws and also see, as I daily do, vast schemes of chicane grinding the faces of the poor, and wars brutally involving the death of millions whose lives are precious to them because of the love of power on the part of some one or many, I am not so sure. Illusions hold too many; lust and greed, vast and bleary-eyed, dominate too many more. Ignorance, vast and almost*

*unconquerable, hugs and licks its chains in reverence. Brute strength
sits empurpled and laughs a throaty laugh.*

This essay moved me very much. Now as I look back upon my first
reading of it, I believe that more than anything else, I then hungered to
feel that I might "escape the confusion of time and the feebleness of
earthly memory."

Many experiences, impressions, aspirations all prepared me to be receptive to Dreiser's work. In 1927, I procured a Modern Library edition of
Free and Other Stories, with an "Introduction" by Sherwood Anderson.
Anderson's tribute to Dreiser further prepared me for his work. And
when I read these stories, especially "Free," it was as though I were being
clearly told what I had in some vague way come to know. Then, in New
York, that same year, I read a number of Dreiser's books, including all
of the novels which he had published up to that time. I was employed as
an advertising salesman, selling ads in R. R. Donnelley's Classified Telephone Directory, *The Red Book.* Prizes were to go to the salesmen with
the highest percentages achieved by the end of a sales campaign. I was in
line to receive one of these prizes, a sum that would amount to at least
one hundred and fifty dollars. My salary was thirty-five dollars a week:
this prize money was considerable, then, in proportion to what I was
earning. But during the final weeks of the campaign, I became so absorbed in reading Dreiser's books that I went to the New York Public
Library daily, or else remained in my own room to read these works. I
did not get my prize, but I did go through a considerable portion of his
collected work. The impression these made on me was deep and profound.
However, I did not borrow Dreiser's attitudes, acquire some so-called
method of writing, nor accept a deterministic view of men which regards
them as rats in traps or cages. More than anything else, I felt wonder and
awe: I was strengthened in my feeling that human emotions, feelings,
desires, aspirations are valuable and precious. I gained more respect for
life, more sympathy for people, more of a sense of human feelings and
thoughts as of major value in this, our common life. I recall one illustration of this. During this same period, I read much of Nietzsche. I remember how, whenever I was too strongly inclined to think and act in terms
of Nietzschean arrogance, I would think of the Dreiserian world. The
impression Dreiser left was too strong for me to fall unchecked into an
acceptance of the Nietzschean idea of the superman.

Sitting then and talking with Dreiser, there was in my mind this recurrent feeling of sadness. as I recognized that he had aged. When he
spoke of his work, he was really speaking of the final books that he would
write.

A few further impressions might here complete my personal account of him. When he talked, he was simple, direct, and unpretentious. He had assurance. I had the feeling that if there was anything I might say which would be of use to him, he would take it and use it in his own way. He remained a man with curiosity, and he had various comments to make. He spoke of Edgar Lee Masters, and of rumors which had been current to the effect that Masters was poor. He grew cranky, almost angry. He said that we needed action by the government, the creation of a cabinet position and a man in the cabinet to deal with art and literature. He decried the fact that no governmental measures had been taken to provide for indigent artists in their old age. This was on his mind, more than immediate world problems. Of the latter, he said nothing.

As we talked, I grew increasingly hungry. It had been my understanding that we would lunch together. But Dreiser said nothing about our going out to eat. So we talked. But finally, I was too hungry to go on, and suggested that we go out and have a bite. He remarked that he never ate lunch, and had to remain in his room because of business appointments. And then, I shook hands with him, and left.

II

Dreiser's letters to me, written between 1943 and the time of his death, were usually short. In them there was feeling, warmth and friendliness. They include references to his work which, I think, may give some sense of Dreiser, the writer, during his last years. In quoting from them, I shall mainly cite such passages.

On July 4th, 1944, after he had returned from his last visit to New York, he wrote me a letter in longhand, acknowledging an article of mine dealing with the work of Ring Lardner, which I had sent him. His last paragraph read:

> *That was to me an entertaining conversation I had with you in New York. Only the extreme pressure of practical and necessitous matters kept me from calling on you at Pleasantville. But there'll be another time and another conversation.*

Earlier, on November 5, 1943, I had received a letter from him, in which he commented on remarks I had made in a letter in which I had mentioned some literary Philistines. He wrote:

> *. . . most certainly I agree on what you say concerning Philistinism. But it makes up so large a portion of the known world. And when it turns to literature, painting, music or what not—when the*

practitioners in these fields . . . manage to attract any attention at all, the fat is in the fire. For what the Philistine desires, of course, is to build himself a petty fame at the expense of the artist whoever he may be. In sum, very early in my work, I found that there was nothing to do about him, or them.

They raved and raved. Some, to be sure, died off in the course of time—and that was that. Others were discharged from their jobs only to be replaced by new if not worse authorities fresh from high school or the sticks or both. And often, in my own case, I used to marvel at the pettiness of their complaints or the savagery of their assaults. But I got past that—paid no attention to them and, like a moving procession, I saw them move off into the shadows of nothingness and disappear.

Some, truly enough, were able and valuable, but I do not wish to name them because I do not care for any more clatter. Writing, as is, is hard enough. . . .

On January 20th, 1944, there is a letter in which he discussed an article I had written on Dostoevsky, and he mentioned that he greatly favored *The Idiot,* and wished that it would be done into a play: he added that when young, in his late twenties, *Poor People* had "thrilled" him, "and would do so again, I feel."

I wrote him inquiring about the scientist Jacques Loeb, and asking him if he had read Loeb's writing in Chicago. On May 10, 1945, he answered:

Dear Farrell

In answer to your inquiry about Chicago, no I did not read Loeb in Chicago.

It was later in New York when I was living in Tenth Street, around 1910 or 12. I came across some magazine articles by him, which I read with great interest. (Also one of his books.) I then wrote him telling him of my interest in his work. I also told him of some chemical and physical observations of my own. He answered my letter inviting me to come and see him at the Rockefeller Institute. I went. And from then on until the time of his death he either wrote me occasionally or sent me some pamphlets or printed deductions of his own.

I am very much obliged to you for sending me your article on An American Tragedy. *It is a fine piece of work, and I am delighted to have it. I can tell you one thing though. You are letting yourself in (or perhaps you already know that) for a lot of critical drubbing, for all of the kind words you print concerning me. . . .*

In May of the same year, I also received a telegram from him, which read:

COULD YOU POSSIBLY READ MY LATEST BOOK THE BULWARK FOR ME
I NEED AN HONEST ADVANCE OPINION WIRE COLLECT

DREISER

I agreed to do this, and wrote him to say that I would take the manuscript along with me on a vacation trip I was planning. On May 26th, 1945, he wrote, thanking me. Here is his letter in part:

> Dear Farrell
>
> You are very kind and good natured to take on The Bulwark, particularly on your vacation, and I certainly would not have imposed it on you at this time if it had not been for the urgency of my need for your honest opinion.
>
> As you will see it is not the third volume of The Trilogy. However, I do have the third volume well under way, really about three-fourths of it, which I have now decided to take out of my store house and finish. I hope to have it done late next Fall or Winter.
>
> The Bulwark is a story I have carried in mind for many, many years—all of thirty. And I will be very grateful to obtain your opinion. . . .

I was slow in reading the manuscript because of many activities engaged in on my trip. On June 20th, 1945, he said in a letter:

> While I did not expect an immediate answer from you, I sent the Manuscript to you because I felt that you would criticize it eventually, and I really wanted an advance criticism, if possible.
>
> The reason for that is that I sent it to an old friend of mine, —— and she found either a change of style, or I couldn't decide whether it was a change of subject matter which made the difference to her. However, that was my reason for bothering you with the script as I know that you would make clear whether she was wrong or right.
>
> The novel has a time limit on it so far as the publication is concerned. Since they seem to feel that a few cuts here and there might be valuable, it makes me wish to hear what you have to say, because at least in your case I will have a clear and unbiased criticism.
>
> Whatever your opinion is in connection with this book as to subject matter, treatment or interpretation, it will be of benefit, not harm to me, because I will find out what particular things might be advan-

tageously remedied. So if you can speed up the examination of the book, I will certainly take it as a great favor.

I was quite impressed with *The Bulwark*. In my judgment, it was on a level with Dreiser's other novels, all of which I admired. I wrote him a long and detailed analysis of the novel. Concerning this service to Dreiser, I trust I might add that I regarded performing it both as an honor and as a duty. Apparently, the criticism of his friend had confused his own attitudes and judgment. He wanted to make a test of his book, and to see whether another opinion would conform or not with the objections of his friend. Reading the novel, I guessed one of the reasons for her objection. In the analysis which I sent Dreiser, I observed that since Hemingway had come on the scene, many writers and readers used and responded to dialogue differently from what had been the case when he was a younger writer. In the works of Hemingway, and of many who have come after him, dialogue is used to carry much of the burden of narrative, and to reveal psychological states which many earlier writers would describe in the third person. I further discussed the difference between his use of dialogue and that of Hemingway and of post-Hemingway writers. Dreiser's dialogue was illustrative, and often would follow after generalized description or analysis, revealing a point related to the generalized analysis or description which immediately preceded it. Further, his dialogue would be used to highlight and bring out scenes. In use and in texture, Dreiser's dialogue is different from that in many post-Hemingway works. Many contemporary readers are accustomed to the use of dialogue as it has evolved in our fiction during these last twenty-five years. As I have indicated above, I supposed that here was one of the objections of Dreiser's old friend. I called her on the telephone, and confirmed my guess. Commenting on these aspects of the novel, I wrote Dreiser to the effect that, in my opinion, his literary habits were set, and that it would be a mistake for him to try and alter the manner in which he wrote dialogue and used it as a device or instrument in the construction of his stories. In other words, I suggested that he should ignore criticisms or suggestions about his use of dialogue which were based on the desire to read dialogue of a post-Hemingway type. I suggested changes in his dialogue only in detail, and in specific scenes.

I liked those aspects of *The Bulwark* which his old friend objected to the most. These were the passages which reveal Dreiser's own mysticism, and which recount the mystical and religious feelings of his chief protagonist, Solon Barnes. The mystical or religious features of *The Bulwark* came as no surprise to me. I had been aware that Dreiser was not the thoroughgoing determinist and naturalist which many of his critics have described him to be. I did not think that he should change, or in any way seriously alter those parts of the novel which had mystical or religious overtones. Dreiser always tried to give his readers a sense of the full or whole nature of his major characters. Solon Barnes is a man with much sweetness. This sweetness comes out in Dreiser's accounts of Solon's marital relationship. And Solon's sweetness is bound up with the man's religious and mystical feelings. To have changed or deleted these parts of the book would, in my view, have been to ruin it. I urged him not to do much revision of these parts. Also, Dreiser felt with Solon Barnes. Dreiser, in his last days, was growing more mystical and religious. Regardless of anything he may have said concerning religion or mysticism when he was younger, this was the attitude that he was now developing. This was part of the final statement that Theodore Dreiser would make as he drew near the end of his life-long and wondering search for some theory of existence. Briefly, he wanted to express through this novel, and through his characterization of Solon Barnes, something of his own feelings, his own views. And I was convinced that he had done this in a characterization which was poignant and tragic. The solace and strength which Solon Barnes gained from heeding his "inner light" was this man's "bulwark." Apparently, in all of this, my interpretation and suggestions were at variance with those of Dreiser's old friend. And I am inclined to think that it was on this point, more than on any matters of style or detail, or even of construction, that Dreiser wished for an opinion. For the rest, I made a number of concrete suggestions concerning words, phrases, scenes and some anachronisms, and said that perhaps he should consider these when he revised the book.

On June 27th, 1945, he wrote, thanking me for my letter about *The Bulwark,* and stated that he considered my observations and deductions helpful.

And on July 5th, he wrote: ". . . I am now winding up *The Stoic,* which will be finished in about two months." And then, on October 13th, 1945, he wrote:

> About the cutting (of The Bulwark. *JTF*) I feel now that Mr. Elder (of Doubleday Doran & Co.) will do a good job of it. He seems to me to be of much the same opinion as you are about it. He has also written me that he has been in touch with you and appreciates your point in the matter.

Then on October 24th, 1945, there is this paragraph in one of his letters:

> As for myself, I have just finished the long missing third volume of the Trilogy, concerning which you inquire. Believe it or not, it is

*actually finished, and in due course will fall into your kindly hands
. . . so that as to its merits, as well as its defects, I will hear the truth.
And good or bad, that is always welcome to me.*

On December 9th, 1945, I was to discuss *The Genius* on the programme,
"Invitation to Learning," along with Bernard de Voto and Max Lerner.
Drieser wrote a note on November 27th, 1945, saying that he would be
listening to this programme, and added a little paragraph concerning his
opinion of the programme as a whole. I quote: ". . . At times it is quite
interesting. Then, again, as you say it is most stuffy."

The programme, dealing with *The Genius,* seemed to go very well. In
passing, I might remark that Max Lerner, as chairman of it, was quite
excellent. When I spoke, I made some effort to relate Dreiser, and his
hero, Eugene Witla, to the background of the 1890's. It was with pleasure
that all three of us spoke, knowing Dreiser would be listening. We all
admired his work, and we were proud to know that we could publicly
express this admiration while he was still living, and able to hear our discussion. At the same time, we were not doing this with any desire to
flatter. I personally was deeply gratified that I could appear on this programme. While I did not consider myself a disciple, I did know that I, as
well as many other American writers, owed him a spiritual debt. To be
able to repay that debt in a public sense could not but move one. I am
happy to know that Dreiser was pleased. The next day, in a telegram to
me, he said in part:

CONGRATULATIONS ON YOUR PART IN INVITATION TO LEARNING PROGRAM
WHEN YOU SO KINDLY AND GENEROUSLY WIELDED YOUR CRITICAL CUDGELS
IN MY BEHALF . . . YOUR KINDLY CONSIDERATION OF THE CIRCUMSTANCES
WHICH SURROUNDED ANY WOULD BE WRITER OF THE NINETIES OF WHICH I
HAPPEN TO BE ONE SO IN VIEW OF THE LACK OF ORIGINAL CHRISTMAS
GREETINGS HERE'S HOW I FEEL THAT YOU ARE HONEST AND YOUR DEDUC-
TIONS SOUND REGARDLESS OF WHOM YOUR DEDUCTIONS CONCERN IS THERE
ANY CHANCE OF GETTING A COPY OF THE SCRIPT OR RECORDS OF PROGRAM
· THEODORE DREISER

On December 3rd, 1945, he had written me:

I am sending by Express a copy of The Stoic. *It is actually finished,
and since I am interested to get your opinion as to its worth or lack of
worth, I am sending you the first copy.*

*In a way you wished this on yourself, as you expressed the desire
several times to read it as soon as possible. However, there is no rush
on it. Read it at your own convenience, and I will be deeply grateful.*

*I realize that you have pressing work of your own, and that naturally
comes first.*

Anyhow, read it when you can, and write me about it later.

On December 14th, 1945, in another letter, there were Christmas
greetings.

I began reading *The Stoic* as soon as it arrived on December 10th, and
I read thirty-three chapters the first night. The next morning, I sent off a
hasty letter to Dreiser, saying in part:

". . . It reads excitingly, seems to me to be a solidly built story, and to
have pace and progression. . . . Normally, I have found that I read your
books more slowly than other novels. Here I note that I read much more
rapidly than in your other works. . . ."

On December 19th, 1945, I wrote Dreiser a long letter, describing my
impressions of *The Stoic*. I began with a few suggestions of an editorial
character, suggestions which concerned small details, and I stated that I
would make more of these to Mr. Elder. I declared that the book was, to
me, very impressive until the end. Concerning the end, I made two suggestions. I proposed that at the end, when Berenice, Cowperwood's mistress, has succeeded in having a hospital built to the man's memory, the
emotional impact should be deepened. I proposed that this be rewritten,
suggesting that it be done in the mood of the ending of *Sister Carrie*,
where Carrie sits in her hotel room, a successful actress, rocking and wondering, wondering what life is about. Also, Dreiser had appended a postscript on good and evil. I remarked that I thought this should be either
rewritten or else not used. I remarked that I did not accept it as a moral
attitude which could not be answered, but declared more to the point, that,
coming at the end of a trilogy, it should be written and thought out more
carefully. The postscript, let me add, was not necessary to the rest of the
novel. It was a personal statement of Dreiser's.

III

Early in the morning of December 29th, 1945, I was awakened by a loud
ring of the doorbell. When one is awakened at such an hour, one expects
bad news. A telegram came. It read in part:

TEDDY WAS TAKEN ILL 3AM AND RALLIED FOR AWHILE BUT PASSED AWAY
650 PM TODAY . . .

HELEN DREISER

I was writing a memorial article on Dreiser for *The Saturday Review
of Literature*. A letter from Theodore Dreiser arrived in the mail. I read
it, with my manuscript before me. Dated December 24th, 1945, it read:

Dear Farrell:
I don't know how to thank you enough for your criticism of The
Stoic. *I know that you are very right about most of the editorial
exceptions. I also think you are dead right about the last chapter in
regard to Berenice. As I wrote Elder, I simply stopped writing at the
end because I was tired, after writing the two volumes. Your suggestions are sound and logical, and I will re-write the last chapters.*
*As to the essay on Good and Evil, well that is something that can
be discussed at length, and there is plenty of time for that. . . .*

I understand that in the last few days of his life, Dreiser had gone back
to the revision of the ending of *The Stoic*. There was not time enough for
the completion of this revised chapter.

There is one impression which I have most strongly now, after having
gone through these letters. I think of the man who wrote them, spending
the last of his strength in these novels, *The Bulwark* and *The Stoic*.
Phrases and sentences take on a poignant meaning for me. "Writing, as
is, is hard enough . . . it is not the third volume of the Trilogy. However, I do have the third volume well under way, really about three-
fourths of it. . . . I hope to have it done next Fall or Winter. . . . As for
myself, I have just finished the long missing third volume of the
Trilogy. . . . Believe it or not, it is actually finished. . . . *The Stoic*. It is
actually finished. . . . I simply stopped writing at the end because I was
tired. . . . Good and Evil, well that is something that can be discussed at
length and there is plenty of time for that. . . ."

One can visualize him, pondering on good and evil to the end—as he
had at forty, when he sat, looking across the Hudson River from New
Jersey, pondering and writing *Hey-Rub-a-Dub-Dub*.

Early Newspaper Reviews

Louisville *Times*
Louisville, Ky., November 30, 1900

. . . *a plain woman* . . .

Out in the highways and hedges of life you find a phase of realism that
has not found its way into many books. It is sometimes morbid and sometimes forbidding. At its best it is grim and shadowy. It reeks of life's
sordid endeavor; of the lowly home and the hopelessly restricted existence.
Its loves, its joys, its sorrows, are narrow. There is little sunshine. It is plain
realism.

When a man puts this sort of thing in a book he cannot expect to hear
the plaudits of an admiring host or know the lavish tribute that goes out
to men who write successful fiction. But he is an artist nevertheless. Fiction must reflect life, and all life does not present itself in the drawing-
room, in the palace car or in the luxurious home. Because Theodore
Dreiser has chosen to tell of the other side, not the "other half" about
which so much has been written, but the other side of the social scale, he
may not have brilliant success, but he will have the credit that must be
accorded a man who has written faithfully and impressively.

"Sister Carrie" is the name of his book. It is a homely name; there is
no suggestion of the girl with the laughing eye and the glowing cheek,
and there is no thought of rustling silk and dancing lace. Instead, there
comes into the mind the picture of a plain woman, plain in the sense of
being of the great common people. And you are not mistaken.

Only once before in our recent fiction has this life been exploited, and
then it was done by the brilliant young realist, Frank Norris. What happened in San Francisco in the brutal dentist's home happens in Chicago
with "Sister Carrie." Where "McTeague" ended in hopeless tragedy and
thrilling detail, "Sister Carrie" closes with a superficial triumph. But even
then there is the shadow of a man's mistaken life and the inevitable sorrow of bitter defeat.

"Sister Carrie" is the story of a poor girl who gets into the glamor and
the excitement of a great city. She is caught up in its dizzy whirl. She is
exposed to temptation and she falls. What she does, what she says, what
she lives for, are all told with minute detail and vivid realism. There is not

the remarkable detail that has made Norris a master in his way, but it is the fine attention to the little things that makes Dreiser a factor in that sort of fiction which must be read and which we must have. It is a remarkable book, strong, virile, written with the clear determination of a man who has a story to tell and who tells it. Doubleday, Page & Co., publishers, New York.

Commercial Advertiser
New York, N. Y., December 19, 1900

. . . *civilization is at bottom an economic fact* . . .

It may well be said at the very outset that the titular heroine of *Sister Carrie* is a very frequent and commonplace type, unredeemed by even a touch of the basic honesty and inner charm of Du Maurier's *Trilby,* and yet the imperfect sketch which Mr. Dreiser has rendered of her detracts but little from the value of his work, for the reason that she plays a subordinate part in the development of the story. She is interesting as an unconscious tool in the shaping of events and as exhibiting in her own career the occasional absurd disproportion of motives to results. The extraordinary power with which this novel is vested, and which should, but probably will not, give it wide recognition, has little to do with the delineation of foolish worldly wise Carrie; the power of the novel resides in a concrete and detailed proof of a truth too little understood.

The facts of the life of George Hurstwood, for some time the lover of Carrie, constitute a series of pictures, vivid to intensity, hard to deny, and illustrative of the maxim of Turgot: "Civilization is at bottom an economic fact." Hurstwood, as we first see him, is a prosperous business man of a prevalent type. Perhaps he has too much girth, is a trifle flabby-fleshed; is used too much to social success, too little to hardening effort. Still he is the eminently well-groomed, pleasant-faced man, whose contemporaries we negligently admire every day of our lives, in the cafes, the brokers' offices and at dinner, because of their unassuming but well-marked success, their buoyancy and their *savoir faire*. Of these men the workers of hand and brain have always been envious. By what diverse law are these happier soldiers of fortune enabled to turn genial ways into gold, and by a facile twist of wit wrench to their own use the lantern of Aladdin? What is the economic bottom of it and of them? For there is an economic bottom to the matter, a tragic truth, which justifies, because it proves necessary, the sweat of the delvers.

There comes to George Hurstwood, at that period of early middle life when, as psychologists tell us, radical changes of habit and thought are most likely to appear, a sudden and violent species of mental vertigo.

Sister Carrie is the occasion. The primal cause rests back somewhere in the essential instability of the man's showy and amusing life. The attractions of Carrie are unusual, but a more potent reason for madness lies in the fact that she is possessed (*vi et armis*) by a casual, dense and insignificant drummer. It may be that if Hurstwood had led a delver's life, he would have had a delver's friends, those enduring ones who bind a man down and stand wardens when wildness is upon him. But a club life breeds club friends, and club friends are for entertainment only. Between sun and sun, and with none to hinder or much care, Hurstwood threw away his social position, his property and his occupation, all for the benefit of a miscellaneously mooded girl, as graceful as a cat, and, like a cat, tolerant of humanity only that she might gain a sunshiny corner in some well cushioned bay-window. A little too late Hurstwood saw the entire matter in its correct light; and though he bitterly regretted that part of it which involved throwing his honor after his goods, it did not change his attitude toward the girl. There was that much to his credit. He recognized that he was in every way bankrupt and must start life afresh simply on the basis of whatever effective power and personality he possessed.

After they had fled from Chicago and settled in New York things went along smoothly for a time. Hurstwood had still some ready money, and with that he reembarked in a small way in the liquor trade. But the owner of the building presently concluded to sell out and Hurstwood was again put out of business, with most of his small remaining capital gone. Still he was not greatly discouraged; something surely would turn up. He had always borne himself effectively before men, and it was absurd that he should fail to do so in time of stress. But the money dwindled steadily and they moved to cheaper quarters. When he came to seek for a position he found that the suavity of a man of affairs is suspicious unless accompanied by credentials. He found also that the good positions were not only taken, but had endless applicants in line for them, and that for the poor positions he was unfitted by manner, habit and inclination. After many days of fruitless quest for something in his line he began to drop into hotel corridors "just to rest a minute." Then he began to stay home in the mornings, then all day. This resulted partially from complete discouragement and partially because he did not realize the precariousness of his position. While at home it did not seem to him worth while to shave often or to wear good clothes, but he often did Carrie's marketing errands, that he might feel that his going and coming really counted. The money continued to dwindle; they ceased to count by hundreds or by dollars; the cent became the unit of their arithmetic.

Goaded on by necessity and by Carrie's reproaches, Hurstwood determined to get work in any line or of any kind. He became a motorman, a porter. But, screw up his courage as he would, he found the work demanded more endurance than he had to give. These proofs of his incompetence shocked him. The shadow of his successive efforts frightened him from further effort. His debonaire manner, his air of commanding attention, deserted him. Even his shoulders fell forward and his feet shuffled. With this shrinkage of his social being came a corresponding and pitiful shrinkage in his personality. The tumble-down clothes he wore struck the poison of decay into his whole system. A sort of universal numbness took possession of him. This was instanced in one way by the absence of the keen sense of shame which he had formerly felt for his position. Finally, like the predatory animals, he ceased all pretense of making return for his necessities. At first this took the form of puny accounts with small bakers and costermongers with whom he and Carrie had traded; of being "out" when they called to collect and of sitting hunched up in his chair, repeating to himself with nerveless derision, "They can't get blood out of a turnip." In these days of vacancy the panorama of his past prosperity often rolled itself down on the empty stage of his life to amuse him, and he saw himself well-dressed, smiling and amiable again, and encored for the excellence of his stories.

As a result of this mental process of shrinkage and reversion, Hurstwood's earthy, honest love for Carrie turned to kindliness and languid goodwill. But to Carrie, Hurstwood became the veritable "old man of the sea." Perhaps there was in this a naive adherence to the old tribal conception of power as the sole requisite and justification of conquest and possession. Perhaps Carrie divined that it would be an anomaly in natural law for a woman to continue with a man who was thoroughly down, powerless to protect her, and who was therefore, properly speaking, no longer a man. Perhaps she did not believe in that alleged immortality of love which passes understanding and alters not; perhaps she knew there was no such thing. Perhaps, and this is more likely, she thought simply that as he had broken his implied contract to support her, he was not entitled to further consideration except by gratuitous favor. In any event, the life she was leading "was not gay," while her desire was boundless for comfort, position and a view of the wider world. After she had luckily obtained a position as chorus girl in a theatre, she loyally, for some weeks, gave him part of her earnings. But the thing cloyed. So much to him was so much chopped from that little margin over bare living expenses, which represented daintiness and a degree of ease. For that reason, and because he was as he was, she left him.

Hurstwood drifted down to the Bowery. In a vague and indeterminate way, hastened only when hunger drove, he acquired the simple art and learning of the army of the unemployed. This consisted in each man keeping as fast hold as he might upon a misty, rayless life. By day one sat, when weather permitted, upon the park benches and read such scraps of papers as fate blew along. In winter it was more of a problem, though the lodging houses opened for a small sum. The matter of judging benevolent faces, whose owners would donate what was requisite to shove a little further along a lax existence, was not difficult. At about 11 it was proper to join the wavering line who waited each night for free bread at the Vienna bakery. Occasionally Hurstwood saw posters of Carrie, who, it appeared, had made a great success on the stage. Once when it was very cold and he was desperate, he waylaid her near the stage door and she gave him a little money. But as months dragged on, each became to the other a dislimning memory. For his part he was too utterly flaccid to have any over-clear ideas—except, to be sure, that strangely pleasant and oft-recurring panorama of the now far past. She, on her side, had gained place and friends and dainty ways and finally—last luxury of the well-used—a complete code of aesthetics. An extra snap of adversity brought to Hurstwood the *coup de grace*. He had long desired it, but the habit of keeping on was persistent. One night, however, he said for the last time, "What's the use?" and concluded there was none. A boat which set out from Twenty-seventh Street east took his nameless body to its grave.

Beyond a certain distance on the road to destitution, there is a vanishing point for self-respect. "Physical disgrace" and social meanness are at once indicative and productive of moral squalor. And therefore the cloistered philosophers erred when they stated with due eloquence that solely in the spirit of a man, and not in his material well-being, manhood consists. To maintain in some sort the reserve of social power which makes possible mental freedom is a just instinct of self-preservation. If bankruptcy, absolute not relative, and including the loosing of each social grip, ensues, what may a man do? For the enmity of the fates is a variable, only the answering force of the man may be built up measure by measure. To build up this force and buttress it with friends and efficiency in work is to attempt to over-top the unknown variable; man can not do more, or know the result before the event. It is only certain that all the advantages and probabilities are with the workers. And though they can not afford to vaunt their immunities, the Hurstwoods will in comparison forever be unlucky. And if a thousand of them are becalmed in prosperity, and never meet a gale, yet a negative demonstration is of more effect and is not thereby invalidated.

The novel named *Sister Carrie*—Heaven knows why—says these things, and truly.

New York *Times*
New York, N. Y., January 15, 1901

. . . *the game as it is played* . . .

"The mere living of your daily life," says Theodore Dreiser, "is drastic drama. To-day there may be some disease lurking in your veins that will end your life to-morrow. You may have a firm grasp on the opportunity that in a moment more will slip through your fingers. The banquet of to-night may crumble to the crust of the morning. Life is a tragedy."

"But isn't that a rather tragic view to take?" I asked. "Hasn't each man something in himself that makes life worth living? If, as you say, you want to write more than anything else, isn't that power or ability to write something that would make life worth while under all circumstances?"

"No, not under all circumstances, because you can't use ability except under certain favorable conditions. The very power of which you speak may, thwarted, only serve to make a man more miserable. I have had my share of the difficulties and discouragements that fall to the lot of most men. I know something of the handicap of ill health and the necessary diffusion of energy. A man with something imperative to say and no time or strength for the saying of it is as unfortunate as he is unhappy. I look into my own life and I realize that each human life is a similar tragedy. The infinite suffering and deprivation of great masses of men and women upon whom existence has been thrust unasked appalls me. My greatest desire is to devote every hour of my conscious existence to depicting phases of life as I see and understand them."

"What are you trying to show in what you write? Do you point out a moral?" I inquired.

"I simply want to tell about life as it is. Every human life is intensely interesting. If the human being has ideals, the struggle and the attempt to realize those ideals, the going back on his own trail, the failure, the success, the reason for the individual failure, the individual success—all these things are interesting; interesting even where there are no ideals, where there is only the personal desire to survive, the fight to win, the stretching out of the fingers to grasp—these are the things I want to write about— life as it is, the facts as they exist, the game as it is played! I said I was pointing out no moral. Well I am not, unless this is a moral—that all humanity must stand together and war against and overcome the forces of nature. I think a time is coming when personal gain will rarely be sought at the expense of some one else."

"Where among people is there the greatest readiness to stand by one another, among the rich or the poor?" I asked.

"Among the poor, they are by far the most generous. They are never too crowded to take in another person, although there may be already three or four to share the same room. Their food they will always share, even though there is not enough to go around."

"Are you writing something else?" I inquired.

"I have another book partly finished but I don't know when I shall get it done. I have not the time to work on it, much as I want to."

"Have you been satisfied with the reception of *Sister Carrie*?"

"Well, the critics have not really understood what I was trying to do. Here is a book that is close to life. It is intended not as a piece of literary craftsmanship, but as a picture of conditions done as simply and effectively as the English language will permit. To sit up and criticise me for saying "vest," instead of "waistcoat"; to talk about my splitting the infinitive and using vulgar commonplaces here and there, when the tragedy of a man's life is being displayed, is silly. More, it is ridiculous. It makes me feel that American criticism is the joke which English literary authorities maintain it to be. But the circulation is beginning to boom. When it gets to the people they will understand, because it is a story of real life, of their lives."

Post Standard
Syracuse, N. Y., February, 1901

. . . *the hopeless granite wall* . . .

With more than enough realism and less than a sufficient sense of humor, Theodore Dreiser tells us in *Sister Carrie* (Doubleday) that a country girl without money and without what we call bringing up, once came to Chicago, failed to find work which suited her, went to live with a drummer, abandoned him for a handsomer man, though married, and finally drifted into an artistic career on the stage. Mr. Dreiser aims to depict the sordidness of municipal life and the artistic yearnings. I imagine that he would be flattered by being called the Zola of the United States. He is so realistic that he gives the street and number of his characters, adopts their slang for his own, and fills pages with conversations in which the heroine says chiefly, "Oh, I don't know." This is a very usual and harmless remark in conversation, but it does not lend much zest to fiction.

With a generous adoption of the principle of absorbing whatever you want, wherever you find it, Mr. Dreiser in describing the drummer in the early part of the story, clips a page entire from Mr. Ade's *Fables in Slang,* namely, the description of the ways of Gus of Milwaukee with the women. Occasionally Mr. Dreiser's language is ridiculous, as when describing Carrie's feelings when a nice young man has left her, he remarks that "the coach seemed lorn."

Yet, on the whole, there is something about *Sister Carrie* which deserves to be talked about. Mr. Dreiser has served a useful apprenticeship as a newspaper man in various cities of this country. He knows the aspect of the hopeless granite wall that seems to surround the unsuccessful in a great city. The decline of Hurstwood, Carrie's second venture, who comes to New York without a reputation, and drifts downward from the position of a small business man to that of a vagrant, finally dying miserably, is touching, and, no doubt, truthful. The description of the street car strike in Brooklyn is better than most of the newspaper reports of the time.

Newark *Sunday News*
Newark, N. J., September 1, 1901

. . . *the impression is simply one of truth* . . .

Unfortunately the title of this book gives no hint of its interest, and neither does it bear the faintest relation to the story. The heroine is not a nun, nor has her story any family circle for its setting. On the contrary, her life is distinctly non-conventional, and the portrayal of it begins after she has left home.

But the fitting monograph on this suggestive subject of titles has yet to be written.

In the case of *Sister Carrie,* the title is the weakest thing about the book. From its first sentence and throughout its most inconsiderable length the story holds the reader. It is one to sit up over late at night and ponder by day. Told with an unsparing realism and detail it has all the interest of fact; and the terrible inevitableness of fact, also. Perhaps no better word picture of a man's downfall has ever been painted than is to be found within these pages. The evolution of the hanger-on, the beggar, the social outcast, here finds its final portrayal. From the successful man of affairs to the beneficiary of city charities; from a respected member of society to the veriest outcast; from a being instinct with energy and ambition to a wretched, broken creature—every step of the long downward course is followed and illuminated as though by a gleaming searchlight. The possibility of it all is horrible; an appalling arraignment of human society. And yet there is here no word of preachment; there are scarce any philosophic reflections or deductions expressed. The impression is simply one of truth, and therein lies at once the strength and the horror of it.

The conception and portrayal of character in *Sister Carrie* would be striking in any case, but for a writer, in his first book, to show this power of individualism so highly developed, is really remarkable. The faculty for character development is shown in the evolution of the outcast from the man of position, and in the evolution of the shop girl into the charming and successful woman. And the sketching in of minor personalities is no less skillfully effected. The Chicago drummer is a living, breathing and talking creature. The reader not only sees him, but actually feels his personal atmosphere. The man Hanson, a thrifty Swede-American, is strangely real, and so is his wife, with her subdued air. Scarce a character does not justify his presence by lending an added interest to the story.

This talent for character drawing has been altogether devoted to the portrayal of decidedly second-rate people—second rate as to character, mental capacity and culture. There is no strong nor noble nature in the book; neither is there any lady or gentleman. The effect is depressing, and the reader longs for some relief from the commonplace talk, and material standards, and shallow thinking of these very real and convincing people. If they were less real and convincing, the need of relief would not be so great. In the slight sketch of Ames there is just a gleam of something better—far too small a gleam to lighten the general effect, however.

Perhaps this is the most serious criticism to be made upon the book— this, and its utter lack of any approach to a literary manner of fiction. The word style is here purposely avoided, because the style is, in many ways, excellently strong, convincing, clear, at times, even nervous.

But one does not wish to have a writer express himself in the same way as do his somewhat uncultivated characters. For him to do so, robs his work of literary flavor—a thing still precious, and in favor of which there is always setting in a strong reaction, as against the temporary popularity, with some readers, of the manner which repudiates any thought of choice and discretion in the use of words. Among some of the inelegancies (not to say vulgarities) one noted, are the following:

"Swashed around with a great air."

"He was crazy to have Carrie alone."

"As he spruced around their chambers."

"He wondered how he would get ahead of the drummer."

Having quoted these examples of illiterate diction, it is but fair to try to convey some idea of Mr. Dreiser's power in portraying emotional situations.

The following bit of analysis, as found in its setting, is admirable: "He thought he saw in her drooping eye, her unstable glance, her wavering manner, the symptoms of a budding passion."

And who would not recognize the truth in the following through: "Now, as he spoke, his voice trembled with that peculiar vibration which is the result of tensity. It went ringing home to his companion's heart."

But good examples of emotional expression abound throughout the book, and, of course, lose their effect when disconnected.

Quite as happy, and possibly more rare, is this writer's ability to suggest those delicate mental conditions in which the thought, or sentiment, of one person reacts silently upon that of another:

"Once or twice he held his peace, hoping that in silence her thoughts would take the color of his own. . . . Presently, however, his silence controlled the situation. The drift of his thoughts began to tell.

"She was listening, smiling, approving, and yet not finally agreeing. This was due to a lack of power on his part, a lack of that majesty of passion which sweeps the mind from its seat."

The multiplication of these interpretations of mood impresses the reader, and gives him penetrating glimpses into the minds of the men and women who figure in the story.

It is somewhat singular that one with so much knowledge of human nature as Mr. Dreiser evidently possesses would fail to appreciate the power and depth of certain feminine instincts. The heroine, Carrie, is a sensitive, rather pure-minded girl, and possessed of the rudiments of the artistic temperament—therefore possessed, also, of capacity for suffering. Besides this, she came from a respectable and sheltered home. Yet, after having yielded up that which woman holds most precious, and for the loss of which nothing compensates her heart, this strange heroine feels but the slightest pangs of remorse or shame. Her mental state finds itself expressed in a very few words by the writer:

"Ah," thought Carrie, with mournful misgivings, "what is it I have lost?" And in the brief depicting of her thought which follows there is an utter lack of intensity. She briefly and "infrequently" repines her lost estate, exactly as the average woman might repine some indiscretion which had temporarily wounded her self-complacence.

The construction of the book is excellent as to management of plot, but somewhat elaborated as to detail. While one cannot find fault with the realistic style as such, yet an undue insistence upon detail may seriously mar the effect and power of a book. In the part of *Sister Carrie* which deals with the financial straits of the heroine and Hurstwood, the prolongation of the agony is somewhat unnecessary, even for realistic effect. Even this peculiarity of parts of the book renders it in no sense dull. One is not tempted to skip a single line. Yet all effect of luminous fusion is necessarily sacrificed to such a minute dealing with detail.

The effects of this book are, upon the whole, secondary, while its merits are those which betray great talent—possibly genius. Certainly the writer whose first book is strong and interesting, both in conception and in development, true to life in its portrayal of character, and powerful in its emotional parts, can have no limits placed by any critic upon his possible accomplishment.

Commercial Advertiser
New York, N. Y., September 18, 1901

. . . *in England* . . .

Mr. Theodore Dreiser's *Sister Carrie,* which was not only one of the best novels published last year by Doubleday, Page and Company, but one of the strongest and best-sustained pieces of fiction that we have read for a long time, curiously enough attracted comparatively little notice in this country. In England, however, where it has just appeared in Mr. Heinemann's Dollar Library of American Fiction, it is winning golden opinions from the critics. The *Daily News* calls it "a cruel, merciless story, intensely clever in its realism, and one that proves the author to be a writer of unusual ability." *The Daily Chronicle* brackets it with Will Paine's kindred, but less powerful, *Story of Eva,* and says in conclusion: "It is a grimly gray story of life, and life near the bone. And it proves Mr. Dreiser an author to be reckoned with and never to be overlooked—a true artist." The opinion of the *Athenaeum* is on the whole rather the best of all. It sums the book up as "a creditable piece of work, faithful and rich in the interest which pertains to genuinely realistic fiction," and adds, "it is further of interest by reason that it strikes a keynote and is typical, both in the faults of its manner and in the wealth and diversity of its matter, of the great country which gave it birth. Readers there are who, having perused the three hundred and odd pages which go to the making of *Sister Carrie,* will find permanent place upon their shelves for the book beside M. Zola's *Nana.*"

New York *Evening Sun*
New York, N. Y., June 18, 1907

. . . *though he writes he does not read much* . . .

Mr. Dreiser and His Critics.

Young novelists ought not to allow themselves to be interviewed, because they are liable to make as bad mistakes about the nice things said of their work as they are with regard to the warnings addressed to them by kind yet conscientious critics.

Mr. Theodore Dreiser wrote a book called *Sister Carrie* when he was very young. We have never heard his age, and guessed it from his prose. The story was suppressed here because, as was reported, the publisher's grandmother or maiden aunt, or somebody like that, thought that it was in bad taste. Of course it really wasn't. It was simply crude and rough and immature. However, it was republished the other day, and treated very nicely by the reviewers. It was still a powerful story badly told. For, strange as it may seem, Mr. Dreiser showed that he was as faulty a critic of his own work in 1907 as in 1900. Indeed, so thoroughly satisfied was he with the book that, as far as we could make out, he had not changed a single word or cut out a single line of the childish philosophy contained in the original.

This was bad enough. But it was worse to find that our young friend had lost his temper and was reported as reviling the whole race of critics as follows in the columns of a literary review:

"Well, the critics have not really understood what I was trying to do. Here is a book that is close to life. It is intended, not as a piece of literary craftsmanship, but as a picture of conditions done as simply and effectively as the English language will permit. To sit up and criticise me for saying "vest" instead of "waistcoat"; to talk about my splitting the infinitive and using vulgar commonplaces here and there, when the tragedy of a man's life is being displayed, is silly. More, it is ridiculous. It makes me feel that American criticism is the joke which English literary authorities maintain it to be. But the circulation is beginning to boom. When it gets to the people they will understand, because it is a story of real life, of their lives."

Charity and real respect for Mr. Dreiser, as a promising, or at one time promising, young author leads us to suppose that though he writes he does not read much. Otherwise he would be aware that some of the books which have been most "close to life," which have dealt with "the tragedy of a man's life," have been composed with the greatest possible care and with a painful regard for the proprieties of a good style. What is more, his novel, as a picture of conditions "done as simply and effectively as the English language will permit," would have gained vastly by the elimination of all the eloquence and fine writing which we and others found so irritating.

Before Mr. Dreiser completes his second book a short course in home reading would be desirable. There is, we think, a translation of the *Letters of Flaubert*. In them he would find an account of how that great man labored to find at all times the fitting word. In the *Moll Flanders* of Defoe, from whom the sainted R. L. Stevenson learned how to persuade the American and English public that he was an original genius as a prose writer, Mr. Dreiser would learn how to do a thing "simply and effectively." And from the books of Sir Henry Maine, an author unfortunately read only by law students, he might find an object lesson in the application to literature of the mathematical process known as the elimination of the constants and learn something of the virtue of austerity.

After such a course we are sure that Mr. Dreiser's gents will cease to be swell dressers, and will give up wearing the pants, vests, prince alberts and tuxedos of the slop shops.

New York *Press*
New York, N. Y., July 3, 1907

. . . *a minor curiosity* . .

A "PURPOSE" NOVEL. It is not often nowadays that a novel has so interesting and curious a story of its own as is possessed by Theodore Dreiser's *Sister Carrie*. We are informed that it was published originally in 1900 by a local firm, but no sooner had a feminine relative of one of the firm read it than she decreed the book must be suppressed, and suppressed it was, in this country at least. But it met with so favorable a reception from the English reviewers that the author evidently persisted until he found a publisher, evidently with no opinionated feminine relatives, who has just issued it again. After reading *Sister Carrie* we can understand easily the shock it gave the first publisher's relative. But we think the shock might have come from another cause than her reported objection to the moral atmosphere of this "novel with a purpose." We saw nothing particularly objectionable in the frank portrayal of Sister Carrie's living with the genial commercial traveler on his promise to marry her, or in her enforced desertion of him and flight with Hurstwood, the suave manager of the "elegant resort" in Chicago. Those incidents interested us and even more so did Carrie Madenda's stage life in New York and the gradual tragedy of Hurstwood's decline from a man of affairs to a Bowery wreck, with suicide as his end. Indeed, as a picture of an actress of a certain type, a woman of little intelligence and practically no moral sense, we think Carrie Madenda may take rank with Henry James's heroine of a finer type in *The Tragic Muse* and Anthony Hope's *A Servant of the Public*. But we were shocked by one element in this novel and that was the fashion of the writer's English. We cannot recall such vulgar forms of expression in any book we have ever read. As it stands, this novel may remain a minor curiosity of literature, in that its author could have observed life with so much truth and yet could not observe ordinary usages of good English. These solecisms are so strangely out of touch with everyday speech that they give to the book a character that can be described only as naive.

The Critical Battle

Stuart P. Sherman

THE BARBARIC NATURALISM OF
MR. DREISER

The layman who listens reverently to the reviewers discussing the new novels and to the novelists discussing themselves can hardly escape persuasion that a great change has rather recently taken place in the spirit of the age, in the literature which reflects it, and in the criticism which judges it. The nature of the supposed revolution may be briefly summarized.

The elder generation was in love with illusions, and looked at truth through a glass darkly and timorously. The artist, tongue-tied by authority and trammelled by aesthetic and moral conventions, selected, suppressed, and rearranged the data of experience and observation. The critic, "morally subsidized," regularly professed his disdain for a work of art in which no light glimmered above "the good and the beautiful."

The present age is fearless and is freeing itself from illusions. Now, for the first time in history, men are facing unabashed the facts of life. "Death or life," we cry, "give us only reality!" Now, for the first time in the history of English literature, fiction is become a flawless mirror held up to the living world. Rejecting nothing, altering nothing, it presents to us—let us take our terms from the bright lexicon of the reviewer—a "transcript," a "cross-section," a "slice," a "photographic" or "cinematographic" reproduction of life. The critic who keeps pace with the movement no longer asks whether the artist has created beauty or glorified goodness, but merely whether he has told the truth.

Mr. Dreiser, in his latest novel, describes a canvas by a painter of this austere modern school: "Raw reds, raw greens, dirty gray paving stones—such faces! Why, this thing fairly shouted its facts. It seemed to say: 'I'm dirty, I am commonplace, I am grim, I am shabby, but I am life.' And there was no apologizing for anything in it, no glossing anything over. Bang! Smash! Crack! came the facts one after another, with a bitter, brutal insistence on their so-ness." If you do not like what is in the picture, you

From *The Nation*, December 2, 1915.

are to be crushed by the retort that perhaps you do not like what is in life. Perhaps you have not the courage to confront reality. Perhaps you had better read the chromatic fairy-tales with the children. Men of sterner stuff exclaim, like the critic in this novel, "Thank God for a realist!"

Mr. Dreiser is a novelist of the new school, for whom we have been invited off and on these fourteen years to thank God—a form of speech, by the way, which crept into the language before the dawn of modern realism. He has performed with paint. He has presented the facts of life "one after another with a bitter, brutal insistence on their so-ness," which marks him as a "man of the hour," a "portent"—the successor of Mr. Howells and Mr. James. In the case of a realist, biographical details are always relevant. Mr. Dreiser was born of German-American parents in Terre Haute, Indiana, in 1871. He was educated in the Indiana public schools and at the State University. He was engaged in newspaper work in Chicago, St. Louis, New York, and elsewhere, from 1892 to 1910. He has laid reality bare for us in five novels published as follows: "Sister Carrie," 1901; "Jennie Gerhardt," 1911; "The Financier," 1912; "The Titan," 1914; and "The Genius," 1915. These five works constitute a singularly homogeneous mass of fiction. I do not find any moral value in them, nor any memorable beauty—of their truth I shall speak later; but I am greatly impressed by them as serious representatives of a new note in American literature, coming from that "ethnic" element of our mixed population which, as we are assured by competent authorities, is to redeem us from Puritanism and insure our artistic salvation. They abundantly illustrate, furthermore, the methods and intentions of our recent courageous, veracious realism. Before we thank God for it, let us consider a little more closely what is offered us.

I

The first step towards the definition of Mr. Dreiser's special contribution is to blow away the dust with which the exponents of the new realism seek to becloud the perceptions of our "reverent layman." In their main pretensions, there are large elements of conscious and unconscious sham.

It should clear the air to say that courage in facing and veracity in reporting the facts of life are no more characteristic of Theodore Dreiser than of John Bunyan. These moral traits are not the peculiar marks of the new school; they are marks common to every great movement of literature within the memory of man. Each literary generation detaching itself from its predecessor—whether it has called its own movement Classical or Romantic or what not—has revolted in the interest of what it took to be a more adequate representation of reality. No one who is not drunken with the egotism of the hour, no one who has penetrated with sober senses into the spirit of any historical period anterior to his own, will fall into the indecency of declaring his own age preëminent in the desire to see and to tell the truth. The real distinction between one generation and another is in the thing which each takes for its master truth—in the thing which each recognizes as the essential reality for it. The difference between Bunyan and Dreiser is in the order of facts which each reports.

It seems necessary also to declare at periodic intervals that there is no such thing as a "cross-section" or "slice" or "photograph" of life in art—least of all in the realistic novel. The use of these catchwords is but a clever hypnotizing pass of the artist, employed to win the assent of the reader to the reality of the show, and, in some cases, to evade moral responsibility for any questionable features of the exhibition. A realistic novel no more than any other kind of a novel can escape being a composition involving preconception, imagination, and divination. Yet, hearing one of our new realists expound his doctrine, you might suppose that writing a novel was a process analogous to photographing wild animals in their habitat by trap and flashlight. He, if you will believe him, does not invite his subjects, nor group them, nor compose their features, nor furnish their setting. He but exposes the sensitized plate of his mind. The pomp of life goes by, and springs the trap. The picture, of course, does not teach nor preach nor moralize. It simply re-presents. The only serious objection to this figurative explanation of the artistic process is the utter dissimilarity between the blank impartial photographic plate, commemorating everything that confronts it, and the crowded inveterately selective human mind, which, like a magnet, snatches the facts of life that are subject to its influence out of their casual order and redisposes them in a pattern of its own.

In the case of any specified novelist, the facts chosen and the pattern assumed by them are determined by his central theory or "philosophy of life"; and this is precisely criticism's justification for inquiring into the adequacy of any novelist's general ideas. In vain, the new realist throws up his hands with protestations of innocence, and cries: "Search me. I carry no concealed weapons. I run life into no preconceived mould. I have no philosophy. My business is only to observe, like a man of science, and to record what I have seen." He cannot observe without a theory, nor record his observations without betraying it to any critical eye.

As it happens, the man of science who most profoundly influenced the development of the new realistic novel—Charles Darwin—more candid than the writers of "scientific" fiction—frankly declared that he could not observe without a theory. When he had tentatively formulated a general law, and had begun definitely to look for evidence of its operation, then first the substantiating facts leaped abundantly into his vision. His "Ori-

gin of Species" has the unity of a work of art, because the recorded observations support a thesis. The French novelists who in the last century
developed the novel of contemporary life learned as much, perhaps, from
Darwin's art as from his science. Balzac emphasized the relation between
man and his social *milieu;* the Goncourts emphasized the importance of
extensive collection of "human documents"; Zola emphasized the value
of scientific hypotheses. He deliberately adopted the materialistic philosophy of the period as his guide in observation and as his unifying principle in composition. His theory of the causes of social phenomena, which
was derived largely from medical treatises, operated like a powerful magnet among the chaotic facts of life, rejecting some, selecting others, and
re-disposing them in the pattern of the *roman naturaliste.* Judicious
French critics said: "My dear man," or words to that effect, "your representations of life are inadequate. This which you are offering us with so
earnest an air is not reality. It is your own private nightmare." When they
had exposed his theory, they had condemned his art.

Let us, then, dismiss Mr. Dreiser's untenable claims to superior courage
and veracity of intention, the photographic transcript, and the unbiassed
service of truth; and let us seek for his definition in his general theory of
life, in the order of facts which he records, and in the pattern of his representations.

II

The impressive unity of effect produced by Mr. Dreiser's five novels is
due to the fact that they are all illustrations of a crude and naïvely simple
naturalistic philosophy, such as we find in the mouths of exponents of
the new *Real-Politik*. Each book, with its bewildering masses of detail, is
a ferocious argument in behalf of a few brutal generalizations. To the
eye cleared of illusions it appears that the ordered life which we call civilization does not really exist except on paper. In reality our so-called society is a jungle in which the struggle for existence continues, and must
continue, on terms substantially unaltered by legal, moral, or social conventions. The central truth about man is that he is an animal amenable
to no law but the law of his own temperament, doing as he desires, subject only to the limitations of his power. The male of the species is characterized by cupidity, pugnacity, and a simian inclination for the other sex.
The female is a soft, vain, pleasure-seeking creature, devoted to personal
adornment, and quite helplessly susceptible to the flattery of the male. In
the struggles which arise in the jungle through the conflicting appetites
of its denizens, the victory goes to the animal most physically fit and
mentally ruthless, unless the weaklings, resisting absorption, combine
against him and crush him by sheer force of numbers.

The idea that civilization is a sham Mr. Dreiser sometimes sets forth explicitly, and sometimes he conveys it by the process known among journalists as "coloring the news." When Sister Carrie yields to the seductive drummer, Drouet, Mr. Dreiser judicially weighs the advantages and disadvantages attendant on the condition of being a well-kept mistress. When the institution of marriage is brushed aside by the heroine of "The Financier," he comments "editorially" as follows: "Before Christianity was man, and after it will also be. A metaphysical idealism will always tell him that it is better to preserve a cleanly balance, and the storms of circumstance will teach him a noble stoicism. Beyond this there is nothing which can reasonably be imposed upon the conscience of man." A little later in the same book he says: "Is there no law outside of the subtle will· and the power to achieve? If not, it is surely high time that we knew it— one and all. We might then agree to do as we do; but there would be no silly illusion as to divine regulation." His own answer to. the question, his own valuation of regulation, both divine and human, may be found in the innumerable contemptuous epithets which fall from his pen whenever he has occasion to mention any power set up against the urge of instinct and the indefinite expansion of desire. Righteousness is always "legal"; conventions are always "current"; routine is always "dull"; respectability is always "unctuous"; an institution for transforming schoolgirls into young ladies is presided over by "owl-like conventionalists"; families in which parents are faithful to each other lead an "apple-pie order of existence"; a man who yields to his impulses yet condemns himself for yielding is a "rag-bag moralistic ass." Jennie Gerhardt, by a facile surrender of her chastity, shows that *"she could not be readily corrupted by the world's selfish lessons* on how to preserve oneself from the evil to come." Surely, this is "coloring the news."

By similar devices Mr. Dreiser drives home the great truth that man is essentially an animal, impelled by temperament, instinct, physics, chemistry—anything you please that is irrational and uncontrollable. Sometimes he writes an "editorial" paragraph in which the laws of human life are explained by references to the behavior of certain protozoa or by reference to a squid and a lobster fighting in an aquarium. His heroes and heroines have "cat-like eyes," "feline grace," "sinuous strides," eyes and jaws which vary "from those of the tiger, lynx, and bear to those of the fox, the tolerant mastiff, and the surly bulldog." One hero and his mistress are said to "have run together temperamentally like two leopards." The lady in question, admiring the large rapacity of her mate, exclaims playfully: "Oh, you big tiger! You great, big lion! Boo!" Courtship as presented in these novels is after the manner of beasts in the jungle. Mr. Dreiser's leonine men but circle once or twice about their prey, and spring, and pounce; and the struggle is over. A pure-minded serving-maid, who is suddenly held up in the hall by a "hairy, axiomatic" guest and "masterfully" kissed upon the lips, may for an instant be "horrified, stunned, *like a bird in the grasp of a cat.*" But we are always assured that "through it all something tremendously vital and insistent" will be speaking to her, and that in the end she will not resist the urge of the *élan vital.* I recall no one of all the dozens of obliging women in these books who makes any effective resistance when summoned to capitulate. *"The psychology of the human animal,* when confronted by these tangles, these ripping tides of the heart," says the author of "The Titan," "has little to do with so-called reason or logic." No; as he informs us elsewhere with endless iteration, it is a question of chemistry. It is the "chemistry of her being" which rouses to blazing the ordinarily dormant forces of Eugene Witla's sympathies in "The Genius." If Stephanie Platow is disloyal to her married lover in "The Titan," "let no one quarrel" with her. Reason: "She was an unstable chemical compound."

Such is the Dreiserian philosophy.

III

By thus eliminating distinctively human motives and making animal instincts the supreme factors in human life, Mr. Dreiser reduces the problem of the novelist to the lowest possible terms. I find myself unable to go with those who admire the powerful reality of his art while deploring the puerility of his philosophy. His philosophy quite excludes him from the field in which a great realist must work. He has deliberately rejected the novelist's supreme task—understanding and presenting the development of character; he has chosen only to illustrate the unrestricted flow of temperament. He has evaded the enterprise of representing human conduct; he has confined himself to a representation of animal behavior. He demands for the demonstration of his theory a moral vacuum from which the obligations of parenthood, marriage, chivalry, and citizenship have been quite withdrawn or locked in a twilight sleep. At each critical moment in his narrative, where a realist like George Eliot or Thackeray or Trollope or Meredith would be asking how a given individual would feel, think, and act under the manifold combined stresses of organized society, Mr. Dreiser sinks supinely back upon the law of the jungle or mutters his mystical gibberish about an alteration of the chemical formula.

The possibility of making the unvarying victoriousness of jungle-motive plausible depends directly upon the suppression of the evidence of other motives. In this work of suppression Mr. Dreiser simplifies American life almost beyond recognition. Whether it is because he comes from Indiana, or whether it is because he steadily envisages the human animal, I cannot say;

I can only note that he never speaks of his men and women as "educated" or "brought up." Whatever their social status, they are invariably "raised." Raising human stock in America evidently includes feeding and clothing it, but does not include the inculcation of even the most elementary moral ideas. Hence Mr. Dreiser's field seems curiously outside American society. Yet he repeatedly informs us that his persons are typical of the American middle class, and three of the leading figures, to judge from their names— Carrie Meeber, Jennie Gerhardt, and Eugene Witla—are of our most highly "cultured" race. Frank Cowperwood, the hero of two novels, is a hawk of finance and a rake almost from the cradle; but of the powers which presided over his cradle we know nothing save that his father was a competent official in a Philadelphia bank. What, if anything, Carrie Meeber's typical American parents taught her about the conduct of life is suppressed; for we meet the girl in a train to Chicago, on which she falls to the first drummer who accosts her. Eugene Witla emerges in his teens from the bosom of a typical middle-class American family—with a knowledge of the game called "post office," takes the train for Chicago, and without hesitation enters upon his long career of seduction. Jennie Gerhardt, of course, succumbs to the first man who puts his arm around her; but, in certain respects, her case is exceptional.

In the novel "Jennie Gerhardt" Mr. Dreiser ventures a disastrous experiment at making the jungle-motive plausible without suppressing the evidence of other motives. He provides the girl with pious Lutheran parents, of fallen fortune, but alleged to be of sterling character, who "raise" her with the utmost strictness. He even admits that the family were church-goers, and he outlines the doctrine preached by Pastor Wundt: right conduct in marriage and absolute innocence before that state, essentials of Christian living; no salvation for a daughter who failed to keep her chastity unstained or for the parents who permitted her to fall; Hell yawning for all such; God angry with sinners every day. "Gerhardt and his wife, and also Jennie," says Mr. Dreiser, "accepted the doctrines of their church without reserve." Twenty pages later Jennie is represented as yielding her virtue in pure gratitude to a man of fifty, Senator Brander, who has let her do his laundry and in other ways has been kind to her and to her family. The Senator suddenly dies; Jennie expects to become a mother; Father Gerhardt is brokenhearted, and the family moves from Columbus to Cleveland. This first episode is not incredibly presented as a momentary triumph of emotional impulse over training—as an "accident." The incredible appears when Mr. Dreiser insists that an accident of this sort to a girl brought up *under the conditions stated* is not necessarily followed by any sense of sin or shame or regret. Upon this simple pious Lutheran he imposes his own naturalistic philosophy, and, in analyzing her psychology before the birth of her illegitimate child, pretends that she looks forward to the event "without a murmur," with "serene, unfaltering courage," "the marvel of life holding her in trance," with "joy and satisfaction," seeing in her state "the immense possibilities of racial fulfillment." This juggling is probably expected to prepare us for her instantaneous assent, perhaps a year later, when a healthy, magnetic manufacturer, who has seen her perhaps a dozen times, claps his paw upon her and says, "You belong to me," and in a perfectly cold-blooded interview proposes the terms on which he will set her up in New York as his mistress. Jennie, who is a fond mother and a dutiful daughter, goes to her pious Lutheran mother and talks the whole matter over with her quite candidly. The mother hesitates—not on Jennie's account, gentle reader, but because she will be obliged to deceive old Gerhardt; "the difficulty of telling this lie was very great for Mrs. Gerhardt"! But she acquiesces at last. "I'll help you out with it," she concludes—"with a little sigh." The unreality of the whole transaction shrieks.

Mr. Dreiser's stubborn insistence upon the jungle-motive results in a dreary monotony in the form and substance of his novels. Interested only in the description of animal behavior, he constructs his plot in such a way as to exhibit the persistence of two or three elementary instincts through every kind of situation. He finds, for example, a subject in the career of an American captain of industry, thinly disguised under the name of Frank Cowperwood. He has just two things to tell us about Cowperwood: that he has a rapacious appetite for money, and that he has a rapacious appetite for women. In "The Financier" he "documents" those two truths about Cowperwood in seventy-four chapters, in each one of which he shows us how this hero made money or how he captivated women in Philadelphia. Not satisfied with the demonstration, he returns to the same theses in "The Titan," and shows us in sixty-two chapters how the same hero made money and captivated women in Chicago and New York. He promises us a third volume, in which we shall no doubt learn in a work of sixty or seventy chapters—a sort of huge club-sandwich composed of slices of business alternating with erotic episodes—how Frank Cowperwood made money and captivated women in London. Meanwhile Mr. Dreiser has turned aside from his great "trilogy of desire" to give us "The Genius," in which the hero, Witla, alleged to be a great realistic painter, exhibits in 101 chapters, similarly "sandwiched" together, an appetite for women and money indistinguishable from that of Cowperwood. Read one of these novels, and you have read them all. What the hero is in the first chapter, he remains in the hundred-and-first or the hundred-and-thirty-sixth. He acquires naught from his experience but sensations. In the sum of his experiences there is nothing of the impressive mass and coherence of activities bound together by principles and integrated in character, for all his days have been but as isolated beads loosely strung on the thread of his desire. And so after the production of the hundredth document in the case of Frank Cowperwood, one is ready to cry with fatigue: "Hold! Enough! We believe you. Yes, it is very clear that Frank Cowperwood had a rapacious appetite for women and for money."

If at this point you stop and inquire why Mr. Dreiser goes to such great lengths to establish so little, you find yourself once more confronting the jungle-motive. Mr. Dreiser, with a problem similar to De Foe's in "The Apparition of Mrs. Veal," has availed himself of De Foe's method for creating the illusion of reality. The essence of the problem and of the method for both these authors is the certification of the unreal by the irrelevant. If you wish to make acceptable to your reader the incredible notion that Mrs. Veal's ghost appeared to Mrs. Bargrave, divert his incredulity from the precise point at issue by telling him all sorts of detailed credible things about the poverty of Mrs. Veal's early life, the sobriety of her brother, her father's neglect, and the bad temper of Mrs. Bargrave's husband. If you wish to make acceptable to your reader the incredible notion that Aileen Butler's first breach of the seventh article in the decalogue was "a happy event," taking place "much as a marriage might have," divert his incredulity by describing with the technical accuracy of a fashion magazine not merely the gown that she wore on the night of Cowperwood's reception, but also with equal detail the half-dozen other gowns that she thought she might wear, but did not. If you have been for three years editor-in-chief of the Butterick Publications, you can probably perform this feat with unimpeachable versimilitude; and having acquired credit for expert knowledge in matters of dress and millinery, you can now and then emit unchallenged a bit of philosophy such as "Life cannot be put in any one mould, and the attempt may as well be abandoned at once. . . . Besides, whether we will or no, theory or no theory, the large basic facts of chemistry and physics remain." None the less, if you expect to gain credence for the notion that your hero can have any woman in Chicago or New York that he puts his paw upon, you had probably better lead up to it by a detailed account of the street-railway system in those cities. It will necessitate the loading of your pages with a tremendous baggage of irrelevant detail. It will not sound much like art. It will sound more like one of Lincoln Steffens's special articles. But it will produce an overwhelming impression of reality, which the reader will carry with him into the next chapter where you are laying bare the "chemistry" of the human animal.

IV

It would make for clearness in our discussions of contemporary fiction
if we withheld the title of "realist" from a writer like Mr. Dreiser, and
called him, as Zola called himself, a "naturalist." While asserting that all
great art in every period intends a representation of reality, I have tried
to indicate the basis for a working distinction between the realistic novel
and the naturalistic novel of the present day. Both are representations of
the life of man in contemporary or nearly contemporary society, and
both are presumably composed of materials within the experience and
observation of the author. But a realistic novel is a representation based
upon a theory of human conduct. If the theory of human conduct is adequate, the representation constitutes an addition to literature and to social history. A naturalistic novel is a representation based upon a theory
of animal behavior. Since a theory of animal behavior can never be an
adequate basis for a representation of the life of man in contemporary
society, such a representation is an artistic blunder. When half the world
attempts to assert such a theory, the other half rises in battle. And so one
turns with relief from Mr. Dreiser's novels to the morning papers.

Sherwood Anderson

AN APOLOGY FOR CRUDITY

For a long time I have believed that crudity is an inevitable quality in the production of a really significant present-day American literature. How indeed is one to escape the obvious fact that there is as yet no native subtlety of thought or living among us? And if we are a crude and childlike people how can our literature hope to escape the influence of that fact? Why indeed should we want it to escape?

If you are in doubt as to the crudity of thought in America, try an experiment. Come out of your offices, where you sit writing and thinking, and try living with us. Get on a train at Pittsburg and go west to the mountains of Colorado. Stop for a time in our towns and cities. Stay for a week in some Iowa corn-shipping town and for another week in one of the Chicago clubs. As you loiter about read our newspapers and listen to our conversations, remembering, if you will, that as you see us in the towns and cities, so we are. We are not subtle enough to conceal ourselves and he who runs with open eyes through the Mississippi Valley may read the story of the Mississippi Valley.

It is a marvelous story and we have not yet begun to tell the half of it. A little, I think I know why. It is because we who write have drawn ourselves away. We have not had faith in our people and in the story of our people. If we are crude and childlike, that is our story and our writing men must learn to dare to come among us until they know the story. The telling of the story depends, I believe, upon their learning that lesson and accepting that burden.

To my room, which is on a street near the loop in the city of Chicago, come men who write. They talk and I write. We are fools. We talk of writers of the old world and the beauty and subtlety of the work they do. Below us the roaring city lies like a great animal on the prairies, but we do not run out to the prairies. We stay in our rooms and talk.

And so, having listened to talk and having myself talked overmuch, I grow weary of talk and walk in the streets. As I walk alone, an old truth comes home to me and I know that we shall never have an American

From *The Dial*, November 8, 1917.

literature until we return to faith in ourselves and to the facing of our own limitations. We must, in some way, become in ourselves more like our fellows, more simple and real.

For surely it does not follow that because we Americans are a people without subtlety, we are a dull or uninteresting people. Our literature is dull, but we are not. One remembers how Dostoevsky had faith in the simplicity of the Russians and what he achieved. He lived and he expressed the life of his time and people. The thing that he did brings hope of achievement for our men.

But let us first of all accept certain truths. Why should we Americans aspire to a subtlety that belongs not to us but to old lands and places? Why talk of intellectuality and of intellectual life when we have not accepted the life that we have? There is death on that road and following it has brought death into much of American writing. Can you doubt what I say? Consider the smooth slickness of the average magazine story. There is often great subtlety of plot and phrase, but there is no reality. Can such work live? The answer is that the most popular magazine story or novel does not live in our minds for a month.

And what are we to do about it? To me it seems that as writers we shall have to throw ourselves with greater daring into the life here. We shall have to begin to write out of the people and not for the people. We shall have to find within ourselves a little of that courage. To continue along the road we are travelling is unthinkable. To draw ourselves apart, to live in little groups and console ourselves with the thought that we are achieving intellectuality, is to get nowhere. By such a road we can hope only to go on producing a literature that has nothing to do with life as it is lived in these United States.

To be sure, the doing of the thing I am talking about will not be easy. America is a land of objective writing and thinking. New paths will have to be made. The subjective impulse is almost unknown to us. Because it is close to life, it works out into crude and broken forms. It leads along a road that such American masters of prose as James and Howells did not want to take, but if we are to get anywhere, we shall have to travel that road.

The road is rough and the times are pitiless. Who, knowing our America and understanding the life in our towns and cities, can close his eyes to the fact that life here is for the most part an ugly affair? As a people we have given ourselves to industrialism, and industrialism is not lovely. If anyone can find beauty in an American factory town, I wish he would show me the way. For myself, I cannot find it. To me, and I am living in industrial life, the whole thing is as ugly as modern war. I have to accept that fact and I believe a great step forward will have been taken when it is more generally accepted.

But why, I am asked, is crudity and ugliness necessary? Why cannot a man like Mr. Dreiser write in the spirit of the early Americans, why cannot he see fun in life? What we want is the note of health. In the work of Mark Twain there was something wholesome and sweet. Why cannot the modern man be also wholesome and sweet?

To this I make answer that to me a man, say like Mr. Dreiser, is wholesome. He is true to something in the life about him, and truth is always wholesome. Twain and Whitman wrote out of another age, out of an age and a land of forests and rivers. The dominant note of American life in their time was the noisy, swaggering raftsman and the hairy-breasted woodsman. To-day it is not so. The dominant note in American life to-day is the factory hand. When we have digested that fact, we can begin to approach the task of the present-day novelist with a new point of view.

It is, I believe, self-evident that the work of the novelist must always lie somewhat outside the field of philosophic thought. Your true novelist is a man gone a little mad with the life of his times. As he goes through life he lives, not in himself, but in many people. Through his brain march figures and groups of figures. Out of the many figures, one emerges. If he be at all sensitive to the life about him and that life be crude, the figure that emerges will be crude and will crudely express itself.

I do not know how far a man may go on the road of subjective writing. The matter, I admit, puzzles me. There is something approaching insanity in the very idea of sinking yourself too deeply into modern American industrial life.

But it is my contention that there is no other road. If one would avoid neat, slick writing, he must at least attempt to be brother to his brothers and live as the men of his time live. He must share with them the crude expression of their lives. To our grandchildren the privilege of attempting to produce a school of American writing that has delicacy and color may come as a matter of course. One hopes that will be true, but it is not true now. And that is why, with so many of the younger Americans, I put my faith in the modern literary adventurers. We shall, I am sure, have much crude, blundering American writing before the gift of beauty and subtlety in prose shall honestly belong to us.

H. L. Mencken

THE DREISER BUGABOO

Dr. William Lyon Phelps, the Lampson professor of English at Yale, opens his chapter on Mark Twain in his "Essays on Modern Novelists" with a humorous account of the critical imbecility which pursued Mark in his own country down to his last years. The favorite national critics of that era (and it extended to 1895, at the least) were wholly anaesthetic to the fact that he was a great artist. They admitted him, somewhat grudgingly, a certain low dexterity as a clown, but that he was an imaginative writer of the first rank, or even of the fifth rank, was something that, in their insanest moments, never so much as occurred to them. Phelps cites, in particular, an ass named Professor Richardson, whose "American Literature," it appears, "is still a standard work" and "a deservedly high authority"—apparently in colleges. In the 1892 edition of this *magnum opus,* Mark is dismissed with less than four lines, and ranked below Irving, Holmes and Lowell—nay, actually below Artemus Ward, Josh Billings and Petroleum V. Nasby! The thing is fabulous, fantastic—but nevertheless true. Lacking the "higher artistic or moral purpose of the greater humorists" (*exempli gratia,* Rabelais, Molière, Aristophanes!), Mark is put off by this Prof. Balderdash as a laborious buffoon . . . But stay! Do not laugh yet! Phelps himself, indignant at the stupidity, now proceeds to prove that Mark was really a great moralist, and more, a great optimist . . . Turn to "The Mysterious Stranger" and "What is Man?"! . . .

College professors, alas, never learn anything. The identical pedagogue who achieved this nonsense about old Mark in 1910 now seeks to dispose of Theodore Dreiser in the precise manner of Richardson. That is to say, he essays to finish him by putting him into Coventry, by loftily passing him over. "Do not speak of him," said Kingsley of Heine; "he was a wicked man." Search the latest volume of the Phelps revelation, "The Advance of the English Novel," and you will find that Dreiser is not once mentioned in it. The late O. Henry is hailed as a genius who will have "abiding fame"; Henry Sydnor Harrison is hymned as "more than a

From *The Seven Arts,* August, 1917.

clever novelist," nay, "a valuable ally of the angels" (the right-thinker complex! art as a form of snuffling!), and an obscure Pagliaccio named Charles D. Stewart is brought forward as "the American novelist most worthy to fill the particular vacancy caused by the death of Mark Twain" —but Dreiser is not even listed in the index. And where Phelps leads with his baton of birch most of the other drovers of rah-rah boys follow. I turn, for example, to "An Introduction to American Literature," by Henry S. Pancoast, A.M., L.H.D., dated 1912. There are kind words for Richard Harding Davis, for Amelie Rives, and even for Will N. Harben, but not a syllable for Dreiser. Again, there is "A History of American Literature," by Reuben Post Halleck, A.M., LL.D., dated 1911. Lew Wallace, Marietta Holley, Owen Wister and Augusta Evans Wilson have their hearings, but not Dreiser. Yet again, there is "A History of American Literature Since 1870," by Prof. Fred. Lewis Pattee, instructor in "the English language and literature" somewhere in Pennsylvania. Fred has praises for Marion Crawford, Margaret Deland and F. Hopkinson Smith, and polite bows for Richard Harding Davis and Robert W. Chambers, but from end to end of his fat tome I am unable to find the slightest mention of Dreiser.

So much for one group of heroes of the new Dunciad. That it includes most of the acknowledged heavyweights of the craft—the Babbitts, Mores, Brownells and so on—goes without saying; as Van Wyck Brooks has pointed out in *The Seven Arts,* these magnificoes are austerely above any consideration of the literature that is in being. The other group, more courageous and more honest, proceeds by direct attack; Dreiser is to be disposed of by a moral *attentat.* Its leaders are two more professors, Stuart P. Sherman and H. W. Boynton, and in its ranks march the lady critics of the newspapers with much shrill, falsetto clamor. Sherman is the only one of them who shows any intelligible reasoning. Boynton, as always, is a mere parroter of conventional phrases, and the objections of the ladies fade imperceptibly into a pious indignation which is indistinguishable from that of the professional suppressors of vice.

What, then, is Sherman's complaint? In brief, that Dreiser is a liar when he calls himself a realist; that he is actually a naturalist, and hence accursed. That "he has evaded the enterprise of representing human conduct, and confined himself to a representation of animal behavior." That he "imposes his own naturalistic philosophy" upon his characters, making them do what they ought not to do, and think what they ought not to think. That he "has just two things to tell us about Frank Cowperwood: that he has a rapacious appetite for money, and a rapacious appetite for women." That this alleged "theory of animal behavior" is not only incorrect, but immoral, and that "when one half the world attempts to assert it, the other half rises in battle." [*The Nation,* Dec. 2, 1915. Also included in this collection.]

Only a glance is needed to show the vacuity of all this irate flubdub. Dreiser, in point of fact, is scarcely more the realist or the naturalist, in any true sense, than H. G. Wells or the later George Moore, nor has he ever announced himself in either the one character or the other—if there be, in fact, any difference between them that anyone save a pigeon-holing pedagogue can discern. He is really something quite different, and, in his moments, something far more stately. His aim is not merely to record, but to translate and understand; the thing he exposes is not the empty event and act, but the endless mystery out of which it springs; his pictures have a passionate compassion in them that it is hard to separate from poetry. If this sense of the universal and inexplicable tragedy, if this vision of life as a seeking without a finding, if this adept summoning up of moving images, is mistaken by college professors for the empty, meticulous nastiness of Zola in "Pot-Bouille"—in Nietzsche's phrase, for "the delight to stink"—then surely the folly of college professors, as vast as it seems, has been underestimated. What is the fact? The fact is that Dreiser's attitude of mind, his manner of reaction to the phenomena he represents, the whole of his alleged "naturalistic philosophy," stem directly, not from Zola, Flaubert, Augier and the younger Dumas, but from the Greeks. In the midst of democratic cocksureness and Christian sentimentalism, of doctrinaire shallowness and professorial smugness, he stands for a point of view which at least has something honest and courageous about it; here, at all events, he is a realist. Let him put a motto to his books, and it might be:

> *O ye deathward-going tribes of men!*
> *What do your lives mean except that they go to nothingness?*

If you protest against that as too harsh for Christians and college professors, right-thinkers and forward-lookers, then you protest against "Oedipus Rex."

As for the animal behavior prattle of the learned headmaster, it reveals on the one hand only the academic fondness for seizing upon high-sounding but empty phrases and using them to alarm the populace, and on the other hand, only the academic incapacity for observing facts correctly and reporting them honestly. The truth is, of course, that the behavior of such men as Cowperwood and Eugene Witla and of such women as Carrie Meeber and Jennie Gerhardt, as Dreiser describes it, is no more merely animal than the behavior of such acknowledged and undoubted human beings as Dr. Woodrow Wilson and Dr. Jane Addams.

The whole point of the story of Witla, to take the example which seems to concern the horrified watchmen most, is this: that his life is a bitter conflict between the animal in him and the aspiring soul, between the flesh and the spirit, between what is weak in him and what is strong, between what is base and what is noble. Moreover, the good, in the end, gets its hooks into the bad: as we part from Witla he is actually bathed in the tears of remorse, and resolved to be a correct and godfearing man. And what have we in "The Financier" and "The Titan"? A conflict, in the ego of Cowperwood, between aspiration and ambition, between the passion for beauty and the passion for power. Is either passion animal? To ask the question is to answer it.

I single out Dr. Sherman, not because his pompous syllogisms have any plausibility in fact or logic, but simply because he may well stand as arche- type of the booming, indignant corrupter of criteria, the moralist turned critic. A glance at his paean to Arnold Bennett [New York *Evening Post*, Dec. 31, 1915] at once reveals the true gravamen of his objection to Dreiser. What offends him is not actually Dreiser's shortcomings as an artist, but Dreiser's shortcomings as a Christian and an American. In Bennett's volumes of pseudo-philosophy—e.g., "The Plain Man and His Wife" and "The Feast of St. Friend"—he finds the intellectual victuals that are to his taste. Here we have a sweet commingling of virtuous con- formity and complacent optimism, of sonorous platitude and easy cer- tainty—here, in brief, we have the philosophy of the English middle classes—and here, by the same token we have the sort of guff that the half- educated of our own country can understand. It is the calm, superior numskullery that was Victorian; it is by Samuel Smiles out of Hannah More. The offense of Dreiser is that he has disdained this revelation and gone back to the Greeks. Lo, he reads poetry into "the appetite for women"—he rejects the Pauline doctrine that all love is below the dia- phragm! He thinks of Ulysses, not as a mere heretic and criminal, but as a great artist. He sees the life of man, not as a simple theorem in Cal- vinism, but as a vast adventure, an enchantment, a mystery. It is no wonder that respectable schoolteachers are against him. . . .

The Comstockian attack upon "The 'Genius'" seems to have sprung out of the same muddled sense of Dreiser's essential hostility to all that is safe and regular—of the danger in him to that mellowed Methodism which has become the national ethic. The book, in a way, was a direct challenge, for though it came to an end upon a note which even a Meth- odist might hear as sweet, there were provocations in detail. Dreiser, in fact, allowed his scorn to make off with his taste—and *es ist nichts fürchtlicher als Einbildungskraft ohne Geschmack*. The Comstocks arose to the bait a bit slowly, but none the less surely. Going through the volume with the terribly industry of a Sunday-school boy dredging up pearls of smut from the Old Testament, they achieved a list of no less than 89 alleged floutings of the code—75 described as lewd and 14 as profane. An inspection of these specifications affords mirth of a rare and lofty variety; nothing could more cruelly expose the inner chambers of the moral mind. When young Witla, fastening his best girl's skate, is so overcome by the carnality of youth that he hugs her, it is set down as lewd. On page 51, having become an art student, he is fired by "a great warm-tinted nude of Bouguereau"—lewd again. On page 70 he begins to draw from the figure, and his instructor cautions him that the female breast is round, not square —more lewdness. On page 151 he kisses his girl on mouth and neck and she cautions him: "Be careful! Momma may come in"—still more. On page 161, having got rid of mamma, she yields "herself to him gladly, joyously" and he is greatly shocked when she argues that an artist (she is by way of being a singer) had better not marry—lewdness double damned. On page 245 he and his bride, being ignorant, neglect the principles laid down by Dr. Sylvanus Stall in his great works on sex hygiene —lewdness most horrible! But there is no need to proceed further. Every kiss, hug and tickle of the chin in the chronicle is laboriously snouted out, empanelled, exhibited. Every hint that Witla is no vestal, that he indulges his unchristian fleshliness, that he burns in the manner of I Corinthians, VII, 9, is uncovered to the moral inquisition.

On the side of profanity there is a less ardent pursuit of evidence, chiefly, I daresay, because their unearthing is less stimulating. (Besides, there is no law prohibiting profanity in books: the whole inquiry here is but so much *lagniappe*.) On page 408, describing a character called Daniel C. Summerfield, Dreiser says that the fellow is "very much given to swearing, more as a matter of habit than of foul intention," and then goes on to explain somewhat lamely that "no picture of him would be complete without the interpolation of his various expressions." They turn out to be *God Damn* and *Jesus Christ*—three of the latter and five or six of the former. All go down; the pure in heart must be shielded from the knowledge of them. (But what of the immoral French? They call the English *Goddams*.) Also, three plain *damns,* eight *hells,* one *my God,* five *by Gods,* one *go to the devil,* one *God Almighty* and one plain *God.* Altogether, 31 specimens are listed. "The 'Genius'" runs to 350,000 words. The profanity thus works out to somewhat less than one word in 10,000. . . . Alas, the Comstockian proboscis, feeling for such offendings, is not as alert as when uncovering more savoury delicacies. On page 191 I find an overlooked *by God.* On page 372 there are *Oh, God, God curses her,* and *God strike her dead.* On page 373 there are *Ah, God, Oh, God,* and three other invocations of God. On page 617 there is *God help me.*

On page 720 there is *as God is my judge*. On page 723 there is *I'm no damned good. . . .* But I begin to blush.

When the Comstock Society began proceedings against "The 'Genius'," a group of English novelists, including Arnold Bennett, H. G. Wells, W. L. George and Hugh Walpole, cabled an indignant caveat. This bestirred the Authors' League of America to activity, and its executive committee issued a minute denouncing the business. Later a protest of American *literati* was circulated, and more than 400 signed, including such highly respectable authors as Winston Churchill, Percy Mackaye, Booth Tarkington and James Lane Allen, and such critics as Lawrence Gilman, Clayton Hamilton and James Huneker, and the editors of such journals as the *Century,* the *Atlantic Monthly* and the *New Republic.* Among my literary lumber is all the correspondence relating to this protest, not forgetting the letters of those who refused to sign, and some day I hope to publish it, that posterity may not lose the joy of an extremely diverting episode. Meanwhile, the case moves with stately dignity through the interminable corridors of jurisprudence, and the bulk of the briefs and exhibits that it throws off begins to rival the staggering bulk of "The 'Genius' " itself.

In all this, of course, there is a certain savoury grotesquerie; the exposure of the Puritan mind makes life, for the moment, more agreeable. The danger of the combined comstockian professorial attack, to Dreiser as artist, is not that it will make a *muss*-Presbyterian of him, but that it will convert him into a professional revolutionary, spouting stale perunas for all the sorrows of the world. Here Greenwich Village pulls as Chautauqua pushes; already, indeed, the passionate skepticism that was his original philosophy begins to show signs of being contaminated by various so-called "radical" purposes. The danger is not one to be sniffed in. Dreiser, after all, is an American like the rest of us, and to be an American is to be burdened by an ethical prepossession, to lean toward causes and remedies. Go through "The 'Genius' " or "A Hoosier Holiday" carefully, and you will find disquieting indications of what might be called a democratic trend in thinking—that is, a trend toward short cuts, easy answers, glittering theories. He is bemused, off and on, by all the various poppycock of the age, from Christian Science to spiritism, and from the latest guesses in eschatology and epistemology to *art pour l'art.* A true American, he lacks a solid culture, and so he yields a bit to every wind that blows, to the inevitable damage of his representation of the eternal mystery that is man.

Joseph Conrad, starting out from the same wondering agnosticism, holds to it far more resolutely, and it is easy to see why. Conrad is, by birth and training, an aristocrat. He has the gift of emotional detachment.

The lures of facile doctrine do not move him. In his irony there is a disdain which plays about even the ironist himself. Dreiser is a product of far different forces and traditions, and is capable of no such escapement. Struggle as he may to rid himself of the current superstitions, he can never quite achieve deliverance from the believing attitude of mind—the heritage of the Indiana hinterland. One half of the man's brain, so to speak, wars with the other half. He is intelligent, he is thoughtful, he is a sound artist—but always there come moments when a dead hand falls upon him, and he is once more the Indiana peasant, snuffing absurdly over imbecile sentimentalities; giving a grave ear to quackeries, snorting and eye-rolling with the best of them. One generation spans too short a time to free the soul of man. Nietzsche, to the end of his days, remained a Prussian pastor's son, and hence two-thirds a Puritan; he erected his war upon holiness, toward the end, into a sort of holy war. Kipling, the grandson of a Methodist preacher, reveals the tin-pot evangelist with increasing clarity as youth and its ribaldries pass away and he falls back upon his fundamentals. And that other English novelist who springs from the servants' hall—let us not be surprised or blame him if he sometimes writes like a bounder.

As for Dreiser, as I hint politely, he is still, for all his achievement, in the transition stage between Christian Endeavor and civilization; between Warsaw, Indiana, and the Socratic grove; between being a good American and being a free man; and so he sometimes vacillates perilously between a moral sentimentalism and a somewhat extravagant revolt. "The 'Genius'," on the one hand, is almost a tract for rectitude, a Warning to the Young; its motto might be *Scheut die Dirnen*! And on the other hand, it is full of a laborious truculence that can be explained only by imagining the author as heroically determined to prove that he is a plain-spoken fellow and his own man, let the chips fall where they may. So, in spots, in "The Financier" and "The Titan," both of them far better books. There is an almost moral frenzy to expose and riddle what passes for morality among the stupid. The isolation of irony is never reached; the man is still a bit evangelical; his ideas are still novelties to him; he is as solemnly absurd in some of his floutings of the code American as he is in his respect for Bouguereau, or in his flirtings with New Thought, or in his naive belief in the importance of novel-writing. . . .

But his books remain, particularly his earlier books—and not all the ranting of the outraged orthodox will ever wipe them out. They were done in the stage of wonder, before self-consciousness began to creep in and corrupt it. The view of life that got into "Sister Carrie," the first of them, was not the product of a deliberate thinking out of Carrie's problem. It simply got itself there by the force of the artistic passion behind it;

its coherent statement had to wait for other and more reflective days. This complete rejection of ethical plan and purpose, this manifestation of what Nietzsche used to call moral innocence, is what brought up the guardians of the national tradition at the gallop, and created the Dreiser bugaboo of today. All the rubber-stamp formulae of American fiction were thrown overboard in these earlier books; instead of reducing the inexplicable to the obvious, they lifted the obvious to the inexplicable; one could find in them no orderly chain of causes and effects, of rewards and punishments; they represented life as a phenomenon at once terrible and unintelligible, like a stroke of lightning. The prevailing criticism applied the moral litmus. They were not "good"; *ergo,* they were "evil."

The peril that Dreiser stands in is here. He may begin to act, if he is not careful, according to the costume forced on him. Unable to combat the orthodox valuation of his place and aim, he may seek a spiritual refuge in embracing it, and so arrange himself with the tripe-sellers of heterodoxy, and cry wares that differ from the other stock only in the bald fact that they are different. . . . Such a fall would grieve the judicious, of whom I have the honor to be one.

Randolph Bourne

THE ART OF

THEODORE DREISER

Theodore Dreiser has had the good fortune to evoke a peculiar quality of pugnacious interest among the younger American intelligentsia such as has been the lot of almost nobody else writing to-day unless it be Miss Amy Lowell. We do not usually take literature seriously enough to quarrel over it. Or else we take it so seriously that we urbanely avoid squabbles. Certainly there are none of the vendettas that rage in a culture like that of France. But Mr. Dreiser seems to have made himself, particularly since the suppression of "The 'Genius',", a veritable issue. Interesting and surprising are the reactions to him. Edgar Lee Masters makes him a "soul-enrapt demi-urge, walking the earth, stalking life"; Harris Merton Lyon saw in him a "seer of inscrutable mien"; Arthur Davison Ficke sees him as master of a passing throng of figures, "labored with immortal illusion, the terrible and beautiful, cruel and wonder-laden illusion of life"; Mr. Powys makes him an epic philosopher of the "life-tide"; H. L. Mencken puts him ahead of Conrad, with "an agnosticism that has almost passed beyond curiosity." On the other hand, an unhappy critic in *The Nation* last year gave Mr. Dreiser his place for all time in a neat antithesis between the realism that was based on a theory of human conduct and the naturalism that reduced life to a mere animal behavior. For Dreiser this last special hell was reserved, and the jungle-like and simian activities of his characters were rather exhaustively outlined. At the time this antithesis looked silly. With the appearance of Mr. Dreiser's latest book, "A Hoosier Holiday," it becomes nonsensical. For that wise and delightful book reveals him as a very human critic of very common human life, romantically sensual and poetically realistic, with an artist's vision and a thick, warm feeling for American life.

This book gives the clue to Mr. Dreiser, to his insatiable curiosity about people, about their sexual inclinations, about their dreams, about the homely qualities that make them American. His memories give a picture of the floundering young American that is so typical as to be almost epic.

From *History of a Literary Radical*, B. W. Huebsch, 1920.

No one has ever pictured this lower middle-class American life so win-
ningly because no one has had the necessary literary skill with the lack of
self-consciousness. Mr. Dreiser is often sentimental, but it is a sentimentality that captivates you with its candor. You are seeing this vacuous,
wistful, spiritually rootless, Middle-Western life through the eyes of a
naïve but very wise boy. Mr. Dreiser seems queer only because he has carried along his youthful attitude in unbroken continuity. He is fascinated
with sex because youth is usually obsessed with sex. He puzzles about the
universe because youth usually puzzles. He thrills to crudity and violence
because sensitive youth usually recoils from the savagery of the industrial
world. Imagine incorrigible, sensuous youth endowed with the brooding
skepticism of the philosopher who feels the vanity of life, and you have
the paradox of Mr. Dreiser. For these two attitudes in him support rather
than oppose each other. His spiritual evolution was out of a pious, ascetic
atmosphere into intellectual and personal freedom. He seems to have
found himself without losing himself. Of how many American writers
can this be said? And for this much shall be forgiven him,—his slovenliness of style, his lack of *nuances,* his apathy to the finer shades of beauty,
his weakness for the mystical and the vague. Mr. Dreiser suggests the
over-sensitive temperament that protects itself by an admiration for crudity and cruelty. His latest book reveals the boyhood shyness and timidity
of this Don Juan of novelists. Mr. Dreiser is complicated, but he is complicated in a very understandable American way, the product of the
uncouth forces of small-town life and the vast disorganization of the
wider American world. As he reveals himself, it is a revelation of a certain broad level of the American soul.

Mr. Dreiser seems uncommon only because he is more naïve than most
of us. It is not so much that his pages swarm with sexful figures as that he
rescues sex for the scheme of personal life. He feels a holy mission to slay
the American literary superstition that men and women are not sensual
beings. But he does not brush this fact in the sniggering way of the popular magazines. He takes it very seriously, so much so that some of his
novels become caricatures of desire. It is, however, a misfortune that it
has been Brieux and Freud and not native Theodore Dreiser who has
saturated the sexual imagination of the younger American intelligentsia.
It would have been far healthier to absorb Mr. Dreiser's literary treatment
of sex than to go hysterical over its pathology. Sex has little significance
unless it is treated in personally artistic, novelistic terms. The American
tradition had tabooed the treatment of those infinite graduations and
complexities of love that fill the literary imagination of a sensitive people.
When curiosity became too strong and reticence was repealed in America,
we had no means of articulating ourselves except in a deplorable pseudo-

scientific jargon that has no more to do with the relevance of sex than the chemical composition of orange paint has to do with the artist's vision. Dreiser has done a real service to the American imagination in despising the underworld and going bravely to the business of picturing sex as it is lived in the personal relations of bungling, wistful, or masterful men and women. He seemed strange and rowdy only because he made sex human, and American tradition had never made it human. It had only made it either sacred or vulgar, and when these categories no longer worked, we fell under the dubious and perverting magic of the psycho-analysts.

In spite of his looseness of literary gait and heaviness of style Dreiser seems a sincere groper after beauty. It is natural enough that this should so largely be the beauty of sex. For where would a sensitive boy, brought up in Indiana and in the big American cities, get beauty expressed for him except in women? What does Mid-Western America offer to the starving except its personal beauty? A few landscapes, an occasional picture in a museum, a book of verse perhaps! Would not all the rest be one long, flaunting offense of ugliness and depression? "The 'Genius'," instead of being that mass of pornographic horror which the Vice Societies repute it to be, is the story of a groping artist whose love of beauty runs obsessingly upon the charm of girlhood. Through different social planes, through business and manual labor and the feverish world of artists, he pursues this lure. Dreiser is refreshing in his air of the moral democrat, who sees life impassively, neither praising nor blaming, at the same time that he realizes how much more terrible and beautiful and incalculable life is than any of us are willing to admit. It may be all *apologia,* but it comes with the grave air of a mind that wants us to understand just how it all happened. "Sister Carrie" will always retain the fresh charm of a spontaneous working-out of mediocre, and yet elemental and significant, lives. A good novelist catches hold of the thread of human desire. Dreiser does this, and that is why his admirers forgive him so many faults.

If you like to speculate about personal and literary qualities that are specifically American, Dreiser should be as interesting as any one now writing in America. This becomes clearer as he writes more about his youth. His hopelessly unorientated, half-educated boyhood is so typical of the uncritical and careless society in which wistful American talent has had to grope. He had to be spiritually a self-made man, work out a philosophy of life, discover his own sincerity. Talent in America outside of the ruling class flowers very late, because it takes so long to find its bearings. It has had almost to create its own soil, before it could put in its roots and grow. It is born shivering into an inhospitable and irrelevant group. It has to find its own kind of people and piece together its links of comprehension. It is a gruelling and tedious task, but those who come through it contribute, like Vachel Lindsay, creative work that is both novel and indigenous. The process can be more easily traced in Dreiser than in almost anybody else. "A Hoosier Holiday" not only traces the personal process, but it gives the social background. The common life, as seen throughout the countryside, is touched off quizzically, and yet sympathetically, with an artist's vision. Dreiser sees the American masses in their commonness and at their pleasure as brisk, rather vacuous people, a little pathetic in their innocence of the possibilities of life and their optimistic trustfulness. He sees them ruled by great barons of industry, and yet unconscious of their serfdom. He seems to love this countryside, and he makes you love it.

Dreiser loves, too, the ugly violent bursts of American industry,—the flaming steel-mills and gaunt lakesides. "The Titan" and "The Financier" are unattractive novels, but they are human documents of the brawn of a passing American era. Those stenographic conversations, webs of financial intrigue, bare bones of enterprise, insult our artistic sense. There is too much raw beef, and yet it all has the taste and smell of the primitive business-jungle it deals with. These crude and greedy captains of finance with their wars and their amours had to be given some kind of literary embodiment, and Dreiser has hammered a sort of raw epic out of their lives.

It is not only his feeling for these themes of crude power and sex and the American common life that makes Dreiser interesting. His emphases are those of a new America which is latently expressive and which must develop its art before we shall really have become articulate. For Dreiser is a true hyphenate, a product of that conglomerate Americanism that springs from other roots than the English tradition. Do we realize how rare it is to find a talent that is thoroughly American and wholly un-English? Culturally we have somehow suppressed the hyphenate. Only recently has he forced his way through the unofficial literary censorship. The vers-librists teem with him, but Dreiser is almost the first to achieve a largeness of utterance. His outlook, it is true, flouts the American canons of optimism and redemption, but these were never anything but conventions. There stirs in Dreiser's books a new American quality. It is not at all German. It is an authentic attempt to make something artistic out of the chaotic materials that lie around us in American life. Dreiser interests because we can watch him grope and feel his clumsiness. He has the artist's vision without the sureness of the artist's technique. That is one of the tragedies of America. But his faults are those of his material and of uncouth bulk, and not of shoddiness. He expresses an America that is in process of forming. The interest he evokes is part of the eager interest we feel in that growth.

Thomas K. Whipple

ASPECTS OF A PATHFINDER

The importance of Theodore Dreiser as a writer is chiefly historical. That is to say, he belongs to that class of men, such as Edmund Waller, "Ossian," and Charles Brockden Brown, who for a time enjoy a considerable vogue, but whom later generations, after the novelty and the immediate applicability have worn off their work, find unreadable. Such men usually excel in some one particular: they introduce or perfect a trick of style; they exploit a new province of human life; they develop an odd, unknown mode of feeling. But shortly their specialty is mastered by other writers, by men perhaps of less originality, but of solider and better rounded talents; and, save by the historian of literature, the partial and incomplete work of the pioneer is forgotten.

So it must be, I think, with Dreiser. He is important because he was among the first to establish a point of view which has become more and more prevalent. As Sherwood Anderson says in the dedication to *Horses and Men,* Dreiser has made a path through the wilderness, and now the path is becoming a street—a street that shows signs of growing overcrowded. But it is unlikely that future readers will care to acquaint themselves at first hand with the work of the trail-breaker. The labor of reading Dreiser is too arduous and not sufficiently profitable. Too often, while engaged with one of his novels, one has that sense of grinding despair which comes in nightmares when one is being pursued over endless wastes of soft sand. The experience, however instructive, is too painful to be sought out by normal humanity.

Even Dreiser's admirers admit his shortcomings as a writer of novels. His style is atrocious, his sentences are chaotic, his grammar and syntax faulty; he has no feeling for words, no sense of diction. His wordiness and his repetitions are unbearable, his cacophonies incredible. The following sentence is a specimen of what he can achieve:

> *He had vaulting ambitions and pretensions, literary and otherwise, having by now composed various rondeaus, triolets, quatrains, son-*

From *Spokesmen: Modern Writers and American Life,* D. Appleton & Co., 1928.

nets, in addition to a number of short stories over which he had lit-
erally slaved and which, being rejected by many editors, were kept
lying idly and inconsequentially and seemingly inconspicuously about
his place—the more to astonish the poor unsophisticated "outsider."

He violates English and even American idiom; he often shows himself
ignorant of the meaning of words, as when he uses *satiation* for *satisfac-*
tion or *fearsome* for *afraid*. He freely mingles the most colloquial expressions with poetic archaisms. Worst of all is his liking for the cheap,
tawdry, and banal, for phrases that are trite and florid, for "below-stairs"
writing in the manner of Bertha M. Clay and the Duchess or of the society
column in a country newspaper.

Nor is his command of the art of fiction superior to his command of
language. Of narrative form he seems to have no conception at all, of the
clean, lucid telling of a story. He is constantly forgetting the plan or structure of his work, for he can resist no temptation to wander off into
bypaths, sometimes of rambling general reflection and of philosophical
disquisition, sometimes of social and economic history, even into explana-
tions of biological laws and analogies. Perhaps because he takes for
granted a total ignorance of everything on the part of his readers, he can
let nothing pass without explanation. If he mentions Christian Science, he
must devote pages to its theology and technique. But worse than his fancy
for straying is his habit of amassing what is unimportant and insignificant. Because he cannot bring himself to leave out anything, he heaps up
mountains of pointless detail. We must be told everything about every
character, no matter how minor—where and when he was born, what sort
of house he lives in, what articles of furniture he has in it and what is
their material and design, what his business is and whether he is prospering, how often he goes to church, and so on. But there is no need to
dwell on these aspects of Dreiser's work; they are commonplaces of criticism, and they have been abundantly and amusingly discussed and illustrated by Mencken, Dreiser's foremost champion.

Mencken, however, seems to regard these foibles as of little consequence,
as petty irritations that the reader must try to put out of mind. I cannot
agree: no author's style is unimportant, for it is always characteristic.
Dreiser's style is a personal expression in which inevitably many of his
qualities show themselves. Surely he could not write as he does if there
were not in his mind something correspondingly muddled, commonplace,
undiscerning, cheap, and shoddy. When he says in *The Financier* of an
interior decorator:

> *His eyes brooded great, deep things concerning the illimitable*
> *realm of refinement in which he was working,*

the passage can be no mere slip of the pen, nor can that at the end of *The "Genius"*:

> *"What a sweet welter life is—how rich, how tender, how grim, how like a colorful symphony."*
> *Great art dreams welled up into his soul as he viewed the sparkling deeps of space.*

That sentence alone, if there were no other evidence, would suffice to show that the man who wrote it, however much he might talk about art and beauty, had no conception of either the one or the other. Indeed, that is what all his writing shows. Its lack of any sort of beauty—beauty of form, of imagery, of rhythm—indicates not only that Dreiser himself is devoid of aesthetic sense, but also—what is even more serious—that he has no natural knack for writing. If he had turned to sculpture, say—an art for which he had presumably as much aptitude as for writing—would he have received respectful attention from so intelligent a critic as Mencken? One doubts it, for statues must at least stand up; and it is easy to imagine the sort of figures Dreiser would have carved—like parodies by Goldberg of Rodin's "Thinker." Dreiser's defects are too grave to be dismissed as peccadilloes. After all, an author must in the nature of the case work in literary form, in words and nothing else; and we are forced to take his words for what they are worth, inasmuch as we have no other means of learning what he may have in his mind.

An excellent instance of this truism is Dreiser's characterization. For all we know, his people may live with the utmost distinctness in his mind, but if he lacks means of communication he cannot convey his conception to us with any sharpness. Perhaps he can really create them in his imagination—we cannot tell; all we can know is whether or not he gives us a well defined idea of them. I do not find that he does. On the whole, his minor characters stand out more clearly than his protagonists: Drouet, for example, the drummer in *Sister Carrie,* or old Butler, the Irish politician in *The Financier,* or Clyde's father and mother in *An American Tragedy.* Dreiser has done no better portraiture than some of the sketches in *Twelve Men.* His heroines, Carrie Meeber and Jennie Gerhardt, leave an impression of something soft and yielding, of a gently passive substance, and somewhat the same indeterminateness hangs about Clyde Griffiths. Perhaps their vagueness is part of the author's intention, but he can scarcely have meant them to be quite so blurry as they are, especially as the blur seems more in the drawing than in the subjects of the pictures.

His earlier heroes, on the other hand, Cowperwood of *The Financier* and *The Titan* and Eugene Witla of *The "Genius,"* are all but monstrosities, memorable but unreal. Cowperwood in particular is a bogey-man. The difficulty in both instances is that Dreiser has attempted to go beyond his own powers and is therefore reduced to the poor expedient of telling us about his heroes instead of presenting them, of asserting, that is, that men possess qualities which the author is incapable of portraying directly. The result is a hopeless confusion, an odd effect as of a twice-exposed negative; or rather, we feel as if we were hearing things we cannot believe about a real person with whom we have some acquaintance. Cowperwood, so far as we are permitted to see him for ourselves unprejudiced by the author's comments, is dull, coarse, and mean, with the mentality but not the picturesqueness of a card-sharper or a tricky horse-trader, animated only by avarice and lust. There were such men no doubt who became wealthy and powerful during the Gilded Age of America; and Dreiser's novels would be admirably to the point if they were conceived and executed to illustrate the saying of Charles Francis Adams:

> *I am more than a little puzzled to account for the instances I have seen of business success—money-getting. It comes from a rather low instinct. Certainly, so far as my observation goes, it is rarely met with in combination with the finer or more interesting traits of character. I have known, and known tolerably well, a good many "successful" men—"big" financially—men famous during the last half-century; and a less interesting crowd I do not care to encounter. Not one that I have ever known would I care to meet again, either in this world or the next; nor is one of them associated in my mind with the idea of humour, thought, or refinement.*

So to the reader's eyes looks Frank Cowperwood—but not to Dreiser's. Dreiser sees him as a radiant figure, of keen intellect and irresistible charm, witty and urbane, as dynamic as he is ruthless and unscrupulous, attracting and mastering men and women by his fascination and by an innate power which emanates from him in a sort of glow. He looks like a figure of wish-fulfillment, in whom the author has embodied and realized all the desires to which circumstances have denied satisfaction in his own life. Cowperwood is the sort of man Dreiser would like to have been; at any rate, he is endowed with all the gifts and graces of mind and body, and among them a discriminating passion for art. Precisely here Dreiser's failure is most disastrous, I think, because Cowperwood's creator has himself no comprehension of art. In short, Dreiser has attempted to depict a man rich in many of the traits in which Dreiser is himself most deficient —and the discordance between the sordid dullard he presents and the resplendent demigod he describes robs the figure of all reality.

The central character of *The "Genius,"* Eugene Witla, is equally uncon-
vincing, and even less interesting, as he is weak and vacillating and deficient in self-control. But he is supposed, at any rate, to be something of a
"genius," to have the capabilities of a great painter, and to possess wit and
social charm. He fascinates every one in the book—every one but the
reader, who no more believes in Witla's virtues than he does in Cowperwood's, and for the same reason. Dreiser is again beyond his depth, or
above his level. Drummers and shop girls, farmers, small storekeepers,
bartenders, and clerks he does well with; but when he departs from that
species he only emphasizes his own limitations. The lower middle class in
the Midwest, in city and country and village, he knows and understands,
but he succeeds with no other class and no other locality. His excursions
to New York and Philadelphia are failures. And even in his own field his
characterization, though I do not wish to deny it considerable merit, cannot be called first rate. Sherwood Anderson's portrayal of the same types,
for instance, makes Dreiser's look slack, fumbling, and superficial.

I have dwelt at some length on Dreiser's characterization because his
admirers, though they grant his other shortcomings as a writer, insist that
he can depict people. Mencken is one; yet Mencken's admiration turns out
on closer examination to be not for the people themselves so much as for
the circumstances in which they are placed, for the whole complex rather
than for the individuals. That is, it is Dreiser as social historian rather
than Dreiser as creator of character that Mencken and the others praise.
And therein they are right, for whatever one may deny to Dreiser one cannot deny him an amazing capacity for observation which goes far to
conceal if not to atone for his defects as a creator. Even if indefatigability
of observation cannot altogether make up for lack of discernment and
imagination, or industry for bad taste and dullness of intelligence, those
qualities give Dreiser's work an importance as social record which it lacks
as fiction. *The Titan* and *The Financier* have the same merit as the official
biographies of multimillionaires which are composed by hard-working
but uninspired paid biographers. An epic sweep has often been attributed
to Dreiser's novels, and correctly so, for they have the range and vastness
which pertains to any minute record of an enormous area of human life.
They are titanic undertakings, reminding one of huge natural phenomena; to traverse "these vast steppes and pampas of narration," to borrow Mencken's phrase, is like exploring the state of Nevada. And they
have all been assembled, grain by grain, by never tiring, ant-like labor of
observation.

These great talus-heaps of detail bear witness also to a voracious curiosity and an insatiable interest in everything, an interest so universal that
to it nothing, nothing whatever, seems dull or tiresome. This unfailing

zest is one sign of Dreiser's omnivorous love of life—of all of it, of all existence, good or bad, beautiful or ugly. To him it is all exciting, because it is all strange. His is a romantic love of reality, charged with wonder and awe. This sense of novelty is one of the clearest signs that Dreiser has freshness, originality, and independence of mind; this unflagging relish for what is and this feeling of its mystery is one token of the fundamental trait in Dreiser's nature—his inexhaustible flow of emotion. From it spring his love of life, his energy, his observation; it is the moving and guiding force in all he does and says. He may like to consider himself a bold and penetrating thinker, but, as Mencken points out, "his ideas always seem to be deduced from his feelings." Everything he sees or touches he bathes in emotion. It is a source to him at once of strength and of weakness.

Many readers regard Dreiser's emotionality as mere sentimentality, but not, I think, justly. For his feeling is genuine, not spurious, and unlike the sentimentalist he does not gloat over it, revel in it, savor it with delight for its own sake. Nor is he blinded by it: it does not prevent him from seeing reality. If it sometimes gives an unpleasant effect, the reason is twofold: in the first place, the childish crudity of his expression lends an appearance of falsity. For example, when he cries out, once apropos of Chicago and once at the climax of *An American Tragedy:*

> *A very bard of a city this, singing of high deeds and high hopes, its heavy brogans buried deep in the mire of circumstance. Take Athens, O Greece! Italy, do you keep Rome!*
> *But that look in the eyes of Roberta! That last appealing look! God! He could not keep from seeing it! Her mournful, terrible screams! Could he not cease from hearing them—until he got out of here anyhow?*

it is difficult but also, I think, necessary to believe that words so inadequate could be called forth by true emotion. In the second place, Dreiser's feeling often looks false because it seems excessive, out of all normal proportion; and indeed it often is contrary to any normal scale of values. It is like the feeling of an adolescent, which to an adult looks absurd because it overrates what an adult takes for granted, but which is none the less genuine.

Granting Dreiser's imperfect means of communication and his disproportion, one must still insist that in his power of feeling lies his chief claim to greatness. Whatever their delinquencies, his novels leave as their final effect an impression of tremendous passion which makes itself felt even through the slag and dross of his writing. Especially of course this passion shows itself in his tragic sense, in his profound consciousness of the tragedy inherent in all existence, in the very scheme of things—tragedy inescapable, essential, universal—a tragedy perceived by many but by few so strongly, so overwhelmingly felt as by Dreiser. This one quality the author of *Jennie Gerhardt* has in common with the authors of *Œdipus the King* and of *King Lear*.

If one should dream that such a world began
In some slow devil's heart, that hated man,
Who should deny him?

Such is the feeling that actuates Dreiser's work. His brooding pity penetrates all life as he sees it, affecting every human being, from the most glittering superman to the forlornest prostitute. It is not only that most human hopes and desires are sure to be disappointed, and that those that are fulfilled bring no satisfaction—it is less that we do not get what we want than that misfortune hunts out even the most obscure and the most resigned, that even though we ask nothing we are still born to trouble as the sparks fly upward. Dreiser is especially acute in his perception of man's extraordinary capacity for suffering, a capacity for suffering which lends dignity, if not a touch of greatness, to even the weakest and most contemptible of Dreiser's creatures. Naturally, this aspect of his work cannot well be illustrated by quotation; yet, after all that has been said as to his shortcomings, I should like to cite a passage that shows Dreiser at his best, and that shows that at times when he contents himself with utter plainness he can be both effective and moving. The passage concerns a "small, homely, hardworked woman, whose pinching labor of former years had removed nearly all traces of feminine charm," who has just been told by her husband that he is going to be sent to the penitentiary for embezzlement.

His wife went out of the room after a time; but it was only to go into another bedroom and stare out of a window onto the faded grass of the fall. What was to become of her and her husband? She always thought of him and herself and children as a collective unit. There were four children, all told, fortunately well grown now. They would be very poor again, and, worst of all, disgraced. That was what hurt her. She stared and twisted her bony little hands. Her eyes did not moisten, but an ineffable sadness filled them. Sometimes the mediocre and the inefficient attain to a classic stature when dignified by pain.

If only such writing were less rare in Dreiser's work, there would be no excuse for saying that his importance is chiefly historical. And it is true that not even the exacerbation roused by an enforced reading of his books can prevent one from feeling that one has been in the company of a man of unusual dimensions, a man of originality and of great depth and volume of feeling, a man filled with wonder, awe, and pity; yet when one turns again from the author to the novels and surveys those misbegotten Leviathans whose vital spirits are so ill-adjusted to their bulk, one realizes again that it is the man, not his work, that one chiefly admires. That no doubt is why his defenders have paid so much more attention to Dreiser as a man, as an innovator, as a sociologist, than they have paid to him as a novelist. Furthermore, the period in which he began writing made his virtues, even his negative virtues, shine brilliantly by contrast.

To understand the ardent championship which Dreiser has received, one must mentally place him in the period of his first work, remembering that *Sister Carrie* appeared in 1900 and *Jennie Gerhardt* in 1911, and that among the favorite and most typical novels of the time were *When Knighthood Was in Flower, Graustark,* and *Rebecca of Sunnybrook Farm.* No wonder Dreiser was welcomed by the enlightened few. At least, he meant well. At least, he was not facile, conventional, superficial, thoughtlessly optimistic. He did not content himself with the pleasant telling of a pretty story, with the embroidering of rosy decorations. At a time when refreshment and distraction were all that was asked of literature, he manfully resisted the demand. Too much respect cannot be paid to his unyielding steadfastness and integrity. Instead of dealing in confectionery, he set out to tell the whole truth about American life as he saw it, even though he saw it as unpleasant; and he brought to his task a granitelike honesty and a strong sense of fact, seeing for himself and seeing directly, seldom the dupe of general illusions or preconceptions. Dreiser's project was so fresh and strange, so boldly original, that it made all the few who undertook it famous. The critics who approved of the attempt were not so ungrateful as to question its literary success; indeed, they could not afford to, in the bitter war which was being waged by their party against the moralists and the censors. And ever since, they have been writing about Dreiser as if this were still the early Roosevelt period. They have busied themselves with defending his conception of the purpose and nature of fiction, not with weighing his actual achievement.

To insist upon the imperfection of that achievement is not to deny that in many non-literary ways Dreiser's work is of the very greatest moment. As portrayer, critic, and product of American society, no one is more important and, unintentionally, more illuminating. He has few rivals as social historian. The future student of our way of living will have little difficulty in reconstructing from Dreiser's books the Midwest of the late nineteenth and early twentieth centuries, in its finance, politics, business, and daily private life. There are phases of Midwestern life which Dreiser does not touch, but those he treats he treats with authority. American life as he renders it has two outstanding features: chaos and tragedy. It is a free-for-all of personal aggrandizement, a wild struggle to get what each can out of the general grab-bag. Without plan, purpose, or sense, it lacks even the rudimentary organization of the wolf pack. The strongest, the ablest and most unscrupulous win the prizes—a futile victory because it brings no lasting satisfaction. The others, the dull, the weak, the bewildered, who do not even know what they want, who are hampered by all sorts of meaningless moral prejudices, who mill helplessly about, kicked and trodden upon—they are doomed from the outset. In such a disorder there is no place for purpose; such a milieu offers—can in the nature of things offer—no rewards which would appeal to a rational being, no valid reasons for living. Its only prize is economic success; when that has been won, there is nothing for the victor but further and superfluous economic success. The best Dreiser's world has to give is primal elementary pleasure —the pleasure of fighting, of luxury, of sensual gratifications; it is no more humane than the aboriginal jungle of saber-toothed tiger and woolly elephant.

It is a tragic world because it is futile and wasteful, because all people have aspirations and possibilities which cannot be fulfilled in it. Those are happiest on the one hand whose instincts are most primitive and on the other whose aspirations are feeblest; the former get the most, the latter ask the least. It is a tragedy, like most modern American tragedy, of spiritual frustration, of degeneration and decay. How could it be otherwise? Where in such an environment is there chance for the proper growth and development of human personality? What food, what experience, does it offer for human nature to feed upon? It is indifferent to experience, to humaneness of living, because from start to finish it is dominated by the practical ideal: one could ask no better picture than Dreiser's of a practical society. Its material manifestations, its towns and cities and the like, are hideous, sordid, and squalid, because it is indifferent to beauty, to sensuous experience. It is an intellectual vacuum, because what thought it has is either concentrated in self-seeking or dissipated in a blind consolatory cheerfulness which is the negation of thought. Its only aesthetic pleasure is the millionaire collector's delight at having outbid his rivals at an auction. It is destitute of religion; a stale, insipid tribal moralism has replaced the love of God. Naturally in such a country the inhabitants, save for their grasping-muscles, remain undeveloped; and therefore they have no real social life. Existing as they do, not in a social cosmos but in a social chaos, social experience is impossible for them. They drift about, helpless, detached atoms, attracting and repelling one another, with no more cohesion than so many billiard balls. The social aspect of Dreiser's world is the saddest of all, and serves well to emphasize the obvious import of Dreiser's portrayal of American life: namely, that a world given over to practicality is inevitably a tragic world, because it denies full humanity to human beings.

Dreiser himself, however, does not make this deduction. On the contrary, since he can imagine no other mode of living, he accepts the world he has known, the Age of Exploitation at its worst, as typical of human life everywhere at all times, accepts the Chicago of the nineties as a true microcosm, or microchaos. Therefore his explicit social criticism is curiously one-sided. Since he cannot judge his world by any other standards than its own, he cannot criticize its practice; he can only point out the inconsistency between its practice and its professed beliefs and official creeds. As to the latter, his comment runs along familiar lines; he discusses thoughtless optimism and sentimentality, negative, puritanical, taboo morality, intolerance, conformity, and standardization—in short, all the defenses which a society bent on "making good" builds up in the interest of efficiency to protect itself from being diverted by the claims of life and experience.

Not that Dreiser so explains our inconsistencies. He sometimes attributes them to Anglo-Saxon hypocrisy, that handy bugaboo; at other times, fantastically but characteristically, he is inclined to lay the blame on the influence of the Federal Constitution, an "idealistic" document drawn up by "charming and gracious dreamers"—among whom he singles out particularly the author of *Poor Richard's Almanac*! Because he accepts the practical ideal as inevitable, yet objects to the camouflage with which it must always protect itself to avoid friction and maintain an oblivious illusion, he is led into all manner of self-contradiction. He complains at one moment that Americans are passionately religious and moral, fiercely determined to put the Ten Commandments and the Beatitudes into practice, and the next moment that they pay no attention to right and wrong, now that Americans care nothing for righteousness, and now that they care for nothing else. His social criticism is largely vitiated by this uncertainty, which is due to his inability to view the life about him from a detached position.

This same inability is the determining influence on his philosophy, which, needless to say, is one of naturalism. Henry Adams saw the universe as a chaos of warring forces and man as their victim; E. A. Robinson sees man as a waif, a stray, an alien in a world which is indifferent and even hostile to him. Dreiser would assent to both propositions. He is convinced that man is but one among many natural objects, not differing in his status or destiny from a stone or shrub or beast. Nor can he discover a plan or purpose in nature, with or without reference to humanity: it is a senseless jumbled mass of energies that fight it out among themselves—"accidental, indifferent, and bitterly cruel forces," "haphazard and casual," resulting in "the unsolvable disorder and brutality of life." He writes:

> *I admit a vast compulsion which has nothing to do with the individual desires or tastes or impulses of individuals. That compulsion springs from the settling processes of forces which we do not in the least understand, over which we have no control, and in whose grip we are as grains of dust or sand, blown hither and thither for what purpose we cannot even suspect.*

Dreiser, being a determinist, would deny that he has any ethics, but he has a view of life which comes to much the same thing; since life is senseless and nature immoral, it is best to be rich and powerful, able to buy love and luxury. He has only contemptuous pity for the weaklings who are bound by moral scruples, only admiration for the Titans who at any cost get what they want. Again he comes surprisingly close to Henry Adams, to whom education meant efficiency, or a mastery of the world; both men, that is, indulge in success-worship of the crassest sort, the ideal of the *American Magazine.* In Dreiser, to be sure, this spirit is somewhat chastened, partly by personal experience and partly by reading; in his autobiography he tells how he discovered Spencer and Huxley, and adds:

> *Up to this time there had been in me a blazing and unchecked desire to get on, the feeling that in doing so we did get somewhere; now in its place was the definite conviction that spiritually one got nowhere . . . that one lived and had his being because one had to, and that it was of no importance.*

That is, he came to the conclusion that conspicuous worldly success was of little value, but could think of nothing else of any value at all; therefore, though he resigned himself to his own fate, he consistently in his novels depicts this kind of success as the only thing worth striving for: it may be worth little, but nothing else is worth more.

Though Henry Adams thought that he derived his philosophy from his reading in the natural sciences, we saw reason to suppose that he was really more influenced by his personal experience and especially by his environment, the United States between 1870 and 1900. Dreiser avows openly that his views are based on his own experience, particularly as a newspaper reporter in Chicago and St. Louis, though they were precipitated by his discovering the Victorian popularizers of scientific thought. In other words, Dreiser has merely made explicit the view of life which he found implicit in American society, merely reduced American practice to a philosophical theory. He grew up in the ultra-practical society which he depicts, a society wholly given over to economic individualism, and—once more like Henry Adams—though Dreiser has himself abandoned hope of success in the American sense, he has developed, with the aid of what he knows of science, the practical point of view into a view of life. No other attitude occurs to him as conceivable. Through and through he is a product of a thoroughly practical society.

Dreiser's peculiar state of mind is somewhat explained by the circumstances of his life. He was brought up a Catholic—but apparently in a very odd kind of Catholicism. He describes the view of life which was imposed upon him in his childhood, a view that was too simple and too cheerful to stand the strain of reality, that was hard and fast and exclusively moral. According to his account, he was taught to believe that good and bad were as unmistakable as black and white, that mankind was clearly divided into sheep and goats and that there were few goats, that the virtuous throve and were rewarded in this world and the vicious punished, that the universe was run in accordance with the Sermon on the Mount so as to favor the meek, the peaceful, and the pure in heart. Christianity is still to Dreiser synonymous with sentimental optimism; he has no notion how close he has come at times to writing an early-Christian treatise *De Contemptu Mundi*. Furthermore, he was early inducted into a negative morality: virtue consisted in not drinking or smoking, not dancing, not going to the theater. Sex was by its nature essentially sinful. "We were taught persistently to shun," he says, "most human experiences as either dangerous or degrading or destructive." From this atmosphere he plunged as a reporter into slums and police courts and all sorts of misery, filth, and graft. Later he read Huxley, Tyndall, and Spencer, and found his worst fears justified. He went through the experience so common and so painful in the nineteenth century, of losing his faith. Like his contemporaries, he experienced a reaction—much the same sort of reaction that every one goes through on reaching adolescence and leaving the easy harmless world of childhood, but in Dreiser's case aggravated by many circumstances, among them his advanced age. His awakening came ten years too late, and was that much more severe.

No better illustration than Dreiser could be asked of the statement that in a practical society a writer is drilled throughout his youth in false modes of thought and feeling, usually a sham gentility and a spurious puritanism, so that not until he reaches maturity can he rid himself of these encumbrances and really begin to experience life. That is why in many ways it is as if Dreiser had got stuck mentally in the adolescent age. The pained amazement with which he views human imperfection and inconsistency, the confusion, the morbid emotionalism and excitement, the lack of scale in judging values, the intellectual naïveté, the enthusiasm with which he announces what all adults have always known—all are traits, I believe, of an adolescent state of mind. One is tempted to suggest that Dreiser's is a case of delayed or arrested development, that he has never quite grown up, developed, and matured. He is still capable of arguing with serious heat that an earthquake is not an instance of God's mercy. He has succeeded at best only in half-emancipating himself from his early surroundings. As Mencken vigorously puts it:

> *The truth about Dreiser is that he is still in the transition stage between Christian Endeavor and civilization, between being a good American and being a free man. . . . There is an almost moral frenzy to expose and riddle what passes for morality among the stupid. . . . The man is still evangelical.*

But not only does Dreiser retain a preacher's fervor; as we have seen, though he has managed to give up the nostrums with which practical people quiet themselves and to forego his own self-advancement, he has not managed altogether to free himself from the practical temper. He is still half enslaved.

Dreiser's ignorance, already mentioned in connection with his notions of the Constitution and of Christianity, shows itself also in a more pernicious form. Because he is able to conceive only two views of life, the one in which he was brought up and the one to which he has attained—the two views, one followed and one professed, in the world in which he has lived—in all his thinking he sets up false alternatives and impales himself on a needless dilemma. On the one hand are chaos and jungle, "Nature" undisguised, pessimism, determinism, naturalism; on the other, a fatuous cheeriness, a debased morality, and a religion prostituted to practicality. These two for Dreiser exhaust the realms of human thought. It is most unfortunate. Naturalism—the philosophy of Hardy and Conrad—is a view which lends itself well to powerful and profound literary interpretations of life. Furthermore, Dreiser has assembled superabundant material for a penetrating and radical criticism of American life. Yet as thinker, as social critic, and as artist, he has been rendered all but impotent by the influence of his environment.

More than most men, he has suffered from the absence of an established national literary tradition, with its attendant discipline in taste and critical standards. As a writer, like most American writers, he has "just growed." In consequence, all his art, even to his style, seems to have been molded by the pressure of his surroundings: at least, it is a perfect match for them in its crude and chaotic ugliness, its occasional lapses into a maudlin, barbaric showiness, its immaturity, and its lack of rational control.

In part, perhaps, these qualities in Dreiser's work may be due to an innate want of aesthetic sense, but also they are surely in large measure due to a deprivation of the proper experience. It is true that he shows little appreciation even of natural beauty, which must have been available to him; yet one can scarcely believe that if he had lived in an environment which prized sensuous experience and which was rich in sensuous loveliness, especially of human creation, he could have been so oblivious of the claims of beauty. At any rate, if he had known a society which eagerly busied itself with ideas and which cared much for the disinterested play of thought, he could hardly have remained at so raw a stage of intellectual development. And if he had been part of a social web or fabric, he must have had a more varied and affluent conception of humanity and human possibilities. The folk of his making are uncivilized and undeveloped, and so is he, because he has only an uncivilized and undeveloped experience to draw upon. That he should have been denied an adequate experience is the greater pity for the reason that no one ever had a larger appetite for experience than Dreiser. His zest and gusto for living are his most distinctive traits. He has certainly absorbed what his world had to offer, and, I think, as one contemplates the image of that world in his books, one's final wonder is not that he got so little but so much out of it. Who else, who has had the same world as his to deal with, has succeeded in extracting more?

Therein lies Dreiser's great contribution to American letters and to American life. Before either the literature or the life could attain to vitality, some one had to establish a fruitful, living contact with the American environment, to experience it and realize it to the full. Until such a contact could be made, American life must continue to be meager and anemic, providing little sustenance either for humanity or for art. To make that contact is the main work of contemporary literature, and in this achievement Dreiser has been the foremost figure. I do not forget the abortive movement of the nineties headed by Stephen Crane and Frank Norris; but for some reason it failed to impress permanently either the general public or the writers of the time. The present literary manifestation has far more vigor—and it has Dreiser largely to thank. No doubt he is but the channel through which various forces and tendencies effectuate themselves, and no doubt they would have made themselves felt somehow without him. Yet, because he was the first in time of our contemporaries to express the new spirit, and because of the power and massiveness of his work, he has assumed the position of leader. To occupy such a position is in itself a great feat, and one that could be performed only by a man who possessed distinct elements of greatness.

Sinclair Lewis

OUR FORMULA FOR FICTION

To be really popular and beloved in America, a novel should assert that all American men are still handsome, rich and honest, and powerful at golf; that all the country towns are filled with neighbors who do nothing from day to day except go about being kind to one another; that although American girls may be wild, they change always into perfect wives and mothers, and that geographically America is composed solely of New York, which is inhabited only by millionaires; of the West, which retains unchanged all the boisterous heroism of 1870, and of the South, where everyone lives on a plantation perpetually glossy with moonlight and scented with magnolias.

It is not today vastly more true than it was twenty years ago that such novelists of ours as you have read in Sweden—novelists like Theodore Dreiser and Willa Cather—are authentically popular and influential in America. . . . We still mostly revere writers for the popular magazines who in a hearty and edifying chorus chant that the America of 120 million population is still as simple and pastoral as it was when it had but 40 million; that in an industrial plant with 10,000 employees the relationship between the workers and manager is as neighborly and uncomplex as in a factory of 1840 with five employees; that the relationships between father and son and between husband and wife are precisely the same in an apartment in a 30-story palace today, with three motor cars awaiting the family below, five books on the library shelves and a divorce imminent in the family next week, as were those relationships in the rose-veiled 5-room cottage of 1880; that, in fine, America has gone through a revolutionary change from a rustic colony to a world empire without having in the least changed the bucolic, puritanic simplicity of Uncle Sam.

I am sure you know by now that the award to me of the Nobel Prize was by no means altogether popular in America, doubtless an experience not altogether new to you.

Suppose you had taken Theodore Dreiser. Now to me, as to many other American writers, Dreiser, more than any other man, is marching

An excerpt from Lewis's *Nobel Prize Acceptance Speech, 1930.*

alone. Usually unappreciated, often hounded, he has cleared the trail from Victorian Howellsian timidity and gentility in American fiction to honesty, boldness, and passion of life. Without his pioneering I doubt if any of us could, unless we liked to be sent to jail, seek to express life, beauty and terror.

Yet had you given the prize to Dreiser you would have heard groans from America. Certainly some respectable scholar would complain that in Dreiser's world men and women often were sinful, tragic and despairing instead of being forever sunny, full of song and virtue as befits authentic Americans.

Robert Shafer

An American Tragedy:

A HUMANISTIC DEMURRER

Mr. Theodore Dreiser's critical friends have always been ready to admit his deficiencies as a literary artist, and these deficiencies are really extraordinary. Nevertheless, by universal consent Mr. Dreiser stands at the head of the realistic movement in American fiction, not merely because he is its pioneer, and has endured obloquy and even persecution for the Cause, but primarily on account of his seriousness and singleness of purpose, his depth of keen feeling, and his earnest reflectiveness. His work also anticipates in important respects the efforts of the post-realists and super-realists, so-called, and altogether has a present salience which insistently demands consideration.

The work, however, cannot be assessed—cannot indeed be understood —apart from the man; and fortunately Mr. Dreiser has written much about himself. He was born in 1871 in Terre Haute, Indiana, of German Catholic parents who struggled vainly against poverty. In the schools of another Indiana town he received the elements of an education, but apparently learned little of value to him beyond reading and writing. In boyhood and youth, in school or out, he became acquainted with a number of the better-known writers, chiefly of fiction, of the nineteenth century, but without gaining from them more than momentary entertainment. He has said that as a boy he "had no slightest opportunity to get a correct or even partially correct estimate of what might be called the mental A B abs of life."

If the truth is to be told, one reason for this lay clearly within himself. For he was, as his records show him, a stupid boy and young man, lapped in vague reverie and hazy dreams of enjoyment, and roused slowly to puzzled observation and thought. "No common man am I," he used to tell himself when he was scarcely out of his 'teens, with no evident reason save that with adolescence came an intense craving for freedom

From *Humanism and America*, ed. by Norman Foerster, Farrar and Rinehart, 1930.

from the shackles of common life—freedom to indulge fully his temperamental longing for sensuous and materialised delight. This self-conceit helped to prevent him from learning what could have been learned during his boyhood, and, as he grew older, aroused in him bitter resentment against the limitations of his early environment.

Those limitations, at the same time, were extreme. The Dreiser household was one combining almost unrelieved ignorance with perfect tastelessness, presided over by a father whose consuming interest was a Catholicism degraded into mere ceremonies and prohibitions. Mr. Dreiser explicitly denotes the quality of the purifying influence dominant in the home and community of his youth: "One should read only good books . . . from which any reference to sex had been eliminated, and what followed . . . was that all intelligent interpretation of character and human nature was immediately discounted. A picture of a nude or partially nude woman was sinful. . . . The dance in our home and our town was taboo. The theatre was an institution which led to crime, the saloon a centre of low, even bestial vices. . . . It was considered good business, if you please, to be connected with some religious organisation. . . . We were taught persistently to shun most human experiences as either dangerous or degrading or destructive. The less you knew about life the better; the more you knew about the fictional heaven and hell ditto. . . . In my day there were apparently no really bad men who were not known as such to all the world, . . . and few if any good men who were not sufficiently rewarded by the glorious fruits of their good deeds here and now! . . . Positively, and I stake my solemn word on this, until I was between seventeen and eighteen I had scarcely begun to suspect any other human being of harbouring the erratic and sinful thoughts which occasionally flashed through my own mind."

By the time Mr. Dreiser had fairly formed the suspicion that, despite appearances, other people might not be much better than himself, his family had begun to break up, following the death of his mother, and he himself had been thrust into the world—or rather into Chicago, where the Dreisers by now lived—to earn his way. He did manage to spend one year at Indiana University, to the great improvement of his health, but with no positive intellectual benefit, so that he refused to waste a second year, which he might have had there. He confessed this, it should be said, in no boastful spirit. He was in fact made to realise at Bloomington that there were elements of knowledge which it would be useful to him to acquire—but he found the effort hopeless. His mind could not be constrained, and, besides, the deficiencies of his earlier schooling stood in his way. Hence he returned to Chicago, to become a collector for an easy-payment furniture shop.

It was at this time that his feelings—scarcely yet his imagination or his reason—were awakened by the spectacle of "America on the make." He found that spectacle intensely vital. At the same time, too, he was doing the first reading that really came home to him:—he was reading a daily column of Eugene Field's in a Chicago newspaper. It gave him the notion of doing something like that himself, and sent him hunting for a post on a news-sheet. This he finally obtained, and at the reporter's desk achieved his real education, one not beyond his grasp. His first instructor promptly informed him that "life was a God-damned stinking, treacherous game, and that nine hundred and ninety-nine men out of every thousand were bastards." The truth of this generalisation Mr. Dreiser proceeded to establish for himself, by observation of those of life's realities which constitute news, and by intercourse with fellow-journalists. He discovered that practically all men, high or low, were lying hypocrites, outwardly professing a fine morality, but privately violating this without hesitation whenever it would serve their turn in the pursuit of gain or in the satisfaction of lust.

This was the reality, at any rate, which the young reporter saw, and which, as he says, broadened considerably his viewpoint, finally liberating him "from moralistic and religionistic qualms." So liberated was he, indeed, that he came to judge men "thoroughly sound intellectually" in proportion as he found them "quite free from the narrow, cramping conventions of their day." So liberated was he that he came to see the "religionist" for what he was: "a swallower of romance or a masquerader looking to profit and preferment." He came also to see behind "the blatherings of thin-minded, thin-blooded, thin-experienced religionists" only "a brainless theory." Nor was this the limit of his discoveries. He came further to see that life was not simply a ruthless struggle for material advantages, because, howsoever ruthless and intelligent one's struggle, still, one might be defrauded by sheer accident. Chance seemed, at times, the final ruler of all things—many of the reporter's assignments combining "to prove that life is haphazard and casual and cruel; to some lavish, to others niggardly."

Mr. Dreiser, it is fair to say, was the more ready to learn these lessons of experience because, as he plainly tells his readers, he himself was lustful and passionately eager for the material satisfactions of life. He longed to join in the antics of the rich, who alone, as he judged, were bathed in happiness. He felt, as he gazed enviously upon the gilded sons and daughters of earth, that, from no fault of his, life was tragically cheating him. And this sense of grievance, feeding upon itself, passed easily through a sentimental phase into bitterness, as his reminiscences show: "Whenever I returned to any place in which I had once lived and found things changed, as they always were, I was fairly transfixed by the oppressive sense of the evanescence of everything; a mood so hurtful and dark and yet with so rich if sullen a lustre that I was left wordless with pain. I was all but crucified at realising how unimportant I was, how nothing stayed but all changed. . . . Life was so brief, . . . and so soon, whatever its miserable amount or character, it would be gone. . . . But I, poor waif, with no definite or arresting skill of any kind, not even that of commerce, must go fumbling about looking in upon life from the outside, as it were. Beautiful women, or so I argued, were drawn to any but me. . . . I should never have a fraction of the means to do as I wished or to share in the life that I most craved. I was an Ishmael."

Not always, of course, was Mr. Dreiser sunk in a bitterness induced by self-pity and sentimental regret. Often in moments of successful work or of flattering companionship he was quickly lifted up into a mood of expansive self-satisfaction, equally unbalanced. Then he would say to himself: "I must be an exceptional man. . . . Life itself was not so bad; it was just higgledy-piggledy, catch-as-catch-can, that was all. If one were clever, like myself, it was all right." It was indeed magnificent, so long as the slave of temperament could dream of his heroic future as something assured. But dreams, like life, were unstable, and the fever for self-advancement, becoming intolerable from its intensity, would transmute itself—not every time into frank self-pity—but sometimes into tearful "sympathy for the woes of others, life in all its helpless degradation and poverty, the unsatisfied dreams of people." And from the downtrodden for whom he wept he also drew a lesson. The hideous inequalities both of fortune and of capacity which he saw, proved to him that democracy, like morality, was a sham, a hollow convention, irrelevant, indeed opposed, to the facts of life and practice.

Mr. Dreiser's journalistic career took him from Chicago to St. Louis, and thence, with several stops on the way, to Pittsburgh, during a period of rather more than three years. In these years, he says, speaking of his "blood-moods or so-called spiritual aspirations," he was "what might be called a poetic melancholiac, crossed with a vivid materialistic lust of life." His body, he adds, "was blazing with sex, as well as with a desire for material and social supremacy." It is not surprising, consequently, that he found himself able to entertain carnal desires for several women at the same time—though this at first surprised him, and troubled him also, until his day of liberation from "moralistic qualms." It is not surprising either that he presently was captivated by a charming country girl, several years older than himself, who had no single idea and only one desire in common with him. He had welcomed his liberation from "moralistic and religionistic qualms" the more complacently because of the simplification of thought and conduct to which it pointed. From this time the conduct of life was to be straightforward as well as simple, in accordance with the brutish yet vital law of following your dominant impulse regardlessly, ruthlessly, slavishly. But now this liberation itself was mainly instrumental in plunging him into a new, long-continued, and grievous difficulty. For his simple country maiden, though she was drawn to him as he was drawn to her, was nevertheless rigidly conventional, immovably "moralistic," one of the predestined pillars of an ordered society and a stable family. She steadfastly refused to yield him her body without marriage, and he, alas, was not only unable to support her but deeply unwilling to marry her even if he could.

Clearly this pair did not understand all that divided them in spirit, but, still, Mr. Dreiser knew from the first some portion of the truth. For he knew what love really was: it was a mere "blood-mood"; it was a vivid lust crossed with poetic fires; it was irresistible, of course, but it was like everything else, transient, shifting, evanescent. He already suspected, as he later concluded, that monogamy—marriage indeed of any kind—was a debasing institution which not only killed the love that brought men to it, but also deformed and dwarfed their personalities. It might not harm stupid and lethargic men, but the man of individuality, at least, the highest type of citizen, required utter freedom to follow his vital impulses—required the joys of the sexual act "without any of the hindrances or binding chains of convention." He knew, in fine, that "the tug of his immense physical desire for his beloved" might easily have been satisfied, despite his poverty, without compromising the future, and without doing a hurt to society, had there only been "any such thing as sanity in life," outside of himself. He even knew, after the first raptures of idyllic feeling had passed, that any other beautiful woman would have served his need as well; but, nevertheless, he clung to this one, because in fact no beautiful woman whom he found accessible did keep alive in him the same fever of desire. Yet his beloved remained immovable, and so drew him on, through several years of miserably divided feeling, into a marriage finally accomplished after his carnal fires had cooled, owing to the passage of time and the casual ministrations of certain other fair creatures, more pliant, but unsatisfying.

I dwell upon this painful episode, following Mr. Dreiser's own example, because it tells so much. It was the crucial event of his early life, and it left an ineffaceable scar. The fact is, indeed, that without definite knowledge of this miserable union, it would not be easy to understand how Mr. Dreiser became so obstinately fixed in those notions of life which journalism and its associations gave him and which he was eager to accept. Without definite knowledge of this marriage, further, it would be impossible fully to understand his novels; for none of them could have been written quite as it stands save in the light of this afflictive experience of his, and several, it is extremely likely, could not otherwise have been written at all.

Some knowledge of another side of Mr. Dreiser's life, however, during his years of work for the news-sheets, is also necessary for those who would understand his novels. He has told us that in St. Louis the great literary idol of his associates was Zola, and after Zola, Balzac. These novelists, and especially the former, were constantly held up to him as models by one of his assignment-editors, who made it abundantly clear what Zola stood for. Mr. Dreiser read none of the Frenchman's books at this time, but he did read an unpublished novel by two St. Louis newspaper men which made a deep and lasting impression upon him and which, as he later discovered, was wholly inspired by Zola and Balzac. This was "the opening wedge for him into the realm of realism," and, too, "it fixed his mind definitely on this matter of writing," firing him with a desire to create something of the sort himself. He thought the novel "intensely beautiful," "with its frank pictures of raw, greedy, sensual human nature, and its open pictures of self-indulgence and vice." In these indirect ways, evidently, Zola exerted upon the young reporter an influence real and significant. It was, indeed, probably much more important than the direct influence exerted by Balzac not long thereafter; though the accident which brought Mr. Dreiser to a fevered and ecstatic reading of many of Balzac's novels, while he was in Pittsburgh, marked what was for him "a literary revolution."

The crowning stage of Mr. Dreiser's education, however, was now to come, while he was still in Pittsburgh, with his discovery of certain of the writings of Huxley, Tyndall, and Herbert Spencer. Huxley, Mr. Dreiser credits with finally dispelling the "lingering filaments" of Christianity still trailing about him; and Huxley's work of dispersion was completed by Spencer's *First Principles*. This book wholly "threw him down in his conceptions or non-conceptions of life" by its "questioning or dissolving into other and less understandable things" all that he had deemed substantial. "Up to this time," he says, "there had been in me a blazing and unchecked desire to get on and the feeling that in doing so we did get somewhere; now in its place was the definite conviction that spiritually one got nowhere, that there was no hereafter, that one lived and had his being because one had to, and that it was of no importance. Of one's ideals, struggles, deprivations, sorrows and joys, it could only be said that they were chemic compulsions. . . . Man was a mechanism, undevised and uncreated, and a badly and carelessly driven one at that."

The seeming ill logic of some of these remarks—the sudden concern over spiritual things felt of one who had hitherto devoted himself wholeheartedly to the world by sensuous appearances—is not unimportant. Clearly Spencer's book left an abiding mark on Mr. Dreiser because it represented in a general way the abstract conclusion towards which his own observations had been pointing. Without knowing it, and without any attempt to set his intellectual house in order, he had himself been drifting towards a mechanistic naturalism. Spencer made him aware of this, and if, as he thought, that awareness left him crushed and hopeless, it at least seemed to clear his mind of rubbish, and to give his view-point self-consistency and finality. Nevertheless, he did not come forth a Spencerian; and, indeed, his debt to the *Synthetic Philosophy* may easily be exaggerated—the more easily because it really is important.

Mr. Dreiser emphasizes the fact that his reading of the *First Principles* was followed by an emotional revulsion—a revulsion which the Synthetic Philosopher can scarcely alone have caused. And in truth just at the time when he stumbled upon Spencer his feelings were strained to the breaking-point. He had just returned from a last desperate, yet unsuccessful, effort to seduce his country maiden, which left him crushed, not only by that defeat itself, but by the consciousness that the gratification he was bound to secure was now driving him towards a marriage for which he had no capacity, no desire, and no prospect of sufficient means. Moreover, immediately after his Western visit he had gone, for the first time, to New York, where he had received an extraordinarily vivid impression of all the glories and delights of that worldly success, with its attendant wealth, which he so intensely craved. The sight had fired him to renew his efforts after so grand a reward, but, at the same time, had made him gloomily feel his distance from it, lodging in his mind a stubborn doubt if it could, after all, ever be attained by him. The combined weight of these experiences had intensified his already bitter sense of the world's indifference to his desires and aims, of the world's unconscious cruelty, and of its brutal injustice. He had eagerly embraced the world at his earliest opportunity, had reviled those who opposed themselves to it—and what was the world doing for him, what was it not blindly and carelessly doing against him? He was brought to the point of sheer despair, and was ready to turn upon the world—yet not ready to turn his back upon it. For he had not the slightest conception of any other than sensuous and worldly values, of any other than material gratifications which might bring to him fulness of life. Years ago he had defiantly closed *that* door, without in the least knowing what he was doing, and it was never to be opened to him. He was miserably exasperated by defeat, but the world's appeal was still insistent and compelling, and would be heard and obeyed for many a year, whether or not it became suspect for a siren's call.

In these circumstances the *First Principles* came really as a god-send. The book had the impressive appearance of being the voice of science itself uttering at last the Truth. Yet its weight and authority left undisturbed Mr. Dreiser's worldliness and some of his dear prejudices. It left, indeed, everything as it was with him; but it did appear to rob everything of value, and so, as he thought, left him crushed and hopeless. Actually, however, it offered him a species of consolation for the crushed and hopeless state into which he had already been plunged by his efforts after a "realistic" way of life. A species of consolation;—because, though the dehumanised conception of the world and life presented by naturalism was "cold comfort," still, it did enable one who felt badly used to turn upon the universe and *say,* if not feel, that life was a meaningless and unimportant phenomenon anyhow.

The *Synthetic Philosophy,* Mr. Dreiser tells the world, "eternally verified" his "gravest fears as to the unsolvable disorder and brutality of life." Precisely; as these turns of phrase show, it left his feelings what they had been, likewise his desires and aims, and his sentimental humanitarianism and more. What Spencer gave him was something to fall back upon and *say* in hopeless or disillusioned moments, but something which, leaving him otherwise where he was, even helped to preserve him inviolate from self-criticism or self-discipline. Following the guidance of temperament and mood, he took from Spencer what he wanted, and nothing else; and it so happened that this included little or nothing specifically characteristic of Spencer as against various other naturalistic thinkers. The tone, indeed, of Mr. Dreiser's naturalism, as well as its emphasis upon accident and chaotic disorder, is not only more sophisticated than that of Spencer's, but abruptly contradictory of the Synthetic gentleman's grandiose fancy of one eternal, universal law infallibly working to bring about perfection in all things earthly.

His dark emotional naturalism—and, it may be added, several of the contradictions it has involved him in—bring Mr. Dreiser, as some of his readers have perceived, close to Thomas Hardy, in proportion as he is far from Spencer. He does not mention Hardy in the record of his development which I have been following, but he is said to have confessed to "an enchanted discovery" of that novelist in 1896, and his delight is what was to be expected. As far as one can see, however, his indebtedness to Hardy, though real, is not important.

II

This, in summary form, is the story of Mr. Dreiser's preparation for a novelist's career. His first novel was published in 1900, and his sixth in 1925. Though from an early time he has had warm friends amongst the critics, still, even the most devoted of these have harshly condemned some of his books; and, in general, critical opinion, when not predominantly hostile, has been sharply divided. Nevertheless, in the face of whatever difficulties, Mr. Dreiser has slowly won a leading position in the world of fiction, for reasons which I began by mentioning. And his sixth novel, *An American Tragedy,* was, upon its appearance, widely proclaimed a masterpiece.

Certainly, moreover, *An American Tragedy* is by all odds the best of Mr. Dreiser's novels, though perhaps not the most *interesting*. In it his language is still faulty, as in his earlier books; the quality of his style is mediocre, when not worse; his narrative is badly proportioned;—but, nevertheless, the novel also has excellences which its author had not previously achieved, and which are seldom to be found save in works of a serious and mature artistry. It has a sombre inevitableness, a self-contained adequacy, a restraint, dignity, and detachment which bespeak not merely the experienced craftsman, but also the workman's sure grasp of his theme united with a deeply emotional confidence in its truth and importance. A far higher intelligence is exhibited in its execution than in Mr. Dreiser's play, *The Hand of the Potter* (1918), whose theme is similar in several respects. If one should name a single change indicative of the intelligent masterliness of *An American Tragedy,* perhaps the most significant is the fact that in this book, for the first time, Mr. Dreiser has permitted his characters and events to speak entirely for themselves.

But though *An American Tragedy* marks a really notable advance in technique, and a heightened plausibility thus attained, partly through restraint, still, it exhibits Mr. Dreiser's thought and the essential quality of his realism entirely unchanged. How Mr. Dreiser reached a mechanistic naturalism has above been shown, and how he became conscious of the fact. The appropriate result was that all his novels became tales of human irresponsibility, constructed to illustrate life's contradiction of the hollow conventions of society, and life's obedience to blind laws which make the individual's experience a chaos with an end unrelated to desert. This is the theme of *An American Tragedy,* as of the earlier novels. It is a tale of human irresponsibility, supported by youthful prejudices never relinquished, built up on false antitheses, and capped by a merely circumstantial realism calculated to give the narrative a deceptive air of importance.

Youthful prejudice, for example, transparently dictates the important part played by religion in this novel. Religion is represented as an illusion capable of deceiving only those blind to life's realities—the hopelessly incompetent and unintelligent, those whose advocacy would itself discredit any doctrine. Religion's illusory nature is said to be self-evident, indeed, since it has much to say of Providence, yet manifestly bestows on the convert no worldly rewards, in satisfaction of the real needs and desires with which he is endowed, not by his own design or wish. Convention, too, is represented as a force which sways only the stupid and lethargic, which makes no demands entitling it to respect, and which the intelligent disregard deliberately, the temperamental wilfully. Intelligence itself is pictured as merely an instrument useful for devising methods of self-advancement;—in other words, as the servant of inborn temperament. And temperament is the one irresistible, compelling force in life, to which all else is ultimately obedient. Hence no one is really responsible for anything;—save, perhaps, the novelist who sees this important truth, at length, and by careful selection of appropriate matter is able to picture it for us.

Not even Mr. Dreiser's expert care and long practice, however, are sufficient to enable him to evade a difficulty inherent in the nature of his theme. For the predicament of Roberta Alden is infinitely sad, and her creator narrates her history and murder with an exemplary truthfulness which emphasises that sadness to the full. Nevertheless, the reader's sympathy is not invoked. The girl, on the contrary, is presented as the inevitable resultant of inheritance, environment, and sex, and she lives as an embodied energy rather than as a person. Extraordinary pains are taken, with all the multitudinous details of her story, to balance causes against effects, and she emerges a plausible creature. There is nothing incredible in her being just conventional enough and unwary enough and love-sick enough to suit the story's purpose; but, too, there is nothing in her nature or her history to render either important. Indeed, her grievous distress, leading up to her murder, takes on, under Mr. Dreiser's hand, the same significance as the squirming of an angleworm, impaled by some mischievous boy—no less, but certainly no more.

"Chemic compulsion" draws Roberta Alden as it draws other substances. "Chemic compulsion" epitomises the book. It "just happens"— and this is all—that "chemic compulsion" entangles Roberta with the squid—Clyde Griffiths, the defeated squid. For readers of Mr. Dreiser's "epic" tale, *The Financier,* who recall the apologue of the lobster and the squid cannot fail to recognize Clyde Griffiths as the embodiment of the latter—and his cousin Gilbert as the patient, triumphant lobster. The squid, it need scarcely be said, commands no more sympathy than

Roberta;—indeed, most readers inevitably must sympathise with the spirit of the "irate woodsman's" brutal question during the trial. This undefiled son of the forest asked: "Why don't they kill the God-damned bastard and be done with him?" But, just for this reason, it has to be remembered that Mr. Dreiser exhausts every possible means so to account for Clyde as to preserve him from all blame. The squid is the complete plaything of "chemic compulsion," the paragon of irresponsibility, the perfect exemplar of the truth as the truth has been revealed to his creator.

This being so, it is little less than a miracle that Mr. Dreiser has contrived—through the infinite detail of a merely circumstantial realism—to save Clyde Griffiths' humanity sufficiently to maintain the reader's "suspension of disbelief" until the end of the book. Undoubtedly he has done so, though he has not succeeded in making all readers feel that patience has been adequately rewarded. They have been impressed, as is fitting before so monumental a composition; they have been troubled; they have not been recompensed. Eight hundred and forty pages devoted to the unconscionable prolongation of a mere sensational newspaper story! Remarks to this effect I have heard more than once; and they roughly indicate the real difficulty—the inevitably self-destroying effect of such an effort as Mr. Dreiser's, in proportion as it is successful.

This difficulty, however, does not actually lie in the plot of *An American Tragedy,* as the remark just cited implies. The bare plot of the *Agamemnon* of Æschylus might equally well form the basis of a mere sensational newspaper story, and Clytaemnestra in that play and in the *Choephori* makes for herself, not without seeming justice, the plea that is made for Clyde Griffiths. Not she, but Destiny, she says, through her its helpless instrument slew Agamemnon; and she also pleads that she did not make herself, yet can only act out her inborn nature. But it is not for his plots, nor because he was well acquainted with Mr. Dreiser's view of life, that Æschylus lives on still amongst us. His dramas have a perennial and deep value for mankind because, rejecting the plausible notion of "chemic compulsion," he struggled with profound conviction to convey a very different meaning through their form, characters, and action. Without evading any of its difficulty, he asserted his faith that Moral Law uncompromisingly governs the life of man, making for an order which is divine, in the face of a chaos intrinsically evil, and that men are fully, if tragically, responsible for the consequences of their acts, whatever their motives or compulsions, so that ignorance and self-conceit are equally as criminal as violence.

This is not to say all, of course, but it may suffice to show how Æschylus and, more clear-sightedly, Sophocles cut straight through to the centre of the human problem and propounded a solution which, if not the only one, nor by itself a complete one, is still, strictly speaking, irrefutable, being founded directly upon facts of experience which have not changed with the passing generations;—an unassailable solution, moreover, which gives weight and meaning to every individual and to all of his acts. And hence it is that the bloody and sensational fables of Æschylus and Sophocles, triumphantly formed in full harmony with their meaning, have an interest and value for men which time does not exhaust.

Mr. Dreiser's difficulty is not that he has different facts of experience to interpret;—he has precisely the same facts concerning an essentially unchanged human nature. His difficulty is that his mechanistic naturalism compels him so to select and manipulate facts of experience as to deny, through his narrative, that human life has any meaning or value. The attempt is suicidal, and the more consistently it is carried out the more completely is Mr. Dreiser forced to divest his creatures and their actions of any distinctively human quality and meaning. The more successful he is the more insignificant his work becomes. *An American Tragedy,* as I have said, is more skilfully, faithfully, and consistently executed on the naturalistic level than any of its author's earlier novels, and precisely for this reason it contains no single element of tragedy in any legitimate sense of the word, and it impresses thoughtful readers as a mere sensational newspaper story long drawn out. In other words, in proportion as Mr. Dreiser contrives to accomplish his self-imposed task he has nothing to tell us except that there is nothing to tell about life until it can be reduced even below the apparent level of animal existence, to the point where it becomes a meaningless chaos of blind energies.

Whether or not any real sense of the self-destroying character of this effort, to create a literature as valueless and insignificant as possible, will ever strike Mr. Dreiser's consciousness, I should not venture to guess. But only an obstinate self-conceit, or an invincible stupidity, one imagines, could have kept him from seeing the absurdities into which he was forced, in the course of half-a-dozen sentences, when he recently attempted to draw up a brief statement of his present belief. He wrote: "I can make no comment on my work or my life that holds either interest or import for me. Nor can I imagine any explanation or interpretation of any life, my own included, that would be either true—or important, if true. Life is to me too much a welter and play of inscrutable forces to permit, in my case at least, any significant comment. One may paint for one's own entertainment, and that of others—perhaps. As I see him the utterly infinitesimal individual weaves among the mysteries a floss-like and wholly meaningless course—if course it be. In short I catch no meaning from all I have seen, and pass quite as I came, confused and dismayed."

To this point has Mr. Dreiser's naturalism driven him. If the general sense of this awkward yet mannered statement comprised the truth about him and his work, he would, of course, never have been asked to make it. He would, in all probability, have been confined long ago to an asylum; and he would certainly never have written any of his books. Those books, moreover, have manifestly not been written just for his own entertainment. They have been written because he felt he had something to say— because of his certainty that he had come to know the truth, as men in general knew it not. And with singular faithfulness of purpose and of industry, involving what for him must have been almost superhuman effort, because of his defects of mind and training, he has devoted himself to the struggle to express the truth as he conceived it—that is, to reduce it to consistency and give it coherent form. He has also neglected nothing, within his limits, to make it impressive. He has thus lived a rationally purposive life, reducing at least to symptoms of order the welter of his impressions and impulses, controlling at least fitfully his rebellious temperament, and mastering (or "sublimating") at least partially his almost pathological obsession by sex. For the sake of self-expression—or, as I shall presently suggest, of self-justification—he has thus achieved an appreciably disciplined life, and so has in his own person, against his own literary aim, furnished a convincing refutation of his philosophy. He has effectively proved that *An American Tragedy* gives form to a view of life as gratuitous as it is unmeaning.

Fortunately it is now realised by an increasing number of people that naturalistic philosophies are merely speculative ventures, which derive no valid support from "modern science." And it has, besides, been shown above how little "science" had to do with the formation of Mr. Dreiser's naturalistic prejudice. Mr. Dreiser, on his own showing, was first awakened to a sense of life as a problem to be solved by his discovery of the radical contrast between the ethical standards of his father and his church (as he understood its teaching), and his own spontaneous impulses and desires. His haphazard, undirected education gave him an unexcelled opportunitiy to learn that there were many others like himself, that they seemed to be the most vigorous members of their communities, and that they never hesitated to transgress every ethical standard, when they could get away with it, in their struggle for self-advancement and self-gratification. He treasured every impression which seemed to be on his side against ethical standards by which he stood condemned. His self-esteem had been gravely shocked by the discordance he had discovered, and he now found the means to restore it and, indeed, to strengthen it, by appeal from home and church to the larger world. Not he was in the wrong of it, but the "senseless," "impossible" theories which would have convicted him of shameful tendencies. "In shame there is no comfort, but to be beyond all bounds of shame," says one of Sidney's Arcadians, and this Mr. Dreiser might thenceforth have taken for his motto.

Governed by this apolaustic prejudice, he has since continued his transparent course of seeing only what he has desired to see, or rather of admitting the reality of only what suited him, while setting down all else as either hypocrisy or delusion. And while it is true that no one escapes the necessity of bringing only a selective attention to bear upon the outer world, it by no means follows that we are all alike cut off from "reality." On the contrary, it does mean that the basis of our selective attention, the interests and purposes served by it, are of fundamental importance. And the disastrous effect of Mr. Dreiser's apolaustic prejudice is that it encouraged him in slavery to mere temperament, in helpless surrender to the chaotic flow of "natural" impulses, while it brought to his attention from the outer world only what fed itself, the antics of complicated beasts with strange illusions. The trouble with what he thus saw is not that it was non-existent, some gross trick of the fevered imagination;—it was there to be seen—it is there, in grievous plenty. No, the trouble is that none of it has positive significance. The naturalism which it fathers lights up the animal in man, but tells man nothing of that which positively distinguishes him from the beast—more, it vindictively denies that anything save hypocrisy and delusion does so distinguish him. And while it seeks to dissolve our humanity, it ends, as it ends in Mr. Dreiser, in a bottomless morass of misrepresentation and despair. This is the American tragedy of our confused age which constitutes the real import of Mr. Dreiser's masterpiece.

John Chamberlain

THEODORE DREISER REMEMBERED

Last spring, driving east from Chicago, I passed through Warsaw, Indiana, a sleepy town situated close to three small, lovely lakes. There was something familiar about the place, something that made me feel certain I had been there before. And then, suddenly, I remembered: I had read about Warsaw in Theodore Dreiser's autobiography of childhood, "Dawn." Dreiser had lived there in his early teens; there he had read Shakespeare, Ouida, "Tom Jones," Laura Jean Libby, General Lew Wallace's "Ben Hur," Dickens, Carlyle and "Moll Flanders" in higgledy-piggledy confusion in the local library. There one of his sisters had conceived an illegitimate child; there his mother, a vague, sweet, struggling, ineffectual creature, had tried to keep the remnants of her family together on practically nothing. And there young Theo had skated and swum, had mooned about the beauty of the lakes and the Tippecanoe River, and had dreamed about high-born girls while having an experience with the baker's willing daughter.

It was easy to imagine the culture of Warsaw two or three generations ago; you could read it in the architecture, which was a little more solid than Rochester's to the south, or that of Coldwater, Michigan, to the north. Quite obviously the culture had been Puritan-commercial; that could be taken for granted. But—or so one fancied—the spirit of the place wasn't too pushing, or too intolerant. The local church sociables were really sociable; it was, in short, the sort of town that would neither accept the Dreisers nor persecute them. Nor would it bring these impoverished newcomers from southern Indiana into the Puritan-commercial orbit.

I had not read Dreiser in a long time and I had not been thinking of him. But the five minutes spent driving through Warsaw suddenly explained to me Dreiser's whole relation to the literature of his times and to the movement of ideas that killed the rule of the genteel tradition in America. This was not the result of an attempt at mystical penetration on my part; I was no Keyserling catching an idea from a cross-wind merely because the car had slowed down to fifteen miles an hour. What had hap-

From *After the Genteel Tradition,* ed. by Malcolm Cowley, W. W. Norton & Co., 1936.

pened was that the half-remembered facts of "Dawn" suddenly shuffled themselves into a significant pattern. Dreiser, it became wholly obvious to me for the first time, had not consciously attacked the sway of the genteel tradition when he wrote "Sister Carrie." That book had been a natural; it was a yea-saying to what he had learned in Warsaw, not a nay-saying to the conventional New England schoolmarm. Indeed, his own school teachers had been both sympathetic and helpful.

Consider the facts in the case. The young Theodore had not been accepted by Puritan-commercial folk; therefore he was not loaded down in childhood with hampering theories of the correct way in which to live and act and write. The great moral paradox of the age—how to square the competitive parable of the talents with other teachings of the New Testament—did not trouble him, since he was not preached at by elders who were quick to urge young people to succeed, and to be good Christian men and women at the same time. Nor did he suffer because of exclusion: Warsaw did not hound him. He got through the impressionable years without undue infection from the missionary spirit of the American Tract Society and the novels of the period. Instead he followed his instincts: for sentimentalism (Ouida, Laura Jean Libby), and for good, raw, healthily vulgar stuff ("Tom Jones," "Moll Flanders"). The Ouida strain and the "Tom Jones" strain persist as dominants in all the Dreiser books. If young Theodore had anything to rebel against, anything to give him the mark of negativism, it was the Catholic Church, whose creed was interpreted with a dogmatic literalness by his narrow and repellent father. But the father, who did not come with his family to Warsaw, lacked the intelligence to apply the Catholic creed to books or to daily life; his dogmatism remained largely *in vacuo*. Hence Dreiser's opposition to his father never centered on anything concrete. It developed merely into an animus against philosophy in general and so served to confirm him in an empirical habit of mind.

The women of Dreiser's novels are generally of two types—the uncritical, naturally sweet sort who give in for reasons of sympathy rather than of passion, and the prim, fussy daughters of the genteel. The first type— Carrie Meeber, Jennie Gerhardt, Roberta Alden, even Aileen Butler, the contractor's daughter, of "The Financier" and "The Titan"—is compounded of Dreiser's memories of his mother and his sisters; the second type is obviously drawn from the model of his first wife, a Missouri girl who was his first contact with the genteel. But the girl from Missouri had nothing to do with the shape of "Sister Carrie" or "Jennie Gerhardt"; these books are positive acts, affirmations of life hungering for experience. Not until he wrote "The Genius" and, later on, "An American Tragedy," did Dreiser mix animus with his ink. The animus is probably the reason for his heavy insistence on the role of environment in accounting for the character of Clyde Griffiths. Simply because the conscious nay-sayer protests too much, it has been easy to attack the conception of the young Clyde as "inevitably" the product of his early environment. Other young men with evangelical backgrounds failed to kill their sweethearts in similar dilemmas. Theory, in Dreiser's later years, commenced to ride his feeling for personality; he did better work when he was concerned with projecting personality, leaving the moralizing for isolated passages that stand as blemishes without destroying the force of his creation.

It is the early Dreiser that interests me—the Dreiser of "Carrie" and "Jennie," of the Cowperwood stories, and of the autobiographical narrative, "A Book About Myself," which has been republished as "Newspaper Days." I read "A Book About Myself" when I was just out of college, a young innocent who had little idea of what made the wheels go round in America. With its detailed account of wandering through Chicago, St. Louis, Toledo, Pittsburgh, and New York in the nineties, "A Book About Myself" made the complexity of the modern industrial scene understandable—one could see from Dreiser's weltering, wondering, patient pages how it came into being. Dreiser's memories of the Pittsburgh of the Homestead Strike were especially galvanic; I had scarcely known, before reading "A Book About Myself," that such a thing as labor strife existed. (We were then living in the New Era, and I had been too young to take any particular notice of the troubles of 1918-21.) "A Book About Myself" was just the thing to give a fledgling newspaper reporter a sense of orientation. As for the novels—"Carrie," "Jennie," "The Titan," "The Financier"—they helped to confirm the impressions gained from "A Book About Myself." But they don't stand intensive rereading; one recalls them too easily. They have no stubborn subtleties of the sort that only yield themselves up on the third trip; hence my main affection for Dreiser is that he once helped me and did such a good job of it that I need his help no longer. Along with Scott Fitzgerald, Ring Lardner and others, he taught me to see through the genteel tradition, to shake myself free of the belated colonialism of the late nineteenth century in New England. He taught me to discount as wish fulfillment the ideas of Stuart P. Sherman, who seemed to think Carrie Meebers and Jennie Gerhardts and Frank Cowperwoods were impossible.

Not that Dreiser's anatomy of American life is final; no live person's should be. Finality means the end of curiosity, and Dreiser has always been curious. Even his late attempt to square Marxism with his own notions of "equity" leaves plenty of room for discovery, for rearranging his patterns to account for new intrusions in fact. He is still the empiricist. This habit of mind was what distinguished him, along with Stephen

Crane, from all his important novelist contemporaries. And because of this habit of mind and a set of reflexes that had not been conditioned by the dominant ethos, the young Dreiser went forth, equipped as no other novelist of the late nineteenth century, to understand emerging industrial America. When he looked at a "captain of industry" or a "promoter," he was under no inner compulsion to square what he saw with an ethic picked up in Sunday-school years. Herein he broke with more tender-minded contemporary novelists who were also fascinated by the problem of industrial power—with Frank Norris, William Allen White, Robert Herrick, and a host of lesser figures. The lesser figures were content to shut their eyes and glorify; they did the groundwork that resulted in the Coolidge cult of Service. To Norris, White and Herrick, more sensitive men, the industrialist was too patent a force to be ignored, yet they couldn't digest him without serious qualms of conscience.

The business man was justified by the parable of the talents, yes; but there was this matter of the plain words of the New Testament. What to do about the paradox? William Allen White solved it, in "A Certain Rich Man," by having his hero, John Barclay, give away the "dirty dollars" that he had amassed during his lifetime. Frank Norris, after dwelling on the power and the nerve and the skill of his market operator in "The Pit," engineered a similar last-minute conversion. And Robert Herrick caused his "American citizen," the sausage-maker Van Harrington, to think his way through to a new Darwinian competitive ethic—something which an actual Van Harrington would probably have never bothered his head about. All three of them—White, Norris and Herrick—felt constrained by their upbringing to take their eyes off the object: the industrialist, who usually felt justice and destiny to be on his side. They misinterpreted the man of destiny when they gave him the moral qualms of the brooding novelist. And the Puritan-commercial culture was paradoxically to blame for both the man of destiny and his misinterpreter. The man of destiny went forth armed with the parable of the talents and a Calvinistic conviction of divine election; as John D. Rockefeller put it, "God gave me my money." And the novelist, who chose to accent the New Testament, couldn't believe that John D. said that with a good conscience. Dreiser was the first novelist to realize that. Lacking the conviction of commercial election himself, lacking also an uneasy belief that America must be squared with the New Testament, he could simply look and report and imagine.

It is true that as a young man Dreiser had his moments when he lacked the objective vision. He confesses, willingly enough, that he often yearned for the things that wealth could buy; he had an adolescent itch for gaudy clothes, for fine estates, for dinners in lobster palaces. But he soon satisfied himself that he lacked personal capacity for the sort of life that would bring him these things, and when he eventually did make money—as editor of the *Delineator* and as the author of a couple of popular successes —he used it to finance his writing, not to imitate the Philadelphia millionaires whose antics he had studied in the nineties. His own early desires enabled him to understand the longings of Carrie and Jennie, of Cowperwood and Clyde Griffiths; as Louis Kronenberger puts it, he has frequently used the novel to kill the thing he originally loved. Clyde Griffiths may be taken as a portrait of the young man Dreiser might have been if events had not decreed otherwise. Simply because Dreiser created Griffiths in a confessional mood, the portrait has authenticity and symbolic truth. Clyde Griffiths may not represent America in its better moments, but he represents one American aspiration, at any rate. The fact that Dreiser did not himself go the way of Clyde Griffiths, however, riddles the deterministic philosophy which the book is intended to underscore.

I have said nothing about the barbarities of Dreiser's style; there is nothing left to say about them that hasn't been said a hundred times and more. I have said nothing about the effect that Thomas Henry Huxley and Balzac had on him, for a rereading of "Dawn" convinces me that Dreiser would have come to "Sister Carrie" and "The Titan" without their aid. Nor is there anything very specific to say about Dreiser's effect on later generations of American writers. In so far as his novels served as rallying points for the critics of the genteel—Mencken, Huneker, Vance Thompson—they have helped nearly everyone from Sherwood Anderson on down to Faulkner in a very general way. Dreiser, along with David Graham Phillips, the Shaw of "Mrs. Warren's Profession," Brieux, Emma Goldman, Freud and Mabel Dodge Luhan as *salonniere,* helped make it possible for our novelists to admit sex as an explosive element to their fictional worlds. But American writing, in the twenties, turned vigorously away from the Dreiserian conception of fiction. Fitzgerald, Lardner, Hemingway, Thornton Wilder, Elizabeth Roberts, Katharine Anne Porter, Kenneth Burke, Erskine Caldwell, Robert Cantwell—none of these believes in the power of massed detail. Nor does Dos Passos, who has sometimes been called Dreiserian in his scope. For Dos Passos' latest method is to pare his narratives to the bone; he gets his sense of profusion simply by putting four or five narratives between the same covers. Printed as an independent novel, the story of Charley Anderson, for example, would seem a clipped, un-Dreiserian thing. As a craftsman, Dreiser has made little mark. He remains, for me, a part of an education in ideas.

Lionel Trilling

REALITY IN AMERICA

It is possible to say of V. L. Parrington that with his *Main Currents in American Thought* he has had an influence on our conception of American culture which is not equaled by that of any other writer of the last two decades. His ideas are now the accepted ones wherever the college course in American literature is given by a teacher who conceives himself to be opposed to the genteel and the academic and in alliance with the vigorous and the actual. And whenever the liberal historian of America finds occasion to take account of the national literature, as nowadays he feels it proper to do, it is Parrington who is his standard and guide. Parrington's ideas are the more firmly established because they do not have to be imposed—the teacher or the critic who presents them is likely to find that his task is merely to make articulate for his audience what it has always believed, for Parrington formulated in a classic way the suppositions about our culture which are held by the American middle class so far as that class is at all liberal in its social thought and so far as it begins to understand that literature has anything to do with society.

Parrington was not a great mind; he was not a precise thinker, or, except when measured by the low eminences that were about him, an impressive one. Separate Parrington from his informing idea of the economic and social determination of thought and what is left is a simple intelligence, notable for its generosity and enthusiasm but certainly not for its accuracy or originality. Take him even with his idea and he is, once its direction is established, rather too predictable to be continuously interesting; and, indeed, what we dignify with the name of economic and social determinism amounts in his use of it to not much more than the demonstration that most writers incline to stick to their own social class. But his best virtue was real and important—he had what we like to think of as the saving salt of the American mind, the lively sense of the practical, workaday world, of the welter of ordinary undistinguished things and people, of the tangible, quirky, unrefined elements of life. He knew what

From *The Liberal Imagination,* Viking Press, 1945.

so many literary historians do not know, that emotions and ideas are the sparks that fly when the mind meets difficulties.

Yet he had after all but a limited sense of what constitutes a difficulty. Whenever he was confronted with a work of art that was complex, personal and not literal, that was not, as it were, a public document, Parrington was at a loss. Difficulties that were complicated by personality or that were expressed in the language of successful art did not seem quite real to him and he was inclined to treat them as aberrations, which is one way of saying what everybody admits, that the weakest part of Parrington's talent was his aesthetic judgment. His admirers and disciples like to imply that his errors of aesthetic judgment are merely lapses of taste, but this is not so. Despite such mistakes as his notorious praise of Cabell, to whom in a remarkable passage he compares Melville, Parrington's taste was by no means bad. His errors are the errors of understanding which arise from his assumptions about the nature of reality.

Parrington does not often deal with abstract philosophical ideas, but whenever he approaches a work of art we are made aware of the metaphysics on which his aesthetics is based. There exists, he believes, a thing called *reality;* it is one and immutable, it is wholly external, it is irreducible. Men's minds may waver, but reality is always reliable, always the same, always easily to be known. And the artist's relation to reality he conceives as a simple one. Reality being fixed and given, the artist has but to let it pass through him, he is the lens in the first diagram of an elementary book on optics: Fig. 1, Reality; Fig. 2, Artist; Fig. 1′, Work of Art. Figs. 1 and 1′ are normally in virtual correspondence with each other. Sometimes the artist spoils this ideal relation by "turning away from" reality. This results in certain fantastic works, unreal and ultimately useless. It does not occur to Parrington that there is any other relation possible between the artist and reality than this passage of reality through the transparent artist; he meets evidence of imagination and creativeness with a settled hostility the expression of which suggests that he regards them as the natural enemies of democracy.

In this view of things, reality, although it is always reliable, is always rather sober-sided, even grim. Parrington, a genial and enthusiastic man, can understand how the generosity of man's hopes and desires may leap beyond reality; he admires will in the degree that he suspects mind. To an excess of desire and energy which blinds a man to the limitations of reality he can indeed be very tender. This is one of the many meanings he gives to *romance* or *romanticism,* and in spite of himself it appeals to something in his own nature. The praise of Cabell is Parrington's response not only to Cabell's elegance—for Parrington loved elegance—but also to Cabell's insistence on the part which a beneficent self-deception may and even should play in the disappointing fact-bound life of man, particularly in the private and erotic part of his life.[1]

The second volume of *Main Currents* is called *The Romantic Revolution in America* and it is natural to expect that the word romantic should appear in it frequently. So it does, more frequently than one can count, and seldom with the same meaning, seldom with the sense that the word, scandalously vague as it has been used by the literary historians, is still full of complicated but not wholly pointless ideas, that it involves many contrary but definable things; all too often Parrington uses the word romantic with the word romance close at hand, meaning *a* romance, in the sense that *Graustark* or *Treasure Island* is a romance, as though it signified chiefly a gay disregard of the limitations of everyday fact. Romance is refusing to heed the counsels of experience (p. iii); it is ebullience (p. iv); it is utopianism (p. iv); it is individualism (p. v); it is self-deception (p. 59)—"romantic faith . . . in the beneficent processes of trade and industry" (as held, we inevitably ask, by the romantic Adam Smith?); it is the love of the picturesque (p. 49); it is the dislike of innovation (p. 50) but also the love of change (p. iv); it is the sentimental (p. 192); it is patriotism, and then it is cheap (p. 235). It may be used to denote what is not classical, but chiefly it means that which ignores reality (pp. ix, 136, 143, 147, and *passim*); it is not critical (pp. 225, 235), although in speaking of Cooper and Melville, Parrington admits that criticism can sometimes spring from romanticism.

Whenever a man with whose ideas he disagrees wins from Parrington a reluctant measure of respect, the word romantic is likely to appear. He does not admire Henry Clay, yet something in Clay is not to be despised—his romanticism, although Clay's romanticism is made equivalent with his inability to "come to grips with reality." Romanticism is thus, in most of its significations, the venial sin of *Main Currents;* like carnal passion in the *Inferno,* it evokes not blame but tender sorrow. But it can also be the great and saving virtue which Parrington recognizes. It is ascribed to the transcendental reformers he so much admires; it is said to mark two of his most cherished heroes, Jefferson and Emerson: "they were both romantics and their idealism was only a different expression of a common spirit." Parrington held, we may say, at least two different views of romanticism which suggest two different views of reality. Sometimes he speaks of reality in an honorific way, meaning the substantial stuff of life, the ineluctable facts with which the mind must cope, but sometimes he speaks of it pejoratively and means the world of established social forms; and he

[1] See, for example, how Parrington accounts for the "idealizing mind"—Melville's—by the discrepancy between "a wife in her morning kimono" and "the Helen of his dreams." Vol. II, p. 259.

speaks of realism in two ways: sometimes as the power of dealing intelligently with fact, sometimes as a cold and conservative resistance to idealism.

Just as for Parrington there is a saving grace and a venial sin, there is also a deadly sin, and this is turning away from reality, not in the excess of generous feeling, but in what he believes to be a deficiency of feeling, as with Hawthorne, or out of what amounts to sinful pride, as with Henry James. He tells us that there was too much realism in Hawthorne to allow him to give his faith to the transcendental reformers: "he was too much of a realist to change fashions in creeds"; "he remained cold to the revolutionary criticism that was eager to pull down the old temples to make room for nobler." It is this cold realism, keeping Hawthorne apart from his enthusiastic contemporaries, that alienates Parrington's sympathy —"Eager souls, mystics and revolutionaries, may propose to refashion the world in accordance with their dreams; but evil remains, and so long as it lurks in the secret places of the heart, utopia is only the shadow of a dream. And so while the Concord thinkers were proclaiming man to be the indubitable child of God, Hawthorne was critically examining the question of evil as it appeared in the light of his own experience. It was the central fascinating problem of his intellectual life, and in pursuit of a solution he probed curiously into the hidden, furtive recesses of the soul." Parrington's disapproval of the enterprise is unmistakable.

Now we might wonder whether Hawthorne's questioning of the naive and often eccentric faiths of the transcendental reformers was not, on the face of it, a public service. But Parrington implies that it contributes nothing to democracy, and even that it stands in the way of the realization of democracy. If democracy depends wholly on a fighting faith, I suppose he is right. Yet society is after all something that exists at the moment as well as in the future, and if one man wants to probe curiously into the hidden furtive recesses of the contemporary soul, a broad democracy and especially one devoted to reality should allow him to do so without despising him. If what Hawthorne did was certainly nothing to build a party on, we ought perhaps to forgive him when we remember that he was only one man and that the future of mankind did not depend on him alone. But this very fact serves only to irritate Parrington; he is put out by Hawthorne's loneliness and believes that part of Hawthorne's insufficiency as a writer comes from his failure to get around and meet people. Hawthorne could not, he tells us, establish contact with the "Yankee reality," and was scarcely aware of the "substantial world of Puritan reality that Samuel Sewall knew."

To turn from reality might mean to turn to romance, but Parrington tells us that Hawthorne was romantic "only in a narrow and very special sense." He was not interested in the world of, as it were, practical romance, in the Salem of the clipper ships; from this he turned away to create "a romance of ethics." This is not an illuminating phrase but it is a catching one, and it might be taken to mean that Hawthorne was in the tradition of, say, Shakespeare; but we quickly learn that, no, Hawthorne had entered a barren field, for although he himself lived in the present and had all the future to mold, he preferred to find many of his subjects in the past. We learn too that his romance of ethics is not admirable because it requires the hard, fine pressing of ideas, and we are told that "a romantic uninterested in adventure and afraid of sex is likely to become somewhat graveled for matter." In short, Hawthorne's mind was a thin one, and Parrington puts in evidence his use of allegory and symbol and the very severity and precision of his art to prove that he suffered from a sadly limited intellect, for so much fancy and so much art could scarcely be needed unless the writer were trying to exploit to the utmost the few poor ideas that he had.

Hawthorne, then, was "forever dealing with shadows, and he knew that he was dealing with shadows." Perhaps so, but shadows are also part of reality and one would not want a world without shadows, it would not even be a "real" world. But we must get beyond Parrington's metaphor. The fact is that Hawthorne was dealing beautifully with realities, with substantial things. The man who could raise those brilliant and serious doubts about the nature and possibility of moral perfection, the man who could keep himself aloof from the "Yankee reality" and who could dissent from the orthodoxies of dissent and tell us so much about the nature of moral zeal, is of course dealing exactly with reality.

Parrington's characteristic weakness as a historian is suggested by his title, for the culture of a nation is not truly figured in the image of the current. A culture is not a flow, nor even a confluence; the form of its existence is struggle, or at least debate—it is nothing if not a dialectic. And in any culture there are likely to be certain artists who contain a large part of the dialectic within themselves, their meaning and power lying in their contradictions; they contain within themselves, it may be said, the very essence of the culture, and the sign of this is that they do not submit to serve the ends of any one ideological group or tendency. It is a significant circumstance of American culture, and one which is susceptible of explanation, that an unusually large proportion of its notable writers of the nineteenth century were such repositories of the dialectic of their times—they contained both the yes and no of their culture, and by that token they were prophetic of the future. Parrington said that he had not set up shop as a literary critic; but if a literary critic is simply a reader who has the ability to understand literature and to convey to others what he understands, it is not exactly a matter of free choice whether or not a cultural historian shall be a literary critic, nor is it open to him to let his virtuous political and social opinions do duty for percipience. To throw out Poe because he cannot be conveniently fitted into a theory of American culture, to speak of him as a biological sport and as a mind apart from the main current, to find his gloom to be merely personal and eccentric, "only the atrabilious wretchedness of a dipsomaniac," as Hawthorne's was "no more than the skeptical questioning of life by a nature that knew no fierce storms," to judge Melville's response to American life to be less noble than that of Bryant or of Greeley, to speak of Henry James as an escapist, as an artist similar to Whistler, a man characteristically afraid of stress—this is not merely to be mistaken in aesthetic judgment; rather it is to examine without attention and from the point of view of a limited and essentially arrogant conception of reality the documents which are in some respects the most suggestive testimony to what America was and is, and of course to get no answer from them.

Parrington lies twenty years behind us, and in the intervening time there has developed a body of opinion which is aware of his inadequacies and of the inadequacies of his coadjutors and disciples, who make up what might be called the literary academicism of liberalism. Yet Parrington still stands at the center of American thought about American culture because, as I say, he expresses the chronic American belief that there exists an opposition between reality and mind and that one must enlist oneself in the party of reality.

II

This belief in the incompatibility of mind and reality is exemplified by the doctrinaire indulgence which liberal intellectuals have always displayed toward Theodore Dreiser, an indulgence which becomes the worthier of remark when it is contrasted with the liberal severity toward Henry James. Dreiser and James: with that juxtaposition we are immediately at the dark and bloody crossroads where literature and politics meet. One does not go there gladly, but nowadays it is not exactly a matter of free choice whether one does or does not go. As for the particular juxtaposition itself, it is inevitable and it has at the present moment far more significance than the juxtaposition which once used to be made between James and Whitman. It is not hard to contrive factitious oppositions between James and Whitman, but the real difference between them is the difference between the moral mind, with its awareness of tragedy, irony, and multitudinous distinctions, and the transcendental mind, with its passionate sense of the oneness of multiplicity. James and Whitman are unlike not in quality but in kind, and in their very opposition they serve to complement each other. But the difference between James and Dreiser is not of kind, for both men addressed themselves to virtually the same social and moral fact. The difference here is one of quality, and perhaps nothing is more typical of American liberalism than the way it has responded to the respective qualities of the two men.

Few critics, I suppose, no matter what their political disposition, have ever been wholly blind to James's great gifts, or even to the grandiose moral intention of these gifts. And few critics have ever been wholly blind to Dreiser's great faults. But by liberal critics James is traditionally put to the ultimate question: of what use, of what actual political use, are his gifts and their intention? Granted that James was devoted to an extraordinary moral perceptiveness, granted too that moral perceptiveness has something to do with politics and the social life, of what possible practical value in our world of impending disaster can James's work be? And James's style, his characters, his subjects, and even his own social origin and the manner of his personal life are adduced to show that his work cannot endure the question. To James no quarter is given by American criticism in its political and liberal aspect. But in the same degree that liberal criticism is moved by political considerations to treat James with severity, it treats Dreiser with the most sympathetic indulgence. Dreiser's literary faults, it gives us to understand, are essentially social and political virtues. It was Parrington who established the formula for the liberal criticism of Dreiser by calling him a "peasant": when Dreiser thinks stupidly, it is because he has the slow stubbornness of a peasant; when he writes badly, it is because he is impatient of the sterile literary gentility of the bourgeoisie. It is as if wit, and flexibility of mind, and perception, and knowledge were to be equated with aristocracy and political reaction, while dullness and stupidity must naturally suggest a virtuous democracy, as in the old plays.

The liberal judgment of Dreiser and James goes back of politics, goes back to the cultural assumptions that make politics. We are still haunted by a kind of political fear of the intellect which Tocqueville observed in us more than a century ago. American intellectuals, when they are being consciously American or political, are remarkably quick to suggest that an art which is marked by perception and knowledge, although all very well in its way, can never get us through gross dangers and difficulties. And their misgivings become the more intense when intellect works in art as it ideally should, when its processes are vivacious and interesting and brilliant. It is then that we like to confront it with the gross dangers and difficulties and to challenge it to save us at once from disaster. When intellect in art is awkward and dull we do not put it to the test of ultimate or immediate practicality. No liberal critic asks the question of Dreiser whether *his* moral preoccupations are going to be useful in confronting the disasters that threaten us. And it is a judgment on the proper nature of mind, rather than any actual political meaning that might be drawn from the works of the two men, which accounts for the unequal justice they have received from the progressive critics. If it could be conclusively demonstrated—by, say, documents in James's handwriting—that James explicitly intended his books to be understood as pleas for co-operatives, labor unions, better housing, and more equitable taxation, the American critic in his liberal and progressive character would still be worried by James because his work shows so many of the electric qualities of mind. And if something like the opposite were proved of Dreiser, it would be brushed aside—as his doctrinaire anti-Semitism has in fact been brushed aside—because his books have the awkwardness, the chaos, the heaviness which we associate with "reality." In the American metaphysic, reality is always material reality, hard, resistant, unformed, impenetrable, and unpleasant. And that mind is alone felt to be trustworthy which most resembles this reality by most nearly reproducing the sensations it affords.

In *The Rise of American Civilization,* Professor Beard uses a significant phrase when, in the course of an ironic account of James's career, he implies that we have the clue to the irrelevance of that career when we know that James was "a whole generation removed from the odors of the shop." Of a piece with this, and in itself even more significant, is the comment which Granville Hicks makes in *The Great Tradition* when he deals with James's stories about artists and remarks that such artists as James portrays, so concerned for their art and their integrity in art, do not really exist: "After all, who has ever known such artists? Where are the Hugh Verekers, the Mark Ambients, the Neil Paradays, the Overts, Limberts, Dencombes, Delavoys?" This question, as Mr. Hicks admits, had occurred to James himself, but what answer had James given to it? "If the life about us for the last thirty years refused warrant for these examples," he said in the preface to volume XII of the New York Edition, "then so much the worse for that life. . . . There are decencies that in the name of the general self-respect we must take for granted, there's a rudimentary intellectual honor to which we must, in the interest of civilization, at least pretend." And to this Mr. Hicks, shocked beyond argument, makes this reply, which would be astonishing had we not heard it before: "But this is the purest romanticism, this writing about what ought to be rather than what is!"

The "odors of the shop" are real, and to those who breathe them they guarantee a sense of vitality from which James is debarred. The idea of intellectual honor is not real, and to that chimera James was devoted. He betrayed the reality of what is in the interests of what ought to be. Dare we trust him? The question, we remember, is asked by men who themselves have elaborate transactions with what ought to be. Professor Beard spoke in the name of a growing, developing, and improving America. Mr. Hicks, when he wrote *The Great Tradition,* was in general sympathy with a nominally radical movement. But James's own transaction with what ought to be is suspect because it is carried on through what I have called the electrical qualities of mind, through a complex and rapid imagination and with a kind of authoritative immediacy. Mr. Hicks knows that Dreiser is "clumsy" and "stupid" and "bewildered" and "crude in his statement of materialistic monism"; he knows that Dreiser in his personal life—which is in point because James's personal life is always supposed to be so much in point—was not quite emancipated from "his boyhood longing for crass material success," showing "again and again a desire for the ostentatious luxury of the successful business man." But Dreiser is to be accepted and forgiven because his faults are the sad, lovable, honorable faults of reality itself, or of America itself—huge, inchoate, struggling toward expression, caught between the dream of raw power and the dream of morality.

"The liability in what Santayana called the genteel tradition was due to its being the product of mind apart from experience. Dreiser gave us the stuff of our common experience, not as it was hoped to be by any idealizing theorist, but as it actually was in its crudity." The author of this statement certainly cannot be accused of any lack of feeling for mind as Henry James represents it; nor can Mr. Matthiessen be thought of as a follower of Parrington—indeed, in the preface to *American Renaissance* he has framed one of the sharpest and most cogent criticisms of Parrington's method. Yet Mr. Matthiessen, writing in the *New York Times Book Review* about Dreiser's posthumous novel, *The Bulwark,* accepts the liberal cliché which opposes crude experience to the mind and establishes Dreiser's value by implying that the mind which Dreiser's crude experience is presumed to confront and refute is the mind of gentility.

This implied amalgamation of mind with gentility is the rationale of the long indulgence of Dreiser, which is extended even to the style of his prose. Everyone is aware that Dreiser's prose style is full of roughness and ungainliness, and the critics who admire Dreiser tell us it does not matter. Of course it does not matter. No reader with a right sense of style would suppose that it does matter, and he might even find it a virtue. But it has been taken for granted that the ungainliness of Dreiser's style is the only possible objection to be made to it, and that whoever finds in it any fault at all wants a prettified genteel style (and is objecting to the ungainliness of reality itself). For instance, Edwin Berry Burgum, in a leaflet on Dreiser put out by the Book Find Club, tells us that Dreiser was one of those who used—or, as Mr. Burgum says, utilized—"the diction of the Middle West, pretty much as it was spoken, rich in colloquialism and frank in the simplicity and directness of the pioneer tradition," and that this diction took the place of "the literary English, formal and bookish, of New England provincialism that was closer to the aristocratic spirit of the mother country than to the tang of everyday life in the new West." This is mere fantasy. Hawthorne, Thoreau, and Emerson were for the most part remarkably colloquial—they wrote, that is, much as they spoke; their prose was specifically American in quality, and, except for occasional lapses, quite direct and simple. It is Dreiser who lacks the sense of colloquial diction—that of the Middle West or any other. If we are to talk of bookishness, it is Dreiser who is bookish; he is precisely literary in the bad sense; he is full of flowers of rhetoric and shines with paste gems; at hundreds of points his diction is not only genteel but fancy. It is he who speaks of "a scene more distingué than this," or of a woman "artistic in form and feature," or of a man who, although "strong, reserved, aggressive, with an air of wealth and experience, was *soi-disant* and not particularly eager to stay at home." Colloquialism held no real charm for him and his natural tendency is always toward the "fine":

> . . . *Moralists come and go; religionists fulminate and declare the pronouncements of God as to this; but Aphrodite still reigns. Embowered in the festal depths of the spring, set above her altars of porphyry, chalcedony, ivory and gold, see her smile the smile that is at once the texture and essence of delight, the glory and despair of the world! Dream on, oh Buddha, asleep on your lotus leaf, of an undisturbed Nirvana! Sweat, oh Jesus, your last agonizing drops over an unregenerate world! In the forests of Pan still ring the cries of the worshippers of Aphrodite! From her altars the incense of adoration ever rises! And see, the new red grapes dripping where votive hands new-press them!*

Charles Jackson, the novelist, telling us in the same leaflet that Dreiser's style does not matter, remarks on how much still comes to us when we have lost by translation the stylistic brilliance of Thomas Mann or the Russians or Balzac. He is in part right. And he is right too when he says that a certain kind of conscious, supervised artistry is not appropriate to the novel of large dimensions. Yet the fact is that the great novelists have usually written very good prose, and what comes through even a bad translation is exactly the power of mind that made the well-hung sentence of the original text. In literature style is so little the mere clothing of thought—need it be insisted on at this late date?—that we may say that from the earth of the novelist's prose spring his characters, his ideas, and even his story itself.[2]

To the extent that Dreiser's style is defensible, his thought is also defensible. That is, when he thinks like a novelist, he is worth following—when by means of his rough and ungainly but no doubt cumulatively effective style he creates rough, ungainly, but effective characters and events. But when he thinks like, as we say, a philosopher, he is likely to be not only foolish but vulgar. He thinks as the modern crowd thinks when it decides to think: religion and morality are nonsense, "religionists" and moralists are fakes, tradition is a fraud, what is man but matter and impulses, mysterious "chemisms," what value has life anyway? "What, cooking, eating, coition, job holding, growing, aging, losing, winning, in so changeful and passing a scene as this, important? Bunk! It is some form of titillating illusion with about as much import to the superior forces that bring it all about as the functions and gyrations of a fly. No more. And maybe less." Thus Dreiser at sixty. And yet there is for him always the vulgarly saving suspicion that maybe, when all is said and done, there is Something Behind It All. It is much to the point of his intellectual vulgarity that Dreiser's anti-Semitism was not merely a social prejudice but an idea, a way of dealing with difficulties.

No one, I suppose, has ever represented Dreiser as a masterly intellect. It is even commonplace to say that his ideas are inconsistent or inadequate. But once that admission has been made, his ideas are hustled out of sight while his "reality" and great brooding pity are spoken of. (His pity is to be questioned: pity is to be judged by kind, not amount, and Dreiser's pity —*Jennie Gerhardt* provides the only exception—is either destructive of its object or it is self-pity.) Why has no liberal critic ever brought Dreiser's ideas to the bar of political practicality, asking what use is to be made of

[2] The latest defense of Dreiser's style, that in the chapter on Dreiser in the *Literary History of the United States,* is worth noting: "Forgetful of the integrity and power of Dreiser's whole work, many critics have been distracted into a condemnation of his style. He was, like Twain and Whitman, an organic artist; he wrote what he knew—what he was. His many colloquialisms were part of the coinage of his time, and his sentimental and romantic passages were written in the language of the educational system and the popular literature of his formative years. In his style, as in his material, he was a child of his time, of his class. Self-educated, a type or model of the artist of plebeian origin in America, his language, like his subject matter, is not marked by internal inconsistencies." No doubt Dreiser was an organic artist in the sense that he wrote what he knew and what he was, but so, I suppose, is every artist; the question for criticism comes down to *what* he knew and *what* he was. That he was a child of his time and class is also true, but this can be said of everyone without exception; the question for criticism is how he transcended the imposed limitations of his time and class. As for the defense made on the ground of his particular class, it can only be said that liberal thought has come to a strange pass when it assumes that a plebeian origin is accountable for a writer's faults through all his intellectual life.

Dreiser's dim, awkward speculation, of his self-justification, of his lust for "beauty" and "sex" and "living" and "life itself," and of the showy nihilism which always seems to him so grand a gesture in the direction of profundity? We live, understandably enough, with the sense of urgency; our clock, like Baudelaire's has had the hands removed and bears the legend, "It is later than you think." But with us it is always a little too late for mind, yet never too late for honest stupidity; always a little too late for understanding, never too late for righteous, bewildered wrath; always too late for thought, never too late for naive moralizing. We seem to like to condemn our finest but not our worst qualities by pitting them against the exigency of time.

But sometimes time is not quite so exigent as to justify all our own exigency, and in the case of Dreiser time has allowed his deficiencies to reach their logical, and fatal, conclusion. In *The Bulwark* Dreiser's characteristic ideas come full circle, and the simple, didactic life history of Solon Barnes, a Quaker business man, affirms a simple Christian faith, and a kind of practical mysticism, and the virtues of self-abnegation and self-restraint, and the belief in and submission to the hidden purposes of higher powers, those "superior forces that bring it all about"—once, in Dreiser's opinion, so brutally indifferent, now somehow benign. This is not the first occasion on which Dreiser has shown a tenderness toward religion and a responsiveness to mysticism. *Jennie Gerhardt* and the figure of the Reverend Duncan McMillan in *An American Tragedy* are forecasts of the avowals of *The Bulwark,* and Dreiser's lively interest in power of any sort led him to take account of the power implicit in the cruder forms of mystical performance. Yet these rifts in his nearly monolithic materialism cannot quite prepare us for the blank pietism of *The Bulwark,* not after we have remembered how salient in Dreiser's work has been the long surly rage against the "religionists" and the "moralists," the men who have presumed to believe that life can be given any law at all and who have dared to suppose that will or mind or faith can shape the savage and beautiful entity that Dreiser liked to call "life itself." Now for Dreiser the law may indeed be given, and it is wholly simple—the safe conduct of the personal life requires only that we follow the Inner Light according to the regimen of the Society of Friends, or according to some other godly rule. And now the smiling Aphrodite set above her altars of porphyry, chalcedony, ivory, and gold is quite forgotten, and we are told that the sad joy of cosmic acceptance goes hand in hand with sexual abstinence.

Dreiser's mood of "acceptance" in the last years of his life is not, as a personal experience, to be submitted to the tests of intellectual validity. It consists of a sensation of cosmic understanding, of an overarching sense of unity with the world in its apparent evil as well as in its obvious good. It is no more to be quarreled with, or reasoned with, than love itself— indeed, it is a kind of love, not so much of the world as of oneself in the world. Perhaps it is either the cessation of desire or the perfect balance of desires. It is what used often to be meant by "peace," and up through the nineteenth century a good many people understood its meaning. If it was Dreiser's own emotion at the end of his life, who would not be happy that he had achieved it? I am not even sure that our civilization would not be the better for more of us knowing and desiring this emotion of grave felicity. Yet granting the personal validity of the emotion, Dreiser's exposition of it fails, and is, moreover, offensive. Mr. Matthiessen has warned us of the attack that will be made on the doctrine of *The Bulwark* by "those who believe that any renewal of Christianity marks a new 'failure of nerve.'" But Dreiser's religious avowal is not a failure of nerve—it is a failure of mind and heart. We have only to set his book beside any work in which mind and heart are made to serve religion to know this at once. Ivan Karamazov's giving back his ticket of admission to the "harmony" of the universe suggests that *The Bulwark* is not morally adequate, for we dare not, as its hero does, blandly "accept" the suffering of others; and the Book of Job tells us that it does not include enough in its exploration of the problem of evil, and is not stern enough. I have said that Dreiser's religious affirmation was offensive; the offense lies in the vulgar ease of its formulation, as well as in the comfortable untroubled way in which Dreiser moved from nihilism to pietism.[3]

The Bulwark is the fruit of Dreiser's old age, but if we speak of it as a failure of thought and feeling, we cannot suppose that with age Dreiser weakened in mind and heart. The weakness was always there. And in a sense it is not Dreiser who failed but a whole way of dealing with ideas, a way in which we have all been in some degree involved. Our liberal, progressive culture tolerated Dreiser's vulgar materialism with its huge negation, its simple cry of "Bunk!," feeling that perhaps it was not quite intellectually adequate but certainly very *strong,* certainly very *real.* And now, almost as a natural consequence, it has been given, and is not unwilling to take, Dreiser's pietistic religion in all its inadequacy.

Dreiser, of course, was firmer than the intellectual culture that accepted him. He *meant* his ideas, at least so far as a man can mean ideas who is

[3] This ease and comfortableness seem to mark contemporary religious conversions. Religion nowadays has the appearance of what the ideal modern house has been called, "a machine for living," and seemingly one makes up one's mind to acquire and use it not with spiritual struggle but only with a growing sense of its practicability and convenience. Compare *The Seven Storey Mountain,* which Monsignor Sheen calls "a twentieth-century form of the *Confessions* of St. Augustine," with the old, the as it were original, *Confessions* of St. Augustine.

incapable of following them to their consequences. But we, when it came to his ideas, talked about his great brooding pity and shrugged the ideas off. We are still doing it. Robert Elias, the biographer of Dreiser, tells us that "it is part of the logic of (Dreiser's) life that he should have completed *The Bulwark* at the same time that he joined the Communists." Just what kind of logic this is we learn from Mr. Elias's further statement. "When he supported left-wing movements and finally, last year, joined the Communist Party, he did so not because he had examined the details of the party line and found them satisfactory, but because he agreed with a general program that represented a means for establishing his cherished goal of greater equality among men." Whether or not Dreiser was following the logic of his own life, he was certainly following the logic of the liberal criticism that accepted him so undiscriminatingly as one of the great, significant expressions of its spirit. This is the liberal criticism, in the direct line of Parrington, which establishes the social responsibility of the writer and then goes on to say that, apart from his duty of resembling reality as much as possible, he is not really responsible for anything, not even for his ideas. The scope of reality being what it is, ideas are held to be mere "details," and, what is more, to be details which, if attended to, have the effect of diminishing reality. But ideals are different from ideas; in the liberal criticism which descends from Parrington ideals consort happily with reality and they urge us to deal impatiently with ideas—a "cherished goal" forbids that we stop to consider how we reach it, or if we may not destroy it in trying to reach it the wrong way.

Saul Bellow

DREISER AND THE TRIUMPH OF ART

Dreiser is not very popular now, unfortunately, and Professor Matthiessen's book will not restore his popularity though it defends him with some real feeling against the usual charges of crude writing, faulty thought, and ridiculous prejudices. Part of this biography is disingenuous, the political part; Matthiessen pretended to see no difference between radicalism and Communism and refused to see that William Z. Foster is not the heir of Eugene V. Debs. Dreiser understood many things better than he did politics; so probably, did Matthiessen. But Dreiser would not have made, in the writing of a novel, an error of the kind Matthiessen tragically allowed himself to make in this study. It is true that it was left unfinished, but there is no hint in it of a possible different treatment of this political problem; there is only the pitiful obstinacy of a "position," that marvelous dishonesty of modern politics. Through it, you sense Matthiessen's confusion and pain.

His admirers grant that Dreiser was a great novelist who wrote badly. But it is very odd that no one has thought to ask just what the "bad writing" of a powerful novelist signifies. Matthiessen says that his groping after words corresponded to the groping of his thought, "but with both words and thought borne along on the diapason of a deep emotion." This is something of a start, but Matthiessen does not attempt to go very deeply into the matter.

Dreiser's novels are best read quickly. You pass rapidly through the pages, almost as if you were reading a newspaper, but great things remain. Occasionally you are arrested by a powerful phrase; but Dreiser is never entirely free from the habits of a feature-story writer, the old-fashioned sort, like Brisbane, who has fed on Gustavus Myers and Ingersoll and on Congressional rhetoric. When he is at his worst he is not even a slick feature-story writer. His passion for the subject failing him, Dreiser can never rest on writing itself; he has not that skill. But there are few modern writers whose passion for the subject is so steady. And then his journalistic habits are often useful; by means of them he captures things

From *Commentary*, May, 1951. A review of F. O. Matthiessen's *Theodore Dreiser*.

that perhaps could not be taken in other ways—common expressions, flat-nesses, forms of thought, the very effect of popular literature itself.

I think it is fair to judge a writer in part by the way he breaks through his first defects, the stiffness of his beginner's manner, his romanticism or sentimentality or modishness, his early thicknesses or thinnesses. In writing, as in personal history, what a man overcomes is a measure of his quality. An individual of any category or class performs an important and a fascinating service when he drives beyond the ordinary limitations of his type. Dreiser is, before our eyes, a newspaperman deepened, serious, finally showing a capacity that unites him with men of a very different sort who started out in a very different way. Each comes to the essential accompanied by all his accidents. A writer in America is likely to be an "irregular."

The majority of modern novelists with their care for the poetry of detail, and in their craving for stability, have not made much progress toward the greatest contemporary facts. How many European novels today have the power of the factual accounts of deportations, camps, escapades, battles, hitherto unknown relations? Considering how hideously life has been shaken, it is remarkable perhaps that any novels are being written at all in, say, France and Italy. And it is understandable that writers should try to preserve the old sort of accomplishments. But how can the *écrivain artiste* keep pace with these phenomena? Even before the war, he had fallen far behind. The social meaning of his great skill was conservative; it was an effort to contain, in the military meaning of the word, great disturbances. A very talented novelist, Alberto Moravia, in his recent book, *Conjugal Love,* shows how reality is bound to revenge itself on the writer, the cultivated artist, *l'écrivain artiste,* when he keeps it at several removes. It will force him to discover the emptiness of his accomplishments, the vanity of his stability.

I often think the criticisms of Dreiser as a stylist at times betray a resistance to the feelings he causes readers to suffer. If they can say that he can't write, they need not experience these feelings. And I think, too, that the insistence on neatness and correctness is one of the signs of a modern nervousness and irritability. When has clumsiness in composition been felt as so annoying, so enraging? The "good" writing of the *New Yorker* is such that one experiences a furious anxiety, in reading it, about errors and lapses from taste; finally what emerges is a terrible hunger for conformism and uniformity. The smoothness of the surface and its high polish must not be marred. One has a similar anxiety in reading a novelist like Hemingway and comes to feel in the end that Hemingway wants to be praised for the offenses he does not commit. He is dependable; he never names certain emotions or ideas, and he takes pride in that—it is a form of honor. In it, really, there is submissiveness, acceptance of restriction.

Many American novelists, moreover, reveal in their extreme concern with expression that they are greatly oppressed by details. When they lack the strength that can encompass and lift up these details—facts of our American, modern reality—they are inclined to put into accomplishments of style what is really a helplessness or recoil. Ugliness and banality growing huge, there is the fear that no poetry can inhabit the same space. So single, isolated perceptions wound the novelist, colors oppress him, factories bear him to the ground, business and advertising make him suffer, cellophane sticks in his throat. He will then "handle" by his writing his various pains. A good example of this sort of "handling" is the trip from West Egg described in F. Scott Fitzgerald's *The Great Gatsby*. Dreiser had no need for this use of language because of his greater lifting power. He depended on principles, not on taste. It was something other than taste that helped him during the crushing years of poverty and near-insanity in the New York slums. He returned to sanity and life, disfigured, I believe, but with the important knowledge of how life could be supported, and this was a knowledge that carried fairly easily facts that were too great a burden to other writers.

This important knowledge was not what Dreiser thought it was. When he is writing about his principles, in language awkwardly borrowed from Herbert Spencer or Huxley, they are gone the instant he invokes them. They reveal themselves sometimes incidentally in a power of lament— "And off he walked, very gay and dapper and assured because of a recent and seemingly durable success of his own." But they are most plain where the line of fate surpasses clearly the confusion of many wishes and efforts, and when Dreiser bitterly, grudgingly, admits his *amor fati*. This is what is so moving in him, his balkiness and sullenness, and then his admission of allegiance to life. The fact that he is a modern American gives an extreme contour to this allegiance; it is made after immersion in the greatest difficulties and reasons for pessimism and with all the art of which he is capable, art stubbornly insisted upon under the severest discouragements. His history is that of a man convinced by his experience of "unpoetic reality" of the need to become an artist.

John Berryman

DREISER'S IMAGINATION

For decades Theodore Dreiser loomed large as one of the few world figures in our fiction. Then his immense frame so deteriorated, especially
after his death in 1945, that when a detailed biography was produced by
Robert H. Elias in 1949 an influential book reporter could question
whether Dreiser was a subject of general interest to the public at all. In
1951, with "Theodore Dreiser" (William Sloane), a posthumous study by
one of America's most respected literary historians, the late F. O. Matthiessen of Harvard, the question was conclusively answered. Dreiser's shifting, somber, dubious life is hardly one to be dealt with briefly (as it has to
be in this account), but that it has to be dealt with, and that it is of great
general interest there is no longer any doubt.

The earlier part of that life has been handled impressively by Dreiser
himself in several books ("Dawn," "Newspaper Days," "Twelve Men")
very like his novels and not much less interesting. Small wonder if
Matthiessen's opening chapters are somewhat perfunctory, but it is to his
credit that even here he helps to clarify Dreiser's story.

Born in Indiana in 1871, Dreiser was a German immigrant's son. His
father was a strict Catholic and his mother loving and easy-going. His
education was wretched by any standard and he proved to have small gift
for language, and very modest ability as a newspaper reporter. At 27, as
Matthiessen says clearly, he showed exactly no promise of becoming a
writer of note. When presently he wrote his first novel, "Sister Carrie"
(World), he had to be prodded by a friend, Arthur Henry (as Louis
Bouilhet prodded Flaubert into "Madame Bovary"). And when it was
virtually suppressed upon publication in 1900, Dreiser sank into a depression that lasted three years and wrote no more fiction for ten.

Instead, upon recovery, Dreiser became an optimistic and extremely successful director of popular magazines, soliciting from other writers, including Mencken, just the sort of emasculated trash he had despised. For six
years he rode the facile American waves. Then, at 39 he wrote "Jennie

From *Highlights of Modern Literature,* ed. by Francis Brown, New American Library of
World Literature, Inc., 1954. A review of F. O. Matthiessen's *Theodore Dreiser.*

Gerhardt" (World) and, behold, he had learned nothing and forgotten nothing and was just the same and nearly as good as before.

Matthiessen emphasizes, without attempting to explain, the mystery of Dreiser's resumption of his talent and integrity after an entire decade of wasted or degraded activity. He says very little, however, about a mystery more cardinal still—namely, Dreiser's blank failure thereafter to develop as an artist. Four long novels followed, and then, at last, two others—one better, the rest worse, but all essentially like the early novels.

It has not escaped notice that Dreiser wrote like a hippopotamus. His ineptitude, in fact, has been so long familiar that perhaps we have not been sufficiently surprised that an important author, writing badly over a lifetime, should continue to do so without an attempt at redemption or amelioration. Probably the two mysteries are related, and we might try to approach them through a consideration of Matthiessen's chapters on the individual novels.

The usual decline of an author's reputation following his death was dramatized in Dreiser's case by an increasingly feeble or contemptuous response to the posthumously issued novels, "The Bulwark" (1946) and "The Stoic" (also World, 1947). The critical chapters here ought to help arrest this decline.

Matthiessen is hardest on "The Genius," which he calls Dreiser's poorest novel, the one "least rewarding to reread." This strikes as very severe a man who has read it four or five times just for pleasure—never, I confess upon reflection, with admiration precisely, but with the febrile, self-indulgent eagerness Dreiser is apt to induce. But Matthiessen is right, of course, or if not quite right he has only forgotten "The Stoic."

Mr. Matthiessen is nearly always right. He attributes Dreiser's formidable descriptive power to a freshness of eye and obstinate memory fused with a deep sense of changingness which made it seem historically important to preserve appearance. He analyzes handsomely the debts to Balzac and Spencer, and the devices, such as they are, used by the novelist to organize his materials. He remarks that "One of the reasons why Dreiser's characters often take on a grave magnitude lies in their refusal to be hurried, a refusal on his part as well as on theirs."

He denies genuine stature to Frank Cowperwood and does not conceal a progressive weakening through the financial trilogy. He notes that Dreiser's naïveté above a certain social level is simply the price we pay for the marvelous keenness of longing represented in his characters for successive levels of luxury and achievement far above them, but still below most of his cultivated readers. Matthiessen is right above all in insisting on the word "rhythm" as a key to Dreiser's method.

It is well to have this position—which looks like a critical haven—stated by someone as scrupulous, as cautious as Matthiessen, who had seldom much to say on his own as a literary scholar and stuck close to his texts. He describes Dreiser's style as a matter of "the groping after words corresponding to a groping of the thought, but with both words and thought borne along on the diapason of a deep emotion"—of a "deep grounding, at its best, in the rhythm of his emotions." This seems to me to be profound, the only way, indeed, of accounting for immense effects achieved by means so banal and shabby.

The question, then, is to identify the emotion or emotions. Here we can be in no doubt. Matthiessen speaks in other passages of Dreiser's most recurrent theme as that of "the outsider." Yet is the theme really a figure? Is it not rather the feelings that swarm, hardly distinguished, through the figure of the outsider—the bright, vague longing or aspiration or *yearning* that every reader will probably recognize as Dreiser's central and characteristic emotion?

This emotion is American. We remember it less broodingly in sharper, more polished works by Dreiser's contemporaries, in the early novels of Sinclair Lewis, in "The Great Gatsby." The objects vary—money and fame and love—but the clustered, helpless emotions persist without change even through their gratification—because it was the emotions and not their objects that mattered.

What distinguishes Dreiser from his contemporaries is a kind of stupidity, a kind of unself-consciousness, that forbade him ever to employ these emotions until they had passed thoroughly under the mastery of his elephantine memory. He could deal only with the past. Not surprisingly, therefore, he displayed no promise, and he could not be corrupted. We recall Mencken's mature description of him as "granitic, without nerve," with no cunning but with a "truly appalling" tenacity.

There was no question of "integrity" at all. He could be discouraged, and so do nothing, or he could be busy with other things, and so not write. Yet once his imagination came into play at all it brought up the one fixed emotion, and the tides of a real life, long past, billowed through him again.

Stupidity is a weapon, for an artist, almost as powerful as intelligence— as a social man can be protected against bores by a mild deafness. The same stupidity, or unself-consciousness, prevented Dreiser from ever improving his style. Probably the notion never occurred to him, and thus no artifice ever arose to interfere with the almost unconscious *overwhelming* way in which his finest work sweeps the reader with it. A test of Dreiser, as of any large writer, is how he handles what matters most. The magnificence of his supreme achievement has not always been distinguished from the merely fascinating readability of his early novels. His masterpiece—I would agree with what I take to have been Matthiessen's opinion—is "An American Tragedy," and the center of it is the murder (legal and moral up to a point, and then only moral). The darkening rhythm of these phantasmal scenes has hardly been surpassed in fluidity since "Life on the Mississippi." "And then, as planned that night between them—a trip to Grass lake. . . . And yet * * * And then * * *." The prose is artless and unlike Mark Twain's except that both embody freely American plain speech; the comparison is between their perfect attention to the nervous rhythms of their heroes' desires. It is worth mention, too, that "no"-style may on occasion be preferable to some aspects of Melville's lengthy and deplorable affair with Shakespeare.

One of Matthiessen's shrewdest remarks about this wonderful book is this: "As Clyde plots murder in spite of himself, Dreiser goes to the opposite extreme from the writer of a detective story. Everything that Clyde does is so inept that he is discovered at once." But, all the same, the kind of interest that Dreiser's work evokes and satisfies resembles more the interest we take in a detective story than the interest we take in Hemingway or Jane Austen. It is a little feverish.

Some readers will remember a devastating passage in E. M. Forster's "Aspects of the Novel" (Harcourt, Brace) where the author is relating the action of some novel by Walter Scott. "And then?" he says, and tells you what comes next. "And then?" "And then?" But suddenly the novel was over, and you must not—says Forster acidly—ask that question too often. In Scott, no doubt, one follows an artificial series of events, and in Dreiser a natural, but the kinds of interest gratified are the same: a gossip interest, an "And then?"

Greater writers, frankly, do not evoke this interest so keenly or simply —although it has become fashionable, as storytelling decays among us, to pretend that they do. One does *not*, that is, rush on from chapter to chapter of "Anna Karenina" just to see what happens.

One great author who admittedly does evoke this interest is Dostoevsky, and it is with Dostoevsky that Dreiser must be compared. He poorly stands the comparison when his major work is placed against one by no means the Russian's greatest—"Crime and Punishment." As Matthiessen says, Clyde Griffiths is no Raskolnikov, and Dreiser knew no such heights of understanding as those upon which Dostoevsky created his ultimate chapters.

An English view will enforce the abyss of difference. H. G. Wells, who ought one day to be recognized as a judge of modern fiction with few peers, described "An American Tragedy" perfectly as "a far more than life-size rendering of a poor little representative of American existence, lighted up by a flash of miserable tragedy * * * It gets the large, harsh superficial truth" and is "one of the great novels of this century." Dreiser commanded pathos without the tragic dimension. Perhaps he insisted too much upon personal ideas.

Still, Dreiser at present has other interests for us. Matthiessen's second real achievement is the careful study in his concluding chapters of Dreiser's politics and philosophy. Thoroughly grounded himself in American radical thought, and sympathetic with the broodings of an inquirer, Matthiessen has unraveled as well as anyone could the tangled paths by which Dreiser approached simultaneously a membership in the American Communist party and a cloudy position somewhere in the universe of neo-Christian mysticism. A long comparison with Clarence Darrow is more helpful here than were the frequent comparisons earlier with Whitman, Melville and others.

The whole painful discussion, which does not avoid, for example, Dreiser's slow development away from anti-Semitism, is relevant to Matthiessen's tragic death and ought to be read by everyone interested in either man. "Contemplating for ourselves," Matthiessen writes, "the extremes to which both Darrow and Dreiser had gone in their skepticism, we are faced with the grave question of how long positive values can endure only as the aftershine of something that has been lost."

An essential horror in life, in modern life, which Dreiser did not ever really face in his fiction, faces us quietly in these last chapters, and we can only mourn two honest men.

Alfred Kazin

THEODORE DREISER: HIS EDUCATION

AND OURS

The fortunes of literature can reverse the fortunes of life. The luxury that
nourished Edith Wharton and gave her the opportunities of a gentle-
woman cheated her as a novelist. It kept her from what was crucial to the
world in which she lived; seeking its manners, she missed its passion.
Theodore Dreiser had no such handicap to overcome. From the first he
was so oppressed by suffering, by the spectacle of men struggling aimlessly and alone in society, that he was prepared to understand the very
society that rejected him. The cruelty and squalor of the life to which he
was born suggested the theme of existence; the pattern of American
life was identified as the figure of destiny. It was life, it was immemorial, it
was as palpable as hunger or the caprice of God. And Dreiser accepted it
as the common victim of life accepts it, because he knows no other,
because this one summons all his resources.

Winter, Dreiser wrote in his autobiography, had always given him a
physical sense of suffering. "Any form of distress—a wretched, down-at-
heels neighborhood, a poor farm, an asylum, a jail, or an individual or
group of individuals anywhere that seemed to be lacking in the means of
subsistence or to be devoid of the normal comforts of life—was sufficient
to set up in me thoughts and emotions which had a close kinship to actual
and severe physical pain." He grew up in the friendly Indiana country of
the eighties, in the very "Valley of Democracy" to be rhapsodized by
Booth Tarkington and Meredith Nicholson; but he never shared its leg-
endary happiness. His father, a crippled mill superintendent who was
unable to provide for the family of fifteen, was a rigidly devout Catholic.
The family separated periodically, the father going to Chicago to pick up
work, the mother and younger children living in one small town after
another. The bugaboo of social disapproval and scandal followed them
insistently; at one time the mother kept a boardinghouse and a sister furnished the village gossips with a first-rate scandal. The family poverty was

From *On Native Grounds,* Harcourt, Brace, 1942.

such that the town prostitute, his brother Paul's mistress, once sent them food and clothes, and even arranged for their removal to another city.

Dreiser grew up hating the shabby and threadbare rationale of the poor as only their sensitive sons learn to hate it; he hated his father and pitied his mother because she seemed so ineffectual in the face of disaster. The shining success in the family was his brother Paul, who became a popular vaudeville artist and composer. It was a painful, brooding boyhood, whose livid scars were to go into the first chapters of *An American Tragedy;* a boyhood touched by the lonely joys of wallowing in Ouida and *Tom Jones,* but seared by the perennial separations of the family and its grim and helpless decline. There was stamped upon Dreiser from the first a sense of the necessity, the brutal and clumsy dispensation of fate, that imposed itself upon the weak. He hated something nameless, for nothing in his education had prepared him to select events and causes; he hated the paraphernalia of fate—ill luck, the shadowy and inscrutable pattern of things that ground effort into the dust. He did not rebel against it as one who knows what the evil is and how it may be destroyed; he was so over-powered by suffering that he came to see in it a universal principle.

As Dreiser wandered disconsolately through the nineties, a reporter and magazine writer in New York and Chicago, St. Louis and Pittsburgh and Toledo, he began to read the pronouncements of nineteenth-century mechanism in Darwin and Spencer, in Tyndall and Huxley. They gave him not a new insight but the authority to uphold what he had long suspected. They taught him to call a human life a "chemism," but they did not teach him the chemical nature of life; they suggested that man was an "underling," a particle of protoplasm on a minor planet whirling aimlessly in the solar system, which for such a mind as Dreiser's was an excellent way of calling man what Dreiser had from his earliest days known man to be—a poor blind fool. The survival of the fittest was not a lesson in biology to be gathered in Darwin; it was the spectacle of the nineties as Dreiser watched and brooded over it in the great industrial cities that had within the memory of a single generation transformed the American landscape. For whatever the middle-class environment of his boyhood had given him, it was not laissez-faire theology. Capitalism had denied the young Dreiser its prizes, but it had not blinded him to its deceptions. All about him in the convulsive nineties, with their railroad strikes and Populist riots, Dreiser saw American society expanding as if to burst, wealth rising like mercury in the glass, the bitter shambles of revolt, the fight for power. While Robert Herrick was peering anxiously through his academic window and Edith Wharton was tasting the pleasures of Rome and Paris, while David Graham Phillips was reporting the stale scandals of New York high society for Pulitzer and Frank Norris was eagerly devouring the history of California for *The Octopus,* Dreiser was walking the streets of Chicago, the dynamic, symbolic city which contained all that was aggressive and intoxicating in the new frontier world that lived for the mad pace of bull markets and the orgiastic joys of accumulation. He was not of that world, but he understood it. Who could resist the yearning to get rich, to scatter champagne, to live in lobster palaces, to sport the gaudy clothes of the new rich? It was easy enough for those who had made a religion of their desire; it was easier still for a poor young writer who had been so hurt by poverty and the poor that the call of power was the call of life.

What Dreiser learned from that world was that men on different levels of belief and custom were bound together in a single community of desire. It was not the plunder that excited him, the cheating and lying, the ruthlessness and the pious excuses; it was the obsession with the material. A subtler mind, or a less ambitious one, might have cackled in derision; but Dreiser was swept away by the sheer intensity of the passion for accumulation. In *The Titan* he was to introduce a staggering procession of Chicago buccaneers on 'change with the same frowning, slow, heavy earnestness with which Abraham might have presented his flocks to God. He was fascinated by the spectacular career of Charles T. Yerkes, the most dazzling financier of his day, whose reckless energy and demoniac thirst for money spelled the highest ambition of his culture. Power had become not an instrument but a way of life. The self-conscious tycoons sat a little insecurely before their gold plate, their huge and obvious pictures, giggled perhaps in rare moments at their ostentatious and overdressed wives; but to Dreiser they represented the common soul's most passionate hopes made flesh. The symbols of power had become monumental, stocks and bonds blown feverishly into imitation French châteaux, the luxury of yachts, and conquerors' trips to Europe.

These evidences of success were something Dreiser could neither approve nor disapprove. Secretly, perhaps, he may have admired them for taking the American dream out of the literary testaments and crowning it with a silk hat; but what caught him was the human impulse that stole through the worst show of greed and gave it as natural and simple a character as local pride or family affection. As he wrote the story of Frank Algernon Cowperwood (Yerkes himself) in *The Financier* and *The Titan,* his plan was to build by tireless research and monumental detail a record of the industrial-commercial ethic. Though both novels were published at the height of the Progressive agitation, they have nothing in common with the superficial distaste that ruled David Graham Phillips's books, or with the sensitive homilies of Robert Herrick's. For the muckraking novel of the Theodore Roosevelt era assumed as its first premise that the society it excoriated was a passing condition; the novelists of the period based their values either on the traditional individualism and amenity of an agricultural and small owner's way of life (which was the ideal of the Progressive movement), or on the ideal society of Socialism, as did London and Sinclair. Dreiser would neither tinker with that society nor reject it. It was the only society he knew, the only society he had been allowed to understand; it was rooted in the same rock with poverty and mischance, strength and valor; it was life in which, as he wrote, "nothing is proved, all is permitted."

It was this very acceptance that gave him his strength. Since he could conceive of no other society, he lavished his whole spirit upon the spectacle of the present. Where the other novelists of his time saw the evils of capitalism in terms of political or economic causation, Dreiser saw only the hand of fate. Necessity was the sovereign principle. "We suffer for our temperaments, which we did not make," he once wrote, "and for our weaknesses and lacks, which are no part of our willing or doing." There was in nature "no such thing as the right to do, the right not to do." The strong went forward as their instinct compelled them to; the weak either perished or bore life as best they could. Courage was one man's fortune and weakness another man's incapacity.

In a lesser novelist this very dependence upon fate as a central idea might have been disastrous; it would have displayed not an all-encompassing intensity but mere ignorance. Dreiser rose to the top on the strength of it. He raised Cowperwood-Yerkes to the level of destiny, where another might have debased him below the level of society. Cowperwood becomes another Tamburlane; and as one remembers not the cities that Tamburlane sacked, but the character that drove him to conquest and the Oriental world that made that character possible, so one sees Cowperwood as the highest expression of the acquisitive society in which he rules so commandingly. His very spirit may seem repulsive; his ostentation, his multitudinous adulteries, his diabolism, his Gothic pile in Philadelphia and Renaissance palace in New York, merely a display of animalism. But we do not indict him for his ruthlessness and cunning; we despise his rivals because they envy him the very brutality with which he destroys them. When Cowperwood slackens (it cannot be said that he ever fails), it is not because his jungle world has proved too much for him, but because it is not enough. He has exhausted it by despoiling it, as he has exhausted his wives, his partners, his friends, and the sycophantic ingenuity of the architects to the rich. One remembers that poignant episode in which Cowperwood confesses to Stephanie Platow that his hunger for life increases with age but that men have begun to judge him at their own value. He must accept less from life because he has surged beyond its traditional limitations.

It was by a curious irony that Dreiser's early career became the battle-ground of naturalism in America. He stumbled into the naturalist novel as he has stumbled through life. It is doubtful that he would have become a novelist if the fight for realism in American letters had not been won before he arrived on the scene; but when he did, he assumed as a matter of course that a tragic novel so indifferent to conventional shibboleths as *Sister Carrie* was possible. Frank Norris became a naturalist out of his admiration for Zola; Stephen Crane, because the ferocious pessimism of naturalism suited his temperament exactly. Naturalism was Dreiser's instinctive response to life; it linked him with the great primitive novelists of the modern era, like Hamsun and Gorki, who found in the boundless freedom and unparalleled range of naturalism the only approximation of a life that is essentially brutal and disorderly. For naturalism has always been divided between those who know its drab environment from personal experience, to whom writing is always a form of autobiographical discourse, and those who employ it as a literary idea. The French naturalists, and even their early disciples in America, found in its clinical method, its climate of disillusion, their best answer to romantic emotion and the romantic ideal. Naturalism was the classicism of the nineteenth century. Flaubert, Zola, Stephen Crane, and Frank Norris were all suckled in the romantic tradition; they turned to naturalism to disown romantic expansiveness, lavishness of color, and the inherent belief that man is capable of molding his own destiny. To a Flaubert and a Stephen Crane the design became all; it was the mark of fatality in human life rather than life as a seamless web of imponderable forces that interested them. Much as Pope proclaimed in *An Essay on Man* that

> *In human works, though laboured on with pain,*
> *A thousand movements scarce one purpose gain . . .*

> *So Man, who here seems principal alone,*
> *Perhaps acts second to some sphere unknown,*

so the classic naturalists furnished case histories of suffering to describe the precise conditions under which, as a citizen of the urban industrial world, modern man plans his life, fumbles in the void, and dies.

What Dreiser gave to the cause of American naturalism was a unique contribution. By exploding in the face of the Genteel Tradition, *Sister Carrie* made possible a new frankness in the American novel. It performed its function in literary history by giving the "new" morality of the nineties the example of solid expression; but it liberated that morality quite undeliberately. The young Dreiser, as John Chamberlain has put it, "had not been accepted by Puritan-commercial folk; therefore he was not loaded down in childhood with hampering theories of the correct way in which to live and act and write." The same formless apprenticeship and labored self-education which kept him from the stakes of modern society shielded him from its restrictions. He had no desire to shock; he was not perhaps even conscious that he would shock the few people who read *Sister Carrie* in 1900 with consternation. It would never have occurred to Dreiser that in writing the story of Hurstwood's decline he was sapping the foundations of the genteel. With his flash, his loud talk and fine linen, his rings and his animal intelligence, Hurstwood was such a man as Dreiser had seen over and over again in Chicago. The sleek and high-powered man of affairs automatically became Dreiser's favorite hero. To tell his story was to match reality; and the grossness and poignance of that reality Dreiser has known better than any other novelist of our time.

Dreiser's craftsmanship has never been copied, as innumerable writers have copied from Stephen Crane or even from Jack London. There has been nothing one could copy. With his proverbial slovenliness, the barbarisms and incongruities whose notoriety has preceded him into history, the bad grammar, the breathless and painful clutching at words, the vocabulary dotted with "trig" and "artistic" that may sound like a salesman's effort to impress, the outrageous solecisms that give his novels the flavor of sand, he has seemed the unique example of a writer who remains great despite himself. It is by now an established part of our folklore that Theodore Dreiser lacks everything except genius. Those who have celebrated him most still blush a little for him; he has become as much a symbol of a certain fundamental rawness in American life as Spanish villas on Main Street, and Billy Sunday.

Yet by grudging complete homage to him, Americans have innocently revealed the nature of the genius that has moved them. As one thinks of his career, with its painful preparation for literature and its removal from any literary tradition, it seems remarkable not that he has been recognized slowly and dimly, but that he has been recognized at all. It is because he has spoken for Americans with an emotion equivalent to their own emotion, in a speech as broken and blindly searching as common speech, that we have responded to him with the dawning realization that he is stronger than all the others of his time, and at the same time more poignant; greater than the world he has described, but as significant as the people in it. To have accepted America as he has accepted it, to immerse oneself in something one can neither escape nor relinquish, to yield to what has been true and to yearn over what has seemed inexorable, has been Dreiser's fate and the secret of his victory.

An artist creates form out of what he needs; the function compels the form. Dreiser has been one of the great folk writers, as Homer, the author of *Piers Plowman,* and Whitman were folk writers—the spirits of simplicity who raise local man as they have known him to world citizenship because their love for him is their knowledge of him. "It was wonderful to discover America," Dreiser repeated once after another, "but it would have been more wonderful to lose it." No other writer has shared that bitterness, for no other has affirmed so doggedly that life as America has symbolized it is what life really is. He has had what only Whitman in all the history of the American imagination had before him—the desire to give voice to the Manifest Destiny of the spirit, to preserve and to fulfill the bitter patriotism of loving what one knows. All the rest have been appendages to fate.

Alexander Kern

DREISER'S DIFFICULT BEAUTY

Although from the point of view of the aesthetic critic it seems invalid to judge an author's imaginative work by his ideas, Dreiser is lightly regarded today partly because of his unfashionable philosophical and political position. Faulkner was neglected for years by the liberal critics because of his supposed ideas, and now something of the same disregard of Dreiser is occurring because new ideologies have become dominant.

Certainly the most destructive recent attack, that of Mr. Lionel Trilling (first in *The Nation,* April 20, 1946, and reprinted with some changes in *The Liberal Imagination*) on Dreiser's mind, style, ideas, and late political and religious beliefs, seems to be as much ideological as aesthetic, as the following quotation will make clear:

> *To the extent that Dreiser's style is defensible, his thought is also defensible. That is, when he thinks like a novelist he is worth follow-ing—when by means of his rough and ungainly but effective style he creates rough, ungainly but effective characters and events. But when he thinks like, as we say, a philosopher, he is likely to be not only fool-ish but vulgar. He thinks as a modern crowd thinks when it decides to think: religion is nonsense, "religionists" are fakes, tradition is a fraud, what is man but matter and impulses, mysterious chemisms, and what values has life anyway?*

But as Mr. Trilling recognizes, even the crudeness of Dreiser's thought may have formed the basis for a significant literary achievement which has survived the death of the naturalist movement of which Dreiser was a major part. And, as Eliseo Vivas in his excellent article, "Dreiser, an Inconsistent Mechanist" (*Ethics,* July, 1938) has ably demonstrated, Dreiser's effectiveness as a novelist does not depend upon his naturalistic views.

Though oversimplification does violence to the subtlety of Mr. Trilling's complex analysis, his basic objection seems to be that Dreiser joined the Communist Party and simultaneously adopted an improper religious posi-

From *Western Review,* Winter, 1952.

tion, which permitted him to "accept" the suffering of the universe. This, says Mr. Trilling, is the result of

> . . .*the liberal criticism in the direct line of Parrington, which establishes the social responsibility of the writer and then goes on to say that, apart from his duty of resembling reality as much as possible, he is not really responsible for anything, not even for his ideas. The scope of reality being what it is, ideas are held to be mere "details," and, what is more, to be details which, if attended to, have the effect of diminishing reality. But ideals are different from ideas; in the liberal criticism which descends from Parrington ideals consort happily with reality and they urge us to deal impatiently with ideas—a "cherished goal" forbids that we stop to consider how we reach it, or if we may not destroy it in trying to reach it the wrong way.*

But criticizing Dreiser's muddled political views still does not prove that he is a bad artist. Both Dreiser's Communism and Ezra Pound's Fascism are undesirable, but we should not use politics to prove that either of these men makes no contribution to literature. This, of course, begs the question of the significance of an author's ideas in relation to his literary ability, for most critics seem to be influenced in their evaluations by ideological commitments. Still we should make an effort to achieve the maximum detachment.

A further complication in separating ideological from literary judgments lies in the fact that the author's views may shape his techniques. It seems clear that Dreiser's method of characterization, his characteristic emotional effects, and his elaborate use of detail, even his lack of a sense of humor, are all related to his theories. This is not true of his style; what it most lacks is command of sound, a deficiency which is not the necessary concomitant of any set of philosophical ideas. But in any case the style is the first aesthetic barrier, and the reader for whom style is important is likely to think that Dreiser's verbal crudity alone vitiates his work and that he has no other technical equipment. Neither opinion seems valid. In the first place Dreiser's style often succeeds, and in the second place he has other qualities which make up for the lack of an impressive verbal command.

The mere badness, the awkwardness of Dreiser's prose, is obvious. Mr. Trilling is right, moreover, in emphasizing that it is pretentious, "literary in the bad sense," shining "with paste gems." Like Whitman, Dreiser, in compensating for a lack of education and culture, strove painfully for an elaborate vocabulary, and like Whitman, is at his worst when his style is least natural. (That this unhappy result is not necessarily the consequence of such a background is indicated by Mark Twain's brilliant colloquial style.) Furthermore, Dreiser's prose is sometimes weakest in important places, as at the conclusion of his novels, where it is strained and bald. Yet, as Mr. Trilling also knows, Dreiser's writing is often effective.

But the importance of the question of Dreiser's style can easily be over-estimated. Thus Mr. Ransom in "The Understanding of Fiction" (*Kenyon Review*, Spring, 1950) writes, "we should not approve of any fictionist who does not possess a prose style," and then points out that Dreiser nearly falls into this classification. Yet this type of view can cause trouble. If a fine prose style is made essential to successful fiction, there is the danger of judging all literature as if it were metaphysical poetry, a view which makes T. S. Eliot and Joseph Frank overrate a novel like *Nightwood*. Not all novels are of the same type, and not all types will be characterized by the same excellences. Professors Crane, Keast, and Olson, the Chicago critics, have a point when they argue that criteria are needed to enable the critic to distinguish between the several types of excellence of different artistic media. A novel is not to be preferred automatically on the basis of one criterion alone.

Mr. Ransom, who is much more conscious than most critics of the problems of aesthetic theory, seems to have sensed some of these objections. In "The Understanding of Fiction" he has admitted the limit of stylistic considerations by saying, "The human importance of the art-work is that it 'touches the heart.'" This opens to consideration the various means by which the reader's emotions can be engaged and permits emphasis upon a variety of aspects of the art of fiction.

Though Mr. Ransom characteristically asserts that it is style alone which "can touch the heart," other parts of his argument seem to indicate that this is not the case. He says that an object in fiction, to be embraced, must be a certain sort of "concrete object, a stock object with which we are already familiar in our sentimental experience." And it is his view that style is what makes an object concrete. The difficulty here is his definition of style, a definition which seems to be broader than he really intends.

> *Running over in our minds some memorable fiction, I believe we are likely to identify it with certain instances, or at least certain remembered complexes, or concentrations which consist in linguistic maneuvers in the first place (i.e. on the surface) and of feeling-tones of effects in the second place (when it comes to our responses); and not with gross or over-all effects such as plot or ideologies. We do not make this discovery more truly about a play of Shakespeare. And if we are challenged to defend our judgment of the work we do not take up the book in order to refresh ourselves on the plot or the moral but*

*in order to find specific passages, the right passages, for our peculiar
evidence. Can we not say that fiction, being literature, will have style
for its essential activity?*

Then Mr. Ransom quotes as an instance a passage from the end of
Daisy Miller. But its appreciation depends upon our knowledge of the
entire novel, of the characters of the two speakers, and of Daisy. For anyone who has not read the book, the quotation completely fails to convey
what Mr. Ransom intends. To the degree that interdependence of a particular and its general context is style, Dreiser too has a style.

If, as Mr. Ransom also suggests, more than a "passion for techniques,
for the formal pyrotechnics of language" enters into the reader's reception
of the novel, what are some of the other elements which might be considered and to what degree does Dreiser command them? I suggest the following: skill in characterization, effective presentation of nature and life,
projection of the dramatic-scene, patterns of action, controlled invention,
and multivalence, or appeal on more than one level. Examining him under
these categories may help to explain why Allen Tate in 1944 ranked Dreiser with Faulkner and Hemingway as the only American novelists of
major importance after World War I.

Naturally Dreiser's most effective work will be considered and the number of books reduced to three or four. The ones which retain our interest
are *Sister Carrie, Jennie Gerhardt, An American Tragedy,* and to a lesser
extent *The Financier.* The major works in terms of the criteria listed, will
stand up under close inspection.

Take first characterization. It has been objected that Dreiser's characters
are types, or case histories externally and mechanically treated, and that
they do not engage our interest because they have no dignity. Although it
can be argued that the naturalist all too frequently deals with types, Dreiser, giving more than his theory demands, both individualizes his minor
characters and successfully shapes his major characters in the round. That
this does not seem obvious is due to his habit of constantly generalizing
about how certain types of character react in certain situations. Yet these
generalizations are based upon specific, often brilliant insights which
transcend the technique by which they are conveyed.

It is frequently said that the naturalists cannot treat intellectuals, that
they are limited in depiction of character to externals, and that they cannot handle internal monologue. True, Dreiser's chief figures are not intellectuals (neither are Hemingway's); but not all his characters are handled
externally. The characters of *An American Tragedy* are not developed
solely from an external point of view. Roberta's desperate reflections when

she is waiting for a letter from Clyde and cannot show her feelings to her family; Clyde's conflict when he first thinks of the idea of murder; Sondra's worries about whether she should write to Clyde in prison— surely all these are memorable examples of his presentation of internal experience. But since such thoughts are put into a form of indirect discourse, they seem described rather than reported.

Dreiser's characterization has sometimes seemed mechanical because he depends on chemisms or chemic compulsions to explain the source of motivation. But if Dreiser has the "gift for searching an individual life to its depths" as Alfred Kazin believes, it is not important whether he classifies his discoveries in terms of humors, chemisms, or Freudian complexes. What is important is the clear observation of these motives in action within the perspective of the novel as a whole.

Moreover, Dreiser feels for his characters and makes us feel with them; he is able to develop his wide range of individuals with such sympathy that they engage our emotions. This is true even of Cowperwood when he is caught having taken some six hundred thousand dollars from the city treasury. Jennie is a "bad woman," a type we disapprove of, yet we are deeply moved by her individual plight. In fact we find ourselves so involved in the problem of even so weak a character as Clyde that we try to tell him what he ought to do to help himself. This ability to project characters with sympathy, which Dreiser shares with Tolstoy, is so lacking in Dos Passos and O'Neill that their more coldly presented characters seem, finally, much more case histories than do Dreiser's.

Though it would be absurd to expect from naturalism the Aristotelian ethical concept of character, we do obtain a definite notion of the dignity of human nature from Dreiser, and this in a sense higher than that his figures are fellow sufferers with us in life. Hurstwood retains his dignity by turning on the gas instead of accepting passively his own collapse. And Clyde shows integrity at the end. After he has written a statement saying he has found consolation in religion, he is man enough to recognize his doubts about his own conversion, and we respect him for his honesty.

But character in a novel has meaning only in context, and in supplying this context Dreiser is a master. He is most notable, of course, for his picture of the manifold complexity of institutions. A brilliant documentor of business life, he has, as Philip Rahv says, a "Balzacian grip on the machinery of money and power." Of the effects of poverty he has been unsurpassed by American novelists, and he has the further merit of being a pioneer in this approach. We can understand, after Carrie's bleak experiences in job hunting, in working in the sweat-shop, and in her subsequent illness, why she became Drouet's mistress. And Hurstwood's collapse into beggary, as he loses his social role and his self confidence, is one of the finest and most convincing sequences in American fiction. Thus Dreiser's settings, both material and institutional (he uses nature mainly for figures of speech), are so carefully built that they seem actual. Like Balzac and Tolstoy, he constructs a real world, broad in scope and large in conception, peopled with a wide range of convincing characters.

He is able to engage very powerfully our affections for these characters, to make us feel strongly their emotions and especially his emotion for them. These emotions are romantic but not sentimental, and though Trilling feels that Dreiser's pity is often self-pity, his work is not one long and dreary autobiography filled with cries of pain. Indeed this pity is produced by a tragic view of life which holds that man's best efforts and attempts are often vain. Notable examples are the death of Jennie's mother, her own final isolation and loneliness, and the conclusion of *An American Tragedy*. There is in such places an eliciting of feelings which are elemental, which come from greater depths than the unearned level of stock response. They are universal and are gained by an appeal which comes not from naming an appropriate word but from a carefully built complex of experience which gains a complex response.

On the other hand intensity is a quality which Dreiser does not usually show. He is, for one thing, too steadily expository. Since no motivation has to be pushed quite so hard as the exclusively deterministic, the result is that the form of motivation often obtrudes, as in the closing of the safe door when Hurstwood removed the money. Consequently, though Dreiser is not more didactic than Eliot in his dramas, he fails to achieve the intensity which comes with complete artistic integration.

Obviously also, Dreiser is not a specialist in the use of such technical devices as imagery and symbolism. Though he occasionally uses symbols, they are rarely maintained. The combat of the lobster and the squid in *The Financier* and the song of the weir-weir bird in *An American Tragedy* are typical and obtrusive. The repeated use of Carrie's rocking and musing in her chair until it becomes symbolic of her unsatisfied longing is, on the other hand, a more successful device, but one of the sort that Dreiser rarely employs.

Nor does he specialize in economy. Rather he provides an almost overwhelmingly massive accretion of detail. This is an effect not particularly amenable to textural analysis, but still it is an effect, and valid. When we emphasize the need of economy in writing, it is well to remember that Henry James, despite his early strictures, is said by Edith Wharton to have read Whitman's poetry aloud with satisfaction. Yet Dreiser's detail is more effective than Whitman's, because it is placed in a dramatic framework of narrative forms which dictate the shape and size of the result. So, as Mr. Rahv says, Dreiser achieves a "prosiness so primary in texture that when taken in bulk it affects us as a kind of poetry of the commonplace."

In addition, Dreiser shows a mastery of plot structure, which is with him historical and temporal rather than spatial. His tensions with society were not such as produced a disintegration of his world, and the deeply hidden stratum of his optimism was at last clearly revealed in his posthumous fiction. But still within the old chronological framework, and despite the accretion of detail, there was room for considerable patterning both to increase the reader's anxiety and re-enforce the theme. Complication of action often stretches the reader's tension, as when Carrie quarrels with Drouet before she goes off with Hurstwood, or when Jennie's father is burned and thrown out of work before she accepts money from her lover, or most notably when Clyde and Roberta find no way to terminate her pregnancy. The product of such structural thickening is a Dostoevskyan power which ineluctably seizes our emotions.

Though Dreiser naturally used the Nineteenth Century novel form without technical innovations, his subconscious if not his conscious artistry built up narrative structures of considerable complexity. Thus, Clyde's flight when the automobile runs over the little girl is preparation for his choice of murder as an escape from his later involvement. Or again, though Clyde is shocked by his mother's protection of his sister when she becomes pregnant, we are prepared for the irony that he is willing to accept his mother's aid when she comes to his defense. And Dreiser often succeeds in moulding this material into patterns of action with enough architectonic skill to achieve a cumulative effect of no little significance.

His understanding of poverty and of the consequences of erotic passion without economic security allows him to present a picture of modern life which is as pertinent and meaningful as the painting of the ash-can school of artists, whom he knew and resembled.

Finally, his invention is something very apt. Sondra's typed letter to Clyde in prison is an excellent example, since it concentrates for him and for us the entire futility of his crime and makes clear that to gain her he did the one thing which would effectively cut her off from him forever. Even the phrasing of the note is well conceived. While the girl might not have used the third person form, Dreiser's doing so gives precisely the right tone of her detachment.

> *Clyde—This is so that you will not think that someone once dear to you has forgotten you. She has suffered much too. And though she can never understand how you could have done as you did, still, even now, although she is never to see you again, she is not without sorrow and sympathy and wishes you freedom and happiness.*

While multivalence in the sense of appeal to different future periods can not be demonstrated, there is the related sense of present appeal on several levels to be considered. Though such an appeal is empirical rather than technical, it seems important because works which have survived have always interested different audiences and generally fairly large ones. The critical problem in Dreiser's case is not to ascertain what gradually gained him popularity, for it is obvious that he can tell a story. The problem is rather to recognize what elements he has to offer in addition to the most obvious.

His work shows the ability to convey the meaning of a serious if unsubtle view of life, to create a convincingly real world peopled with human characters, to project their emotions with a power which engages our affections, and to wrest a kind of difficult beauty from unpromising materials despite a technique which only partially served its purpose.

Studies

Malcolm Cowley

SISTER CARRIE: HER FALL AND RISE

When he finished his first novel, *Sister Carrie,* Theodore Dreiser was a big, shambling youngster of twenty-nine with an advancing nose, a retreating chin, and a nature full of discordancies. He was dreamy but practical, rash but timid, persistent in his aims but given to fits of elation or dejection. His manners must have been frightful, in spite of the hours he had spent in boyhood poring over Hill's *Manual of Etiquette.* He was full of understanding and sympathy for the weakness of others, including drunkards, wastrels, and criminals, but sometimes he failed to show generosity toward those he regarded as rivals, with the result that his career was full of sudden friendships and estrangements.

He was an appealing young man in many ways and yet, on the basis of what he afterward wrote about himself, he could hardly be called an admirable character. He was possessed by cheap ambitions: his early picture of the good life was to own what he called "a lovely home," with cast-iron deer on the lawn; to drive behind "a pair of prancing bays," and to spend his evenings in "a truly swell saloon," with actors, song writers, and Tammany politicians, amid "the laughter, the jesting, the expectorating, the back-slapping geniality." His taste was worse than untrained; it was actively bad except in fiction, and when he was offered the choice between two words, two paintings, two songs, or two pieces of furniture, he took the one that looked or sounded more expensive. In his "affectional relations," as he called them, he was a "varietist," to use his expensive word for a woman-chaser; and he makes it clear that he treated some women abominably after he caught them. If the character of Eugene Witla in *The "Genius"* is a self-portrait, as it seems to be, then his neighbors must have said rightly that his first wife was a saint to put up with him.

Yet Dreiser painted the portait knowing that it would be recognized; and in other books he described his transgressions in the first person. Once in his life he stole money; he needed a new overcoat and held out $25

From *New Republic,* May 26 and June 23, 1947. Copyright 1947 by Malcolm Cowley.

from his weekly collections for a Chicago furniture house. That petty crime must have been the hardest to confess to his readers, but he told the story in all its details, including his terror and shame when the theft was discovered. In writing of himself or his background he had a massive honesty that was less a moral than a physiological quality. It was his whole organism, not his conscious mind or his moral code, that made him incapable of any but minor falsehoods. Several times he tried writing false stories for money, but the words wouldn't come; and later in his career he found it physically impossible to finish some of the novels he had started, if their plots took a turn that seemed alien to his experience. He wasn't satisfied with easy answers. "Chronically nebulous, doubting, uncertain," he says of himself, "I stared and stared at everything, only wondering, not solving." It would take him thirty years to find—in his own life—the right ending for his last novel, *The Bulwark*.

There were always persons who believed in him and came to his help at critical points in his career. There was his mother first of all, a woman who could read a little but couldn't sign her name until Dorsch, as she called him, and his youngest sister learned to write in the second grade of a German-language parochial school; they taught her to form the letters. But the mother understood her Dorsch sympathetically; and later when he confided to her that he wanted to be a writer more than anything else in the world, she made her painful little sacrifices so that he could read and study. Then there was the teacher at the Warsaw, Indiana, high school who was so impressed by this earnest and fumbling student that later she rescued him from his underpaid work at the warehouse in Chicago where he was showing symptoms of tuberculosis; she arranged to have him admitted to Indiana University and paid most of the expenses for his one college year out of her savings.

There was a copyreader on the *Chicago Globe,* a quietly raging cynic who took a fancy to Dreiser, insisted that he be hired, and taught him to write signed stories. There were various newspaper editors, including Joseph B. McCullagh of the St. Louis *Globe-Democrat,* who trained him and pushed him ahead. There was Arthur Henry, formerly of the *Toledo Blade,* who encouraged him to write *Sister Carrie;* the writing faltered and stopped for two months when Henry went away, then started again when Henry returned, read the early chapters and said, yes, it was going fine. There was most of all his brother Paul, who helped him in his recurrent fits of depression; he would go searching for Theodore, find him hiding in a cheap lodging house, force money on him and invent a job that he could fill. Then, in later years, there were all the publishers (including Horace Liveright) who offered him large sums in the form of advance royalties on novels that in most cases were never written; who gave him the money as a business venture, partly, but also as a token of respect for the work he had done.

Largely as a result of these interventions that saved him time and again, Dreiser came to have a mystical faith in his star. What he said of Eugene Witla might have been applied to himself: "All his life he had fancied that he was leading a more or less fated life, principally more. He thought that his art was a gift, that he had in a way been sent to revolutionize art in America, or carry it one step forward. . . ." It was, however, only during his periods of elation that Dreiser regarded himself as a favored ambassador of fate. When he became dejected, "he fancied," as Dreiser said of Witla and presumably of himself, that "he might be the sport or toy of untoward and malicious powers, such as those which surrounded and accomplished Macbeth's tragic end, and which might be intending to make an illustration of him." Hurstwood, in *Sister Carrie*, was such an "illustration." Cowperwood, the financier of a later book, was Dreiser riding the storm and battling among the Titans.

The result was a curious self-confidence. James Oppenheim wrote a poem about the time when he and Dreiser watched an amazing sunset over the Hudson. "Could you describe that, Dreiser?" he asked. "Yes, that or anything," was the answer. Dreiser could describe anything, from the stupid to the sublime, because in a sense he could describe nothing; he never learned to look for the exact phrase. One sometimes feels that he would have been a great philosopher if he had acquired the art of thinking systematically, instead of merely brooding over ideas, and a great writer if he had ever learned to write. Or might one call him a great inarticulate writer? There are moments when Dreiser's awkwardness in handling words contributes to the force of his novels, since he seems to be groping in them for something on a deeper level than language; there are crises when he stutters in trite phrases that are like incoherent cries.

His memoirs make it clear that what he respected in himself was the intensity of his emotions and his sense of what he calls, in another trite phrase, "the mystery and terror and wonder of life." He often heard voices. One of them—it was the voice of Chicago—spoke to him in his youth, and later he transcribed its words into a sort of elemental poetry. "I am the pulsing urge of the universe," it said to him. "All that life or hope is or can be or do, this I am, and it is here before you! Take of it! Live, live, satisfy your heart!"

A phrase often applied to Dreiser by others is "standing alone" or "marching alone." "It was always Dreiser standing alone who won the battle against the censors," I heard a publisher say. In his Nobel Prize address, Sinclair Lewis told the Swedish Academy that Dreiser "more than any other man, marching alone, usually unappreciated, often hated, has cleared the trail from Victorian and Howellsian timidity and gentility in American fiction to honesty and boldness and passion of life." Although Dreiser deserved the tribute, its phrasing was inexact. He marched forward and at last won the battle, but he was seldom alone, except in the fits of dejection when he hid away from the world. Even then there was always someone who sought him out, gave him money or encouragement and insisted that he go back to writing. Indeed, these helpers appeared so often at critical moments that one is tempted, like Dreiser himself, to regard them as emissaries of the powers that watched over him.

There were, however, less supernatural reasons for the support he received, and they also help to explain the abuse and hatred that made it necessary. In those days a new social class was appearing in the larger American cities. It consisted of young men, chiefly from the Middle West, who were indifferent to the past and felt that their aspirations had never been portrayed in American literature. They knew that Dreiser was one of them, in his faults as well as his virtues, and they sensed that he would be loyal to his class. It was class loyalty that they expected of him, not personal gratitude. If he wrote great novels, they would not deal with foreigners and aristocrats, or with bygone days, and they would not be written politely for women and preachers. Instead the books would describe persons like those who helped him, like his brothers and sisters, his teachers, his newspaper friends, and his publishers, who would be appearing for the first time in serious fiction. It was the new men who recognized his integrity and chose him—elected him, one might say—to be their literary representative.

The post was dangerous. Later, when he fought their battles, Dreiser would be exposed to attacks from all those who disliked the vulgarity and what seemed to be the dubious moral standards of the new class from which he came. Instead of "marching alone," he would stand in a double relationship to American society: he would be the spokesman for one group and the scapegoat of others.

II

It was in the summer of 1900 that Dreiser joined forces with Frank Norris for a battle against the genteel tradition in American letters. They lost the battle, lost it disastrously, but they touched the imagination of younger writers and a long time afterward their allies won the war.

Norris in 1900 was newly married and working hard to finish his biggest novel, *The Octopus*. Meanwhile he was helping to support himself by reading manuscripts for the new publishing house of Doubleday, Page and Company, which had issued his *McTeague* the year before. One of the manuscripts he carried home was that of a first novel called *Sister Carrie.* "I have found a masterpiece," he said to his first caller in the office one morning. "The man's name is Theodore Dreiser."

"I know him," the caller interrupted.

"Then tell him what I think of it. It's a wonder. I am writing him to call."

A few weeks earlier Dreiser had found a masterpiece, too. He had read *McTeague* and had been excited to learn that another novelist was trying to present an unretouched picture of American life. When he went to see Norris in the Doubleday office, he found that they were of almost the same age—Norris was thirty, Dreiser was twenty-nine—and that they shared the same literary convictions. There was, however, an essential difference between them. Norris had reached his convictions by an intellectual process, largely as a result of reading Zola and deciding that Zola's methods could be applied to American material. Dreiser, on the other hand, insisted that he hadn't read Zola when he wrote his first novel. He had become a Naturalist almost without premeditation, as a result of everything his life had been or had lacked. Unlike Norris he couldn't choose among different theories or move from the drably pitiful to the boisterous to the sentimental. He wrote what he did because he had to write only that or keep silent.

It was his newspaper friend Arthur Henry who first persuaded him to write fiction. They used to work at the same table encouraging each other, and they each finished five or six stories. Dreiser's stories were accepted, not by genteel magazines like the *Century* and *Scribner's,* but by the new ten- and fifteen-cent monthlies that were less concerned with ideality and good manners. Henry then insisted that he write a novel. Dreiser protested that he couldn't afford the time, that he was too busy earning a living, that no novel of his would be published—and besides, he didn't have a plot; but still he kept pleasantly brooding over the notion. One day in October, 1899, he found himself writing two words on a clean sheet of paper: "Sister Carrie."

"My mind was blank except for the name," he told his first biographer, Dorothy Dudley. "I had no idea who or what she was to be. I have often thought there was something mystic about it, as if I were being used like a medium." Then suddenly he pictured Carrie Meeber on the train to Chicago; it was a vision that came to him, he said, "as if out of a dream." But the dream was also a memory, for much of his own life went into the novel. In one sense Carrie was Dreiser himself, just as Flaubert once said that *he* was Mme. Bovary; the little Mid-western girl had Dreiser's mixture of passivity and ambition, as well as his romantic love for cities. More definitely she resembled one of his sisters, the one who ran off to Chicago, met a successful businessman, the father of two or three grown children—like Hurstwood in the novel—and eloped with him to New York.

Hurstwood's degradation after losing Carrie was another memory, connected with Dreiser's misfortunes in 1895, after he lost his job on the New York *World*. Unable to find other work, he had lived in cheap lodging houses and—before he was rescued by his brother Paul—had pictured himself as sinking toward squalor and suicide. But there was more of Dreiser in the book than simply the two chief characters: there was his obsessive fear of poverty, there was his passion for gaslight and glitter, and there was his hatred for the conventional standards by which his big family of brothers and sisters had been judged and condemned. Most of all there was his feeling for life, his wonder at the mysterious fall and rise of human fortunes.

Sister Carrie had the appearance of being a naturalistic novel and would be used as a model for the work of later naturalists. Yet it was, in a sense, naturalistic by default, naturalistic because Dreiser was writing about the life he knew best in the only style he had learned. There is a personal and compulsive quality in the novel that is not at all naturalistic. The book is felt rather than observed from the outside, like *McTeague;* and it is based on dreams rather than documents. Where *McTeague* had been a conducted tour of the depths, *Sister Carrie* was a cry from the depths, as if McTeague had uttered it.

It was a more frightening book to genteel readers than *McTeague* had been. They were repelled not only by the cheapness of the characters but even more by the fact that the author admired them. They read that Hurstwood, for example, was the manager of "A gorgeous saloon . . . with rich screens, fancy wines and a line of bar goods unsurpassed in the country." They found him an unctuous and offensive person, yet they also found that Dreiser described him as "altogether a very acceptable individual of our great American upper class—the first grade below the luxuriously rich." Genteel readers didn't know whether to be more offended by the judgment or by the language in which it was expressed, and they must have felt more than a premonition that Hurstwood and his creator belonged to a new class that threatened the older American culture. Most of all they resented Carrie Meeber. They had been taught that a woman's virtue is her only jewel, that the wages of sin are death; yet Carrie let herself be seduced without a struggle, yielding first to a traveling salesman, then to Hurstwood; and instead of dying in misery she became a famous actress. *McTeague* had offended the proprieties while respecting moral principles; every misdeed it mentioned had been punished in the end. *Sister Carrie,* on the other hand, was a direct affront to the standards by which respectable Americans had always claimed to live.

The battle over Carrie started even before the book was published. Dreiser had first given the manuscript to Henry Mills Alden, the editor of *Harper's Magazine,* who had already bought some of his articles. Alden said he liked the novel, but he doubted that any publisher would take it. He turned it over to the editorial readers for Harper and Brothers, who sent it back to the author without comment. Next the manuscript went to Doubleday, Page and Company, where it had the good fortune to be assigned to the man who could best appreciate what Dreiser was trying to do. "It *must* be published," Norris kept repeating to anyone who would listen. His enthusiasm for *Sister Carrie* won over two of the junior partners, Henry Lanier and Walter Hines Page, and with some misgivings they signed a contract to bring it out that fall. Then Frank Doubleday, the senior partner, came back from Europe and carried the proof sheets home with him to read over the weekend. Mrs. Doubleday read them too, and liked them not at all, but her part in the story is not essential. Her husband could and did form his own opinion of *Sister Carrie.* He detested the book and wanted nothing to do with it as a publisher.

There has been a prolonged argument over what happened afterwards, but chiefly it is an argument over words like "suppression"; most of the facts are on record. Doubleday spoke to his junior partners, who had great respect for his business judgment, and they summoned Dreiser to a conference. Norris managed to see him first. "Whatever happens," he said in effect, "make them publish *Sister Carrie,* it's your right." Dreiser then conferred with the junior partners, who tried to persuade him to surrender his contract. "Crushed and tragically pathetic," as Lanier remembers him, he kept insisting that the contract be observed. It was a binding document and it was observed, to the letter. *Sister Carrie* was printed, if only in an edition of roughly a thousand copies. It was bound, if in cheap red cloth with dull black lettering. It was listed in the Doubleday catalogue. It was even submitted to the press for review, if only, in most cases, through the intervention of Frank Norris. When orders came in for it, they were filled. It wasn't "suppressed" or "buried away in a cellar," as Dreiser's friends afterwards complained, but neither was it displayed or advertised or urged on the booksellers. I think it was in the travels of Ibn Batuta that I once read the account of some Buddhist fishermen whose religion forbade them to deprive any creature of life, even a sardine. Instead of killing fish, they merely caught them in nets and left them to live as best they could out of water. That is about what happened to *Sister Carrie,* which wasn't, incidentally, the first or the last book to receive such treatment from publishing houses that changed their collective minds. One couldn't quite say that it was killed; it was merely deprived of light and air and left to die.

Favorable reviews might have rescued it, but with two or three exceptions the reviews were violently adverse and even insulting. "The story leaves a very unpleasant impression," said the Minneapolis *Journal.* "You would never dream of recommending to another person to read it," said the *Post-Intelligencer* in Seattle. *Life,* the humorous weekly, was serious about Carrie and warned the girls who might think of following in her footsteps that they would "end their days on the Island or in the gutter." *Sister Carrie,* said the Chicago *Tribune,* "transgresses the literary morality of the average American novel to a point that is almost Zolaesque." The *Book Buyer* accused Dreiser of being "the chronicler of materialism in its basest forms. . . . But the leaven of the higher life remains," it added, "nowhere stronger than with us."

The book-buying public, most of which yearned for the leaven of the higher life, had no quarrel with the reviewers. The Doubleday records show that 1,008 copies of the book were bound, that 129 were sent out for review and that only 465 were sold. After five years the other 414 copies, with the plates from which they had been printed, were turned over to a firm that specialized in publishers' remainders. That was the end of the story for Doubleday, but not for Dreiser. As soon as he could scrape together $500, he bought the plates of his own novel. He succeeded in having it reprinted by the B. W. Dodge Company in 1907 and by Grosset and Dunlap in 1908. Later it would be reissued in successively larger editions by three other publishers—in 1911 by Harper and Brothers, the firm that had first rejected it, then in 1917 by Boni and Liveright, and in 1932 by the Modern Library—and it would also be translated into most of the European languages. For Dreiser the battle over *Sister Carrie* lasted for more than a quarter-century and ended with his triumph over the genteel critics.

Yet the first years were full of disasters, in spite of the help that Dreiser and his book received from Frank Norris. One English publisher remembered Norris as a man who was "more eager for Dreiser's *Carrie* to be read than for his own novels." Besides trying to get American reviews for the book, Norris kept writing about it to England. A London edition of *Sister Carrie* appeared in 1901 and was enthusiastically praised. "At last a really strong novel has come from America," exclaimed the *Daily Mail;* and there were echoes of the judgment in other English papers.

There was a different sort of echo in New York, a buzz of angry gossip about English critics and their fantastic notions of American fiction. Without the London edition, *Sister Carrie* might have been forgotten for years, but now it was arousing a quiet wave of condemnation among persons who had never seen a copy of the novel. Dreiser found that magazine editors were suddenly uninterested in his articles and stories, which had once been widely published; the new ones were coming back with rejection slips. One editor said, "You are a disgrace to America." The *Atlantic Monthly* wrote him that he was "morally bankrupt" and could not publish there. At the office of *Harper's Magazine* Dreiser happened to meet William Dean Howells, who had always been friendly since the day when Dreiser had interviewed him for another magazine. This time Howells was cold. "You know, I don't like *Sister Carrie*," he said as he hurried away. It was the first occasion on which he had failed to support a new work of honest American fiction.

In 1900 Howells had surrendered to the trend of the times. The great house of Harper, which had dominated American publishing, went bankrupt in that year, and Howells feared that he had lost his principal source of income. But the firm was soon reorganized, with new capital furnished through the elder J. P. Morgan and with new editors for most of its magazines. Colonel Harvey, the new president, was determined to make the house yield dividends. He had an overnight conference with Howells, asked him to continue writing for *Harper's Magazine* on a yearly salary, and told him, incidentally, that the battle for realism was lost. Howells, who had been battling for realism since 1885, sadly agreed with Colonel Harvey. Whatever fire there had been in his critical writing was also lost after 1900, though perhaps that was merely because he was growing old. He still had his style, which was better than that of any other living American writer except Mark Twain. He had his almost official position as dean of American letters, but he was no longer the friend and patron of young writers in revolt.

The failure of *Sister Carrie* in its first edition was part of a general disaster that involved the whole literary movement of the 1890's. One after another, the leaders of the movement had died young or else had surrendered to genteel conservatism. The first of them to go was the novelist H. H. Boyesen, a pioneer of social realism and once a famous figure, although his name is seldom mentioned today except in literature courses; Boyesen died in 1895. Next to go, in 1898, was Harold Frederic, the peppery rebel from upstate New York who, in *The Damnation of Theron Ware,* had written the first American novel that questioned the virtue of the Protestant clergy. Stephen Crane, the one genius of the group, died in 1900 at the age of 29, the victim of consumption, malaria, hard work, and hard living. The dramatist James A. Herne had tried and failed to be the American Ibsen; but at least he had written the immensely popular *Shore Acres* and other plays that introduced daily American life to the American stage. He died in 1901, worn out and discouraged after the presidential campaign of the preceding year, in which he had fought for Bryan and against the annexation of the Philippines. Then Norris died in the autumn of 1902, at the beginning, so it seemed, of a grandly successful career; but he had already given signs, in *The Pit,* of abandoning his naturalistic doctrines.

All these, except Herne, were comparatively young men and there were very few left to carry on the literary movement they had started. Hamlin Garland, after fulminating against the conservatives in art and politics, had gone over to the enemy by easy stages. Editors had taken him out to dinner and convinced him that his passion for reform was weakening his novels as works of art. Unfortunately Garland was no artist; when he lost his crusading passion he lost everything. Henry B. Fuller, the Chicago realist, remained faithful to his own standards; but his novels hadn't sold and he wrote very little for a dozen years after 1900. And it was not only the rebel authors, almost all of them, who had died or fallen silent or surrendered. The little magazines that flourished in New York, Chicago, and San Francisco during the 1890's had also disappeared, and the new publishing houses had become conventional or had gone out of business. Serious writing on American themes declined into a sort of subterranean existence. Speaking generally, the best American books of the following decade would either be privately printed—like *The Education of Henry Adams*—or else they would be written in Europe.

Meanwhile Dreiser had narrowly escaped the fate of his brothers in arms. After *Sister Carrie* was accepted, he had begun working simultaneously on two other novels, in a frenzy of production; but slowly he had been overcome by the feeling that he was unwanted and a failure. He had destroyed one of his two manuscripts, put the other aside, sent his wife to her family in Missouri, and retired to a furnished room in Brooklyn, where he sat day after day brooding over the aimlessness of life and trying to gather enough courage to commit suicide. This time again he was rescued by his brother Paul, who gave him new clothes and sent him to a sanitarium. After his recovery he became a magazine editor and climbed rapidly in his profession, until, as head of the Butterick publications, he was earning $25,000 a year. It was a long time, however, before he felt strength enough in himself to write another novel.

The story of *Sister Carrie* had a curious sequel. Imperceptibly the standards of the American public had been changing in the years after 1900, and Dreiser himself had been gaining an underground reputation based on his one book. When his second novel, *Jennie Gerhardt,* appeared in 1911 it was a critical and even to some extent a popular success. The struggle for naturalism came into the open again. Dreiser had new allies in the younger writers, and by 1920 they had ceased to be rebels; instead they were the dominant faction. It was a long and—at least until the late 1930's —a rather triumphant chapter in the history of American letters that began with the lost battle over *Sister Carrie*.

James T. Farrell

DREISER'S *Sister Carrie*

Sister Carrie was finished in May, 1900. It has become one of the most historic books in modern American literature, and its widespread acceptance as an American classic marks a major victory that has been won for American letters against the Philistines. With his first novel, Theodore Dreiser demonstrated that he was head and shoulders above the contemporaries of his own generation. No other writer in America during the present century has exerted so great a moral force on his successors. No other novelist has done more than Dreiser to free American letters.

His most serious and bitter struggle came with *Sister Carrie*. Thanks to the enthusiasm of Frank Norris, it was accepted by a major New York publishing house. According to the story of this event related now, however, the manuscript was read by the wife of one of the partners of that firm—a social worker interested in moral uplift. To her, the novel was immoral because the heroine did not suffer "the wages of sin." She insisted that it be withheld from publication. Dreiser, urged on by Frank Norris, demanded that the publishers fulfill the contract they had signed with him. A lawyer advised the firm that, while they had legally committed themselves to printing the book, they were under no obligation to *sell* it. They printed *Sister Carrie* with the intention of storing it away in a cellar, but Norris did send about a hundred copies to reviewers. Some years later *Sister Carrie* was republished and placed on sale and Dreiser once more was denounced as immoral. Concerning the position of the American novelist in that period, Dreiser himself has written:

"I think it nothing less than tragic that these men, or boys, fresh, forceful, imbued with a burning desire to present life as they saw it, were thus completely overawed by the moral hypocrisy of the American mind and did not even dare to think of sending their novels to an American publisher. . . . You couldn't write about life as it was; you had to write about it as somebody else thought it was—the ministers and farmers and dullards of the home."

From *The League of Frightened Philistines*, Vanguard Press, 1945.

But Dreiser won his battle, and today he is a living American literary tradition. He helped to raise American life, its contrasts of grandeur and misery, its streets and cities, its tragedies and its vulgarities, to the level of world literature. Such, briefly, is the general significance of Theodore Dreiser in twentieth-century American writing.[1]

But how does his first novel read today? Is it merely a novel of historic significance, or does it retain its value now, so many years after it was written?

Sister Carrie is saturated with the life of America during the eighteen-eighties and the eighteen-nineties. It truly re-creates a sense of an epoch: it

---

[1] At the present time circumstances prevent me from attempting any expanded analysis of Dreiser's work in relation to the writing that immediately precedes him. This is a task I hope to fulfill in the future. Then I hope to discuss his work in relation to that of his important contemporaries and immediate predecessors. Here I wish mainly to make one remark. Dreiser's writing, as a whole, reveals a probing effort to identify social forces, to grasp them, and then to correlate them with human destiny. This is one of the aspects of his work that somewhat differentiates him from such of his predecessors as Henry James, Stephen Crane, and Harold Frederic. In Henry James, a major motif is awareness. Awareness, self-discovery, is also central in Stephen Crane's *The Red Badge of Courage*. Harold Frederic's *The Damnation of Theron Ware* likewise deals, in terms of tragedy, with the theme of awareness. His minister, Theron Ware, gains a sense of values superior to those of a rural, Protestant New York community. These superior values are represented in a doctor who embodies an attitude of science, in a girl whose views are those of the *fin de siècle* esthetics of Europe, and in a priest who represents a sophisticated and liberalized interpretation of Roman Catholicism as a civilizing traditional stream of attitudes and ideas. But the Damnation of Theron Ware results from the fact that he is incapable of assimilating and developing in accordance with the values and attitudes he senses in these three figures. A European and a decayed, rural American pattern of life are juxtaposed in terms of characterizations. Dreiser, as contrasted with these three writers, is most clearly seen as a point of departure. His determinism, more emphasized in *The Financier* and *The Titan* can be analyzed as embodying two important elements: (1) He accepted as science generalizations based on the ideas of nineteenth-century materialism. From these he adduced a deterministic idea, and this, in turn, was represented as biologic determinism. In *The Financier* and *The Titan* this biologic determinism is usually explained by the word "chemisms." Paradoxically enough, Dreiser's appeal to "chemisms" is made quite frequently in specific contexts concerning motivations of characters, where we can now see that the real rationale of these motivations can be most satisfactorily explained by Freudianism. Often his "chemisms" are overall generalizations of impulses of which the character is not aware. In this respect Dreiser asserted a biologic determinism, which, in terms of our present state of knowledge about man, is crude. (2) The other and decidedly more important element in Dreiser's determinism is social. He sought to grasp the working and operation of social laws as they affect human fates. His critics often fail to analyze his determinism; they fasten on his generalizations and interpret his work on the basis of these generalizations. And they oppose to such deterministic generalizations moral and philosophical banalities about free will that are mere commonplaces, commonplaces that are usually derived from a false posing of the problem of free will and determinism—as if this were really an either-or proposition. Dreiser can be described as the American novelist who reflected *social-Darwinism* in his work.

is like a door which permits us entry into the consciousness of an America that is no more. But it is no mere document. It is a powerful and tragic story, created with an unrelenting logic. Dreiser was so far ahead of his time that his first novel is just as fresh and alive today as when it was writ-ten. Many will disagree with me here. Dreiser's style has often been con-demned. I myself do not find it so disturbing as do many of his critics. That his writing is uneven, is marred by clumsy passages, is verbose, and is careless and sentimental, I grant. Dreiser obviously concentrates on details rather than on style. He is one of those writers who is more impor-tant for what he says than for how he says it. In *Sister Carrie* he often relies on the clichés of the time; this is noticeable in the chapter headings. At the same time, he has moments—passages in which there is eloquence and beauty. Mr. Dreiser's style clearly suggests that he is a self-made writer. A man with little formal education, he had to discover things for himself. He sought to grasp and to represent what to him was an Amer-ican chaos, and he reflects this in his style as well as his content. Beauty, tragedy, pathos, rawness, sentimentality, clichés—all are smelted together. In connection with his work, one can use the word "forged"; he wrote his novels as if he were "forging" images of American life. He took the chaos he saw and out of it tried to build an image of life. To me, there is a raw beauty in his very effort.

Furthermore, though the fact has often been overlooked, there is even a logic and a point for his reiterated moralizations that are included in the narrative; they are not always irrelevant, as many critics have maintained. In order to appreciate *Sister Carrie* in our time it is necessary to appreciate it against the background of its own time.

Dreiser has told the story of his life in other books, and we know how he came to Chicago—callow, eager, hopeful, brooding, with little educa-tion, anxious to get ahead in life. He saw the spectacle of luxury in Amer-ican life sharply contrasted with that of dire poverty; he perceived how eyes blinked at misery and how moral hypocrisy was rife. It was not merely natural for Dreiser to moralize about the panorama he saw: it was practically a subjective necessity. Dreiser's moralizations, on the subjective side were the beginnings of thought, feelings, perceptions, which led him to write the novels that have now become part of a literary tradition.

Objectively, when he wrote *Sister Carrie* it was not sufficient for him merely to have told her story as it might be told now, in 1943. In 1900 it was necessary for him to argue Carrie's case, to defend her, to defend his very right to present such material in a novel. It was essential that he break down the reader's resistance to a realistic and tragic story, in order that it might be received on its own merits. There is a logic and a place for his comments, his moralizations, his asides. They belong to the warp and woof of the period he described and in which he wrote.[2]

In *Sister Carrie* money plays a central role. Without money—money as we know it in our society—the story is meaningless and the tragedy is forced. In order to understand the book clearly it is essential that we understand the all-important role that money plays in it.

To the characters, money is a mystery, as it remains to many up to the present. The good-natured salesman, Drouet, discovers that money comes easily. He sells goods. An order is signed. In time, he is paid a commission. It comes almost effortlessly—and is spent accordingly. To Carrie, a poor and yearning country girl going to Chicago, money is the means for getting everything in life for which she aspires. To Hurstwood, in his pleasant and established life, money at first is not even a problem; later it is the instrument that will permit him to satisfy his passion for Carrie; in the end, it is the means to keep his body and soul together—and he must beg for it on the street.

Dreiser's general comments have often been criticized, sometimes justly, because of their lack of validity. But Dreiser was so much clearer about money than most of his contemporaries that one should remark on this. In *Sister Carrie* he writes: "The true meaning of money yet remains to be popularly explained and comprehended. When each individual realizes for himself that this thing primarily stands for, and should be accepted as, a moral due—that it should be paid out as honestly stored energy and not as usurped privilege—many of our social, religious, and political troubles will have permanently passed." Dreiser came very close to a true and clear definition of money when it is to be considered as other than a medium of exchange—that it is congealed labor power. His clarity, his consciousness of the role of money, his refusal to be deceived by the mysteriousness that shrouds the definition of money in the popular consciousness of his time,

[2] The naturalism of Flaubert can be juxtaposed to that of Dreiser, not merely in terms of a narrow notion of style and method but, more importantly, in terms of broad treatment. Flaubert is intensive; Dreiser is extensive. Flaubert writes with concentration, with a sharp eye for detail, and with an extraordinary power of suggestiveness. Dreiser generalizes, explains, argues, points out; he lacks Flaubert's power of concentration. This difference is not merely one of art, or of artistic skill. It is social and cultural. Flaubert could be intensive and could concentrate—thanks to the high level of French culture that was his inheritance. Dreiser's cultural inheritance was relatively negligible. Just as he had to discover for himself, so his sympathetic readers similarly had to discover. This extensiveness of Dreiser's method was not preconditioned solely by the hypocrisy of the Philistines; it was further preconditioned by the fact that more sympathetic, more alert persons, also had to discover the meanings of American life. The consequences of important economic and social developments are not felt and clarified fully and immediately. They must be discovered temporally. In this sense, the extensiveness of Dreiser's method has a social rationale behind it. It reveals a process of self-discovery in American life.

must be grasped if we would understand his work. For no modern American writer has so well dramatized the meaning of money in individual lives.

Above all else, the reason why *Sister Carrie,* to this day, remains so meaningful, so moving and so compelling a novel is Dreiser's portrait of Hurstwood. In Hurstwood, type and individuality merge so well that they are practically indistinguishable. Hurstwood is actually a social function, a kind of glorified major-domo. His entire life flows out of and around his position as the manager of an elegant saloon in the Chicago of the Eighties. What seems to be natural sophistication, manners, *savoir-faire,* is clearly related to his character; Hurstwood's occupation has so firmly molded his character that in his slow, painful, tragic degeneration, the effects remain. From beginning to end, we see in Hurstwood an unfaltering logic.

Here is a character who is all of a piece with himself, with his work, with his station in life. Dreiser understood this man, spiritually and socially; in his creation of him there is perceivable a remarkable unity between the individual and the effect of his position on his character. Chicago was a rising and raw provincial metropolis. Hurstwood belonged in such a place. Such a man going to New York, where celebrities and rich *bons vivants* were so common, was practically doomed to failure. Consequently his passion for Carrie is not the sole reason for Hurstwood's undoing, for his tragic degradation. A man cannot escape from himself, from his own character. Hurstwood's tragedy begins when he abandons his social role in Chicago.

In general, the novel is based on a contrast between grandeur and misery. It also revolves around a further contrast: that of the rise of Carrie and the decline of Hurstwood. Unlike Hurstwood, Carrie is much less an individualized portrait. She is a social type, the "poor working girl" of the banal songs of the period, described realistically rather than sentimentally. What we see in Carrie is a pattern of American destiny. An aspiring girl with little intellect, who is all feeling and aspiration, she follows a typical course. Leaving the country—this was the period when the city was beginning to triumph decisively over the country—she is thrown helplessly into the turmoil of Chicago. She can advance, gain finery and luxury, do what she wants to do, give expression to her feelings only through a path of sin.

When the book was read by the publisher's wife, this pattern of destiny was shocking: it was revolting to the moral concepts of the era. And withal, it was a social prediction. Today New York and Hollywood are full of Sister Carries: in fact, Sister Carrie is, in literature, a forecast of the type that has become the heroine of present-day gossip columns. She has become so familiar that one rarely even pauses to realize that Dreiser, more than forty years ago, revealed the genesis of this type, the motivations and the social factors that have perfected it.[3]

What is at the core in all of Dreiser's major works, including *Sister Carrie,* is the moral depth of the man's writings. Dreiser has always been concerned with the moral consequences implicit in the spectacle of wealth and poverty so apparent in our society. Evil is a problem to him, but he does not treat it in theological terms. To him, evil is social: all his novels are concerned with social history, the social processes of evil. Ambition, yearning, aspiration—these all revolve around this problem, and it in turn revolves around the role of money. He has related social causation—the basic social and economic factors that play a causal role in society—to individual patterns of destiny. His realism is a realism of social structures, and it was in *Sister Carrie* that he gave to American literature the first of his works of this character.

In essence, a book stands the test of time when we can translate its meaning into the experiences of our own time and see that it remains significant and alive. And that, I insist, can be done with *Sister Carrie.* It is one of the major novels in twentieth-century American literature.

[3] Carrie Meeber, Eugene Witla, Frank Cowperwood, and Clyde Griffiths are all young. In the case of Cowperwood, the man's career is described as being past youth, but it is to be observed that he becomes a great financial success while still young. It is interesting to note, in passing, the contrasts between these three characters. Carrie and Clyde both seek the same kind of end —success, advancement. It is suggestive that Carrie, a girl, succeeds, and that Clyde, in a later period, fails and is executed. This contrast in itself suggests the closing in of the chances of success, the increasing stratification of American life. Cowperwood is of an earlier period than Carrie. He violates the social codes, but succeeds—succeeds despite the fact that he is jailed. He is a realistically drawn young man of the period when opportunity was greatest in America. Further, the following contrast is interesting. The road to success for Cowperwood is business and finance, particularly the realm of finance which relates to speculation and manipulation. Carrie's avenue of success, like that of Eugene Witla, is art. For Clyde, the possibility of success is through family connections—rich relatives—and the opportunities they afford him of meeting rich people. Here is an illuminating contrast. It should suggest an additional reason as to why Mr. Dreiser's work is so important in American literature. In his probing effort to grasp forces socially operative in American society, he grasped the patterns of success, the patterns of social change, the way in which American patterns of destiny unfold in consonance with the operation of social forces and social laws.

Robert H. Elias

THE SURVIVAL OF THE FITTEST

Jennie Gerhardt proved to be the first of four new novels completed within five years of Dreiser's leaving Butterick's, but based as it was on material and plans developed some ten years before, it recalled the past more than it reflected the present and disclosed a Dreiser who was troubled by poverty and disaster rather than a Dreiser who had lately relinquished a salary amounting to ten thousand dollars a year.

In his second novel as in his first, Dreiser exhibited characters who were the victims of circumstances or forces beyond their control. Jennie, a member of a poverty-driven family such as was Dreiser's own, is deprived of social distinction and financial security when a United States Senator who wants to marry her and has seduced her dies suddenly and leaves her an unwed mother. Then, supporting herself and her daughter by working as a maid, she attracts one of her employer's house guests, Lester Kane, becomes his mistress, bears his name, and has almost re-established herself when the Kane family, threatening Lester with the loss of his inheritance if he does not give up Jennie, brings an end to the liaison and leaves Jennie with only her daughter to remind her of any love she has ever known. Finally, while Lester, eager for social position, marries an alluring sophisticate, Jennie helplessly endures further misfortune as typhoid claims her child. In the end she has the satisfaction of hearing Lester tell her that his married life has not been happy and that she is the only one he has ever loved, but his realization comes too late to matter, for he is on his deathbed and she can look forward only to "Days and days in endless reiteration."

Although Dreiser implied by this story that individuals as mere human beings were uncertain of fulfilling their purposes, he also implied even more clearly that individuals like Jennie and Lester were the ones most likely to fail. For Jennie is "the idealist, the dreamer," and Lester is good-natured, with "a larger vision of the subtleties that underlie life." And where Jennie lacks "power to strike and destroy . . . to be able to fall upon a fellow-being, tearing that which is momentarily desirable from his

From *Theodore Dreiser: Apostle of Nature*, Alfred A. Knopf, Inc., 1949.

grasp," Lester lacks "the ruthless, narrow-minded insistence on his individual superiority which is a necessary element in almost every great business success." On the other hand, Lester's brother Robert, less imaginative, sensitive, or scrupulous, is an individual who succeeds in his undertakings, and an impression remains that it is primarily persons of feeling and insight who are incapable of successful struggle in the realm of the material.

Yet for one who had achieved what Dreiser had, the idea that success must be completely alien to the artistic temperament was no longer compellingly axiomatic. He had risen too far since *Sister Carrie* to suppose he was destined for failure, and if he had recently been forced to resign his position, he was for that reason only the more concerned with the anatomy of achievement and somewhat more disinterested in his reactions to other strugglers. Life was still something he could call "dramatic" and "more thrilling than the most gorgeous spectacle that man ever planned," but the drama had a different effect from what it had had. Although *Jennie Gerhardt* had been constructed to exhibit the pathetic consequences of accidents, Dreiser could now tell an interviewer that "these accidents merely serve to make . . . (life) more entrancing." And although he had sympathetically portrayed the jobless in *Sister Carrie* and had energetically sought homes for homeless children during his editorship of the *Delineator,* he now viewed misfortune as merely an exciting part of the great play and stated: "I consider the beggar sitting by the roadside one of the most dramatic things that could be imagined. He has a precarious existence and it depends entirely on chance. It is really thrilling to see the way in which he ekes out a living." The temperament of persons like Jennie no longer interested him. In fact, Lester's not marrying Jennie and the death of Jennie's child were incidents Dreiser had to contrive in revising his novel to give the story a "poignancy" which the original tone demanded but which he had not been able to maintain. The process of struggle had become more interesting than struggle's ultimate futility, and those individuals capable of the greatest efforts were necessarily more significant than the passive and neglected failures. It was scarcely surprising, therefore, that even before *Jennie Gerhardt* was completed Dreiser had begun other novels and had chosen to explore the careers, not of helpless women, but of forceful men who possessed both artistic propensities and the characteristics required for material success. And it was simply a measure of his new concerns that when *Jennie* was accepted by Harper & Brothers at the end of April 1911, his next novel, *The "Genius",* was so far advanced that he was able to conclude it only a few months later.

The story of *The "Genius"* was the story of how a sensitive dreamer and artist who disregarded social conventions could fare in a fierce society from which he hoped to remain detached. Originally drafted to concern a St. Louis newspaperman, then changed to concern a painter whose work Dreiser modeled on that of a friend, Everett Shinn, it was in all essential respects an account of Dreiser's own career. Eugene Witla, after a boyhood of romantic daydreaming in the Midwest and yearning for girls he idealizes, lives through a period of disillusionment, reads Spencer, Tyndall, and Huxley, and goes to New York to enjoy the attractions of the city and the blandishments of women. Excited by the insoluble drama about him, he gives his paintings of the spectacle a theatrical appeal and becomes successful enough to marry a Midwestern girl, Angela Blue. There then follow misunderstandings between Eugene and Angela, rebellion by Eugene against Angela's possessiveness, a nervous breakdown, work on a railroad, recovery, and positions first with an advertising company analogous to Street & Smith and second with a publisher of magazines reminiscent of Butterick's. Throughout these events Eugene is the victim of the elements in his character that enable him to succeed. His success as an artist depends on his ability to view the forces of life without being subject to them. But his response to the forces he views is the response of a man moved primarily by the sensuous, and hence of a man repeatedly affected by the sight of lovely eighteen-year-old girls. Continually trying to know the beauty of youth intimately, he is continually disillusioned by its disappointing reality. So long as he can escape disillusionment by new conquests, he can escape melancholy, but so long as he is bound to his wife, who is no longer a mere dream, he cannot escape completely. When finally he encounters a girl, Suzanne Dale, who represents what he believes to be the realization of all dreams, her mother creates trouble that forces him from his position and temporarily separates him from Suzanne; and Angela conceives a baby to compel him to reinterpret his responsibilities, and dies in giving birth. Shocked, bewildered, driven to reflect on his own role in the catastrophe, Eugene seeks salvation in Christian Science and the thought that everything may be regarded as infinite mind, with spirit representing immortal truth and only matter representing mortal error. Subsequently he feels Francis Thompson's "The Hound of Heaven" applies to him, and meditates on the validity of Alfred Russel Wallace's theory of the universe. At the end, while still puzzled by the mystery of life, he is strengthened in his metaphysical tendencies by reading and is "changed notably": now he is "stronger and broader for what he . . . (has) suffered, seen and endured." Writing Suzanne that he is no longer selfish, that love is not all desire, he brings her to him; they marry; and "brooding over the mutation of time and force," he discovers metaphysics beautiful, life calmer and sweeter than he had ever thought it, and a ruling power immanent and "not malicious."

The question dominating the story was a cogent one for Dreiser. Although he himself had not found ultimate salvation in Christian Science and Jug had not died, and his Suzanne Dale had not returned to him, he had suffered a defeat because of his response to sensuous attractions and needed to find a place for himself in which he could see himself as the stronger for what had happened. Hence when he was writing the final chapters of *The "Genius"* he was writing of life as it might be—as, indeed, it ought to be. At the same time, however, the existence of Jug, who had gone away only to regain her health and whom he was not prepared to desert, and the beginning of a new series of amours, which oppressed him with new claims even while they helped him forget old ones, both argued against his soon enjoying Eugene's solution. The answer for Eugene was certainly, in existing circumstances, no answer for Dreiser, and while Dreiser completed the novel and struggled to find himself again, he began to gather material about a man who apparently had encountered few significant limits in his lifetime, a man who had made a fortune in Philadelphia, been imprisoned for embezzling the city's funds, left prison to make a second fortune, gained control of Chicago's street railways, and having lost a fight for long-term franchises, gone to London to fight J. P. Morgan for control of the London subway system, all the while engaging in affairs with a series of mistresses whom he discarded as whim dictated, until at the moment of triumph he fell ill and died, his fortune to be dissipated in law-suits and his art gallery and business enterprises to pass into the hands of others. In this man, Charles Tyson Yerkes, Dreiser had a character who could provide another answer to his question, by demonstrating on the one hand how to succeed and on the other hand what success finally meant; and in Yerkes' career he had material for a trilogy of novels he planned to call *The Financier*.

Dreiser's readiness to plunge into this new project so quickly was of course not entirely the consequence of theoretical implications or marital difficulties. He had considered the idea while completing *Jennie Gerhardt* and had written *The "Genius"* because he could not longer contain within himself the troubles that remained so immediate. But once *Jennie* was accepted for publication, Harper's preferences affected his decisions. While friends to whom he showed the manuscript of *Jennie,* among them James Huneker and Mencken, encouraged him with their praises of the novel to continue writing, Harper's, by displaying interest in *The Financier* rather than in *The "Genius"* as a sequel to *Jennie,* impelled him to proceed at once with the story of Yerkes, for Dreiser was, after all, concerned with making a living; ". . . if there is no money in the game," he wrote to Mencken, "I [am] going to run a weekly."

It was, in fact, on royalties rather than on praise and publishers' preferences that Dreiser, never able to forget Doubleday's actions, depended for convincing encouragement. British writers like Frank Harris, W. J. Locke, and Arnold Bennett reminded the public of *Sister Carrie* by calling it a great book. Mencken, reading the proofs of *Jennie Gerhardt* in order to review it for *Smart Set,* wrote to Dreiser: "Let no one convince you to the contrary: you have written the best American novel ever done, with the one exception of *Huckleberry Finn.*" Most reviewers, once the book was published in October, echoed Mencken's opinions. And Henry Blake Fuller, to whom Dreiser had sent a copy of *Jennie,* welcomed Dreiser into the school of twentieth-century realists, saying: "By the consistent and persistent employment of the approved latter-day method you have reached, cumulatively, results that are remarkable." Yet Dreiser remained uneasy and skeptical about his career. Although *Jennie's* sales surpassed *Carrie's* by totaling almost five thousand during the first month, Dreiser was disappointed and the men at Harper's gave him no reason not to be. The experience of *Sister Carrie* had not been helpful in selling *Jennie Gerhardt,* one of them explained. When Grant Richards, the English publisher, arrived in New York early in November, Dreiser delivered to Richards's hotel an inscribed copy of *Jennie* with a note saying in part: "I hope if you are interviewed you will say something definite about me & Jennie. It seems almost impossible to make my fellow Americans understand that I am alive. I am thinking of moving to London. Once there I will get at least an equal run with Robert Hichens & Arnold Bennet over here." But actually Dreiser was too dispirited to contemplate any kind of trip. He had written thirty-nine chapters of *The Financier*—more than half the first volume—but now was ready to give up the whole trilogy. To go abroad, to travel, to see what Yerkes had seen, he needed money, and *Jennie's* sales were bringing him too little.

Since Dreiser's problem was solely a financial one this time, however, it was far more easily solved than his former psychological ones, and when Dreiser called on Richards the following day, Richards, finding that Dreiser had overestimated the cost of a European tour, evolved a solution agreeable to Dreiser. He went to friends of his at the Century Company and proposed they commission Dreiser to write for the *Century Magazine* three articles on Europe which might eventually be expanded into book length, and at the same time he directed Dreiser to ask Harper's for an advance on *The Financier.* The result was that on November 18 *Century* sent Dreiser a check for a thousand dollars for three articles and the option on any book he might write about the trip, and Harper's, upon his depositing with them the first part of his manuscript, agreed to advance him two thousand dollars on *The Financier* and five hundred dollars against the earnings of *Jennie Gerhardt*. In addition, Harper's prepared to reissue *Sister Carrie*. When Richards suggested to Dreiser that even the Nobel Prize was now within his grasp, Dreiser regained his confidence and on November 22 sailed with Richards on the *Mauretania,* explaining to an interviewer before embarking that in his new novel "I'm doing the man as I see him. . . . And when I get through with him he'll stand there, unidealized and uncursed, for you . . . to take and judge according to your own lights and blindnesses and attitudes toward life." In this spirit he was seeking to observe the "color of life."

From the very beginning of the journey he was presented with a series of tableaux. The restless throng milling about the decks of the ship before the gangways were hoisted reminded him of a great New York hotel lobby at dinner time. A Miss X during the voyage suggested to him "our raw American force." The engine room provided a glimpse of a new, fascinating, and baffling world. When he reached England, appearances continued to dominate his impressions, as he persistently sought to externalize them. He picked up a girl of the streets and proceeded to cross-examine her while he attempted to contemplate the very scene of which he was a part, imagining as he spoke to her how he must seem to her speaking in this fashion. He beheld buildings black with soot, their original white showing only where wind and rain had whipped the spots bare, and thought at first: "How wretched," then afterward: "This effect is charming." He visited London's East End, St. Michael's Church in St. Albans, Canterbury, the House of Commons, Manchester, and after observing an English Christmas crossed the Channel to be excited by the Continent in the same way. It was a place of looks, words, gestures, and buildings. Whether it was the age of Rome, the width of Perugia's streets, the Grand Canal of Venice under a glittering moon, or the vain-glorious German officers at Potsdam, Europe had mainly the effect of a picture postcard.

But the more Dreiser saw, the more restless he became to return home. He worried about his writing, about his expenses, about himself. When he first arrived in England, he began to think he would be uncomfortable in the cold, raw weather and would not be able to write anything. Two days before Christmas he needed medicines for intestinal difficulties. Shortly after that, as he hastened to Paris, he estimated how much he was spending and began to feel insecure. Richards had written him a letter explaining in detail what to tip everyone at the hotels in London; had sent him tickets for Paris and directed his attention to a certain restaurant whose headwaiter was a character; had sent letters to friends in Paris on Dreiser's behalf; had begun negotiating for various dramatic and publication rights for Dreiser's novels—and then Dreiser had taken stock of his situation. The women were expensive. The places he stopped at seemed dear, and he even considered joining a Cook's tour. Moreover, word reached him from the United States that Ridgway had left Butterick, and he now entertained the notion of returning to the *Delineator,* a notion for which Richards took him severely to task. Finally in March he goaded Richards into writing him resentfully:

> *"Handicapped financially" indeed! I wish I had half your complaint. That is where you depress me. "I shall cut Paris after Berlin and sail from some port in England." My God! And then: "No more Europe on the worry basis for me." Heavens, what are you talking about? A nice character, but too temperamental. You ought to travel with a doctor and a hypodermic syringe. You really ought. However . . . My dear friend, you have, in the vernacular of your country, put it across; and now, having put it across, you are worrying about the exact degree which you have achieved. Such things not having been done before from your country you have nothing to compare yourself with, but I at least cannot see what you have to complain of.* As long as you are in the meantime doing stuff, or preparing to do stuff that you feel will satisfy your own conscience, *about which I am not, naturally, in a position to dogmatise.*

Yet, baseless as Dreiser's worries might be, he could not find convincing the assurance of those who had known only comfort and security throughout their lives, and instead of seeing the benefits to him and to his work of what he had been doing, he saw the dangers in the price he was paying for these benefits. He remembered all the writing he wished to do, wrote Mencken asking whether he would read the manuscript of *The Financier,* and although Richards tried to persuade him to visit the Hardy country, decided early in April that he must take the first available ship back to America. This ship happened to be the *Titanic,* but since it was on its maiden voyage, Richards thought it might be uncomfortable and preferred to secure Dreiser passage on the *Kroonland,* which arrived in New York at the end of the month, when Dreiser began at once completing *The Financier.*

During his absence Harper's had had a typescript made of his first thirty-nine chapters and now clamored for the rest. But there was further research to do, and Dreiser hunted through the files of the Philadelphia *Public Ledger* for 1870 and 1871 and drew upon the knowledge of his friend Joseph Hornor Coates in Philadelphia to secure full details of Yerkes's first debacle. He had earlier learned from Coates what clubs his character Frank Algernon Cowperwood should belong to, what parties Cowperwood should give, and where he should give them; now he found out about the layout of the stock exchange, the location of Yerkes's office, the history of Drexel's firm, and facts about 1871 court procedure. In addition Coates referred him to Oberholtzer's biography of Jay Cooke and other standard sources. As the first 350 pages were prepared for the printer by July 2, work on the rest of the book went on into August.

Meanwhile problems had arisen concerning which Dreiser needed Mencken's advice. Dreiser wanted to call his whole trilogy *The Financier*, and the first volume simply "Volume One," but Harper's insisted that was commercially inadvisable. Dreiser wanted to shorten his novel so that it would not run to 800 pages, but Harper's was giving him no time to make adequate cuts. Mencken, however, was abroad when Dreiser returned from Europe, and it was not until May 7 that Dreiser could write to him from New York: "Lord[,] I'm glad to know you[']r[e] back. . . . I wish I could talk to you. I have a whole raft of things to discuss not the least of which is the present plan of publishing this book in 3 volumes—1 volume every 6 months. . . . For heaven sake keep in touch with me by mail for I'm rather lonely & I have to work like the devil." Mencken did keep in touch, and while during the summer Jug returned in what was the final attempt to solve the problem of loneliness, Mencken encouraged him in his work, read galleys, suggested the excision of irrelevant details and the expansion of certain incidents, and assured him: "You have described and accounted for and interpreted Cowperwood almost perfectly. You have made him as real as any man could be. And you have given utter reality to his environment, human and otherwise. No better picture of a political-financial camorra has ever been done. It is wholly accurate and wholly American."

Frank Cowperwood's career is both that of a man who recognizes no restraints or limits and that of a man who illustrates the limitations of all men. In the first volume of the trilogy—finally called simply *The Financier* without reference to other volumes—he is shown up to the time when he leaves Philadelphia for Chicago. Born of a family who regard life "as a business situation or deal, with everybody born as more or less capable machines to take a part in it," Cowperwood early in life proves himself one of the more capable machines; he is a "natural born leader," licks "Spat" McGlathery, and becomes interested not in books but in politics, economics, and what makes the world run. Daily observing a lobster gradually devour a squid in a tank at the fish market, he decides: "That's the way it has to be, I guess." Lobsters live on squids, men live on lobsters, and men even live on one another. From the very first he knows how to make money, and soon grows to regard the stock exchange as the whole world unmasked:

> *Here men came down to the basic facts of life—the necessity of self care and protection. There was no talk, or very little there, of honor. . . . So far as he could see, force governed the world—hard, cold force and quickness of brain. If one had force, plenty of it, quickness of wit and subtlety, there was no need for anything else. . . . To get what you could and hold it fast, without being too cruel, certainly not to individuals—that was the thing to do, and he genially ignored or secretly pitied those who believed otherwise.*

With this attitude and something of an artist's liking for the sensuous, he rises in both the world of finance and the world of women. Only because of the accident of the Chicago fire, which leads to banks' calling in their loans, does Cowperwood, who has been free with the city's funds and has all his resources tied up, come to financial disaster. But even then he is not much disturbed, for his imprisonment is only a nuisance he has to endure because he has been "unfortunate"; and treated as a dignitary during a short term in jail, he is soon pardoned and re-established and is able to profit from the panic of 1873. In the world of women, who along with paintings give him a sense of the color and drama of life, he meets fewer obstacles. He overwhelms one woman, tires of her, makes the daughter of a prominent Philadelphian his mistress, divorces his wife, and eventually marries the girl and leaves a socially impossible environment for Chicago: "Isn't it nice to be finally going?" Aileen Butler, his new wife, says to him. He replies: "It's advantageous, anyhow."

Dreiser, however, thinking of Yerkes's later struggles and of the ironic dissolution of the Yerkes fortune after Yerkes's death, provided an epilogue prophesying "sorrow, sorrow, sorrow" for Cowperwood. No one should think that any one way of living, or any one kind of individual, was to be favored. "We live in a stony universe whose hard, brilliant forces rage fiercely," Dreiser remarked in one place. All individuals were disregarded. Man was but an innocent fly caught in the strands of a horrific spider's web. "His feet are in the trap of circumstances; his eyes are on an illusion." Cowperwood was to become "prince of a world of dreams whose reality was sorrow." At the same time Dreiser was not arguing against effort. He was, rather, emphasizing the elements of life that made its events dramatic for him, and by noting the inevitable tragic irony, reaffirming the value of being sufficiently life's observer to detect illusion.

In other work completed or planned at this time he embodied the same view. "The Lost Phoebe," a short story completed in October 1912, but because of its unhappy ending refused by magazines for almost four years, tells of an old widower who, suddenly believing his wife has returned, searches up hill and down valley until, lured by this will-o'-the-wisp and the memory of a world where love was young, he plunges from a cliff to his death, illustrating that dreams might be futile for the dreamer, but in their futility prove artistic for one who could see through them. *The Bulwark*, a novel he had in mind following the trilogy, was to tell ironically of a puritanical Quaker father whose devotion to the Decalogue does not bring success and does result in the disruption of his family. And his account of his trip to Europe, completed in January 1913 and published in November, was written to sweep away the filmy illusions that blurred the vision of mankind. There is "something really improving in a plain, straightforward understanding of life," he wrote in *A Traveler at Forty*. "For myself, I accept now no creeds. I do not know what truth is, what beauty is, what love is, what hope is. I do not believe any one absolutely and I do not doubt any one absolutely. I think people are both evil and well-intentioned." Life is but "an expression of contraries. . . . I know that there can be no sense of heat without cold; no fullness without emptiness; no force without resistance; no anything, in short, without its contrary. Consequently, I cannot see how there can be great men without little ones, wealth without poverty. . . ." Nature is to be indicted as "aimless, pointless, unfair, unjust. I see in the whole thing no scheme but an accidental one—no justice save accidental justice." And if he is disturbed by reading of a friend's suicide and seeing in it the manifestation of fate, or moved by a drab English manufacturing town to "feel sorry for ignorant humanity," he is also attracted by the contraries for whose sake the despairing and ignorant exist. He likes "people who take themselves with a grand air," finds Americans "wonderful" with their hopes, dreams, and desires, admires plotting labor leaders, "big, raw, crude, hungry men who are eager for gain—for self-glorification," and is so fascinated by the details of the long-familiar history of the amazingly ambitious Borgias that he records in some six pages of small type the family's "raw practicality" with the air of a discoverer.

His disinterested point of view made it impossible for him, of course, to adopt any theory that presupposed uniformity of idea or custom. He wanted only freedom to report the scene as he beheld it. Early in 1912 he had let some of his friends among the Socialists consider *Idyls of the Poor* for publication, and during the summer they had reprinted in the New York *Call* one sketch concerning the unemployed, "The Men in the Dark," which had appeared in the February *American Magazine*. But Dreiser had no mass reform in mind—at most he accepted the views of William Jennings Bryan. He was concerned with the predicament of individuals as individuals rather than as units in a society. He considered forming a "liberal" publishing house. He criticized the American home as a "fetish," saying: "An orphan asylum can bring up a child better than the average mother," and thereby reversing his *Delineator* policies in the interests of saving the individual from a worse kind of uniformity than he had originally opposed. And he defended feminism in the interests of individualism, telling a reporter:

> *I am an intense individualist, and it seems to me that the beauty and interest of life will be increased in proportion to the growing number of great individuals among women as well as among men. I believe that the feminist movement, taken as a whole, has a distinct tendency to strengthen and enrich the individuality of woman.*

He made clear, however, that he was in principle no reformer:

> *I'm not a propagandist in the feminist cause or in any other cause at present. . . . Reform has a tendency to put all but the biggest temperaments in a cocksure intellectual attitude—and that attitude puts one terribly out of harmony with the great underlying life forces. The gods take their revenge on the cocksure.*

To help dispel this mistaken cocksureness he not only returned to the second volume of his trilogy, to be called *The Titan* and to tell of Yerkes in Chicago, but wrote a one-act play, "The Girl in the Coffin," which he sent to Mencken in July 1913 for comment and consideration for *Smart Set*. Its effect was to suggest by bitter irony that life could not be reduced to rules or formulas. A strike leader, Magnet, whose unmarried daughter lies dead of an abortion, refuses to concern himself with a strike that depends on him because he is too grief-stricken over his daughter's death and interested only in detecting her lover. He is persuaded to participate, however, by the strike organizer, Ferguson, who reveals that he too is grief-stricken by the death of one he loves but that despite that misfortune he is working for the strike. At the end, when a little old lady hands Ferguson the girl's ring, the audience discovers that Ferguson is the lover. The curtain is lowered as he stares into the girl's coffin.

Although this play reaffirmed the extent to which individuals are buffeted by the great underlying life forces, Dreiser was not yet prepared to return to his earlier portrayal of man's weakness. When he beheld individuals seemingly favored by accident or fate, individuals who in addition understood that values and destiny were unrelated, he felt he beheld the forces themselves almost incarnate. And although he perceived that even such strength was accidental and must eventually encounter its limits, he could not rid himself of its fascination until he had followed its career nearer to a logical conclusion. Thus, when he hoped for more "great individuals among women as well as among men," he simply renewed the philosophic sanction for the further study of Yerkes.

Such a renewal of purpose was, moreover, timely, since it now became financially desirable to publish the second volume quickly. Reviewers, except for men like Mencken, were markedly less enthusiastic about *The Financier* than they had been about *Jennie*. They noted its length, called it either dull or forthright and true, and at best treated Dreiser as a recognized realistic reporter of life. The sales, after 8,332 copies sold in the last three months of 1912, dropped to 1,569 copies for the next six months and to 1,727 copies for all of 1913, and if the initial sale was better than that of *Jennie Gerhardt,* the sequel was worse, for *Jennie* had at least sold more than five thousand copies during the first six months of 1912. Now, moreover, *Jennie* too had almost ceased to sell, and *Carrie* in its first year under the Harper imprints sold only a few more than two thousand copies and then dropped to fewer than five hundred for 1913. It began to appear that Dreiser would be able to make scarcely enough to pay Harper's advances. In this situation his principal hope seemed to lie in the possibility of *The Titan's* reviving interest in at least *The Financier.* So from the end of 1912 to the beginning of 1914, supported by friends like William Marion Reedy and Edgar Lee Masters, who had been first attracted to Dreiser through *Sister Carrie,* cheered by an eagerness on Mencken's part to print "The Girl in the Coffin," and financed by another two-thousand-dollar advance from Harper's, Dreiser directed all his efforts toward writing *The Titan.*

This time circumstances contributed to his work. Armed with letters of introduction to people who had known Yerkes when he died in 1905, and relying in part on the advice of Edgar Lee Masters, then a practicing lawyer in Chicago, he went to Chicago in December 1912 to consult editors, businessmen, politicians, and other lawyers and to peruse the files of Chicago newspapers. But he had the help of more than persons and papers. He had the help of mood. At last he had permanently separated from Jug, and although she refused to agree to any kind of a divorce and thus prevented him from marrying again until her death in 1942, he was now at least freed from persistent reminders of his obligations. In Chicago he could recall the boyhood romantic dreams he had once experienced there, and as he passed places where he had worked or where he had feared to apply for work, he could feel the force of ancient hopes and the meaning of growth and achievement. Perceiving that Yerkes had been a creator of much that had evoked longings, he could sense the significance of Yerkes's accomplishments and amours. Chicago had, moreover, become a center for painters, writers, actors. He went to Jerome Blum's studio and stood delighted before the exciting, bright canvases. He went to the Cliff Dwellers and talked with Fuller and Hamlin Garland. He went to newspaper offices and met Ben Hecht and Floyd Dell, and with Dell visited Maurice Browne's Little Theater and met some of the actors, among them Kirah Markham, dark and statuesque, who had captivated Dell and whom Dreiser now captivated in turn. In this city where Yerkes had lived with the freedom that Dreiser had long craved, Dreiser now found a woman whose youth, beauty, and artistic sympathies represented a realization of his youthful aspirations, and as he and Miss Markham became drawn to each other, he felt the surge of the adventure and accomplishment that shaped the career of his financier. He told interviewers that "a literal transcript of life as it is" would require of readers a "special kind of guts" and, declaring that such a transcript would show that "most lives are failures," insisted he himself was "not a pessimist": "I am not even sentimentally aroused by suffering. I sympathize with struggling merit more than I do with poverty in general." Art should show, he said, "not only the concentrated filth at the bottom but the wonder and mystery of the ideals at the top." It was, after all, the mind that constructed the schemes that "merit" struggled to carry out.

In his new novel Dreiser made his character increasingly aware of the drama as well as of the amoral nature of living. Cowperwood in *The Titan* wishes not only financial power, but also recognition as a grand, colorful force in the drama. He wants to amass money in order to give him personal advantage. He wants to dominate society in order to live as he pleases. He is faithless to his wife and pursues the wives and daughters of his friends mainly to enjoy the interest of variety and to experience the illusion of beauty and the beauty of illusion. Continuing life in Chicago as he began it in Philadelphia, he snatches land from insignificant and helpless citizens, buys street railways until he has nearly a monopoly, inaugurates an impressive series of liaisons with women who appear more exciting than Aileen, and is on the verge of controlling Chicago's transportation system when the citizenry opposes his efforts and frustrates his purposes. Having by then alienated Aileen, he is apparently a lonely, defeated man until at the very last Berenice Fleming, daughter of a Louisville madame and a girl he has sought to interest since she was fifteen, comes to him and offers to share his life and he promises to live for her alone. Dreiser then interjects: "How strange are realities as opposed to illusion!" and suggests in an epilogue the final days of Cowperwood, "caught at last by the drug of a personality which he could not gainsay."

Dreiser could no more now than in *The Financier* dramatize the meaningful irony of Cowperwood's promise and hope, since another volume was to follow. But another volume was not necessary to make the irony more specific. "Woe to him who places his faith in illusion—the only reality—and woe to him who does not," Dreiser exclaimed. "In one way lies disillusion with its pain, in the other way regret." What consolation there was existed in regarding everything as an inevitable process within which the titans were what mattered. The implications of *The Financier* simply became explicit:

> *At the ultimate remove, God or the life force, if anything, is an equation, and at its nearest expression for man—the contract social—it is that also. Its method of expression appears to be that of generating the individual, in all his glittering variety and scope, and through him progressing to the mass with its problems. In the end a balance is invariably struck wherein the mass subdues the individual or the individual the mass—for the time being. For, behold, the sea is ever dancing or raging. . . . But without variation how could the balance be maintained?*

And Cowperwood, "rushing like a great comet to the zenith, his path a blazing trail . . . did for the hour illuminate the terrors and wonders of individuality." Dreiser had no use for those who would judge Cowperwood's conduct by some moral code or see in it merely evidence of a man interested in profits. He complained to reporters early in 1914 that Chicago's rich men were now interested only in growing rich, that small-town attitudes were dominating the city and producing censors of literature and art, that the spirit that had created Chicago was dead. "A big city is not a little teacup to be seasoned by old maids," he expostulated. "It is a big city where men must fight and think for themselves, where the weak must go down and the strong remain. Removing all the stumbling stones of life, putting to flight the evils of vice and greed, and all that, makes our little path a monotonous journey. Leave things be; the wilder the better for those who are strong enough to survive and the future of Chicago will then be known by the genius of the great men it bred."

But this attention to strength was not only to underscore its limits. Cowperwood would not end life as he began it. The lobster and the squid might illustrate life, but lobsters did not always win. Cowperwood was fated to encounter an opposite force: "for him also the eternal equation—the pathos of the discovery that even giants are but pygmies, and that an ultimate balance must be struck."

This conclusion served once more to reaffirm Dreiser's own role. It was not in the actual struggle or illusion that values lay, nor in the fact of potential equilibrium, but rather in the awareness and appreciation of what struggle, illusion, and equilibrium meant. To only the truly aware could individuality be wonderful and the discovery that giants were but pygmies be pathetic. To only the artist, then, could life be dramatic. Dreiser thus was brought again to the problem of the artist's career, already presented in his unpublished *"Genius"* but now assuming a different importance, and difficulties in publishing *The Titan* only helped redefine the question and gave it immediacy.

Early in March 1914 Harper's, having printed 8,500 sets of sheets to send to the binder and having begun to advertise *The Titan,* suddenly decided to halt publication. Reasons for this singular decision varied. From some of his friends Dreiser heard that Harper's had become fearful of his uncompromising realism; from others, that the treatment of financiers would antagonize men on whom the firm was dependent; from still others, that one of the members of the firm was a friend of Berenice Fleming's prototype and disapproved of what Dreiser had revealed. Dreiser himself was ill in a Chicago hotel at the time and had to leave to two of his friends in New York, William C. Lengel and Anna P. Tatum, the problem of rescuing the book. But whatever the reasons for his difficulty with *The Titan,* it was soon evident in what publishers said that Dreiser was being limited by the very codes *The Titan* challenged. George H. Doran considered the book unsalable and Dreiser a very abnormal American. Mitchell Kennerley called the manner in which Berenice's original had been utilized cheap, slanderous, and sensational. Men at the Century Company said the story was abnormal and impossible. Only the John Lane Company, a British firm recently established in the United States under the managing directorship of J. Jefferson Jones, was interested and they, within three weeks of the Harper decision, enthusiastically accepted the book, advanced Dreiser one thousand dollars, agreed to pay him a twenty per cent royalty, and sought to take over his other books from Harper's, who, however, at once set a prohibitively high valuation upon them.

If Dreiser was jubilant over the Lane acceptance, he was disgusted with the events that had led to it. A month later in Philadelphia, where Kirah Markham was playing at the Adelphi Theater, he criticized the influence of orthodoxy, called socialism misguided, and advocated an intellectual aristocracy. "The tendency here is to put the pyramid on its apex," he complained, "to discard the opinions of those at the highest point of the intellectual scale for the prejudices and stupidity of the multitude. Everything is for the vast, ruling majority. No wonder that Europe laughs at us. The idea that all men are created equal is one of the fundamental errors of our system of Government. For to the distinguishing mind it is quite apparent that the degree of intellectual endowment with which individuals come into this world varies enormously. But to level down is the cry of mediocrity everywhere." At the end of May, writing about his uncompleted trilogy for the New York *Evening Sun,* he noted that usually only the little or common things could be understood by the average man, but explained that the uncommon story of Cowperwood was important:

> *A rebellious Lucifer this, glorious in his sombre conception of the value of power. A night-black pool his world will seem to some, played over by the fulgorous gleams of his own individualistic and truly titanic mind. To the illuminate it will have a very different meaning, I am sure, a clear suggestion of the inscrutable forces of life as they shift and play—marring what they do not glorify—pagan, fortuitous, inalienably artistic. . . .*

Of course, since the artistic element was to be found in the inscrutability, and the inscrutability became evident only when an individual was the victim of the whim of life's forces, it remained for the artist as artist to appreciate the plight. With the eye of the outsider the artist observed the Lucifers and Michaels of the world and gave their struggle relevance. And although Dreiser was willing to contend that "the mind of the great merchant is conscious of the poetry of his work," it was not the merchant's but the poet's role that troubled him. In the fall of 1913 he had begun with a new perspective to revise *The "Genius,"* and now, with continuing financial necessity—for *The Titan* failed to sell in its first year as many copies as *The Financier* had sold in its first few months—he began to prepare it for publication.

F. O. Matthiessen

OF CRIME AND PUNISHMENT

For American fiction, the nineteen-twenties inaugurated a more flourishing period than any Dreiser had previously known. Several of his near contemporaries were coming into their own with a wider public. His most devoted followers, especially Sherwood Anderson, were growing up around him. Among the many new talents which made this decade one of the richest in our literary history, both realists like Sinclair Lewis and naturalists like Dos Passos were conscious of how much Dreiser had helped to prepare their way. It is more surprising to find Scott Fitzgerald saying, at the dawn of his own career: "I consider H. L. Mencken and Theodore Dreiser the greatest men living in the country today."

Dreiser took a varying and complex attitude towards the dominant mood of the 'twenties. He joined in their sweeping arraignment of the past and present inadequacies of American culture, and said flatly: "We are not an artistic nation. All we care about is to be rich and powerful." But this conviction did not lead him, as it did so many younger artists, to flight and exile. The roots of his own life were now inextricably intertwined with half a century of American experience, and, though he noted that much he had gone through had been "inimical to mental freedom and artistic energy," he still could declare America to be "as satisfying to me, as stimulating, I am sure, as Russia ever was to Tolstoy or Dostoevsky . . . or France to Flaubert or de Maupassant."

These examples indicate his realization—out of a wider range of reference than he had previously possessed—that the artist's adjustment to society is never likely to be easy. He was sympathetic with social protest, but reaffirmed his belief that the greatest writers "are not concerned with social amelioration as an end or a motive. Rather their purpose is to present life in the round, good, bad, and indifferent, alike, without thought of change and without hope of improvement. They paint the thing as it is, leaving change to nature or to others." In an introduction to a new edition of *Tono-Bungay* he strongly preferred Wells the novelist to Wells the reformer. This preference was naturally colored by Dreiser's own

From *Theodore Dreiser*, William Sloane Associates, 1951.

recurrent doubts of all efforts to order the world. "As I see him," he stated again in this introduction, "man is much more led or pushed than he is leading or pushing."

He admired the new fiction for the frankness of its record, yet in another twist of mood he saw a serious limitation in its lack of "exaltation." He was also puzzled by the fact that so many of this next generation of realists wanted "to indict life, not picture it in its ordinary beauty. . . . What is lacking in the experience of these young writers to make them think there is no beauty?" By observing where Dreiser believed "beauty" and "exaltation" were now to be found, we may begin to catch the tone of the long novel upon which he was at work and which he hoped would provide what the decade was missing. Beauty did not exist for him in delicate or fragile isolation. He described his characteristic associations with it when he voiced his appreciation of the essays of Llewellyn Powys: "They are so serious, so pathetic, so—in the main—sombre and so beautiful. They are so full of a genuine understanding of life and of a kind of sane sorrow because of the fact that in general things are so necessitous, so hopeless, and so unrewarded. And yet there is a courageous and hence impressive joy in the amazing and ebullient beauty that informs the necessitous and inexplicable and unescapable process which we know as living."

Beauty was to be seized at the heart of tragedy, as was also exaltation: "If there are all the chain cigar stores, chain drug stores, haberdasheries, movie theatres, and big hotels in Manhattan to describe, here are also Hell, Heaven, and Purgatory of the soul." But contemporary writers, held too close by the details of surface description, "rarely climb any such heights as Dante climbed to look out over the tremendous waste of lives." Dreiser had none of the firmness of vision to emulate even from afar *The Divine Comedy*. But he must have been conscious of the fact that he was summoning up all his resources when he changed the title of his novel from *Mirage* to *An American Tragedy*. In an interview in 1921, in which he looked back to his situation at the time of *Sister Carrie,* he revealed the point of view that was to be dominant in his treatment of Clyde Griffiths: "I never can and never want to bring myself to the place where I can ignore the sensitive and seeking individual in his pitiful struggle with nature—with his enormous urges and his pathetic equipment."

Dreiser worked longer and more steadily upon this novel than upon any of his others. This concentration was made possible by the fact that Liveright—who had now brought all his works together under one imprint and in 1923 had reissued *The "Genius"*—was providing him with a four-thousand-dollar annual drawing account. He wrote, as always, with great uncertainty and difficulty. But he had chosen his subject deliberately, and was sure that it was not only right for what he wanted to say, but also very typical of American life. When he had revisited Terre Haute in 1915, he had stayed at the same hotel to which his mother had once come looking for work. He recalled how his brother Rome used sometimes to put on the best clothes he had and idle outside the doorway with a toothpick in his mouth to give the impression that he had just dined there. Looking around the midnight grill, Dreiser watched those the community would call "our most successful men," men "of a solid, resonant, generative materiality. The flare of the cloth of their suits! The blaze of their skins and eyes! The hardy, animal implication of their eyes!" These were lesser Cowperwoods, and Dreiser continued to be attracted by them.

"But," he went on, "what interested me more, and this was sad too, were the tribes and shoals of the incomplete, the botched, the semi-articulate, all hungry and helpless, who never get to come to a place like this at all—who yearn for a taste of this show and flare and never attain to the least taste of it." These were the opposites of Cowperwood, of Dreiser's American version of the surviving fittest. From these other ranks he was to pick Clyde Griffiths, but he would give him a taste of the wealth from which he was excluded, and the weak boy, more sensitive than most and thus more helpless, would be destroyed by it.

In one sense, Dreiser was taking one of the stock legends of American behavior and reversing its happy ending. After the novel's appearance in 1925 he said: "The type of life that produced it has not changed. For years I have been arrested in stories and plays by the poor young man who marries the rich man's daughter. I have had many letters from people who wrote: 'Clyde Griffiths might have been me.'"

He was also writing a documentary novel, as he did in his study of the businessman. But here the core of his material was even more public—not the story of financial operations that a Yerkes would keep as hidden as he could, but what everybody was reading in the newspapers, indeed, the favorite drama of the American people: the story of a murder trial. After pondering several other cases he chose for his document the drowning of Grace Brown by Chester Gillette in Moose Lake, Herkimer County, New York, in 1906. Dreiser's center of interest, to be sure, was not in crime and its detection, but in contemplating a victim of the contemporary American dream. Clyde Griffiths' aspirations to rise in the world, to be a success as measured by money and social position, were those stimulated and sanctioned by twentieth-century capitalist society, and Dreiser instinctively moved his climax, without specifying any dates, into the showy period after the First World War. Before the glittering possibility of marrying Sondra Finchley had flashed upon him, Clyde had become involved, out of his loneliness and repression, in an affair with the mill girl Roberta Alden. If he had had some money of his own, he might have handled the unlooked-for consequence—Roberta's pregnancy—as the harder and more experienced young men of the social set knew how to. But Clyde was caught, and thrashed about in a hopeless effort to escape. What Dreiser studied was the sexual and social forces that overpowered Clyde and swept him before them until, seeing no way out, in his shallow immaturity he finally plotted murder. Yet Roberta's actual death was accidental, since the boat into which Clyde lured her upon the lake overturned at a moment when he had not willed it. The ultimate range of Dreiser's theme thereby became the terrible and baffling problem of justice.

His chief addition to his sources was his detailed presentation, in the first of the three books of his novel, of Clyde's background. The Gillette family, though not wealthy, were not really poor. But Dreiser, in order to carry Clyde's actions beyond the sphere of any merely temperamental aberration, immersed the Griffiths family in poverty as extreme as his own youth had known. As a result, Clyde's world, from the time we first see him as a boy of twelve until his death, is portrayed with a more deliberate and more detailed thoroughness than that of any of Dreiser's other characters. Dreiser shows him as always worked upon by his environment and circumstances, even to the point of being tempted to murder by coming across a newspaper account of a drowning.

In the opening scene he is an unwilling participant in the street service conducted by his preacher father in connection with the itinerant Bible mission he runs. For this vague impractical father Dreiser drew in part upon Asa Conklin, his employer in his first job after his year at college, who had been equally vague and impractical in his schemes for promoting real estate. The emotional center of the Griffiths family is Clyde's mother, who buoys up her husband by her wholehearted if ignorant faith. But Clyde is from the start alien to their values. He observes that his parents are forever proclaiming the care of God for all, and yet they are always "hard-up": "Plainly there was something wrong somewhere." Beginning in this fashion Dreiser makes a sustained contrast between the professed and the actual, as it strikes a boy who will have little regular education and no accurate training for anything.

Each successive episode is designed by Dreiser for its bearing upon Clyde's final tragedy. For instance, his older sister Esta, as tired of the dreariness of their life as he is ("dreary" is one of the recurrent key words here), runs away with a lover. In spite of his parents' grief, Clyde, now in his adolescence, cannot see that "her going was such a calamity, not from the *going* point of view at any rate." Then she is deserted and comes back, and Clyde reflects that this is typical of everything that happens in the family, of their repeated rhythm of failure. But as she bears her illegitimate child, Clyde cannot share in the stock emotion of blaming the whole affair upon the seducer. His confused mixture of feelings foreshadows what they will be in his own affair with Roberta.

The section of this first book that has been praised most often is where Dreiser evokes the splendor for which Clyde longs by making him a bellhop in the Green-Davidson in Kansas City. The vast luxury hotel is a peculiarly fitting symbol for the glamour and the waste of the modern American city, as Henry James had observed in *The American Scene.* Dreiser's way of conveying its spell over Clyde is one of the most matured examples of his method. He is more detached than when he wrote *Sister Carrie.* He can now judge as "gauche" all the senseless overfurnishing which is "without the saving grace of either simplicity or necessity." But his richly stored memory can create to the full Clyde's own amazement and awe at "this perfectly marvellous-marvellous realm." Dreiser is so sympathetically involved with how everything here would strike Clyde's starved imagination that he can take us through the routine of a bell-hop's day as though, once again, it were something out of *The Arabian Nights.* The downpour of small change into his hand "seemed fantastic, Aladdinish really." Dreiser can make us feel what Clyde feels, even through the trite image Clyde uses when complimenting his first girl friend Hortense: " 'An' your eyes are just like soft, black velvet,' he persisted eagerly. 'They're wonderful.' He was thinking of an alcove in the Green-Davidson hung with black velvet."

But the main reason why Dreiser can make us feel touched by Clyde's feelings is that he is aware of how pathetic they really are. For Clyde this hotel is the actual world in contrast with his family's shakily based ideal. But Dreiser, with a firmness of balance he had never quite possessed before, can let us sense at the same time how hopelessly wrong Clyde is in believing that these surroundings mark "a social superiority almost unbelievable." Dreiser observes that here was the "most dangerous" environment for the boy's temperament that could have been found. He was so "insanely eager for all the pleasures which he imagined he saw swirling around him." His "none-too-discerning" mind could so easily be convinced that the chief end of life was having and spending money.

This first book ends with Clyde's initial disaster. A car in which he is riding with a group of the other bell-hops and their girls runs down a child; and Clyde, knowing that the scandal will cost him his job, decides to skip out of town. We see him next three years later, twenty now and very cautious, working at the Union League Club in Chicago. Here by chance he encounters the uncle whom he had envisaged distantly as a "kind of Croesus," Samuel Griffiths, a collar manufacturer of Lycurgus, New York. He is favorably impressed by Clyde's quiet good looks, and, feeling also some compunction over his previous neglect of his brother's family, he listens to the young man's request that he be given an opportunity to make his way in the mill. The shift to an upstate New York town of twenty-five thousand affords Dreiser another sphere in which to demonstrate how completely he has worked out the details of the world in which he has placed Clyde.

He has studied once again the gradations of the economic and social scale. Though secretly somewhat awed by the bigger men he meets in Chicago, in Lycurgus Samuel Griffiths is at the top. The self-made founder of his own business, he already represents a degree of solid conservatism not yet attained by the families of even newer enterprises, such as the Finchley Electric Sweepers. Dreiser also makes a telling contrast between Mr. Griffiths, who is in general tolerant and forbearing, and his son Gilbert, who is self-centered, vain, and meanly arrogant. This is the same kind of difference Dreiser noted in *Jennie Gerhardt* between Archibald and Robert Kane. Eisenstein, whose script for a picture based on *An American Tragedy* was not what Paramount wanted, seized upon the significance of the contrast. He saw that in Mr. Griffiths "there still prevails the patriarchal democratic spirit of the fathers, who have not forgotten how they themselves came to the town in rags to make their fortunes. The succeeding generation is already approximating to a money aristocracy; and in this connection it is interesting to note the difference in attitude towards Clyde adopted by his uncle and cousin respectively." Mr. Griffiths takes it for granted that Clyde should have his chance; Gilbert regards him as an interloper who should be kept out of their inner circle.

Another telling contrast, which occupies Clyde's thoughts through most of the long second book, is between Roberta and Sondra. Roberta is like Clyde in that her whole youth has been grounded in poverty. She has come from her father's farm to work in the mill, afflicted by the same "virus of ambition and unrest" that afflicts Clyde. Until she meets him she still feels herself terribly alone. And when he, as the foreman of the shop in which she is working, begins to show an interest in her, she looks up to him as someone far outside her sphere. This is one of Dreiser's most effective strokes in pointing out the successive rungs of insecurity. For Clyde at this moment is aware that he has not really been accepted by Sondra's family and that he stands firmly nowhere.

The developing relationship between them, entered upon with misgivings by both, is handled with Dreiser's greatest tenderness. He knows how, in their first happiness together, they will feel at the Starlight Amusement Park "a kind of ecstasy all out of proportion to the fragile, gimcrack scene." He is equally in possession of Roberta's whole state of mind from her first deep sense of guilt at yielding herself to Clyde to her agonized realization that she can no longer hold him. The crisis when she discovers that she is going to have a baby, and when Clyde tries in vain to find a doctor who will perform an abortion, is regarded by Dreiser as "an illustration of the enormous handicaps imposed by ignorance, youth, poverty and fear." Dreiser knows Roberta thoroughly, and Clyde's vision of her "steady, accusing, horrified, innocent blue eyes" is likely to remain with the reader as long as anything in the novel.

The contrast with Sondra Finchley is revelatory in more ways than Dreiser seems to have meant it to be. From the first moment Clyde sees her with his cousins, she appears to him "as smart and vain and sweet a girl" as he has ever laid eyes on. These curiously mixed adjectives suggest the quality of the social group in which she is at the center, a faster-moving and more stylish group than is quite approved by the rather conservative Griffiths. Clyde reads about her avidly in the society columns until she decides one day to take him up "as a lark," partly because she realizes how much this will irritate his cousin Gilbert. At this point Clyde determines to break off with Roberta, only to discover that it is already too late. Sondra soon realizes that she is really attracted by Clyde. She is flattered at first by his doglike devotion, but gradually responds to an intensity in him beyond that of the college boys she is used to. But what Clyde finds in his "baby-talking girl" is what Dreiser never manages to convey to us concretely.

Here is the clearest-cut instance of what we have noted recurrently in Dreiser's portrayal of women. He was able to give reality to the kind he had known when he was young. But as soon as he reached above a certain point in the social scale, the details seem superficial and the total effect false. By the mid-nineteen-twenties he had doubtless known many flappers like Sondra, but he still could not make them actual. We therefore have here a strangely double effect. We know what Sondra symbolizes for Clyde, but it is as though we were looking at her from a distance, through the language of the society columns or the eyes of the outsider who does not really understand her. In part this may have been what Dreiser intended. When Clyde attempts to explain at the end the overwhelming fascination Sondra exercised over him, he says: "She seemed to know more than anyone else I ever knew." We have had no evidence of her knowing anything beyond the silliest prattle, and there is the sad irony of Clyde's having been so deluded. But Dreiser's presentation of Sondra is not primarily satirical. He was trying to suggest the social set in its animation as well as its superficiality, and for this he had none of the equipment that was second nature to Scott Fitzgerald. Both words and tune seem wrong this time, and not merely when Sondra coos: "Cantum be happy out here wis Sondra and all these nicey good-baddies?" When Gilbert says, "Spin the big news, Dad," or one of the college boys asks, "Did you hear who is being touted for stroke next year over at Cornell?" we have no illusion that we are listening to possible talk.

The third book, consisting entirely of the trial and its aftermath, raises the chief questions about structure. Dreiser devotes over a hundred thousand words to the account of the trial itself, from the first introduction of the local coroner, leafing through a mail-order catalogue when the telephone rings, to the verdict of guilty. Here the novel becomes documentary in the most literal sense. Many of the lawyers' speeches are based very closely upon what was actually said, and even Roberta's pathetic letters to Clyde, which become the most affecting evidence against him, often reproduce almost verbatim those of Grace Brown. The question, as in all such matters, is what Dreiser made of his sources, and here opinion has been very divided. For some readers interest breaks down under the sheer weight of details; for others the exhaustiveness of Dreiser's treatment is what builds up to an effect of final authority. Eisenstein, for instance, admired the whole novel for being "as broad and shoreless as the Hudson . . . as immense as life itself," and regarded it in its total structure as an "epic of cosmic veracity and objectivity."

It is certainly the most carefully planned of all Dreiser's novels, and though its movement is slow, it advances magisterially from beginning to end. He made use of a simple but effective "framing" device to suggest the bounds of Clyde's world, virtually duplicating his opening and closing chapters. In each he takes us into the deep canyon of a big city on a languorous summer night, and shows us the Griffiths family group lifting their voices in song "against the vast scepticism and apathy of life." He could hardly have produced a more concentrated impression of the overpowering and dwarfing metropolitan desert—of "such walls," as he remarks parenthetically, "as in time may linger as a mere fable." They are no fable here. They are the stone and steel of Kansas City at the beginning, and of San Francisco at the end. But at the end Clyde's place has been taken by Esta's boy, now eight years old.

Dreiser also introduced a few more developed devices of foreshadowing than he had tried before. For example, when Clyde first meets Roberta outside the factory, he invites her out in an amusement park boat, and she asks "Will it be perfectly safe?" Thus is she launched upon the utter insecurity of her relationship with him which will end only when, at a far more distant and deserted spot, she will step down into the boat of her death. A comparable way of causing us to look back to the start is the parting gift to Clyde from another man in the death house, a lawyer who, though a refined intellectual in looks and manner, has been convicted of poisoning an old man of great wealth. He leaves Clyde his copy of *Arabian Nights.*

But such thematic devices are still sparse in Dreiser's method, and he depends for his dramatic effects primarily upon the kind of bare contrasts he had used in *Sister Carrie*. One of the strongest of these also bears out how, despite the great length of this novel, many of the individual scenes are very compact. In a chapter of only three pages he affords us two glimpses, first by Roberta of Clyde's world, and then by him of hers. Anguished now by the thought that he is going to desert her, Roberta comes along Central Avenue to see him standing beside the car of one of Sondra's friends, and the girl "affectedly posed at the wheel" is for Roberta "an epitome of all the security, luxury, and freedom from responsibility" which are enticing Clyde away. Put side by side with this is Clyde, riding with his new friends, and getting out of the car to ask directions at a farmhouse. He momentarily stops short in his tracks, and Sondra calls, "What's the matter, Clyde? Afraid of the bow-wow?" He has read the name on the mailbox, Titus Alden, and here in this dilapidated and miserable house, and in the threadbare and beaten figure of the man who he knows must be Roberta's father, he sees the typification of everything that he has most wanted to escape, and that now seems to be extending "its gloomy, poverty-stricken arms" to seize him once more. In both these glimpses, incidentally, clothes still play a central symbolical role.

When one moves from smaller to larger scenes, one gets an increasing sense of the rightness of Dreiser's over-all proportions. The quality of spacing is what makes most memorable a kind of effect he had not attempted before, the suggestion of the remoteness from human contact of the lake to which Clyde lures Roberta. He evokes the desolateness of the spot partly by the very slowness with which he takes the two from their secret meeting in Utica to a pleasant resort, and then to a more remote one, and then to Big Bittern. To heighten its unearthly quality he draws also upon the language of fantasy. Clyde has been compelled here as though "some Giant Efrit" had sprung up in his brain. The water itself is "like a huge, black pearl cast by some mighty hand, in anger possibly." Some of these details may seem stock in themselves, but their cumulative effect is to remove Clyde farther and farther from his charted paths of ordinary reality, to numb his mind to the point where Roberta becomes to him "an almost nebulous figure" in "an insubstantial rowboat upon a purely ideational lake." In this way Dreiser builds up our acceptance of the involuntary nature of the catastrophe.

But the large questions still remain: wherein is this novel particularly American, and wherein is it a tragedy? Ten years after the book's appearance, when a boy named Robert Edwards killed a girl in circumstances running closely parallel to those Dreiser had treated, he was asked to be a special reporter at the trial. He also wrote how he had first reached the

conclusion that he had found in such a case "the real American tragedy."
He went back to his newspaper days when he had begun to observe the
consuming passion of his time to be the desire for wealth. He recalled
how, furthermore, "pride and show, and even waste, were flaunted in a
new and still fairly virgin land—in the face of poverty and want not on
the part of those who would not work, but the poverty and want of those
who were all too eager to work, and almost on any terms." In the light
of such facts he had come to believe that the case of Clyde Griffiths was a
typical result of the fierce competitive spirit. He now reaffirmed how not
only typical but also approved by all the standard *mores* was Clyde's longing to rise.

In the novel itself he had made other generalizations about America. In
dwelling upon Clyde's and Roberta's ignorant lack of preparation for life,
he had observed how both their families in their unthinking narrow moralism were "excellent examples of that native type of Americanism which
resists facts and reveres illusion." Incidentally, he introduced a new source
to which such a boy and girl would turn for their standards of judgment
and taste. Clyde, casting around for any means to escape Roberta, recalls
a fake wedding he had seen in a movie. Roberta, looking forward to their
marriage, is pathetically determined to have the same kind of taffeta afternoon dress that a screen heroine has worn.

In studying the lines of demarcation and stratification in Lycurgus,
Dreiser is aware that they are hardly peculiar to America, but he wants to
give his particular American facts to the full, and even notes—though it is
not central to his purpose—how the native girls in the factory hold themselves aloof from the foreign-born. In his documentation of the trial he
emphasizes how the question of Clyde's guilt or innocence becomes a
mere incident in the struggle between rival politicians. The Republican
District Attorney is also currently a candidate for Judge, so it is natural
for Clyde's Democratic lawyers to oppose him by every means they can.

Many other such details could be cited. European observers were to
comment upon the restlessness and uprootedness of Clyde's life in contrast to the more fixed patterns that still prevailed among them, as also
upon the absence of any traditional culture even in the upper class. But
Dreiser's central thought in putting the word American into his title was
the overwhelming lure of money-values in our society, more nakedly
apparent than in older and more complex social structures. And just as
the flame was more bright and compelling, so were its victims drawn to
it more helplessly.

But are such victims figures for tragedy? There has hardly ever been a
more unheroic hero than Clyde, and Dreiser did everything he could not
to build him up. He is good-looking, to be sure, with his black hair and

white skin and nice smile, and with a wistfully appealing quality that makes him superficially attractive—indeed, not unlike a minor movie hero. But Dreiser keeps repeating that he is essentially selfish, with no steadily deep feelings for others, and with no serious consideration for Roberta in her trouble. Dreiser tells us near the beginning that Clyde, over-impressed by every sign of wealth, revealed "a soul that was not destined to grow up." As he moves into the final debate with himself over what to do about Roberta, his weak and scattered mind is never able to face the real facts. He shows no trace of greater maturity at this time of crisis.

As Clyde plots murder in spite of himself, Dreiser goes to the opposite extreme from the writer of a detective story. Everything that Clyde does is so inept that he is discovered at once. He plans nothing straight and leaves every kind of clue in his wake, even letters in the trunk at his rooming house that spell out the whole situation. These he had kept out of "an insane desire" for anything that showed "a kindness, a tenderness toward him." No wonder the prosecution regards him as possessing only "the most feeble and blundering incapacity." And he is hardly more than a puppet in his own attorneys' hands as he sits listening to the line of defense in which they coach him. They know that they can do nothing with the unlikely truth of the accidental killing without dressing it up. They present him as "a mental and moral coward," who underwent "a change of heart" towards Roberta, and decided to marry her after all. He recites this lie by rote. The charged hostility of the unbelieving courtroom is relieved by "the solemn vengeful voice" of a woodsman: "Why don't they kill the God-damned bastard and be done with him?"

Yet Dreiser does not mean us to share in this judgment, and we do not, despite the immense problem he faced in creating any sympathy for such a pawn. Earlier American writers had dealt with the theme of young men driven to murder by forces stronger than themselves, but their emphases had been very different. Hawthorne's Donatello, in boyish devotion to Miriam, acted in sudden unthinking frenzy to free her from the sinister figure who shadowed her. Melville's Billy Budd, horrified by the falseness of the accusation that he had been plotting mutiny, hit out instinctively, and (as Captain Vere said) it is as though Claggart were "struck dead by an angel of God." James's Hyacinth Robinson, caught between the conflicting claims of his devotion to the Princess Casamassima and the commands of the political underground to perform a revolutionary murder, cannot support the tension, and chooses suicide instead. In each case the study is one of essential innocence, and the weakness of a Hyacinth Robinson is not enough to interfere with our feeling for him.

But Dreiser had gone farther even than Melville in his questioning of free will. In presenting Clyde he gave the most complete illustration of his belief that "the essential tragedy of life" is that man is "a waif and an interloper in Nature," which desires only "to work through him," and that he has "no power to make his own way." He can lead us to respond to Clyde's situation only to the extent that we follow the defense attorney's description of him as "a mental and moral coward" into the further statement: "Not that I am condemning you for anything that you cannot help. After all, you didn't make yourself, did you?" This is the same expression Dreiser had used in *The Hand of the Potter*. One of Clyde's last fumbling reflections in the death house returns again to the essential point: "Would no one ever understand—or give him credit for his human —if all too human and perhaps wrong hungers—yet from which so many others—along with himself suffered?" Powys said of Dreiser: "No man I ever met is so sympathetic with weakness." A crucial element in our final estimate of this novel is how far he can enable us to participate in his compassion.

He has deprived himself of many of the most powerful attributes of traditional tragedy. Rejecting the nineteenth-century myth of the free individual, which his experience has proved to him to be false, he has now gone to the opposite pole in portraying an individual without any purposive will. He has decided that a situation like Clyde's was far more widely typical of America than one like Cowperwood's. But if in a sense Cowperwood was above tragedy, Clyde is below it, since there can be no real drama without conflict. In *Pierre* Melville had made his most devastating critique of optimistic individualism. But caught by his own despair he had also presented a young character so dominated by fate that we do not have the catharsis that can come only out of some mature struggle against doom. Dreiser is not despairing in *An American Tragedy*. He is writing with objective detachment. But as is the case in most of O'Neill's plays, he sees man so exclusively as the overwhelmed victim that we feel hardly any of the crisis of moral guilt that is also at the heart of the tragic experience.

But in considering the final effect of the novel we must not fail to reckon with the several chapters after the trial. For here, as he deals with the long months of waiting in the brutal death house, he makes a detailed study of the religious appeals held out to Clyde by his mother and by a young evangelistic minister. Dreiser describes Mrs. Griffiths as "a figure out of the early Biblical days of her six-thousand-year-old world," and really conveys her as such in her square-shouldered if anguished trust in her son, even after his conviction, and in her unwavering if defeated effort to secure his pardon. It may come as more of a surprise that Dreiser speaks of the Reverend Mr. McMillan as a present-day Saint Bernard or

Savonarola: "a strange, strong, tense, confused, merciful, and too, after his fashion beautiful soul; sorrowing with misery, yearning toward an impossible justice."

Here the qualifications that clog the prose are also a chief source of Dreiser's strength. To a greater extent even than in his earlier books he was determined to hold on with unrelaxed tenacity until he had given the full record, and he did not want his own unbelief to reduce his preacher to a satirized stereotype. The effect of the Reverend Mr. McMillan's efforts to bring consolation to Clyde is, to be sure, ironic. For as he gains the young man's confidence and hears his whole story, he comes to the saddened conclusion that, though Clyde may be technically innocent on legal grounds, his whole tangled train of thoughts and actions makes him deeply guilty in the eyes of God. But he does not turn against Clyde, but labors to bring him to contrition and conversion. He thinks that he has succeeded. But though Clyde, under his prompting, signs a statement to that effect, as he walks to the electric chair he is not at all sure that he really believes. Nor has there been any of the final recognition of his destiny that frees a Hamlet or a Raskolnikov. Clyde is still a cornered animal.

The street scene of the epilogue, paralleling that of the prologue, makes some small but important thematic additions. The father, who has played such a dim part in Clyde's life, looks even more ineffectual than before. The mother is still the one figure in the group who radiates a preserving if blind trust in divine providence, but her face is now "seamed with lines of misery." When her little grandson, "unsoiled and unspoiled and uncomprehending"—and paying no attention to the service—asks her for a dime to buy an ice-cream cone, she gives it to him thinking of Clyde, thinking that she must be "more liberal" with this boy, and not try to restrain him too much. But essentially she has learned nothing, and the whole course of events might easily be repeated. We feel "the vast scepticism and apathy of life" with greatly increased pressure. Dreiser has not shaped a tragedy in any of the traditional uses of the term, and yet he has written out of a profoundly tragic sense of man's fate. He has made us hear, with more and more cumulative power, the "disastrous beating" of the Furies' wings.

This distinction between tragedy and a tragic sense was not made by the reader who saw this novel most nearly with Dreiser's own eyes. Clarence Darrow read it with complete intensity, moved most by Dreiser's "fanatical devotion to truth," and he felt at the end that he had been "gripped in the hands" of such "a master of tragedy . . . as the world has seldom known." He also said: "Of course my philosophy is practically the same as yours." This kinship between Dreiser and Darrow may help us to define a little more thoroughly what it was that *An American Tragedy* brought to articulation out of our life, and what its significance is in the drift of our cultural history.

The philosophy that these two men shared had, of course, been Darrow's before it was Dreiser's. He was fourteen years the senior, also a product of the Middle West, where he likewise experienced poverty and inferior schooling. But his father was the village agnostic of Kinsman, Ohio, well read in Jefferson, Voltaire, and Paine. By the time therefore that Darrow managed to have a year in the Michigan Law School, his mind was already grounded in a firm rationalism such as Dreiser never knew. One of his major experiences was reading Altgeld's *Our Penal Code and Its Victims* (1884), with its compelling demonstration that the poor man does not receive equal justice. The connecting strand in all his various defenses that brought him to national prominence was his conviction that the criminal is not a free agent.

Darrow's final views, as expressed in *The Story of My Life* (1932), are extraordinarily akin to the burden of *An American Tragedy*. They bear out from a different angle why minds growing to maturity in the late nineteenth century felt such a break with earlier American tradition. Faced with the gross inequalities of Chicago financial life, Darrow came to doubt the doctrine of natural rights expressed by his father's eighteenth-century philosophers. He was to go much farther than that in casting off all traditional sanctions, and to regard any belief in a purposive universe as mere delusion. Like Dreiser he could ónly brood upon the "meaninglessness" of existence.

And yet, no matter how far-reaching his scepticism, like Dreiser he preserved a core of deeply humane values. His chief concern was the same as that in *An American Tragedy*: society's immense fallibility in arriving at justice. He considered crime as a sickness to be cured. When he developed his theory of how the cure might be effected, he again voiced some of Dreiser's most pervasive thoughts: "Most men and women are haunted by poverty, and all are helpless in the clutch of a relentless fate . . . To prevent burglary the cause must be removed; it can never be done in any other way."

In regarding the victims of the law he too quoted the line about "the hand of the potter." His most condensed conclusion could have served as an epigraph for Dreiser's treatment of Clyde: "I have always felt sympathy for all living things. . . . I have judged none, and therefore condemned none. I believe that I have excused all who are forced to live awhile upon the earth. I am satisfied that they have done their best with what they had."

This close correspondence between the values of the two men makes us more aware of how representative these values are of their times, more aware too of why Dreiser held them. He viewed a society in which the equality whereon alone democratic justice might be based had been destroyed by the oligarchy of wealth. At this point he was not thinking in political terms; he entertained no ideas of how Clyde's world might be changed; he only contemplated it with somber resignation. Contemplating for ourselves the extreme to which both Darrow and Dreiser had gone in their scepticism, we are faced with the grave question of how long positive values can endure only as the aftershine of something that has been lost. Dreiser began to sense this as the 'twenties moved into the 'thirties, and he was caught up far more directly into political thinking than he had ever been before.

In the meantime *An American Tragedy* was his first immediate popular success, with a sale of twenty-five thousand in its initial six months, which still left it far below the ranks of a best seller. It was banned only in Boston. Mencken, who no longer needed to be Dreiser's champion, summed up the consensus of favorable opinion when he said: "Dreiser can feel, and, feeling, he can move. The others are very skillful with words." Wells agreed with Bennett that here was "one of the greatest novels of this century. It is a far more than life-size rendering of a poor little representative corner of American existence, lighted up by a flash of miserable tragedy . . . It gets the large, harsh superficial truth that it has to tell with a force that no grammatical precision and no correctitude could attain." The word "superficial" is important to note, particularly as coming from a European. The shallowness of a Clyde prevents his history from ever reaching the transfiguration that Dostoevsky dwells upon in the closing pages of *Crime and Punishment*.

But the thoroughness of Dreiser's treatment, the realization we have at the end that his mind has moved inexhaustibly, relentlessly over every relevant detail raises the book to the stature that made Joseph Wood Krutch speak of it as "the great American novel of our generation." There were still many dissenting voices. Clyde's whole experience was too undifferentiated, too unilluminated to compel the attention of some readers already habituated to the masterpieces of the modern psychological novel. But for young men growing up in the 'twenties and 'thirties here was a basic account of the world to which they were exposed.

Granville Hicks

Theodore Dreiser and *The Bulwark*

To appreciate Theodore Dreiser's posthumous novel, *The Bulwark,* we must see it in relation to his life and the body of his work. Certainly it is not the best of his novels, but it is a remarkably appropriate climax to his career. Taken by itself, it would add little to his reputation as a novelist, but it compels us to revise upward our estimate of the man.

The Bulwark is the story of a Quaker boy who grows up in the outskirts of Philadelphia, works hard, prospers in the banking business, marries the girl of his choice, raises a family, and wins an enviable position in the community. Only as his children approach maturity is this Solon Barnes confronted with problems to which the moral code of the Friends seems inadequate. One son and one daughter achieve conventional success, but Solon is too astute to believe that they have found the inner peace known to himself and his wife. The other three children are overt rebels, and all of them have their difficulties, with the youngest blundering into tragedy. Solon's faith is assailed by these disasters, but in the end doubts are dispelled and faith triumphs.

Although the emphases and conclusions seem almost startlingly new, the theme is that to which the whole of Dreiser's career was devoted. His great problem was always the problem of values, and, in particular, the problem of the inadequacy of the middle-class morality of the nineteenth century. He had been taught by his sternly Catholic father to work hard, live austerely, and expect his reward in the hereafter. In the world of his young manhood, he quickly discovered, most people did not live by these standards. What standards, he asked himself, did they live by, and what happened to them in the end? The questions never ceased to fascinate him.

Dreiser's contemporary, Lincoln Steffens, always talked about "my life of unlearning." Every generation has its share of unlearning to do, but perhaps Americans born in the 1860's and 1870's had more than ordinary difficulty in reconciling the world they grew up in with the account their parents and preceptors had given them of the world as it should be.

From *The American Mercury,* June, 1946.

At least for public purposes Lincoln Steffens regarded the process of dis-illusionment as comedy. To Dreiser it was almost unmitigated tragedy. There was a difference in the economic situation of the Steffenses and the Dreisers, and a striking difference in the relations between parents and children. Perhaps, too, Steffens' study of ethics and philosophy helped to soften the shock. Dreiser had to make his own philosophy out of experience and accidental reading, without the straw of formal education. It is not surprising that the confused materialism at which he arrived seemed to him less satisfying than the emphatic certainties of his father's generation.

In *The Bulwark* Dreiser did something that he had never tried to do before and that psychologically he could not have done until time had completed his emancipation. The book, that is, portrays the values of the older generation from its own point of view. Because of this, the first part of the story is quite new. Here is a Dreiserian hero who believes what his parents teach him and sets his feet firmly on the path to respectability and wealth. Solon loves but once, marries the object of his love, and cherishes her until her death. A quiet, earnest, untroubled boyhood leads to a purposeful and, for some years, happy maturity.

In the second part of the novel, however, all the familiar motifs appear. The girls re-enact, in milder versions, the rebellions of Carrie Meeber and Jennie Gerhardt. Stewart, the youngest child, has all of Clyde Griffiths' longing for excitement and luxury, and, like Clyde, is the victim not only of his passions but also of an ironic and Hardyesque accident. Certain of Solon's business associates are cut from the same piece of goods as Frank Cowperwood, and Etta's lover is bloodbrother to Eugene Witla. Here, in short, is the unvarying Dreiserian drama: arrayed on one side are the ideals of pious, moralistic parents, who do not understand their children; on the other are the temptations of luxury and the consequent urge to get money by ruthlessness or dishonesty, together with the temptations of sex.

Dreiser's sympathetic portrayal of the older generation endows the conflict with a poignancy that one cannot feel in his earlier novels. His climax, moreover, goes beyond mere neutrality. Throughout most of the latter part of the book, Dreiser emphasizes Solon's narrowness, and the reader takes the side of Etta and even Stewart against their father, but the conclusion redresses the balance. When Solon sees a beautiful fly eating a beautiful bud—an episode that must have been intended to remind the reader of Cowperwood's famous meditation on the lobster and the squid—he is overcome with awe and wonder. "Surely," he thinks, "there must be a Creative Divinity, and so a purpose, behind all this variety and beauty and tragedy of life." In his business life Solon has remained true to his ideals at no small cost. In his relations with his family he has failed, but he faces his failures and tries to learn from them. Dreiser knew that the central problem remained unresolved, but he was nevertheless determined to make us appreciate Solon's personal triumph. Solon's faith is stronger than ever at the end, and the dignity of his death humbles the more sensitive of his children.

II

Did Dreiser get religion before he died? Those who were close to him in the last year of his life say that, in some sense or other, he did. There is , something warmly personal in his description of Solon's reaffirmation of faith, and one gathers from Mrs. Tjader, his secretary, that Dreiser originally intended to have Solon die a disillusioned man and decided to restore his hero's faith only as his own was awakened. What he believed in is difficult to say, but the novel suggests that he had arrived at a kind of pantheism that he found emotionally satisfying.

Dreiser, as he once observed, was always confused. Although for many years he thought of himself as a materialist, there is not a clear statement of materialism in any of his books, and there are dozens of passages that are quite irreconcilable with any form of naturalism. His political career was a succession of inconsistencies, crowned by the farce of his joining the Communist Party a few months before he died. Every book in which he attempted to give a formal account of his views, from *Hey-Rub-a-Dub-Dub* to *America Is Worth Saving,* is a congeries of contradictions.

In spite of all this, however, Dreiser came close to the root of several important matters. In the first place, he sensed more deeply than any other novelist the psychological consequences of the growth of large cities in America. Few writers have felt more keenly the excitement of the great city, or yearned more passionately for the urban fleshpots, and yet it is preeminently Dreiser who shows us the city as the destroyer of values. He knew as well as anyone the faults of the small communities, but he also knew that in such communities men had developed a way of life that brought some degree of security and satisfaction. The theme is developed early in *Sister Carrie,* and it recurs in every novel thereafter. Again and again Dreiser said in effect, "I cannot live by these standards, but men have lived by them, and it remains to be proven whether there are other standards that make a fruitful life possible." Because the industrialization and urbanization of America are such vast phenomena and so pervasive in their influence, we tend to ignore them as we ignore the climate, but they constitute the great revolution of modern times, more important than any political change, and Dreiser felt the impact of this revolution in every corner of his being.

In the second place, despite his failure to formulate a clear statement

of naturalism, he never got very far away from the crux of the naturalistic problem. If one disregards all the verbose nonsense about "chemic
forces" and the rest, one finds a resolute attempt to see human life as an
integral part of a vast and only partly comprehensible natural process. The
early materialists sought to reduce psychology to biology and biology to
chemistry, and in his vocabulary and sometimes in his thinking Dreiser
borrowed their concepts, but he was never satisfied, and though his dis-
satisfaction often led him into extravagant mysticism, it also kept his
attention focused on the human being as such. There is a passage in *Sister
Carrie,* muddy but interesting, in which he struggles with the problem of
freedom of the will, and in the upshot agrees with the best of the naturalistic philosophers that freedom lies in the understanding of necessity.
Dreiser felt strongly and portrayed fully the power of the inner and outer
forces by which men are pulled this way and hauled that. His own life
was not a life of reason, and few of his characters are reasonable beings.
Yet they are always more than the total of the forces that drive them.

Finally we must say a word about Dreiser's humanitarianism. During
his lifetime he supported a variety of causes, and, whatever mistakes he
may have made, his indignation against injustice did rest firmly on his
sense of the dignity of the individual human being. There are no contemptible persons in Dreiser's novels. Although at times he professed a
Nietzschean scorn of the masses, and stated as a biological fact that less
than 3 per cent of the population was capable of thinking, his sympathies
were quickly roused, and he instinctively made the best case possible for
any person he wrote about. Perhaps one reason why he made Solon
Barnes a Quaker is that the Friends have always been the most generously humanitarian of the Christian sects. At any rate the quotations from
John Woolman's "Journal" do not seem incongruous on Dreiser's pages.
One could no more ask Dreiser for a program of reform than one could
ask him for a system of philosophy, but he did have charity.

"I catch no meaning from all I have seen," Dreiser wrote some twenty
years ago, "and pass quite as I came, confused and dismayed." Perhaps he
changed in the last year or two, and felt both less confusion and less dis-
may. I am not sure, however, that too much importance should be
attached to his conversion. What is important is that, in spite of all his
vagaries, he remained true in essentials to the insights that were vouch-
safed him.

III

Dreiser was a bewildered man, but he had the strength to bear his bewilderment. There is nothing new to be said about his style, for everyone
recognizes its faults and almost everyone knows that they grew out of

the man's basic qualities. Most novelists, if they have any skill with words, are tempted to say more than they know, but Dreiser, whose least encounter with the American language took on the appearance of a wrestling match, stubbornly refused to go beyond himself. I am not trying to suggest that good writing is a vice, but merely that Dreiser's awkwardness was integrally related to his tremendous honesty. Even his banalities do not seem the product of laziness but, rather, the desperate gestures of a man for whom mere words will never suffice.

The Bulwark has all of the old clumsiness, but what is the essentially Dreiserian style is somehow exhibited in a purer vein than ever before. The writing is so commonplace that it becomes austere and even dignified. There are plenty of the old trite phrases, and there are a few pretentious passages, but for the most part the novel is written with a simplicity that begins by being annoying and ends by being impressive. Dreiser never told a story better than in *The Bulwark*.

Yet I have said that *The Bulwark* is not the best of his novels, and in some ways it seems to me the poorest. Certain of his qualities are heightened in the book, but one of the most important of his attributes scarcely makes itself felt, and the novel suffers sharply as a result. What one misses is the sense of a time and a place. Can anyone forget the description of Fitzgerald and Moy's bar in *Sister Carrie* or the account of the Green-Davidson Hotel in *An American Tragedy*? Dreiser's documentation was laborious, and he relied on the piling up of detail, but he got his effect. In *The Bulwark,* on the other hand, the background is invariably a little vague, whether the scene is Solon's bank or Isobel's college or Etta's Greenwich Village. It has always been easy to make fun of Dreiser's concern with trivialities, but the truth is that the commonplace was not commonplace to him and that he could make it fresh and vivid to us. One came to know his people through the minutiae of their lives, and it is strange to read a book of his in which the figures are almost as removed from the vulgar circumstances of place and time as the characters of Henry James.

The explanation lies, at least in part, in the way in which the book was written. Mrs. Tjader tells us that it was begun as early as 1910 and that there were four or five early versions. When Dreiser took up the story again in the winter of 1945, he and Mrs. Tjader pieced the first part of the novel together out of the various fragments, and he then wrote and dictated the last third of the book. As a result, there is a very real uncertainty as to the period in which the action is taking place. The incidents of the latter part of the story are said to occur in the twenties, but there are a hundred details that belong to the years before the first World War. Even, however, if Dreiser had completely revised the novel or had written it afresh, I doubt if he could have documented it as he documented the earlier novels, for by the twenties he was the great American novelist and no longer immersed in the life of the people.

The Bulwark, at least in its final version, was the work of an old man, and its most moving pages portray the old age and death of Solon Barnes. Dreiser has portrayed pathetic old men before now. Solon, however, is not merely pathetic; he is meant to be and is a triumphant figure. As he rises above the vicissitudes of fate by virtue of his inner resources, one believes in his triumph whether or not one believes in the Inner Light.

Whatever its philosophical implications, *The Bulwark* is certainly a rejection of naturalism as a literary theory. Dreiser, it is true, occasionally uses such characteristic phrases as "the import of sex as a force" and "the chemically radiated charm of her," and he even talks about Solon's "psychic religiosity," but these are mere matters of habit or, more probably, vestigial remains of an earlier version, for there is no serious attempt to explain anybody's behavior in terms of physics, chemistry, or biology.

The Bulwark might, indeed, be regarded as the death knell of literary naturalism. It was always a misbegotten theory. However enthusiastically Zola endorsed the formulas of Claude Bernard, he never in practice limited himself to them, and he would have been a mere parody of a novelist if he had. Dreiser owed more to Balzac than he did to Darwin, Spencer, and Haeckel, and even if he had had a more extensive and accurate knowledge of nineteenth century science, he still would not have been able to make great practical use of it. The theorists of naturalism held that the novel could become scientific, but the novelists, fortunately, knew better. Some of the wiser ones took from science what proved to be useful, but they found in science something to add to their art, not a substitute for it. In this country at least naturalism was chiefly a justification of a frankness that was not palatable to middle-class morality. Now that that battle is won, there is not much need for further talk about naturalism.

Dreiser in any case could never be brought comfortably within the naturalistic fold, no matter how hard academicians tried, and it is perhaps as well that *The Bulwark* has come along to make the attempt obviously futile. Even *The Financier* and *The Titan,* which he probably thought of as naturalistic, are Nietzschean rather than Darwinian.

Dreiser was Dreiser and not the exemplar of some theory. He was the lost, bewildered man of the turn of the century, caught between science and faith, between city and town, between the economics of monopoly capitalism and the economics of small-scale competition. With the most painful honesty he set forth the dilemmas of his generation and, by stating what he knew about men, said something about man.

David Brion Davis

DREISER AND NATURALISM REVISITED

If American naturalists have generally scorned theory and self-examination, their critics have been eager to fill the gap and tell the naturalists what naturalism really is. Borrowing frequently from the theories of French writers of an earlier generation, the critics were able to accuse their opponents of attitudes and beliefs traditionally offensive to the American people. While most American naturalists have refused to stand on a platform made by the opposing party, their protests have been ignored by the journals of the genteel tradition, the humanists, and the "new fiction."

Literary naturalism, the critics said, was a celebration of the gross and brutal aspects of man. The writers were really simple souls who lacked tradition and the culture and any suspicion of the depth and dignity of human nature. They were vulgar vanguards in the revolt of the masses; high-school-trained observers with a smattering of nineteenth century science; half-sentimental, half-cynical journalists who tried to make "feature stories" into literature; adolescent iconoclasts who got a thrill out of reducing man to an animal, preaching a naïve determinism, and dwelling on the sordid and ugly sides of life.

Though certain European naturalists defined a theory which could be more accurately described as materialism, a careful examination of the assumptions and aims of early American naturalistic writers and artists shows that the literary taxonomers created an imaginary species. If the American naturalists had been the materialists they were supposed to be, they would have exhibited a tremendous faith in science and the artist as a scientist. The artist would gather facts with the cool indifference of a good biologist. Laws would emerge from the mass of facts and the artist would construct his novel around these predictable, certain rules of human behavior. He would be, essentially, a rationalist, a hard-headed researcher, a tough statistician.

But the paintings and books of the early naturalists in America reveal a generation of sensitive, romantic, dreaming youths—young men obsessed

From "A Reappraisal of Early Naturalism in America," Unpublished paper, Harvard University, 1953.

with ideals and visions and the terrifying suspicion that ideals are unattainable in a modern world. In the place of objective rationalism, one finds intense emotions of sympathy, the recurring image of the unknowable, and a struggling attempt to humanize a strange new world of steel forms and inhuman rhythms.

When one studies anything as blurred and amorphous as a tendency in literature and art, it is a mistake to think in terms of precise categories and static philosophies. There may not be progress in the arts but there is certainly movement. And it is the character of thought to move in dialectical patterns, to shift in attitudes toward authority, tradition, and man's place in the universe. The critic can study what people have said and then trace the direction of this movement and the stages of a process, but he should not classify intellectual races and types and force historical figures to conform.

A vague tendency which eludes exact catalogues and definitions is the pietistic movement in religion. Pietism involved a rejection of human tradition and authority, a reliance on personal experience, and the enthusiasm of those who felt they were shaking off dry, old forms and were penetrating to the inner mystery of things. Outbursts of pietism flared at sporadic intervals during the seventeenth and eighteenth centuries, especially attracting the uneducated classes of Europe, who wanted to push the Reformation to its conclusion. By obliterating the rituals and forms of established religion, the pietists were not moving toward atheism or secular reform. On the contrary, their theology lifted God to an inscrutable height and left man helpless in a determined universe.

Students of American intellectual history often forget that during an era of increasing belief in progress, free will, and morality, many thinkers expressed convictions about human weakness and the inevitability of events without becoming scientific materialists. Even if the pietistic strain had not been transferred to American soil by descendants of Lollards and Anabaptists, Quakers and Moravians, there would probably have been indigenous eruptions. In many denominations there were individuals who worried about human pride and selfishness and tried to work out a vision of sanctity or happiness through harmonizing the self with the inevitable flow of events. These men preached a love of Being in general, of humanity for its own sake rather than for specious moral virtues. Ideal Christian love was a love for the unlovely, and according to the pietistic psychology, the poor and the socially immoral were not necessarily the worst sinners. If ordinary love and virtue were the results of natural law, then true virtue consisted only in the acceptance of the universe as a whole.

As morality and free will became the concern of formal religion, many pietists revolted. But the tendency toward revolt and reform was only a phase in the dialectic of pietism. The rebel Quaker, Elias Hicks, had a strong bent toward extreme Quietism, or the progressive resignation to divine will. He wrote that "God is an impartial being," which meant that man could never discover the divine laws or establish a perfect kingdom. "It is manifest," Hicks said in one of his sermons, "that we should never have a will of our own, independent of his. How presumptuous it is, then, in us to set up our will in contradiction to his, and as it were to dictate to the Almighty!"

This pietistic Quaker was a self-educated man and, according to the *Dictionary of American Biography,* "a tender, humane spirit, quickly touched by either human or animal suffering. . . . A pleader for enlarged rights and opportunities for underprivileged classes of people." Despite the formal religious terminology, his writings contained the kind of piety and spirituality which strongly appealed to two later figures in American literature—Walt Whitman and Theodore Dreiser.

In many respects Whitman was a link between the religious pietism of his Quaker forebears and the secular pietism of writers and painters in the early twentieth century. He was deeply influenced by Elias Hicks and was largely concerned with issues which had been confined to theological debate in an earlier generation. But he was also the prototype of the young naturalistic writer discovering the modern city. If, as H. S. Canby suggests, he had "a Quaker concern for every instance of cruelty, greed or injustice," his voluptuousness was scarcely Quaker.

Whitman's career set an almost standardized pattern for the early naturalists in America. He kept his father at a distance and adored his mother, who had a resigned, pietistic attitude toward the cruelties of life. He immersed himself in sentimental and romantic literature and read indiscriminately, mixing romance with factual books and popular philosophy. This produced a shallow sophistication and the jumbling of technical, foreign, and slang phrases, topped off with rhetoric and exclamation points. Beneath the clichés and incongruous words, however, there lay a very sensitive and emotional spirit, intensely receptive to the new and changing images of urban life.

Whitman went to the city with the habits of a rambling, meditative youth who hoped to give life meaning by a retiring and quiet "concern" for the things he saw. He tramped up and down the great avenues and gazed at the bustling life with a slightly aloof perspective. New York was "turbulent, fleshy, sensual, eating, drinking and breeding." Omnibus jaunts and ferry rides furnished many rough impressions and factual details for *Leaves of Grass.* Life was a great spectacle, and its evanescent forms were the revelations of a divine and creative Force. The "full-sinewed" workers, the ferrymen, the bartenders, the prostitutes, and the drovers made a great pageant which thrilled the soul of Whitman as if they were visions of a Savior or the promise of an afterlife. Despite his celebration of "the body electric" and his fascination with material life, Whitman was not a dispassionate and scientific materialist. He possessed the kind of spiritual "inner light" which could blend and melt the flux of matter around him and then transform the total sensation into a moment of ecstatic beauty.

Despite the injustices he saw in the world, Whitman progressed toward a general love of mankind and an acceptance of the universe as it exists. His earlier raw egotism was given depth by a sense of identification with all humanity, an outpouring of the physical and spiritual self which smoothed the coarse edges of his defiant and seemingly impudent manner. At bottom lay a special doctrine of human *interest:* "A man is interested in anything," Canby points out "when he identifies himself with it. . . ." This was accomplished by entering into other personalities with passion and sympathy. Whitman felt he could accept the responsibility for all men's actions and by his intense and redeeming love, justify himself and his race. His pictures and catalogues of New York life were not mere descriptions but inspired recording of a providential universe.

Whitman extended the pietistic love of Being to include the physical passions and forms. In so doing he gave religious impulses a naturalistic base and spiritualized material love. A generation of dusty leather and polished bronze separated Whitman from the twentieth century. But his spiritual arm reached over the somber concretions of the brown decades and this groping arm found "camerados" in the generation which matured in the decade of bimetallism, depression, and labor crisis. There were hints of the Whitman vision in Thomas Eakins' sturdy realism. But the shadow of Whitman fell heaviest on the naturalistic painters and writers of the first decades of the twentieth century.

II

John Sloan's paintings of New York follow the rough stages of a dialectical pattern which Whitman had traced. The city was first of all a place of awe and wonder, a romantic vision of contrast and innovation. New York was a spectacle in the same sense as the Grand Canyon. Alternating shadows on buildings, the staccato spots of light on moving human heads, plumes of smoke and blazing lights were representative symbols of a swirling flux of material forces, the erosion and accretions, the shifting and buckling strata of human life in a great city. It was a thrill to capture the beauty of a particular moment in the flowing stream of change. Sloan chose rough, clay-like forms, often covered by a veil of fog or smoke or glistening rain to convey the transcience and the beauty of raw, physical New York. The material was out beyond him but he knew it was his eye which found the beauty and selected the image which stood for so much more than a mere artistic pattern. He was not painting as a reformer, but he wanted the viewer to feel the bulk of his shapes and the humanity of his subjects. He wanted one to feel the implacable forces that pushed and pulled objects across his screen, the stifling desolation of tenement life, the weary, hopeless resignation of the immigrant with his pushcart, the bustling impersonality of the warehouses and docks where bewildered strangers were pumped into the blood stream of a strange, throbbing organism, the innocent unconcern of children and pigeons, playing and fluttering in tiny unimportant places beneath the ominous shadows of elevated tracks and fire escapes.

While this first stage was full of the excitement of discovery and the rejection of old subjects and old ways of seeing, a second tendency soon developed. "God must be awfully far away or disinterested," Sloan wrote in the *Gist of Art* (1939), "to let people go on living the way they do in dirt and filthy holes contaminating one another, swarming out to kill when ordered." The spirit of competition was especially troubling. The shop windows displayed riches and finery, and the city people seemed intent on getting ahead even if it meant ignoring the beauty of life and the welfare of their neighbors. It did not seem right for the tenement child to become a tramp or a pushing, grasping office clerk merely because of circumstance. Yet this second stage of the naturalists' attitude was characterized more by an overwhelming compassion than by an urge to reform. Here again, they followed the pattern of Whitman and the earlier pietists. This is not to say that a direct "stream" ran from men like Elias Hicks to John Sloan or that the stages in attitude were a clear-cut, temporal progression. Rather, men like Sloan and Dreiser *reacted* to the fact of the modern city in a pattern which echoed the enthusiasm and sympathy of pietism.

Figures and incidents tended to dominate the paintings of Sloan's second stage. Nursemaids flirting with dark male forms in Madison Square or two working girls chatting in a one-room apartment at three A.M. were typical subjects. Sloan reached out for the deeply human fragments, isolated by the rhythms and shadows of the city. He sympathized with the scrubwomen in the old Astor Library or felt the warm companionship of McSorley's Bar. If traditional religion seemed a precession of stilted, dusty forms built around merely human authorities and myths, a kind of salvation and true religion were still possible in art. Instead of tending toward the rationalism of scientific reform and progress, the second stage in the dialectic resolved itself in a third attitude which combined the first two.

"The artist is a spectator of life," Sloan wrote. "He doesn't need to participate in adventures. The artist is interested in life the way God is interested in the universe." This is a key sentence in the final naturalistic position. Instead of pushing on to muckraking or a scientific recording of nature, the artist must see life as an over-all spectacle and at the same time sympathize with spirits caught in the determined flux of matter. This necessitated a fluctuation between an identification with personalities in specific situations and a retiring, detached perspective where all life, the evil and ugly included, seemed beautiful.

When the artist immersed himself in temporal events he could see the illusion of free will, the tempting possibilities which drove men forward in business. He could feel the delirious lure of ideals, money, fame, and love. But when he retired to his secluded vantage point, he could glimpse the determined panorama and like a Dante gazing into Malebolgia, he felt compassion for the blind, struggling souls. Yet the love which made God seem terrible from the first perspective served to make His creation a vast object of beauty from the second. This was the pietist's "love of Being in general."

III

Theodore Dreiser was unquestionably the central figure of the early naturalistic movement in America; and while his philosophical speculations were often vague, his work exemplified the stages in mood which began in awe and wonder and ended in a compassionate acceptance of the forces of nature. But since Dreiser lacked formal training and artistic discipline, his emotions often shot ahead of his ability to express himself. Especially in his second, or sympathetic cycle, this gap is represented by rhetoric and exclamations. When he identified himself too closely with a character trapped by circumstance, he tended to rely on the most adolescent clichés and forced speculations. This has provoked and tired many sensitive readers and has led them to overlook some of Dreiser's basic assumptions. It was too easy to ignore what he actually wrote and classify him as a Zola-type materialist who occasionally showed inconsistent emotional lapses of pity and sympathy.

Dreiser was the son of a devout Catholic immigrant father and a Mennonite mother. His family environment, he later recorded in *Dawn,* seemed distinguished by "a particularly nebulous, emotional, unorganized and traditionless character." As an intensely romantic and sensitive boy, Dreiser found himself in an uprooted, free-floating limbo between traditional American culture and the rejected, isolated authority of his father. His mother tended toward a pietistic attitude of resignation. "She was, after her fashion, a poet who suffers much, yet unfailingly and irresistibly continues to contemplate beauty—her one enduring and earthly reward, as I came to know." Her internal spirit seemed to glorify the raw facts, the little routines of an otherwise colorless existence, and Theodore drew a certain inspiration from her serenity. He learned that his own personal troubles dissolved in moments of objective contemplation: "I was looking at the clouds, watching the birds, noting the swaying of a tree in the wind, speculating on the doings and thoughts of others. . . . A passing train or boat, even an ambling street car, was ever a delight." There was no necessity of learning about God in books: "Here was my Maker: the creative life force all about me. . . . I am because I wish to be, and this is my way."

But Dreiser knew that only bulky shadows existed outside his own soul and that "some mulch of chemistry" within him transmuted "walls of yellow brick and streets of cedar block into amethyst and gold. . . ." He was possessed by "the mystic something of beauty that perennially transfigures the world!" And while the external life might be insecure and cruel, it was never dull, always full of romance, "so generous, merciful, forgiving."

These were hardly the sentiments of a reformer or a science-obsessed materialist, seeking to *reduce* all thought to "chemisms." Dreiser was a naturalist in the sense that he denied supernaturalism and believed that all reality forms a unified whole with "higher" responses subsequent to lower states of existence. But the belief that mind requires antecedent physical states does not deny the attainment of spiritual insights, of moments of ecstasy or even a kind of omniscience. As George Santayana, a philosophical naturalist, put it in *The Genteel Tradition at Bay* (1931), these are "material functions spiritually realised. . . . No true appreciation of anything is possible without a sense of its *naturalness,* of the innocent necessity by which it has assumed its special and perhaps extraordinary form."

Nor was Dreiser's early reading the logical preparation for a clinical observer. He was fascinated by Poe and Hawthorne, and Laura Jean Libby and Lew Wallace accompanied Emerson and Thoreau in his miscellaneous diet of romantic and transcendental literature. At the Chicago Opera House "Sinbad, the Sailor" and "Ali Baba and the Forty Thieves" aroused his wonder and delight. The glistening towers of Manhattan would later remind him of something from the *Arabian Nights.*

The young Dreiser throbbed with ideals of beauty and romantic fancy. Pathetically shy with girls, he brooded about love, "and by love I do not mean that poetic abstraction celebrated by the religionists—devoid of sex —nor yet the guttural sensuality understood of the materialist. My dreams were a blend of each." It is easy to ignore the fact that he meant his novels to be a blend of each.

When he was supposed to be hunting for a job, Dreiser recalls in *Dawn*, he shuffled about the streets of Chicago, staring at the amazing spectacle:

> *The art of the jumbled streets, the rancid alleys . . . the dirty river, with its dark, inscrutable waters: all moving, soothing, beautiful, rewarding. It was like listening to an enticing symphony. Most of all, the art of the accidental experiences of individuals appealed to me.*

The city shifted and rolled before Dreiser's eyes, all was change, all was uncertain, "only a love of beauty," he felt, "endures." This romantic wandering about the streets of Chicago, and later New York was an experience which Dreiser shared with the naturalistic painters. He recorded many of the moments when, as Robert Henri said, "we seem to see beyond the usual. Such are the moments of our greatest happiness . . . of our greatest wisdom."

In New York Dreiser met William L. Sonntag Jr. and shortly after the young artist's death in 1901 he wrote a tribute in *Harper's Weekly,* telling how Sonntag had taught him to see subtle colors and contrasts in the city. The artist's spirit illuminated a world of chaos and his death was like the sudden extinguishing of a beautiful lamp. The illumined "reality" had been dependent on the artist's vision. Henri had said that "No *thing* is beautiful. But all things await the sensitive and imaginative mind. . . ." A beautiful object seen in a glimpse from a train window might "dissolve into mere materialism" from a different perspective. Dreiser was expressing the same conviction of a mental reality *above* external existence when he commented on George Bellows' "Cliff Dwellers": "Mr. Bellows evokes it all out of that inner intuition which is deeper and finer than all the schools and all the slums with such crowds as these. By contrast they are mere shadows—flotsam and jetsam on the tides of time."

This art spirit of the naturalists was what Santayana meant by "a lyric cry in the midst of business." Both Henri and the philosopher stressed the word "spirit" in relation to beauty in a sense that would have been acceptable to Dreiser. Spirit was not thought of as a physical organ or as an efficacious power, but rather as the distinctively human capacity for beauty through detachment and sympathy. The artist is the man who develops this spiritual sense and thus lifts the flux of material life into a new realm of meaning. In Dreiser's words: "Life, properly and artistically presented, apotheosizes itself and incidentally its handmaiden, the artist."

Dreiser's naturalism progressed through a stage of identification and sympathy to one of resigned contemplation. The shift did not come in a precise, temporal pattern; there was a fluctuation in both his life and fiction. His own early poverty reinforced his sympathy for working people, but as with John Sloan, his detachment and his lack of faith in any panacea long prevented him from overt political action. "Reform has a tendency," he wrote, "to put all but the biggest temperaments in a cocksure intellectual attitude. . . . The gods take their revenge on the cocksure."

When Dreiser was on his "Hoosier holiday" he felt great sympathy for the victims of a terrible flood in Erie, Pennsylvania, and he speculated on the indifference and inscrutable will of God. Yet when contrasts and evils became too great, it seemed to Dreiser that God brought forth great dreamers and idealists who helped to mitigate the injustices. Such were Christ, Saint Francis, John Huss, Savonarola, and Whitman, he proposed in *A Hoosier Holiday*. But even these great men were limited in what they could do for suffering humanity, and in a passage which demonstrates the fluctuation from sympathy to over-all acceptance, Dreiser wrote:

> *We can only sympathize at times where we cannot possibly act,—and we can act and aid where we cannot cure. But of a universal panacea there is only a dream . . . Yet it is because we can and do dream . . . and the fact that they must so often be shattered, that we have art and the joy of this thing called Life. Without contrast there is no life . . . Where would our dreams be . . . If all of that of which we are compelled to dream . . . were present and we did not need to dream?*

In 1923 Dreiser could even feel a nostalgia for the shocking, filthy slums of 1900. The old New York, he then wrote in *The Color of a Great City*, was: "more varied and arresting and poetic . . . The astounding areas of poverty and of beggary even . . . unrelieved as they were by civic betterment . . . as contrasted with the beschooled and beserviced east side of to-day."

Though he rejected superficial ethical judgments, Dreiser was interested in essentially moral problems. Among the distinctive features of modern, urban America were the dazzling opportunities which gripped the imaginative minds of young men. Blind to the chaotic and insecure world of physical fact, these dreaming men projected glorious futures for themselves and succumbed to the pathetic myth that by their own free will they were choosing the most desirable opportunities. For the modern seer, however, schooled in the wisdom of Spencer and Jacques Loeb, the young man's very images and ideals were products of circumstance. His mental processes were somehow out of harmony with the necessities of physical existence and the discord was bound to produce tragedy. Because of the Italian push-cart man's "enduring patience," he had more actual freedom than the petulant young clerk or business man who wears out his heart and brain in a frantic effort to be what he is not. Thus man's only hope, for Dreiser, lay in a knowledge of his helplessness, which could be gained only through art.

If sensitive people were troubled by the grim, determined universe of Spencer, "Have faith to believe that there is a larger intelligence at work which does not care for you or me at all—or if it does, only to this extent, that it desires to use us as a carpenter does his tools. . . ." Man can not fight this power of which he is partly the expression; you can only "do all that you can to keep yourself busy—serenely employed. There is no other answer."

Here, in *A Hoosier Holiday,* Dreiser was voicing a pietistic acceptance of Being, substantially no different from early Quakers or antinomians. Elias Hicks said it was "presumptuous" to assert a will of our own; Dreiser said it was useless "to quarrel with an order which is compulsory and produces all that we know of either joy or pain." Even the violence and contentiousness of Being has compensations in the over-all beauty and variety of life. To see "the physical face of life as beautiful . . . is to be at once strong and wise mentally and physically, to have in the very blood and brain the beauty, glory and power of all that ever was or will be here on this earth."

Far from being a simple, clear recording of external life, art became a central concept in Dreiser's personal religion. Even the writing of *Sister Carrie* was something like translating the Golden Plates: "My mind was blank except for the name. I had no idea who or what she was to be. I have often thought that there was something mystic about it, as if I were being used, like a medium." This was consistent since even the thoughts of a creative writer would be the product of a rigid pattern of circumstance in a deterministic world. There would be something almost providential in the writing of fiction. The creative force of life seemed to kindle itself within an artist's brain and the combustion illumined and brought into full realization a chain of circumstantial events and details which fell by compulsion within the artist's range of vision. Thus no detail, no memory should be deleted or compressed. Artifice might distort the pattern of transcendent reality which the artist strove to create. Thus the tale of Sister Carrie unrolled like a gigantic parchment within Dreiser's consciousness, the providential amalgamation of past experiences, observations, and fears. Matthiessen points out that the smooth flow ceased with the imminent downfall of Hurstwood. Dreiser paused in "abject reverence in the face of misery," feeling "unworthy" to write about Hurstwood's inevitable decline. Yet he had no more power than Hurstwood to alter the course of events. But Dreiser, the compassionate observer, could still see "kindness" in the night of Hurstwood's death. This was the emotion of a pietist, whose aesthetic and moral love of Being transcends any ethical protest or social rebellion.

I V

The naturalists of the early twentieth century were deeply concerned with the problem of uniting art and the turbulent life of urban America. But while they were interested in the subject material of "raw, necessary life," a thin film of romanticism enveloped the slums and waterfronts and generated emotions of excitement and wonder at the sight of tugboats, beggars, or a brightly-lit elevated train. Science was a thrilling study because it shattered the pompous pretensions of self-appointed experts and undermined the arbitrary barriers of traditional morality and religion. Superficial critics said that naturalists lowered man's dignity. Yet many types and classes of people who had been contemptuously ignored by the genteel writers and artists first acquired the dignity of artistic subjects in the works of Sloan and Dreiser. In another sense man assumed more dignity because his world was made more difficult. The following of traditional ethical precepts was no longer a path to sure and easy virtue. The naturalists' world was full of illusion, mistakes, sacrifice, and resignation, and the very complexity of this world challenged man's resources and revealed more dignity than the cut-and-dried world of the idealists, where individuals were good if they wanted to be good. While the naturalists denied freedom of the will, they did not deny a will. This will could be either in or out of harmony with the forces of nature and it is the *natural* bent of the will to strive toward a harmonious relationship. It is entirely possible then to see dignity and tragedy in the struggles of a discordant will, the vain hobbling after an illusion of the spirit like a blind man following a mad dog.

How much more wonderful human nature appears when its achievements are contrasted with its rigid limits! Dreiser was always marvelling at people who, as he wrote in "Sanctuary," "in spite of their unfortunate beginnings, the slime in which primarily and without any willing of their own they had been embedded and from which nearly all were seeking to crawl upwards, and bravely enough, they had heart and faith in life." As an integral part of nature, man absorbed and epitomized its mystery and beauty. "The potter has but so much clay," Dreiser wrote. "He cannot but mold it again and again. And as for the fire, he cannot ultimately prevent it. It goes, somewhat wild or mild, into all he does."

While the urbane George Santayana was temperamentally and culturally far removed from American literary naturalism, he once gave a deep and pertinent description of the sense of piety which runs through the works of Dreiser, Sloan, and Henri:

There is . . . a philosophic piety which has the universe for its object. . . . its extent, its order, its beauty, its cruelty, make it alike impressive . . . the cosmos has its own way of doing things, not wholly rational nor ideally best, but patient, fatal, and fruitful. Great is this organism of mud and fire, terrible this vast, painful, glorious experiment. Why should we not look on the universe with piety?

This was the beauty and piety which the naturalists sought to express, along with the sympathy and wonder they felt when confronting the modern metropolis. That they often failed to convey their true purpose and were interpreted as "apostles of ugliness" does not detract from their meaning. These artists sensed an ancient truth when they discovered the fact that man is not free to determine his temporal destiny but that he is free to achieve happiness in any given moment. The art spirit could make a determined world tolerable. It was not, after all, a pessimist or a seeker of the ugly and sordid who would write as Dreiser did in 1929 in "What I Believe":

I still rise to testify to the aesthetic perfection of this thing. . . . which we call Life. . . . It can and does achieve an aesthetic whole— beauty no less—and via the same elements that are in lice and bedbugs as well as in the most distant suns or sidereal systems—in fire and flowers, in Shelley and Christ.

Eliseo Vivas

DREISER, AN INCONSISTENT MECHANIST

It has become the fashion among the intellectuals to dismiss Dreiser in a lofty and condescending manner. The man, we are informed, is essentially confused. Hence he is not worth reading. He is passé. All the more so since, lacking style, he cannot even be superficially enjoyed. Of course if style is defined in terms of cadence and euphony, in terms of choice of the impeccable image and the inevitable word, Dreiser has no style. But if style is more than this, then he cannot be denied style. For he has archi-tectonic genius. In his lumbering, slow, painful, clumsy way he builds up a story. And when the story is built, the manner fits the matter even to clichés and all. Again, there is no doubt that in an important sense Dreiser is a confused man. But to dismiss him without further qualification is to ignore his depth and his range.

Dreiser's philosophy may be naïve, as his critics have so often pointed out, but it should not be forgotten that "naïve" is a very relative term. In comparison with the views of professional philosophers his ideas are no doubt unacceptable. But they are not foolish or unworthy of consideration. They were held, and not in an essentially different form, by some of the best minds of the last half of the nineteenth century; and essentially in the very form in which he holds them, they are still held by a few professional philosophers. But even if we could be sure that these ideas deserve no con-sideration whatever as systematic philosophy, it cannot be denied that their essential contention that life has no intrinsic meaning, is still one of the basic tenets of contemporary naturalism. In any case, whether naïve or not, Dreiser's philosophy is still of interest to the reader of his novels. That he will continue to have readers, in spite of his present eclipse, we may be certain; because if he is not a philosopher he is a novelist. He has a deep sense of the dramatic movement of human life and a knowledge of its dark urges and baffled quality. He also has a wide range of vision and a deep sense of the relation of man to the cosmos. He is not only an American novelist but a universal novelist, in a very literal sense of the word. The mystery of the universe, the puzzle of destiny, haunts him; and

From *Ethics*, July, 1938. Revised for this volume.

he, more than any of his contemporaries, has responded to the need to relate the haunting sense of puzzlement and mystery to the human drama. No other American novelist of his generation has so persistently endeavored to look at men under the form of eternity. It is no love of paradox, therefore, that prompts the assertion that while Dreiser tries to demonstrate that man's efforts are vain and empty, by responding to the need to face the problem of destiny, he draws our attention to dimensions of human existence, awareness of which is not encouraged by current philosophic fashions. It is then the surest sign of critical naïveté to dismiss Dreiser on the counts of being naïve and lacking style. His prose is indeed fussy, his language a string of clichés; his thought is indeed naïve in many respects. But the prose is the man; his architectonic is superb; and his vision is turned towards horizons the existence of which contemporary novelists seldom suspect. But if all these claims can be asserted consistently the need arises to explain how a man guided by a naïve and unacceptable philosophy can be said to occupy the position he does—can be said to have the depth of insight he possesses.

II

Early in his youth Dreiser read and accepted the then popular materialistic mechanism. The picture of the world which he gained from his youthful reading must have been grasped by him with a deep sense of relief. He hated for deep personal reasons anything remotely allied with religion. Mechanism had the sanction of science. And the theory of evolution, with its emphasis on the ruthlessness of the struggle for survival, was merely an extension on a larger scale of what he himself had observed in Indiana, in Chicago, and in New York. He was untrained in the ways of rigorous analysis; and the materialism he accepted on affective rather than logical grounds was reduced by him to the notion of "chemisms," a word which has no doubt on him a strong and subtle emotive power. Through "chemism" he thinks he explains adequately all phenomena, organic no less than inorganic. Life is chemism, personality is chemism, the emotions are chemisms. There can really be no difference between the urge of the lower animals, human sex desire, and any sentiment that we have agreed to call higher. The animal in the darkness of the forest, Casanova, Dante, and Petrarch, as well as the Marquis de Sade or an Indiana young couple on a swing under an apple tree—they are all examples of chemism, and are fundamentally but the same thing. On his conception of chemism Dreiser grounds an individualistic philosophy. He tells us, not in these terms but to the same effect, that society is a mechanical addition of atomic individuals, each an independent package of force, each a self-contained monad, determined somehow by mechanical forces, pushing or yielding, as it comes into contact with forces larger or smaller than its own. Thus society is but an additive compounding of mechanical forces, dynamically seeking a harmony which is constantly disrupted by the addition of new forces or by the disappearance of old ones. The individuals who additively make up society have each their own urges and their own strength. One seeks power, one peace, one the realization of an artist, the other security. Each encounters obstacles which baffle him or meets with helping currents which aid him toward his goal. The strong ones forge ahead, and the weak ones submit and are the tools of their betters. This is Darwinism at its starkest. When powerful individuals like Cowperwood appear, they disrupt the previously struck balance. The giants who have already arrived, and whose power is threatened by the appearance of a new one, gang up against the newcomer, use the pygmies for their purposes, the conflict quickens, and at the end, whatever the result, a new temporary balance is struck.

In such a pitiless Darwinian world, where might is ultimate lord, he tells us that it is not morality but the appearance of it that counts. The hearty acceptance of ethical principles puts a handicap on the individual in the struggle. But pretense is a useful and invaluable aid. Society is a masked ball—that beauty, dancing so gaily with that man, is an old woman, has false teeth, suffers from arteriosclerosis, and has a bad breath in the morning; and the gallant leading her may be a beggar, or a horse thief, or a rat catcher, or a clever rogue, so cleverly disguised that he can deceive even himself. There you can see a great idealist preaching democracy and the supreme worth of each human personality; everybody wonders at his kindness and admires his gentleness. But we are all easily deceived. He is really a small man with a mean soul; he preaches equality because he hates and fears excellence; and he is a mirror of kindness because he achieves through his generosity the sense of power which big-souled men achieve directly and frankly. He hates selfishness, because it interferes with his own selfishness; and he hates self-assertion, because he cannot tolerate his claims being crossed. He hates men who are arrogant, and loves modest men. But if we only look we can see he is himself the very essence of arrogance. And so with the others. Society is a masked ball. But there is one crime for which there is no forgiveness, no absolution—no man must appear in public without a mask. And a crime still greater, no man must ever tear a mask from another and leave him uncovered.

But this is not the whole picture, for Dreiser tells us that human society is made up of a number of subsocieties arranged hierarchically in terms of power and wealth, and in each one of these subdivisions the same pattern repeats itself. Within each group there are honors to be gained, privileges to be conquered, and relative ease and security to be enjoyed. And in each one, low or high, these are come by in the same way—through cunning, pitilessness, and luck.

In such a pitiless Darwinian world what can morality really mean? Morality is a technique of control, a means of keeping in check those men whose powerful and strong drives would wreck the balance struck by the group; for it is in short a conspiracy of some of the masters and the slaves to keep the parvenu from running amuck. But of course truly strong men disregard the mythical sanctions which may deceive the weak but cannot deceive them. And for that reason no moral code ever fits the facts. One of his characters, obviously speaking for Dreiser himself—for he has expressed the same idea in the first person—was "always thinking in his private conscience that life was somehow bigger and subtler, and darker than any given theory or order of living." And for this reason, "life is to be learned from life, and the professional moralist is at best but the manufacturer of shoddy wares." These wares, shoddy and gratuitous for the strong, have another purpose—they are the sole consolation of the weak and the oppressed. And they may even have an aesthetic value, like the ephemeral rainbows one often catches sight of on the spray over an angry wave; but, like them, though they may be beautiful, they are utterly ineffective for controlling the danger of the sea.

In such a world, what meaning can life have? None of course. In a world which is the product of blind forces, in a world of chemic determinations and mechanical resolutions, how can one expect that life have meaning?

> *Privately his mind was a maelstrom of contradictions and doubts, feelings and emotions. Always of a philosophic turn of mind, this peculiar faculty of reasoning deeply and feeling emotionally were now turned upon himself and his own condition and, as in all such cases where we peer too closely into the subtleties of creation, confusion was the result . . . the world knew nothing. Neither in religion, philosophy nor science was there any answer to the riddle of existence. Above and below the little scintillating plane of man's thought was —what? Beyond the optic strength of the greatest telescope—far out upon the dim horizon of space—were clouds of stars. What were they doing out there? Who governed them? When were their sidereal motions calculated? He figured life as a grim dark mystery, a sad semi-conscious activity turning aimlessly in the dark. No one knew anything. God knew nothing—least of all himself. Malevolence, life living on death, plain violence—these were the chief characteristics of existence. If one failed in strength in any way, if life were not kind*

*in its bestowal of gifts, if one were not born to fortune's pampering
care—the rest was misery. In the days of his strength and prosperity
the spectacle of existence had been sad enough: in the hours of threatened delay and defeat it seemed terrible. . . . The abyss of death!
When he looked into that after all of life and hope, how it shocked
him, how it hurt! Here was life and happiness and love in health—
there was death and nothingness—aeons and aeons of nothingness. . . .*

Dreiser's own life, a life of arduous labor and the most scrupulous artistic
sincerity, has no more meaning than that of anyone else. And this is what
he says of it in the *Bookman,* September, 1928, in a statement of his beliefs:

> *I can make no comment on my work or my life that holds either
> interest or import for me. Nor can I imagine any explanation or
> interpretation of any life, my own included, that would be either true
> —or important, if true. Life is to me too much a welter and play of
> inscrutable forces to permit, in my case at least, any significant com-
> ment. One may paint for one's own entertainment, and that of others
> —perhaps. As I see him the utterly infinitesimal individual weaves
> among the mysteries a floss-like and wholly meaningless course—if
> course it be. In short I catch no meaning from all I have seen, and
> pass quite as I came, confused and dismayed.*

III

In its most important details this is the picture of man and the universe
which Dreiser seems to believe he has discovered in his experiences and
expressed in his novels. But fortunately for his greatness as a novelist, his
explicit intellectual vision of the world is not point by point congruous
with his vision as a novelist. And the philosophy which he has given us in
essays and intercalated in the form of editorial comments in the movement of his dramas is not always true to the record. For there is more to
his own concrete dramatic picture of men and society than he finds room
for in his mechanistic philosophy. And if we miss this more, we miss, I am
afraid, what is truly significant in Dreiser. His mechanism is indeed inadequate, but his dramatic vision of the world within the range of its dis-
criminations is fully ripe and mature. His characters are alive and real,
moving and acting and brooding with all the urge and hesitation, passion
and fear, doubts and contradictions, of fully real human beings. Few contemporary novelists have built up characters as solid, as three dimensional,
as fully bodied, as Dreiser. And the reason he succeeded where others
have failed is that in spite of his naïve mechanism, few novelists respond

to human beings as sensitively as he does. He admires or pities all kinds of men—the forceful money-makers; the weak ones who are born to fail and suffer; the brilliant women who walk in and conquer; the respectable men and the disreputable ones; the masters and the slaves; the happy ones and the victims of meaningless forces who are condemned to live a life of pain, frustration, and denial.

Dreiser not only responds to human beings in a very immediate and sympathetic manner, but what is more important within the limits of his vision, he understands them. And his understanding goes far beyond the chemisms through which he thinks he explains them. For what does it mean to understand a man? Does it not mean to discover some order, some underlying direction, some permanent tendency by reference to which we as observers are able to organize what we know of him, and to decide what is important or relevant and what is not? And this is the reason we read Dreiser and read him with profit, because in spite of his chemisms, and in spite of his poor taste in words and phrases, in spite of his fuzzy prose, and his addiction to unimportant realistic detail—which is never really as unimportant as we in our impatience think it is—we discover in his books insights about human beings we did not have before.

But what is most important of all, his dramatic picture of society and of morality do not corroborate the philosophic theories which he has put forth, and which have caused such violent reaction from conservative critics. His dramatic picture of man is not a picture of the hard atomic entities which his individualistic mechanism tells him they are. Nor does he really see society, when he looks at it dramatically and not editorially, as a mere collection of atomic individuals. His characters are often a-social forces, working for ends destructive of the social equilibrium. But never completely so. Nor is society a mechanical addition of forces. Cowperwood, his reckless Robber Baron, is propelled by a strong will directed to the conquest of power and reckless of the claims of society in its search for satisfaction. But even Cowperwood is not utterly destructive, and his genius, in the pursuit of its own arbitrary ends, has a constructive side to it in quite an objective social sense. Nor is his will utterly arbitrary, nor is he utterly free and a-moral. Less so is Kalvin, a powerful but respectable and conservative business man, and Witla, the genius. We need not go any farther. The personalities and characters of his big men as well as of his small are socially determined, and this in turn means really that it is society that furnishes the shark-man with the precise mold through which his power expresses itself and sets the limits to how far that will shall express itself unchallenged. We do not need to read this into his picture of society; it is there for us to see. Some of his Titans may even be utterly devoid, as he thinks, of ordinary human ties; this is never entirely the case, but grant it. Still these Titans are what they are only in terms of the forces that shaped them, and thus it is that only in the society in which they were reared could they find the necessary outward resistance in terms of which their will can express itself. Grant this, and one has to grant that the ties one has with society are integral and internal, and the relations that exist not external to the individuals which make up society. Thus from his own picture he could have seen that society is an organic pattern and it makes the individual possible as much as the individual makes it possible. If we consider the dramatic picture and disregard the editorial bias, morality is not a club with which the individual is struck down and kept in line. It is, properly conceived, the molds in which the activities of individuals express themselves. There can be no matter without form, no activity without style. And the morality of any society is but the permissible style of activity; the manner in which individuals which are organic parts of it act.

Thus conceived, morality is always larger than the explicit codes through which men say they rule their actions, and life larger than any of its codes and rules, as Dreiser claims. But it cannot be larger than the forms and manners in which it expresses itself. "Life is larger than morality," only if morality is a set of rules, a code, which is fixed once for all and is too rigid to give way. And of course the moralist's wares are then shoddy wares. But it is co-extensive with living if it is conceived as the manner life finds in which to express itself and through which it channels its forces. The mechanistic, atomistic conception of society and the belief that the individual is prior to it in both a logical and existential sense make this notion of morality incomprehensible. But a more acceptable conception of society would urge as part of it the dependences, the interconnections, and the often deep and obscure bonds which underlie many of the stresses felt by men in daily life. Even in overt conflict, interdependences exist and rules of behavior obtain. Men cannot live in utter and complete chaos. There are laws and rules of war as well as of peace. Normally men simply have to trust others and depend on them mutually to some extent at least. Nor are we free, even the least sentimental of us, from loyalties and sympathies and deep-rooted commitments to value. Factors such as these, bonds, ties, forces, deep interconnections, are always found. And they make up society as much as the will of the strong and the yielding of the weak. And they do so in Dreiser's pictures as much as they do in actuality.

Why does he not see this? The phenomenon is common. It is simply the common failure of readjusting theory to facts. Dreiser does not find the moral code in which he was brought up by a narrow and intense father anywhere operative in the world into which, ill equipped but sensitive, he was thrust. Therefore, he concludes, there is no morality. But why is there not? Because emotionally he has never ceased to demand that morality be what he was taught it was—a rigid code, where idealism is always unmistakably good, and selfishness always an unalloyed evil. Yet in his novels Dreiser shows that morality is actually operative in the world, even though it is the editorial philosopher who efficaciously undertakes to squeeze on the palette of the artist the hues with which the latter paints; or, to put it directly, Dreiser does find morality, although his philosophic prejudices succeed to some extent in controlling his artistic vision and limiting it to the lowest and least admirable values. Yet for all his prejudices, his characters are capable of pity, of courage, and occasionally even of idealism, as often as they are of ruthless strength and indifference to their fellows. And for all the successful exercise of arbitrary force with which, with impunity, some men seek to control their fellows, in Dreiser's pages we find that in some sense and to some degree society is nevertheless regulated by immanent moral forces, guided by values that control, however haltingly and weakly, the actions of the strongest no less than of the weakest of men.

Essentially the same can be said of Dreiser's conviction that life has no meaning. Equipped with his materialistic lenses, Dreiser reports he cannot find in the cold ranges of the universe a direction to guide us and give our activity the assurance of transcending significance that we all so profoundly crave. Hence his perplexity, his sense of futility, his monotonous refrain regarding the vanity of effort in such a sorry world. But would he have been as disappointed as he was, were it not for the fact that, in spite of his philosophic commitments, he insisted on purpose, and that his dramatic vision suggested to him, in however confused a way, that his demand was capable of some sort of objective satisfaction? For in spite of his futilitarian philosophy, his characters never genuinely lacked guiding purposes. One of his characters finds the meaning of his activity in success, another in power, another in love, and another in religion. Dreiser himself found it in his uncompromising expression of his vision of life. What other meaning can life have for the novelist than that which is defined by the values his characters espouse? That Dreiser painted men and women as capable of espousing values shows that he saw, although his philosophy did not allow him to acknowledge, that life has in fact purpose. Whether the meaning that his characters find in their lives is anchored in the nature of Being itself or not, is no problem that the novelist (unless he is depicting technical philosophers inquiring into the problem of axiology) need concern himself with; nor is it a problem that as novelist he is equipped to solve. But why, if Dreiser demanded meaning and if he found it in his novels, did he not acknowledge it? Obviously what happened was that

Dreiser the artist was never allowed to challenge the philosophic editor. But fortunately for us, neither did the philosophic lenses of the editor succeed in altogether obfuscating the artist's vision. Dreiser thought he knew that the universe is a purposeless affair; but fortunately for his art he never did learn the lesson his philosophy should have taught him, namely that for a consistent mechanist the very demand for meaning is nonsensical. Fortunately the sincere artist magnificently contradicted the self-taught materialist and found a purpose that, had he been consistent, he could not have found.

Thus Dreiser is a better artist than his philosophy permitted him to be. As philosophic editor, he insisted in pointing out to the reader that the picture he painted was meaningless and that the lives of his characters had no purpose. But within his novels his men and women frequently find that life has a driving significance which overpowers them. Sometimes the meaning it has is sinister; sometimes pathetic; sometimes it almost reaches tragic heights; but meaning it usually has. And if life's meaning is something sad or tragic, in Dreiser's own life, in his enormous capacity for pity, we find an example of a man who, through his work, gave the lie to his own theories.

Charles Child Walcutt

THEODORE DREISER AND THE
DIVIDED STREAM

The Divided Stream of American transcendentalism is the source and indeed the being of what is called the naturalistic movement in our fiction. The essence of transcendentalism is to be found in Emerson's assertion that Nature is the symbol of Spirit. This means that what is Ideal or Absolute as Spirit is translated into physical laws and perfectly embodied (or incarnated) as Nature. But Spirit and Nature are not actually separate for the transcendentalist. They are terms he devises to identify two aspects of the One. Spirit lives in Nature; Nature reveals and embodies Spirit. Modern physicists have come to the same monistic position through their discovery that matter and energy are not different things but only different forms or expressions of the same thing. What seems ultimately to be an electric charge expresses itself as all the forms of the physical universe. Both energy and law are "superior" to matter, but they appear only in or through matter.

Now the transcendentalist called the same elements Spirit and Nature. The former was accessible to Intuition or inspiration; the latter to scientific investigation. Emerson said, "Nature is the symbol of Spirit," and "The axioms of physics translate the law of ethics." Here is the whole system. But the system did not stay whole. The monist stream did not stay One. Just as the language of analysis initially divided it with two words, so time and experience divided it into poles of optimism and pessimism, freedom and determinism, will and fate, social reformism and mechanistic despair. The optimism and idealism of Spirit could not remain identified with the dazzling but terrifying preoccupation with the forces of alien nature, for the Nature which was assumed to be a version of man's spirit and therefore of his will appeared under scientific analysis as a force which first controlled man's will and presently made it seem that his freedom was an illusion, that there was no such thing as will but only chemicals performing reactions which could (theoretically, at least) be pre-dicted.

From *PMLA*, March, 1940. Revised for this volume.

This is the divided stream. It accounts, originally, for America's devotion to facts, to things, to order, efficiency, and knowledge, for her belief that the liberation of the human spirit will be accomplished through the mastery of nature. And it thus accounts for the manner in which our devotion to science and fact has led us to the point where natural law seems to deny freedom and indeed the very concept of Spirit. It accounts for the fact that naturalism has been described, by competent critics, as both "optimistic progressivism" and "mechanistic determinism." Surprisingly enough, it can be both, for a novel that shows a hapless individual destroyed by social or hereditary forces over which he has no control can at the same time and through this very action express outraged idealism and demonstrate the need for reform through either social or scientific knowledge. A step further, however, and we come to the point where naturalism moves through a meaningless cosmos where non-human law is king and the individual can watch and experience and perhaps be destroyed, but cannot finally convince himself that human will or reason can dominate nature.

Theodore Dreiser drank his inspiration from both branches of the divided stream. He has been described as a pessimist, a socialist, a communist; he has been said to embody the antithesis of American transcendentalism; he has himself acknowledged beliefs in the meaninglessness of life, in the moral autonomy of the superman, in the ultimate value and dignity of the individual. In his later works he has placed mind above matter. And even while he was writing his early books he believed in a mystical Cosmic Consciousness that one would hardly have suspected from reading those books. His mixture of despair and idealism, of wonder and fear, of pity and guilt, of chemistry and intuition has given us the most moving and powerful novels of the naturalistic tradition. Examined chronologically, they reveal naturalistic ideas struggling to find a structure by which the novel could move without turning upon crucial ethical choices. They also reveal a continuous *ethical* questioning of tradition, dogma, received morality, and social "justice." Thus they always contain the antithesis of their materialistic premises. Between the poles of this tension is Dreiser's "naturalism." It moves, during his literary career, through phases of objectivity, resignation, and protest toward the groping affirmation of spirit that presides over and, oddly, defeats his final work.

Psychologically, Dreiser is his own divided stream of pity and guilt, of wonder and terror, of objectivity and responsibility. He observes a world without meaning, yet he also responds to a compelling need to believe. Misery in any form moved the young Dreiser to tears. Throughout *A Book About Myself* one of the dominant notes is Dreiser's wondering sympathy for the pain which life inflicts in the form of hunger, weariness, and uncertainty on those whom poverty and suffering have already rendered inarticulate.

Dreiser's repeated references in his early books to the "chemical compound which is youth," the "chemic force" within the mind, "the chemic formula which works to reproduce the species," show that he believed in a sort of mechanistic psychology. He did not pretend to comprehend the workings of the mind, but he was *apparently* sure that there is nothing transcendental in it. This real but as yet unexplained phenomenon of human thought and vitality he deprived of some of its mystery by naming it "chemic." The notion that mental activity is a chemical reaction is not, of course, a full explanation of that activity, and nowhere does Dreiser suggest that it does constitute such a full explanation. He still recognized some wonderful mystery, some all-important force, which gives life its wonder and terror and meaning. Again and again in his autobiography, *A Book About Myself* (1922), he broods over the impermanence of life and his conviction that only living is of absolute value.

> *When one was dead one was dead for all time. Hence the reason for the heartbreak over failure here and now; the awful tragedy of a love lost, a youth never properly enjoyed. Think of living and yet not living in so thrashing a world as this, the best of one's hours passing unused or not properly used. Think of seeing this tinkling phantasmagoria of pain and pleasure, beauty and all its sweets, go by, and yet being compelled to be a bystander, a mere onlooker, enhungered but never satisfied.*

This yearning is everywhere in his books; it is a part of his temperament which we must feel in order to understand the peculiar qualities that he brought to his writing. As a materialist, then, he recognized, in *The "Genius"* (1923), that man is not in control of his destiny:

> *Most of these young men (reporters) looked upon life as a fierce, grim struggle in which no quarter was either given or taken, and in which all men laid traps, lied, squandered, erred through illusion; a conclusion with which I now most heartily agree.*

In this connection the account he gives of his first acquaintance with the works of Herbert Spencer, in about 1893, is worthy of quotation:

> *I fear that I cannot make you feel how these things came upon me in the course of a few weeks' reading and left me numb, my gravest fears as to the unsolvable disorder and brutality of life eternally veri-*

fied . . . There was of course this other (note the dichotomy) matter of necessity, internal chemical compulsion, to which I had to respond whether I would or no. I was daily facing a round of duties which now more than ever verified all that I had suspected and that these books proved. With a gloomy eye I began to watch how the chemical —and their children, the mechanical—forces operated through man and outside him, and this under my very eyes . . . and when I read Spencer I could only sigh. All I could think of was that since nature would not or could not do anything for man, he must, if he could, do something for himself; and of this I saw no prospect, he being a product of these selfsame accidental, indifferent and bitterly cruel forces.

Science did not appeal to Dreiser. He had had so much experience with human misery that it did not seem to him possible to achieve any reasoned explanation of the riddle of life. On the contrary he was endlessly impressed by the instances he saw of life's steady and purposeless flux: "What a queer, haphazard, disconnected thing this living was!" ". . . life is haphazard and casual and cruel; to some lavish, to others niggardly." "But as I wandered about I realized . . . that life was a baseless, shifting thing, its seeming ties uncertain and unstable and that that which one day we held dear was tomorrow gone, to come no more." "The tangle of life, its unfairness and indifference to the moods and longings of any individual, swept over me once more weighing me down far beyond the power of expression." This wonder at the ceaseless, confusing flux of life is elaborated in his book of "philosophy," the very title of which—*Hey Rub-a-Dub-Dub; A Book of the Mystery and Terror and Wonder of Life* (1919)—is an expression of his characteristic attitude toward cosmic forces.[1]

The combination of his observations with his philosophy could produce only moral and ethical agnosticism; and indeed if his autobiography is to be relied upon Dreiser had lost faith in conventional moral codes long before he had come upon the writings of Spencer. We find him declaring, in *A Book About Myself,* that "I am inclined to suspect that the monogamous standard to which the world has been tethered much too harshly for a thousand years or more now is entirely wrong. I do not believe that it is Nature's only or ultimate way of continuing or preserving itself. Nor

---

[1] Dreiser's wide and sympathetic vision of life, his willingness to see and think about its sordid side, make one respect him for failing to arrive at a categorical explanation for the meaning of it all. If the philosopher must withdraw into an ivory tower in order to round out his system, the man who deals with the whole moving pathos of life-as-it-is should not be without some admiration. The practice among academic critics of disposing of Dreiser as a "peasant" or a "journalist" who could not think things through is based, if it has a base, upon ignorance of his personal experience.

am I inclined to accept the belief that it produces the highest type of citizen." And not only did he distrust the unthinking Christian repression of sex—he was concerned with the importance of the sexual urge in normal human life and with the impossibility of giving an authentic or rounded picture of human activity without taking full cognizance of its ubiquitous pressure and stimulation. "Via sex gratification—or perhaps better, its ardent and often defeated pursuit—comes most or all that is most distinguished in art, letters and our social economy, but underneath each and every one of such successes must primarily be written a deep and abiding craving for women, or some one woman, in whom the sex desires of any one person for the time being are centered. 'Love' or 'lust' (and the one is but an intellectual sublimation of the other) moves the seeker in every field of effort," he wrote in *Hey-Rub-a-Dub-Dub*.[2]

A warm, boundless human sympathy; a tremendous vital lust for life with a conviction that man is the end and measure of all things in a world which is nevertheless without purpose or standards; moral, ethical, and religious agnosticism; contact with the scientific thought of the late nineteenth century which emphasized the power and scope of mechanical laws over human desires; belief in a chemical-mechanistic explanation of the human machine; plus an overarching yearning for faith—these are the elements which Dreiser brought to the writing of his novels. Determinism did not attract him as a working hypothesis because he was more interested in the mystery and terror and wonder of life itself than in tracing those forces which might account for and so dispel the mystery.

Knowing Dreiser's life and character one avoids the pitfalls of assuming that his naturalism is derived primarily from other writers. Of literary "influences" it is sufficient to indicate that Dreiser had been urged to read Zola but had not read him when he wrote *Sister Carrie,* although he had been considerably impressed by a Zolaesque novel composed by one of his friends on a Chicago newspaper. On the other hand, he had gorged on Balzac as early as 1893-4. If literary influences were to be pursued, they would obviously point toward realism; but our concern here is to analyze the form which the naturalistic impulse received in his novels, rather than to search out the exact sources of that impulse in his reading.

Dreiser's "naturalism" found expression in four distinct stages. Different ideas about the body of theory just presented appear in succeeding novels and give them different significant forms,—until we come to his last novels, where the predominance of materialistic, non-teleological theory has gone, and in its place appears a solid affirmation of tradition and

---

[2] This book was written in 1919 and consequently shows evidence of familiarity with the Freudian approach to sex. It may be remarked, however, that Dreiser's attitude toward problems of sex is substantially the same in all of his novels from 1900 to 1925.

moral restraint as the values capable of resisting the deteriorating effects of modern society.

II

In the first stage, Dreiser was expounding his conviction of the essential purposelessness of life and attacking the conventional ethical codes which to him seemed to hold men to standards of conduct that had no rational basis in fact, while they condemned others without regard to what Dreiser thought might be the real merits of their situations. The first half of this program—expounding the purposelessness of life—is the backbone of his first novel, *Sister Carrie,* published in 1900. Through a queer juxtaposition of incidents, and with only small regard for the worthiness of their impulses, one character achieves fame and comfort while another loses his wealth, social position, pride, and finally his life.

Into this novel Dreiser has brought all the vivid reality of his own experience with the dreary, beaten, downtrodden life of those who have no money, background, sophistication, and no special talent. With a deep compassion that never assumes the right to pass moral judgment upon the actions of his characters, he shows Carrie Meeber coming to Chicago from the country, drearily passing from one ill-paid and health-breaking job to another, and at length, jobless and depressed by the thought of having to return defeated to the country, setting up housekeeping with Drouet, a "drummer" whom she had met on the train as she first entered the city.

With this social and financial advance, Carrie begins to recognize class differences, to long for "better" things, even to sense Drouet's limitations. Drouet's friend Hurstwood represents the next higher level of culture and wealth. He is manager of a prosperous saloon, he owns a fine house, and his family is eagerly climbing the social ladder. When he meets Carrie he falls desperately in love with her and, in what almost amounts to an abduction, he abandons his family, steals $10,000 from his employer, and flees with her through Canada and into New York.

From this point the fall of Hurstwood and the rise of Carrie are depicted in antiphonal relationship. Hurstwood's degeneration is a remarkable representation of the meaninglessness, almost unmotivated sort of tragedy that art had, until then, conspired to ignore. His wife's grasping jealousy and pettiness impel him towards Carrie, and his being seen with her gives his wife grounds for a divorce action. It is by the merest chance that he finds the safe open on the very night when he had planned to disappear. His theft of the money results from a frantic impulse which he is too weak to resist. When he tries to return the cash to the safe, he finds that the lock has clicked shut. So the theft is consummated by an accident. He is later forced to return the money, but he never recovers his self-esteem. In New

York he takes a half interest in a second-rate saloon and after a time loses his investment. Then he dawdles, first looking for jobs, finally sitting in hotels instead of looking; at length he stays home, reading newspapers endlessly and hoarding the little money he has left. The change in his character from an affluent good-fellow to a seedy miser is convincing and pathetic. Carrie stays with him as long as she can; but when she gets a place in a stage chorus she leaves him in order to room with a girl who is dancing in the same chorus. Hurstwood goes down—to poverty, destitution, begging, starvation, and finally suicide.

As he is drawing nearer to his sordid death, Carrie climbs rapidly until she is earning what was to her an unheard-of salary, living in one of the finest hotels in the city, and receiving proposals and attentions from men as far superior to Hurstwood at his best as he had been to the flashy Drouet: "Even had Hurstwood returned in his original beauty and glory, he could not have allured her." The book ends on a note of uncertainty. Carrie is not to be thought of as having attained any final goal. She is still longing and wondering, "an illustration of the devious way by which one who feels rather than reasons may be led in the pursuit of beauty. Though often disillusioned, she was still waiting for that halcyon day when she should be led forth among dreams become real."

Contemporary reviewers denounced the sordid content and the amoral attitude. They saw no inevitable punishment for transgression and no suggestion that there ought to be, but they missed the moral overtones; for although Dreiser appeals to Nature and rejects conventional moral codes, he also gropes beyond Nature toward a Transcendental concept of Spirit. He defends Drouet's "natural" pursuit of Carrie and suggests that his "conscience" is society's imposition: "He would need to delight himself with Carrie as surely as he would need to eat his heavy breakfast. He might suffer the least rudimentary twinge of conscience in whatever he did, and *in just so far he was evil and sinning*" (italics are mine). But Drouet's spontaneity reflects—or at least promises—something higher than impulse. "We have but an infantile perception of morals. There is more in the subject than mere conformity to a law of evolution. It is yet deeper than conformity to things of earth alone." Later he writes that man will be free when the conflict within him between instinct and will has been resolved,—that is, when the division between imperfect impulse and imperfect reason has been transcended into what the Transcendalists called Reason or Intuition. This development would erase the distinction between nature and Spirit.

A consciously scientific use of detail appears when Dreiser brings chemical physiology to the explanation of Hurstwood's mental condition as he is beginning his final downward plunge:

> *Constant comparison between his old state and his new showed a balance for the worse, which produced a constant state of gloom or, at least, depression. Now it has been shown experimentally that a constantly subdued frame of mind produces certain poisons in the blood, called katastates, just as virtuous feelings of pleasure and delight produce helpful chemicals called anastates. The poisons generated by remorse inveigh against the system, and eventually produce marked physical deterioration. To these Hurstwood was subject.*

This, in small compass, is a clear-cut instance of the influence of science upon Dreiser's method: he is approaching his problem with a new set of instruments. The chemical explanation for mental conditions is of a piece with the amoral outlook and change of focus away from ethical plot-conflict toward the dispassionate *observation* of life. This latter problem brings one to the heart of what is new in the form of *Sister Carrie*.

Structurally, the novel consists of the two life cycles which are opposed to each other in studied balance. What *Sister Carrie* exhibits that is most characteristically naturalistic is the complete absence of ethical plot-complication. The movement of the novel does not depend upon acts of will by the central figures. It is the movement of life—skillfully selected and represented by the artist, to be sure, but still a movement which has little resemblance to the typical plot that begins with a choice or crucial action and ends with the satisfaction of the forces set in motion by that choice. There is no suspense created because the art of the novelist is directed by an entirely different motive. It is the quality of the lives represented that moves the reader, not the excitement of what the characters do. Here Dreiser reflects the impressionism of Crane and strikes a note that we hear later in the work of Sherwood Anderson, where a very different sort of writer has in a different way presented the qualities of experience instead of choices and results. Having deprived his novel of the conventional structure, Dreiser supplies the two cycles—Carrie's rise and Hurstwood's descent. These two cycles embody the principle of change which Dreiser finds fundamental to all life and all natural processes. In a naïve mechanist's novel they would pretend to embody social laws. Not so with Dreiser.

Dreiser, primarily a novelist, never subordinates human values to philosophical implications. The reader is interested in Carrie as a person who faces problems comparable to his own; and if the reader is not to be offended by the course of the story, the successes and failures of the characters must in some way answer to the reader's notion of their worth as human beings. Because of this fact, ethical standards can hardly be eliminated from any novel. Carrie's rise, even though accidental, and not, by conventional standards, "deserved," is welcome because she is an appealing character; and Hurstwood's degeneration, distressing though it may be, is not unbearably offensive because Hurstwood has qualities which cause him to lose some of the reader's sympathy. The philosopher in Dreiser makes concessions to the novelist because his heart is in league with humanity. This is another way of saying that what happens in a piece of fiction must be probable, and probability includes the satisfaction, to some degree, of the moral sense. Hardy's *Return of the Native* appears to turn upon the cruellest coincidences, and yet each character in it experiences a morally probable fate. So with Dreiser. One cannot write stories in which, just as the crisis is approaching, the villain is killed by a falling meteor. Such things may occur in life, but they cannot in novels, which in their design and organization depict a truth that is free from the outrageous accidents of actuality. With these reservations, we may return to the assertion that *Sister Carrie* is organized to demonstrate the essential purposelessness of life. The plot structure of conventional fiction is abandoned for the new organization that answers to Dreiser's view of life.

But though he recognizes the operation of external forces, he is not, in *Sister Carrie,* concerned with an experimental demonstration of the nature of that operation. Rather he is concerned with the pathos of human life and with the constant inscrutable change that attends it. We come, in the last analysis, to a matter of emphasis: one may study the way external forces operate upon men, attempting to lay bare the secrets of their action; or one may see life through the eyes of the objects of these forces, with the wonder and terror of the changes unexplained. Dreiser does a little of both: he shows clearly enough how Hurstwood and Carrie change as they do; but mostly he is concerned with bringing out the shifting, uncertain, mysterious nature of experience as it appears when being acted upon by forces which it cannot fathom and which—most terrible truth—have no purpose that can be related to the purposes of men.

Dreiser believes in a determinism which destroys or modifies the moral view of conduct. He is, further, impressed by the inscrutability of fortune, the lack of meaning and purpose in the action of external forces. Between these two smothering convictions flourishes his affirmation—his belief in the vitality and importance of life. It is upon the latter that one's attention is directed in *Sister Carrie*. The inscrutable variations of fortune serve chiefly to underline the positive quality of life—shifting, elusive, unaccountable—that holds our attention, rather than the spectacle of carefully analyzed forces operating under "experimental" conditions.[3]

[3] The gap between Dreiser's work and the experimental novel of Zola is a wide one, for Dreiser does not make even a pretense of controlling his conditions and discovering truths about the nature of human psychology and physiology. Just where Zola, for example, would

Jennie Gerhardt (1911) is a sort of companion-piece to *Sister Carrie,* with the same major ideas but a shift in emphasis. In the latter, conventional moral codes are assumed to be invalid, while the action is concerned with demonstrating the unpredictable flux of life. In *Jennie Gerhardt* this unpredictable flux is assumed, and the action turns upon the moral and ethical standards according to which society (supposedly) operates. We see how the life of a lovely and sympathetic woman is blighted because her conduct is "officially" immoral; and the effect of the story is to suggest that standard Christian morality is inadequate either to guide or to judge conduct in a world that does not, as Dreiser sees it, answer to the assumptions underlying that code.

Jennie is a girl to whom life "is a true wonderland. . . . From her earliest youth goodness and mercy had molded her every impulse." A wealthy and distinguished Senator discovers her scrubbing floors in his hotel and, enchanted by her beauty and charm, decides to marry her; but he dies suddenly, before the marriage, leaving Jennie pregnant. After the child is born, the disgraced family moves to Cleveland where Jennie presently meets Lester Kane, scion of a wealthy Cincinnati family. He is generous, forceful, direct, and the slightest bit coarse-grained. In spite of his wealth and good breeding, the reader is made to feel that he is, emotionally, less beautifully constructed than Jennie, though he is capable of appreciating her fine nature and is, indeed, worlds beyond her culturally. Most of the book is devoted to their changing relations. He keeps her in various apartments, supplying her liberally with money, always half intending to marry her but never quite making up his mind to disturb the comfortable *status quo.*

Then forces conspire to take Lester away from her. His father dies, leaving Lester's inheritance contingent upon his abandoning Jennie. His family brings all its persuasive force to bear. And, to sweep aside the last hesitation, Lester is attracted by a cultivated and wealthy widow who is deeply in love with him. As always, Jennie is wholly unselfish in wanting Lester to do what is best for himself—and it is he who is uncertain which way to turn, drawn at once by loyalty to Jennie, fascination for Mrs. Gerald, the desire to retain his accustomed wealth and to be active in his father's business, and the influence exerted by his family and the polite society which wants him to become finally "respectable." Social ostracism, combined with the loss of a large part of his independent fortune, which makes Lester's need for a share in his father's estate more pressing, finally

---

theoretically put most emphasis—i.e. in the extraction of laws about human nature—Dreiser is most uncertain and most sure that no certainty can be attained. To him such laws would be fruitless for the very reason that external conditions cannot ever be controlled—a fact of which all his experiences had convinced him.

turn the balance against Jennie—though it is she who urges him to go. At a subsequent meeting he tries to explain his feelings:

> *"I was just as happy with you as I ever will be. It isn't myself that's important in this transaction apparently; the individual doesn't count much in the situation . . . All of us are more or less pawns. We're moved about like chessmen by circumstances over which we have no control. . . .*
>
> *"After all, life is more or less of a farce," he went on a little bitterly. "It's a silly show. The best we can do is to hold our personality intact. It doesn't appear that integrity has much to do with it."* [4]

Stricken with a fatal illness, he calls her to his death bed, where he tells her,

> *"I haven't been satisfied with the way we parted. It wasn't the right thing, after all. I haven't been any happier. I'm sorry. I wish now, for my own peace of mind, that I hadn't done it. . . . It wasn't right. The thing wasn't worked out right from the start; but that wasn't your fault. I'm sorry. I wanted to tell you that. I'm glad I'm here to do it."*

The story ends with Jennie at the station for a last glimpse of the coffin. Her child has died, Lester is gone, she is destitute.

A novel with a "kept woman" for its central figure would be somewhat unusual, but when that kept woman is presented as good and admirable, as possessing positive virtues which raise her quite above the general run of socially minded people, we recognize a novel in which conventional values are challenged, in which an unusual approach is taken to the problem of man in society.

In Jennie's world good intention and beauty of character are not necessarily rewarded. Nor is what is conventionally called evil punished. Hence standard ethics are discredited because they do not represent a realistic interpretation of social relations. They do not constitute the genuine forces which make for social cohesion and regulate the conduct of civilized men. This assumption is fundamental in *Jennie Gerhardt*. As the hero says, "The best we can do is to hold our personality intact." Jennie's goodness is valued more highly than the society which destroys her chance for happiness. Dreiser does not show that there may be extenuating circumstances to pardon the sinfulness of the "fallen woman." He denies that she is sinful; he deplores the moral codes which, failing to restrain her first

[4] This passage is notable as the most explicit statement of belief in the novel. It comes from Lester, but it represents Dreiser's own attitude because it is virtually the thesis of his novel.

slip, inflict a consciousness of guilt upon her ever after; he considers her good and beautiful, and the reader is led to conclude that Lester Kane was foolish (or very unlucky) not to have married her. These conclusions suggest that Dreiser believes in a spiritual truth which exists above the flux and error of actuality. He does not account for it, but he affirms its presence in Jennie and he deplores through his novel the social conditions which blight its growth and free expression.

But the pathos of Jennie's life is the outstanding fact of the novel, the fact upon which may depend any ideas that the reader may gather. As a work of art *Jennie Gerhardt* is highly successful; the ideas upon which it is based serve first of all to create a certain aesthetic effect and do not obtrude themselves in the way of that effect. It is too bad that Jennie should suffer, and the system is to be deplored for making her suffer, but that is not tantamount to saying that the institution of marriage, for example, should be rejected. It would indeed detract from the pathos of Jennie's situation if the author were crusading for change. The conditions which crush her must, for the purpose of the novel, be regarded as unchangeable.

III

In the second stage of his development Dreiser added the idea of the superman to the two main ideas which I have described. When one had found that life was meaningless and morals absurdly inadequate, the next step was to conclude that the only good lay in exercising one's will to power. The philosophy of the superman was conveniently available to enable Dreiser to take this step; and he wrote four novels about the activities of supermen in the modern business world. Nietzsche's philosophy saw in the superman the only hope for the betterment of mankind. Dreiser may have known this aspect of Nietzsche's thought, he may even have begun *The Financier* with the intention of demonstrating some such idea, but his study of the activities of one of the Robber Barons of the late nineteenth century seems finally to have drawn him away from the notion that the financial superman was an indispensable agent in the development of a capitalistic society.

Dreiser's "Trilogy of Desire," composed of *The Financier* (1912), *The Titan* (1914), and *The Stoic* (1947), represents his efforts to set forth the life of a modern financial superman. Although written from the point of view of the superman and begun as a celebration rather than an indictment of him, these novels virtually accomplished Jack London's avowed but unfulfilled purpose in writing the *Sea Wolf*—to show that "the superman cannot be successful in modern life . . . , he acts like an irritant in the social body." This cannot be called Dreiser's purpose, however, for he never arrived at that degree of conviction which would permit him to organize a portion of the social scene and write about it as if he had thought his way through to a final conclusion about its meaning. It is the planlessness and inconclusiveness of life that interested Dreiser. On the other hand, nearly all critics have ceased accusing him of being merely a patient recorder who copied his books tediously from newspaper records. The organizing hand of the artist is always present, but its purpose is not to reduce the complexity of life to a prettily simplified pattern that answers all one's questions about cause and effect, design and purpose.

The Financier and *The Titan* contain perhaps the greatest mass of documentation to be found in any American novels in the naturalistic tradition. They are records of an epoch of American life. The career of Charles T. Yerkes, traction magnate of Philadelphia and Chicago, supplied Dreiser with the materials for his two books. Yerkes is transformed into Frank Algernon Cowperwood, and the novels record his economic and amorous affairs in minutest detail. *The Financier* takes Cowperwood from boyhood up to the panic of 1873. A "superman" devoid of ethical restraints, he goes from business to business, gaining control of the Philadelphia street-railway network, and becoming involved with political graft. He becomes a millionaire and is laying plans to make a billion when the Chicago fire in 1871 causes a panic which wipes out his fortune. Because he seduced the daughter of the political boss, he is at this time abandoned by those in control and made a scapegoat for an indignant populace. After thirteen months in prison he is pardoned just in time to regain his fortune by selling short in the panic of 1873. Here ends *The Financier*.

The Titan is longer and more detailed. It tells how Cowperwood moves to Chicago and, through bribes and cleverness, gains a number of franchises for the distribution of suburban gas. After this coup he launches into a long fight to gain control of all the Chicago street railways. The facts are all there, vividly realized and brought to life. And since the affairs of Cowperwood are part and parcel of this vast economic complex, the recording of its intricacies is documentation in the closest naturalistic tradition. It is setting, condition, and material for the novel; none of it is extraneous, none gratuitous, because it is all a part of Cowperwood's career.

It has been shown in the discussion of both *Sister Carrie* and *Jennie Gerhardt* that Dreiser's determinism is determinism *after the fact*. That is, he does not pretend to go behind an act of so-called will and show all the conditions and pressures of which it is composed. In *The Financier* and *The Titan* there is the same attitude toward man and society, but the situation is greatly altered by a change in one of the factors of the problem. The factor of course is Frank Algernon Cowperwood. Instead of being relatively weak like Carrie, Hurstwood, Jennie, and Lester Kane, Cowperwood is endowed with tremendous energy and ability. He is born to conquer, and he knows it. Toward the end of *The Titan* he is still strong:

> *he seemed a kind of superman, and yet also a bad boy—handsome, powerful, hopeful . . . impelled by some blazing internal force which harried him on and on.*

He is the apotheosis of individualism, the man who moves the mass, which "only moves forward because of the services of the exceptional individual." He answers to the Nietzschean wish "that the significant individual will always appear and will always do what his instincts tell him to do."

At the end of *The Financier* Cowperwood has asserted himself stupendously, made and lost a great fortune, complicated the life of every banker and politician in Philadelphia, and yet, like Jennie and Lester Kane and Hurstwood, has been swept back and forth by environing forces more powerful than even his intelligence and resolution. Being a larger figure, he moves in a more elaborate complex of forces; but the forces elude his foresight and generalship and temporarily strip him of freedom and fortune.

At the end of the great struggle related in *The Titan*, when Cowperwood is temporarily defeated by the enmity his power has evoked, Dreiser expatiates upon the spectacle of his superman's career:

> *Rushing like a great comet to the zenith, his path a blazing trail, Cowperwood did for the hour illuminate the terrors and wonders of individuality. But for him also the eternal equation—the pathos of the discovery that even giants are but pygmies, and that an ultimate balance must be struck. Of the strange, tortured, terrified reflection of those who, caught in his wake, were swept from the normal and the commonplace, what shall we say? Legislators by the hundreds were hounded from politics into their graves; a half-hundred aldermen of various councils who were driven grumbling or whining into the limbo of the dull, the useless and the commonplace.*

These sentences repeat the philosophy outlined earlier in connection with *Sister Carrie* and *Jennie Gerhardt*. The action of the books involves the same wondering uncertainty, the same vision of life as purposeless and unpredictable, the same denial of ethical codes, the same recognition of external pressures which determine the courses of our lives. What distinguishes *The Financier* and *The Titan* from the two previous novels is, as we have seen, the different weight given in them to the human factor in Dreiser's equation of change. Cowperwood is a greater force than Dreiser's earlier characters, but his position in the cosmos is essentially the same.

In conclusion we may consider the ethical import of these books. Hearing about them, one's reaction is that Dreiser must have composed them as an indictment of the business methods of the Robber Barons—to show that they were social menaces who should have been extirpated. Doubtless some such conclusion comes to the reader after he has finished the novels; but so long as he is reading them Cowperwood is the hero. His morals may not be held up as exemplary for American society, but his intelligence and energy make him the center of attention and concern. Further than this, Dreiser is frequently at pains to cast doubt upon the judgments which condemn Cowperwood. Early in *The Financier,* young Cowperwood gets his first lesson in the law of tooth and fang by watching a lobster devour a squid that was placed in a tank with him in a store window. The same novel ends with a parable about the Black Grouper, a fish which survives by virtue of its ability to change color and so deceive enemy and prey alike. We are asked,

> *What would you say was the intention of the over-ruling, intelligent constructive force which gives to Mycteroperca this ability? To fit it to be truthful? To permit it to present an unvarying appearance which all honest, life-seeking fish may know? Or would you say that sublety, chicanery, trickery, were here at work? . . . The indictment is fair.*
>
> *Would you say, in the face of this, that a beatific, beneficent, creative overruling power never wills that which is either tricky or deceptive?*

The conclusion is that Christian ethics are illusory, that people should not be blamed for disobeying a code which, if followed, would render them unfit to survive.

It does not follow from this denial of conventional ethics that a Cowperwood is a boon to society. He may "move the mass," but Dreiser's own story shows that he does not move it to any good end. There is no paradox here. The point is that Dreiser is thinking in terms of the individual without sufficiently considering his social function. He is condemning "Divine Law" without apparently realizing that it often corresponds to natural law. Cowperwood cannot reasonably be condemned to hell-fire for following his natural bent, and it is natural for him to strive for power;

but his social value is another matter. Dreiser denies a beneficent guiding Purpose, and so removes moral blame; but he does not investigate the social function of Cowperwood. If he did, he would unquestionably recognize society's need to restrain such individuals. And he has done so since then.

The *"Genius"* (1915) is cut from the same block as *The Financier* and *The Titan*. Both in form and thesis it resembles those novels so closely that an extended analysis of it is unnecessary. Eugene Witla, the hero of *The "Genius,"* is a superman like Cowperwood. He is an artist rather than a financier, but otherwise he is much the same sort of person. Like Cowperwood, again, he is set loose in the turbulence of modern life and permitted to exercise his superior cunning and resourcefulness untrammeled by moral restraints or inhibiting consideration for others. Like Cowperwood he has his successes and his failures, the forces which thwart his intentions frequently being the combination of weaker people who unite in defiance of his superman self-assertion. And again, Witla's amours occupy a large portion of the story, represent the superabundance of his artistic "genius," and are responsible for several of his misfortunes. Like *The Financier* and *The Titan, The "Genius"* consists of a loosely connected sequence of events related by chronology and by the fact that Eugene Witla participates in them all. The book, furthermore, ends upon a note of wonder and uncertainty which we have found to be characteristics of Dreiser's attitude of life at this stage. And finally, the superman hero is the center of reference and attention throughout the story. His effect upon society is not considered, for Dreiser is still brooding over the place of the individual in his meaningless cosmos. *The "Genius"* is probably also the most personal of Dreiser's books. Revelation replaces theory to a considerable degree.

I V

The third stage in Dreiser's naturalism is marked by his conversion to socialism. Here the ideas that signalized his first stage remain, but instead of advocating individual anarchy, as he tended to do under the aegis of Nietzsche, he has come to believe that something can be accomplished toward the amelioration of social evils if men will unite in a concerted attack upon those evils. *An American Tragedy* (1925) is founded upon this point of view, although we must remember that this, like Dreiser's other novels, is first of all a human story.

An American Tragedy is the story of how Clyde Griffiths goes from singing hymns on the streets of Kansas City, to working as a bellhop in Chicago, to prospering in the collar factory of his wealthy uncle, and, just as he has been taken up by a rich and fascinating society girl, to discovering that his factory girl-friend is pregnant. In desperation, after weeks of torturing worry, he plans to take her boating in the country and "accidentally" drown her. At the final moment he lacks courage to overturn the boat, but Chance—or the situation produced by the two personalities in their particular relation—completes the design in another way: seeing his despairing and horrified expression, Roberta comes toward him in the boat. He strikes out desperately to fend her off and unintentionally hits her with a camera. The boat capsizes, striking Roberta as she falls into the water, and Clyde refrains from saving her.

The rest of the story is devoted to the apprehension, trial, conviction, and execution of Clyde for the murder of Roberta. As the passage referred to above indicates, Clyde himself is not perfectly sure whether or not he is guilty. Before Roberta arose and came toward him in the rowboat, he had certainly decided that he would not commit the crime he had planned. On the other hand, he instituted the expedition with murder in his heart —a fact which exerted great influence upon the final decision of the jury. The prosecution brings dozens of witnesses and traces Clyde's movements minutely. Clyde's only defense is his last-minute change of heart, for which there is no evidence and which is easily counterbalanced by the absolute proof of his murderous intentions.

From an objective point of view one can hardly blame Clyde for an action in which he was largely a weak and helpless participant. Clyde did not wilfully produce the dilemma which called forth his attempt to resolve it. His craving for wealth and social position can be understood—like his complementary lack of ethical standards—in the light of his upbringing. His weakness is contemptible to some readers, but Dreiser certainly does not condemn it. Clyde has a certain power of choice, to be sure, which Dreiser does not reduce to its ultimate chemical constituents as the first naive naturalists thought they might finally be able to do; but that power of choice, though accepted as a factor in the problem, is shown to be conditioned by the many forces among which it exists.

In *An American Tragedy,* however, there is a difference of emphasis which is intimately associated with the structure of the novel. To begin with, Clyde is doubtless the weakest of Dreiser's heroes; he has least of the inexplicable inner drive which makes a commanding personality. He begins, further, with a pitifully meager background and narrow view of life. He is no Cowperwood or Witla superman—he has not even the charm of Carrie or Jennie. And as the novel proceeds there is so careful an attention to detail and so complete a delineation of the various experiences which add to Clyde's miserable store of ideas and ideals that the reader seems to be gaining a full insight into the forces which account for the nature of Clyde's personality. It is because of the simplicity of Clyde's character and the narrowness of his initial outlook that Dreiser is able to go so far behind the phenomenon of his "will" and explain its constituents.

This greater penetration of character goes hand in hand with a considerable difference in structure; for whereas the very essence and meaning of the earlier novels is to be found in the confused and inconclusive buffeting that makes up the lives of Carrie, Jennie, or even Cowperwood, the story of Clyde Griffiths takes its integrated and undeviating way through murder, arrest, trial, and execution. This unity is characteristic of tragedy, which can occur even in a naturalist's world and give form (and even some dignity) to what would otherwise be a dreary and meaningless life.

Although this difference in structure might be attributed merely to its content, there is, furthermore, a difference between the philosophy of the *American Tragedy* and the earlier novels which justifies the assertion that it marks a third distinct stage in Dreiser's naturalism. In *The Financier, The Titan,* and *The "Genius"* Dreiser saw life through the eyes of a superman, to whom it appeared as a welter of forces among which he must try somehow to work out his individual salvation. The damage to society in the career of a Cowperwood may be discovered in the books; but the purpose of those books is not to dwell upon the social evil of his career. Similarly, Eugene Witla's career is seen as an individual's struggle, without particular social implications. In Clyde Griffiths' progress, on the contrary, social implications abound. Dreiser had been converted to socialism since writing *The "Genius";* his American tragedy is a tragedy brought about by the society in which we live. That society is responsible, as the immediate cause, for Clyde's actions. This social consciousness marks the third stage of Dreiser's naturalism. This is not to say that *An American Tragedy* is an indictment of our social order. It is first of all a work of art, the tragedy of Clyde Griffiths, a picture of a life that is tragic because the protagonist is at once responsible (as any human being feels another to be) and helpless (as the philosopher views events). . . . Clyde's tragedy is a tragedy that depends upon the American social system. It shows the unfortunate effects of that system more, for example, than did the defeat of Cowperwood at the end of *The Titan.* In the latter instance a "superman" was battling the opposition aroused by his will to power. In Clyde's case the whole of the American social order, in its normal activity, is brought into the picture.

v

I have deferred discussion of *The Stoic* because, although it completes the "Trilogy of Desire," taking up Cowperwood's career after the Chicago débâcle, it was not published until 1947, thirty-three years after *The Titan.* Dreiser had most of the book written shortly after publication of *The*

Titan, but he kept it by him because he could not, apparently, work it through to a satisfactory conclusion. In the meantime he wrote new sorts of novels which took him into new spheres of thought where it became increasingly difficult to carry through the implications of ideas which were still growing while he wrote the two earlier volumes.

The opening chapters discover Cowperwood taking stock after his expulsion from the Chicago scene. Love and business as usual are interwoven, on this occasion when Berenice Fleming, the most charming and talented woman he has known, whom he has supported through her adolescence, now in the bloom of young womanhood gives herself to him and persuades him also to undertake a new and grander venture in the world of finance. Renewed by the consummation of his love for Berenice, he lays plans to invade the traction business of London, and very soon has set in motion a gigantic scheme to unify and modernize the London underground system.

Complications appear by virtue, as usual, of the impingement of sex upon business. Lord Stane, who is to launch Cowperwood socially as well as bring his large Underground holdings into the financial pool, falls in love with Berenice. On a money-raising trip to America, Cowperwood enters a brief but intense affair with a young dancer. When his wife, Aileen, who has been temporarily shelved, reads of this she threatens to expose Cowperwood in a scandal that will ruin his British operations. But now, when the elements of a highly dramatic involvement are set before us, the story comes to an abrupt and inconclusive ending.

Cowperwood dies of Bright's disease.

Following his death, his fortune of some $12,000,000 is quickly eaten away by taxes, litigation, assessments, litigation, and more litigation. His great house and art collection are auctioned off to pay claims. There is no money to build the hospital he had arranged to leave to the City of New York. Aileen is put out of her house, forced to take an absurdly small settlement, and dies of pneumonia. We hear nothing of what happens to the great London Underground unification. Cowperwood is treated somewhat unkindly by the press, as his enormous fortune and influence evaporate when he is no longer present to maintain them. If he has been a "superman," he has made no permanent impression on society, and his material contribution of street railway systems will not provide alms for oblivion. Any larger significance of his demise is lost because Dreiser devotes most of his attention to the sordid vanity of Aileen, who deserts Cowperwood on his death bed when she learns that Berenice is seeing him.

But most striking and extraordinary of culminations is the turning of Berenice to Yogi in the concluding chapters. Here the divided stream of

American transcendentalism does astonishing things. Wandering in a chaos of pure materialistic flux, Dreiser allows his heroine in these closing chapters to leap to pure Spirit, to Brahma, and to the contemplation and realization of Divine Love. And Dreiser too seems to make the leap, because it appears beyond any question that Berenice carries his thoughts and convictions. She is the most sensitive and intelligent of his characters; she is the only one who makes significant discoveries about the folly and selfishness of even the most cultivated materialistic life; her four years of study with a Guru in India are presented with utter seriousness. This leap of Dreiser's from pure matter to pure Spirit invites various speculations and comments. The philosophical abysses of Brahmanism, with its concepts of unknowable mysteries and endless cosmic cycles of repetition, are psychologically not un-related to the abysses of purposeless flux which terrify the devoted materialist. Nor has it ever been possible to say that Dreiser denied the existence of mysteries. Always in league with humanity, from his earliest book he presented the mazes of the human quest as pathetic and compelling. He sought through his love of men to express the sense of an ideal pattern for which he had sought vainly in nature.

Viewed in artistic terms, however, Dreiser's conclusion of *The Stoic* must be considered grotesque. Berenice is too utterly brilliant and dazzling to be quite real. Her love of fine things, her absorption with herself, her whimsical intelligence, and her courageous defiance of convention in becoming Cowperwood's mistress—these are too many traits to fuse into a convincing personality. In India she ascends through all the levels of Yogi to a direct experience of the supreme Reality—a level from which it is hardly probable that she would return to New York, make the amazing discovery that there is poverty there just as in India, and so devote herself to building and working in the hospital that Cowperwood had planned. The birth of a social consciousness comes naïvely twinned to the discovery of Brahma. Another false start occurs when Berenice finds herself drawn by the culture and charm of Lord Stane. He seems to have the background that Cowperwood lacks. His interests, too, are much broader. And Cowperwood, who had sworn undying love for Berenice, has just been revealed as having a new love affair in New York. But nothing comes of this potential conflict (a favorite in American fiction, by the way), for Berenice decides that Cowperwood's attraction is irresistible. We see her at one moment shrewdly calculating a liaison of vengeance but at the next giving in to pure passion and fascination. After Berenice returned from India to discover that Cowperwood's fortune had vanished into the pockets of lawyers, she "was filled with sorrow as she inwardly viewed the wreckage of all of his plans." Now Cowperwood's plans were largely predacious and materialistic. After her years of study with the Guru, Berenice would have known that Cowperwood's desire to perpetuate his name by leaving a museum was not to be confused with the charity which suffereth all. Yet this is what she appears to do. These are all indications of Dreiser's failure to adapt his materials into an effective pattern. Too many ideas wander about the marches of his action without actually being involved in it.

What finally identifies the structural failure of this book is Dreiser's failure to manage the problem of *scale*. He began by describing financial transactions in a detail that would have carried the volume to 600 pages, but these are casually abandoned in the midst of the barest beginnings of the great London venture. The love entanglements, likewise, are given here and there such minute detail that they create the expectation of an exhaustive presentation; but they turn out to be only samples of a whole that does not take shape. The point of view shifts loosely from person to person at least a dozen times during the story. Minds are invaded and then abandoned with little regard for the values of a controlled point of view. The tired and grainy fragments of the story fall apart. The architectonics of naturalism have disappeared. Having liberated Dreiser's talent, naturalism left him with a cumbersome technique which he could not use for his newer ideas.

If Dreiser's novel appears wooden, it is because the mixture of new ideas and old is grotesque; the style and the techniques of characterization have not accommodated the new ideas. His characters are introduced and described formally—background, occupation, financial status, followed by a few words of generalization about personality or character. For example:

> *Also present were Lord and Lady Bosvike, both young and smart and very popular. They were clever at all sports, enjoyed gambling and the races, and were valuable in any gathering because of their enthusiasm and gaiety. Secretly they laughed at Ettinge and his wife, though at the same time they valued their position and deliberately set themselves out to be agreeable to them.*

This writing has not made use of modern techniques of characterization or modern concepts of personality. It illustrates rather Dreiser's consistent use of the formal Victorian categories, like honesty, diligence, and piety. This makes *The Stoic* seem old-fashioned in 1949; if "naturalism" is new and unusual, then naturalism has vanished from *The Stoic*. Where it most clearly appears is in Dreiser's treatment of love. This is anything but Victorian, for to him love is dependent upon all the social, financial, and personal forces that operate at any moment. It is a tension of lust, ambition, vanity, insecurity, and hate; an alteration in any of these elements will unbalance the tension and set it moving toward a new relationship. Dreiser is not able to exhibit this idea dramatically, but it appears again and again in the thoughts of his characters. Anyone making a new acquaintance of the opposite sex wonders what it would be like to be in love with him and adds up the various financial and social complications. Even in their moments of passion, lovers are busy assessing the *status* of their relation, for nothing is permanent and every action initiates irreversible changes. This fragment of the old Dreiser struggles rather feebly in *The Stoic* with Yogi, traces of socialism, and the writer's weariness. The return to Spirit, although it completes the broken arc of the transcendental tradition, does not furnish here a pattern for coherent fiction.

Dreiser's final novel, although published a year earlier than *The Stoic* was conceived many years later and written long after the greater part of *The Stoic* was finished. *The Bulwark* (1946) appears to represent a transitional stage between the materialism of his earlier work and the Brahminism which appears in the closing pages of *The Stoic*. It deals with three generations of Quakers in Pennsylvania. They go from piety to prosperity to perdition. The protagonist is Solon, of the middle generation, who gets rich, clings to the Inner Light, but sees his children drawn away into various forms of vice and vanity because they cannot resist the material attractions of fine clothes and automobiles or the physical attractions of sex. The novel has a double theme. Sociologically, it shows that the control exercised by a religion of simplicity like Quakerism is powerless against the lures of American materialism. Within Solon it shows the same conflict: Solon contributes to the downfall of his children because he thinks he can serve both God and Mammon. By serving Mammon he makes a lot of money, which opens up the world of ostentation and vice to his children. If they had all lived in poverty, they would not have been tempted. Yet, paradoxically, it is Solon's Quaker background that makes him sober, industrious, and trustworthy—so that he can rise to affluence as a banker. (I do not know what to say about the unquestioned fact that there have been and still are many Quaker families where wealth and simplicity do go together without difficulty, even through several generations. They do not appear in the argument of *The Bulwark*.)

The Bulwark does not reveal the mixture and confusion of communism and Yogi that appear in *The Stoic*. When Solon becomes a successful banker, rich enough to give his children the luxuries they crave, it is not suggested that he is exploiting the poor or living on the unearned increment of usury. His rise is presented as the reward of diligence and devotion. It appears in time that he has erred in believing that the moral sobriety of Quakerism could carry him through financial maneuvers unscathed; but his error is, depending upon how one regards it, either a fatal error that was inescapable under the circumstances or the error of judgment of a man who could not foresee where his commercial involvements would take him. Any Marxian analysis of his experiences must be supplied by the reader. The frivolous outlooks of his children are not attributed to the class struggle but are presented *sub specie aeternitatis;* here, he seems to say, are children growing up with false human values,—values that do not call forth the good of which these children are capable. Their lives are wasted in ostentation and frivolity.

The early Dreiser would have stressed the idea that they were not responsible for their standards; he would have implied that any standards were relative and therefore questionable. Latterly he hurried past these old and easy assumptions to consider what values are good and where they can be found. The Inner Light of Quakerism is not said to be the perfect guide, but it is a guide which made the old people strong and which sustained Solon until he meddled with such powerful gods as Mammon and Moloch. Although Quakerism is not contrasted with Buddhism or Yogi or Platonism, it is clearly presented as a way which made strong Americans; and its strength lies in its qualities of tradition and myth. These compel belief, fidelity, and discipline—without which it would appear that man is not capable of leading a coherent life. The whole book asserts that man must be guided—that is, man in modern America—by powerful attachments to an Authority that he accepts on faith. The rigid morality of Quakerism dampens spontaneity and snubs impulse. To the early Dreiser such repression was bad. Now it is good, for it is a discipline that strengthens the will and quickens the spirit. Dreiser has turned from materialistic monism to Christian dualism, from impulse to control, from nature to spirit, from iconoclasm to traditionalism, from flux to myth.

This is the first novel in which Dreiser has been confronted with the problem of advancing four or five separate actions, instead of concentrating on one person, as in his early novels, and the result is not fortunate. It is, to begin with, difficult for a writer of Dreiser's diffuseness to deal with the birth, early education, adolescence, and "end" of five children and their parents in less than 400 pages. He has performed this task through the small end of a telescope: occasional incidents are dramatized, but most are recounted hastily, in a succession of two and three-page chapters. Characters are developed only to be dropped; others live and die without ever coming to life; others are introduced, forgotten, and then embarrassingly revived for a new occasion. This failure of form reveals a literary artistry that could not keep pace with the changing times. In the historical context of 1900, a straight-line presentation of one incident after another was striking and powerful. Given a prevailing notion of form in the novel, the denial of it becomes a form. The movement of Dreiser's early novels had such a form. But without that-from-which-it-revolts the same work would be either chaotic or commonplace. Here the latter is true, for there is, in this matter, a dialectic at work; whereas in 1900 Dreiser expressed a powerful antithesis, in 1946 the same kind of form is irrelevant because several new syntheses have nullified the tension in which it formerly participated. Nor, in view of the confusion of its plots, can we say that *The Bulwark* is as well constructed as *Sister Carrie*. Today it will be asked, with genuine bewilderment, whether *The Bulwark* is naturalistic. The question would not have been asked in 1900, when it would have struck the pious reader that here was a shockingly detached presentation of moral issues: a boy who strays into vice because he has been repressed at home, who commits suicide rather than bear the shame of having been in jail, who has, in fine, not been equipped to judge wisely and so is not judged by the author. To the world of 1900 this would have seemed an attack upon the very concept of moral responsibility. Today it is commonplace.

As I have already said, Dreiser's greatness as a novelist cannot be accounted for by his naturalism. His greatness is in his insight, his sympathy, and his tragic view of life. Although *The Bulwark* reveals major shifts in his beliefs, and although it is very clumsily contrived, it could still have had all the power and greatness of *Jennie Gerhardt* or *An American Tragedy* if Dreiser had succeeded, to use James's term, in "rendering" his idea. I would not suggest that *The Bulwark* fails because Dreiser abandoned some of his old theories, for much the same view of life is there. Dreiser was bewildered because the world was too complicated and he was not equipped to understand it. Sister Carrie seeks a meaning in her experience, which she cannot find. Solon Barnes has a meaning but cannot live by it, and at the end of the book he is not unlike Carrie in wondering why events have happened as they have.

Thus the fourth stage of Dreiser's naturalism is not naturalism, after all, and it is indeed most instructive to see how easily the style, the method, and the attitudes of the early Dreiser are entirely converted in these final novels to the uses of Authority and Spirit. Having brooded long and sadly over the materialist's world, he turns away from it at the end without greatly changing his tone.

A Selected Bibliography of Dreiser Biography and Criticism

I GENERAL

ADAMIC, LOUIS. "Theodore Dreiser: An Appreciation," *Haldeman-Julius Monthly*, January-March, 1927.

ADAMS, J. DONALD. "The Heavy Hand of Dreiser," *The Shape of Books to Come*. New York, 1944.

———. *The Writer's Responsibility*. London, 1946.

ADCOCK, A. ST. JOHN. "Theodore Dreiser," *The Glory That Was Grub Street*. London, 1928.

ADLER, ELMER, ed. *Breaking Into Print*. New York, 1937.

AGAR, HERBERT. "Cynicism and Sentimentality in America," *New Statesman and Nation*, June 28, 1931.

AHNEBRINK, LARS. "Dreiser's *Sister Carrie* and Balzac," *Symposium*, VII, 1953.

ALGREN, NELSON. "Dreiser's Despair Reaffirmed in *The Stoic*," Philadelphia *Inquirer*, November 23, 1947.

ALLEN, FREDERICK. "Best Sellers: 1900-1935," *SRL*, December 7, 1935.

ALMAN, DAVID. Review of F. O. Matthiessen's *Theodore Dreiser*, Book Find Club Brochure, 1951.

ANDERSON, MARGARET. "Mr. Mencken's Truisms," *Little Review*, January, 1918.

ANDERSON, SHERWOOD. "An Apology For Crudity," *The Dial*, November 8, 1917.

———. "Dreiser," *Little Review*, April, 1916.

———. Introduction to *Free, and Other Stories*. New York (The Modern Library), 1925.

———. Introduction to *Horses and Men*. New York, 1923.

———. *Sherwood Anderson's Memoirs*. New York, 1942.

———. *The Portable Sherwood Anderson*, ed. Horace Gregory. New York, 1949. Contains a letter to Dreiser, and an essay titled "Dreiser."

ANON. Reviews of *America Is Worth Saving*: *Christian Century*, February 26, 1941; *New Yorker*, February 8, 1941; *Social Studies*, November, 1941.

———. "American Writers Look Left," London *Times Literary Supplement*, February 22, 1936.

———. "The Best Short Stories of Theodore Dreiser," *New Yorker*, March 29, 1947.

———. "*Chains*," *Outlook*, June 22, 1927.

———. "*Chains*, Lesser Novels and Stories," *America*, July 16, 1927.

———. "*The Color of a Great City*," *Outlook*, January 9, 1924.

NOTE: *NR = New Republic*; *SRL = Saturday Review of Literature*

———. "Counsel From Hollywood," *Time,* February 3, 1941.

———. "Dark Blue Dreiser," *Literary Digest,* July 26, 1930.

———. "*Dreiser and the Land of the Free,*" *Cresset,* February, 1947.

———. "Dreiser En Passant," *Bookman,* February, 1918. On Stuart P. Sherman's criticism of Dreiser.

———. "*Dreiser Looks at Russia,*" *Dial,* March, 1929.

———. "*Dreiser Looks at Russia,*" *Spectator,* August 24, 1929.

———. "Dreiser on the Sins of Hollywood," *Literary Digest,* May 2, 1931.

———. "Dreiser's Arraignment of Our Intellectual Aridity," *Current Opinion,* May, 1917.

———. "Dreiser's Feud With Kentucky," *Literary Digest,* November 28, 1931.

———. "Dreiser's Novels as a Revelation of the American Soul," *Current Opinion,* September, 1917.

———. "Dreiser the Great," *Newsweek,* March 25, 1946.

———. Editorial on Paul Elmer More's attack on Dreiser. *Review,* April 17, 1920.

———. "Enemies of Society," *NR,* May 8, 1929.

———. "Final Volume," *Cresset,* September, 1948.

———. Reviews of *Free, and Other Stories: Dial,* December, 1918; *Review of Reviews,* October, 1918.

———. "Freer Verse Than Usual," N. Y. *Times,* September 10, 1926.

———. Review of "Indiana: Her Soil and Light" (*The Nation,* October 3, 1923), N. Y. *Times,* October 11, 1923.

———. "It's Nice to Dream About," *Collier's,* October 23, 1926.

———. "The Last of Dreiser," *Pathfinder,* December 3, 1947.

———. "The Last of Dreiser," *Time,* November 10, 1947.

———. "The Liberation of American Literature," London *Times Literary Supplement,* June 15, 1933.

———. "Literary Lunch," *Little Review,* August 2, 1924.

———. "Moods, Cadenced and Declaimed," *Dial,* January, 1929.

———. "Mr. Dreiser's Favorite Hero," *The Nation,* March 8, 1917.

———. "Music and Drama," *Independent,* June 26, 1916.

———. Obituaries: *Newsweek,* January 7, 1946; *Publishers' Weekly,* January 12, 1946; *Time,* January 7, 1946.

———. "Poor Dreiser," *Bookman,* November, 1932. Review of Dorothy Dudley's *Dreiser and the Land of the Free.*

———. "A Re-examination of Dreiser," London *Times Literary Supplement,* December 21, 1951.

———. "The School of Cruelty," *SRL,* February 21, 1931.

———. "The Secret of Personality as Mr. Dreiser Reveals It," *Current Opinion,* March, 1919.

———. "Should It Be Dreiser? Possible Winner of This Year's Nobel Prize in Literature," *Commonweal,* October 22, 1930.

———. "Slap! Slap!" *Literary Digest,* April 11, 1931.

———. "*The Stoic,*" *True,* January, 1948.

———. "Theodore Dreiser," *Bookman,* January, 1924.

——. "Travel at Home," *Independent,* December 4, 1916. Review of *A Hoosier Holiday.*
——. "Travel in America," *Dial,* November 20, 1916. Review of *A Hoosier Holiday.*
——. "Vale," *SRL,* January 5, 1946.
——. "Valedictory," *Time,* March 25, 1946.
——. "What's New," *Senior Scholastic,* April 29, 1946.
——. "Whither the American Writer?" *Modern Quarterly,* Summer, 1932.
ARNAVAN, CYRILLE. "Theodore Dreiser and Painting," *American Literature,* May, 1945.
ARVIN, NEWTON. "Fiction Mirrors America," *Current History,* September, 1935.
ATHERTON, GERTRUDE. "The Alpine School of Fiction," *Bookman,* March, 1922.
AUERBACH, JOSEPH S. *Essays and Miscellanies.* New York and London, 1922.
AUSTIN, MARY. "Sex in American Literature," *Bookman,* June, 1923.
AVERY, MYRTA L. "Success and Dreiser," Autumn, 1938. *Success* was a magazine which Dreiser edited.

BABBITT, IRVING, ET AL. *Criticism in America: Its Function and Status.* New York, 1924.
——. "The Critic and American Life," *Forum,* February, 1928.
BALDWIN, C. S. "Theodore Dreiser," *The Men Who Make Our Novels.* New York, 1924.
BANNING, M. C. "Changing Moral Standards in Fiction," *SRL,* July 1, 1939.
BARBOW, G. "Dreiser's Place On The Screen," *Hudson Review,* Summer, 1952.
BARRET, M. C. "Modern Writers and Religion," *Thinker,* May, 1931.
BEACH, JOSEPH WARREN. *The Outlook for American Prose.* Chicago, 1926.
——. *The Twentieth Century Novel.* New York, 1932.
BECHHOFER, C. E. *The Literary Renaissance in America.* London, 1923.
BELLOW, SAUL. "Dreiser and the Triumph of Art," *Commentary,* May, 1951. Review of F. O. Matthiessen's *Theodore Dreiser.*
BENÉT, WILLIAM ROSE. "Contemporary Poetry," *SRL,* June 29, 1935.
——. "Theodore Dreiser," *Encyclopaedia Britannica* (14th ed.). Chicago, London, Toronto, 1929.
BENNETT, ARNOLD. "The Future of the American Novel," *North American Review,* January, 1912.
——. "Books of the Year," *Savour of Life.* Garden City, N.Y., 1928.
BERG, RUBEN GUSTAFSSON. *Moderna Amerikaner.* Stockholm, 1925.
BERCOVICI, KONRAD. "Romantic Realist," *Mentor,* May, 1930.
BIRD, CAROL. "Theodore Dreiser Speaks," *Writers' Monthly,* May, 1929.
BIRSS, J. H. "Records of Theodore Dreiser: A Bibliographical Note," *Notes and Queries,* September 30, 1933.
BLACKMUR, R. P. "The Economy of the American Writer," *Sewanee Review,* Spring, 1945.
BLACKSIN, IDA. "Theodore Dreiser and the Law," Unpublished M.A. thesis, New York University, 1948.

BLACKSTOCK, WALTER. "Dreiser's Dramatizations of American Success," *Florida State University Studies,* No. 14, 1954.

BLANKENSHIP, RUSSELL. "Theodore Dreiser," *American Literature As an Expression of the National Mind.* New York, 1931.

BODENHEIM, MAXWELL. "On Writing," *SRL,* February 13, 1926. Letter attacking Anderson's article, "Dreiser," *SRL,* January 9, 1926.

BORNSTEIN, JOSEF. "Ein Dichter Besichtigt Russland," *Das Tage Buch,* February, 1929.

BOURNE, RANDOLPH. "The Art of Theodore Dreiser," *History of a Literary Radical and Other Essays.* New York, 1920. Also in *Dial,* June 14, 1917.

———. "The Novels of Theodore Dreiser," *NR,* April 17, 1915.

———. "The Puritan's Will to Power," *The Seven Arts,* April, 1917.

BOWER, MARIE HADLEY. "Theodore Dreiser: The Man and His Times: His Work and Its Reception," Unpublished Ph.D. dissertation, Ohio State University, 1940.

BOYD, ERNEST. *Portraits: Real and Imaginary.* New York, 1924.

BOYNTON, PERCY. "American Authors of Today: Theodore Dreiser," *English Journal,* March, 1923.

———. "Theodore Dreiser," *America in Contemporary Fiction.* Chicago, 1940.

BOYNTON, H. W. "Varieties of Realism," *The Nation,* May 1, 1920.

BRACE, MARJORIE. "Thematic Problems of the American Novelist," *Accent,* Autumn, 1945.

BRAINEN, JOSEPH. "Human Nature in a Crucible," *Jewish Standard,* September 30, 1932.

BROD, AXEL. "Theodore Dreiser," *Tilskueren,* January, 1930.

BROOKS, OBED. "The Problem of the Social Novel," *Modern Quarterly,* Autumn, 1932.

BROOKS, VAN WYCK. "The Literary Life in America," *Emerson and Others.* New York, 1927.

———. *Letters and Leadership.* New York, 1918.

BRUNS, FRIEDRICH. *Die Amerikanische Dichtung der Gegenwart.* Leipzig and Berlin, 1930.

BURGUM, EDWIN BERRY. "The America of Theodore Dreiser," *Book Find News,* March, 1946.

———. *The Novel and the World's Dilemma.* New York, 1947.

BURKE, KENNETH. "A Decade of American Fiction," *Bookman,* August, 1929.

CABELL, JAMES BRANCH. *Some of Us.* New York, 1930.

CAIRNS, WILLIAM B. *A History of American Literature.* New York, 1930.

CALVERTON, V. F. "Art and Social Change," *Modern Quarterly,* Winter, 1931.

———. "Left-Wing Literature in America," *English Journal,* December, 1931.

———. "Marxism and American Literature," *Books Abroad,* April, 1933.

———. "Pathology in Contemporary Literature," *Thinker,* December, 1931.

———. "Proletarianitis," *SRL,* January 9, 1937.

CARGILL, OSCAR. "Naturalists," *Intellectual America.* New York, 1941.

CARNEGIE, DALE. *Five Minute Biographies.* New York, 1937.

CARTER, JOHN. "Dreiser Reduced Literature to Its Own Level," *N. Y. Times Book Review*, August 9, 1925. Review of Burton Rascoe's *Dreiser*.

CESTRE, C. "Theodore Dreiser," *Revue Anglo-Américaine*, August, 1926.

—— and B. GAGNOT. *Anthologie de la Littérature Américaine*. Paris, 1926. Biographical note and translation of Chapter 26 of *The "Genius."*

CHAMBERLAIN, JOHN. "Minority Report of the Novelists," *Farewell to Reform*. New York, 1933.

——. "Theodore Dreiser," *NR*, December 23, 1936.

——. "Theodore Dreiser," *After the Genteel Tradition*, ed. Malcolm Cowley. New York, 1936.

CHANDLER, RAYMOND. "Writers in Hollywood," *Atlantic Monthly*, December, 1945.

CHASE, STUART. Review of *Tragic America*, *Books*, January 24, 1932.

CHESTERTON, G. K. "The Skeptic as Critic," *Forum*, February, 1929.

CHEVALIER, H. M. "Farewell to Purity," *Modern Monthly*, March, 1934.

CHURCH, RICHARD. "The American Balzac," *Spectator*, July 25, 1931.

CLARK, EDWIN. "Self-Revelations," *Yale Review*, June, 1931.

CLEATON, ALLEN and IRENE. *Books and Battles: American Literature, 1920-1930*. Boston, 1937.

COBLENTZ, STANTON A. *The Literary Revolution*. New York, 1927.

COHEN, LESTER. "Theodore Dreiser: A personal Memoir," *Discovery #4*, New York (Pocket Books), 1954.

COLUM, M. M. "Marxism and Literature," *Forum*, March, 1934.

COMBS, G. H. *These Amazing Moderns*. St. Louis, 1933.

CONRAD, LAWRENCE. "Theodore Dreiser," *Landmark*. London, 1930.

COWIE, ALEXANDER. "The New Heroine's Code For Virtue," *American Scholar*, Spring, 1935.

——. *The Rise of the American Novel*, 1938.

COWLEY, MALCOLM. "Naturalism in American Literature," *Evolutionary Thought in America*, ed. S. Persons. New Haven, 1950.

CRAWFORD, BRUCE. "Theodore Dreiser: Letter-Writing Citizen," *South Atlantic Quarterly*, April, 1954.

CRUNCHER, JERRY. "Epitaphs for Living Lions," *Forum*, July, 1928.

DANA, HARRY. "Russia Looks at Dreiser," *New Masses*, February, 1929.

DAVIS, DAVID B. "A Reappraisal of Early Naturalism in America," Unpublished paper, Harvard University, 1953.

DAVIS, ELMER. "The Red Peril," *SRL*, April 16, 1932.

DELL, FLOYD. "American Fiction," *Liberator*, September, 1919.

——. "Talks with Live Authors," *Masses*, August, 1916.

DE MILLE, GEORGE E. "American Criticism Today," *Sewanee Review*, July, 1927.

——. *Literary Criticism in America*. New York, 1931.

DICKSON, LOVAT. "The American Novel in England," *Publishers' Weekly*, October 29, 1938.

DREISER, EDWARD. "My Brother Theodore," *Book Find News*, March, 1946.

DREISER, HELEN. *My Life with Dreiser*. Cleveland, 1951.

DREW, ELIZABETH A. *The Modern Novel: Some Aspects of Contemporary Fiction.* New York, 1926.

DRUMMOND, EDWARD J., S. J. "Theodore Dreiser: Shifting Naturalism," *Fifty Years of the American Novel,* ed. Harold C. Gardiner. New York, 1951.

DUDLEY, DOROTHY. *Forgotten Frontiers: Dreiser and the Land of the Free.* New York, 1932. Republished in 1946 as *Dreiser and the Land of the Free.*

DUFFUS, R. L. "Dreiser," *American Mercury,* January, 1926. Also in *American Criticism: 1926,* ed. William A. Drake. New York, 1926.

DYNAMOV, SERGEI. "Theodore Dreiser Continues the Struggle," *International Literature,* Nos. 2-3, 1932.

EASTMAN, MAX. *The Literary Mind.* New York, 1931.

EATON, W. P. "Revolt From Realism," *Virginia Quarterly Review,* October, 1934.

EDGAR, PELHAM. "American Realism, Sex, and Theodore Dreiser," *The Art of the Novel.* New York, 1933.

ELIAS, ROBERT H. "The Library's Dreiser Collection," *The Library Chronicle,* University of Pennsylvania, Fall, 1950.

———. *Theodore Dreiser: Apostle of Nature.* New York, 1949.

———. "Theodore Dreiser: or, The World Well Lost," *Book Find News,* March, 1946.

ELVEBACK, HELEN B. "The Novels of Theodore Dreiser with an Analysis of His Other Writings," Unpublished Ph.D. dissertation, University of Minnesota, 1946.

ERNST, MORRIS. *To the Pure . . . A Study in Obscenity and the Censor.* New York, 1928.

ERSKINE, JOHN. "American Business in the American Novel," *Bookman,* July, 1931.

FADIMAN, CLIFTON. "Dreiser and the American Dream," *The Nation,* October 19, 1932.

FARRELL, JAMES T. "A Literary Behemoth Against the Backdrop of his Era," *N. Y. Times Book Review,* July 4, 1943.

———. "Social Themes in American Realism," *English Journal,* June, 1946.

———. "Some Aspects of Dreiser's Fiction," *N. Y. Times Book Review,* April 29, 1945.

———. "Some Correspondence With Theodore Dreiser," University of Pennsylvania *General Magazine and Historical Chronicle,* Summer, 1951.

———. "Theodore Dreiser," *Chicago Review,* Summer, 1946.

———. "Theodore Dreiser: In Memoriam," *SRL,* January 12, 1946.

FARRELLY, JOHN. "Finis," *NR,* December 22, 1947.

FAST, HOWARD. Introduction to *The Best Short Stories of Theodore Dreiser.* Cleveland and New York, 1947.

———. "Dreiser's Short Stories," *New Masses,* September 3, 1946.

———. "He Knew the People," *Daily Worker,* December 30, 1945.

FAY, BERNARD. "L'École de l'infortune ou la nouvelle génération littéraire aux États-Unis," *Revue de Paris,* August, 1937.

FELD, ROSE C. Interview with Dreiser. N. Y. *Times Book Review*, December 23, 1923.

FICKE, ARTHUR DAVISON. "Dreiser as Artist," *SRL*, April 17, 1926.

———. "Portrait of Theodore Dreiser," *Little Review*, November, 1915. Poem.

FIELD, L. M. "American Novelists Against the Nation," *North American Review*, June, 1933.

FISCHER, LOUIS. "Russia Adopts Dreiser," N. Y. *Herald Tribune Books*, October 4, 1931.

FISCHER, WALTHER. *Amerikanische Prosa vom Bürgerkrieg bis auf die Gegenwart (1863-1922)*. Leipzig and Berlin, 1926.

FLANAGAN, JOHN T. "Theodore Dreiser in Retrospect," *Southwest Review*, 1946.

FOERSTER, NORMAN. *American Criticism*. Boston and New York, 1928.

FOLLETT, HELEN and WILSON. "The Younger Generation," *Some Modern Novelists*. New York, 1918.

FORD, COREY. *In the Worst Possible Taste*, pseud. John Riddell. New York, 1932.

FORD, FORD MADOX. "Dreiser," *Portraits From Life*. Boston and New York, 1937. Also appeared in part in *American Mercury*, April, 1937.

FRANK, WALDO. "Chicago," *Our America*. New York, 1919.

———. "Our Arts: The Re-Discovery of America: XII," *NR*, May 9, 1928.

———. "Theodore Dreiser: the Colossus of Children," *Time Exposures*, pseud. Search-light. New York, 1926.

FREEMAN, JOSEPH. *An American Testament: A Narrative of Rebels and Romantics*. New York, 1936.

FUESSLE, NEWTON A. "An Admirer of Dreiser," *Reedy's Mirror*, September 8, 1916.

FULLER, HENRY B. "Chicago Novelists," *Little Review*, March 18, 1922.

GALE, ZONA. "Period Realism," *Yale Review*, Autumn, 1933.

GARD, WAYNE. *Book Reviewing*. New York and London, 1927.

GARNETT, EDWARD. "Criticism and Fiction," *Friday Nights*. New York, 1922.

GEISMAR, MAXWELL. "Dreiser and the Dark Texture of Life," *American Scholar*, Spring, 1952.

———. "Theodore Dreiser: The Double Soul," *Rebels and Ancestors; The American Novel, 1890-1915*. Boston, 1953.

GELFANT, BLANCHE H. *The American City Novel*. Norman, Okla., 1954.

GIBBS, DONALD. "Dreiser the Dull," *Forum*, December, 1927.

GILKES, MARTIN. "Discovering Dreiser," *New Adelphi*, December, 1928.

GISSEN, MAX. "What Must America Do?" *NR*, May 26, 1941.

GLAENZER, R. B. "Snap-Shots of American Novelists: Dreiser," *Bookman*, September, 1917. Poem, later in *Literary Snapshots*. New York, 1920.

GLICKSBERG, C. I. "Literature and Science: A Study in Conflict," *Science Monthly*, December, 1944.

———. "Proletarian Fiction in the United States," *Dalhousie Review*, April, 1937.

———. "Two Decades of Literary Criticism," *Dalhousie Review*, July, 1936.

GOLDBERG, ISAAC. *The Man Mencken: A Biographical and Critical Survey*. New York, 1925.

GOLDSCHMIDT, ALFONS. "Holitscher und Dreiser," *Die Weltbuhne*, August 20, 1929.

GRABO, C. H. *The Technique of the Novel.* New York, 1928.

GRAHAM, BESSIE. *The Bookman's Manual.* New York, 1941.

GRATTAN, C. HARTLEY. "Dreiser a Hero," *SRL,* January 14, 1933. Review of Dorothy Dudley's *Dreiser.*

———. "Upton Sinclair on Current Literature," *Bookman,* April, 1932.

GREEN, ELIZABETH and PAUL. *Contemporary American Literature.* Chapel Hill, N.C., 1925.

H. K. "Book Notes," *Left,* January, 1932.

HABBERSTAD, CLAUDE. "Is It?" *NR,* February 19, 1916.

HACKETT, FRANCIS. *Horizons: A Book of Criticism.* New York, 1918.

HAIGHT, ANNE LYON. *Banned Books.* New York, 1935.

HALDEMAN-JULIUS, E. *The Big American Parade.* Boston, 1929.

———. *The First Hundred Million.* New York, 1928.

———. *The Fun I Get Out of Life,* Big Blue Book, No. B-8. Girard, Kan., 1927.

———. *The Outline of Bunk.* Boston, 1929.

HALE, EDWARD E. "The Earlier 'Realism'," *Union College Bulletin,* January, 1932.

HALEY, CARMEN O'NEILL. "The Dreisers," *Commonweal,* July 7, 1933.

HALLOCK, R. P. *The Romance of American Literature,* 1934.

HANSEN, HARRY. Review of *Chains.* N. Y. *World,* May 22, 1927.

———. "Literary Fashions," *Forum,* March, 1933.

HAPGOOD, H. "Is Dreiser Anti-Semitic?" *The Nation,* April 17, 1935. Further discussion in *The Nation,* May 15, 1935.

HARDWICK, ELIZABETH. "Fiction Chronicle," *Partisan Review,* January, 1948.

HARRIS, FRANK. "American Novelists Today: Theodore Dreiser," *Academy,* August 2, 1913.

———. *Contemporary Portraits, Second Series.* New York, 1919.

HARRISON, CARTER H. *Stormy Years.* Indianapolis and New York, 1930.

HART, I. H. "The Most Popular Books of Fiction Year by Year in the Post-War Period," *Publishers' Weekly,* January 28, 1933.

HARTWICK, HARRY. "Hindenburg of the Novel," *The Foreground of American Fiction.* New York, 1934.

HASTINGS, WILLIAM THOMSON, ed. *Contemporary Essays.* Boston and New York, 1928.

HATCHER, HARLAN. *Creating the Modern American Novel.* New York, 1935.

HAY, JOHN. "The Stoic," *Commonweal,* December 19, 1947.

HAZLITT, HENRY. "All Too Humanism," *The Nation,* February 12, 1930.

———. "Art and Social Change," *Modern Quarterly,* Winter, 1931.

———. "Literature as Propaganda," *SRL,* September 16, 1939.

———. "Our Greatest Authors: How Great Are They?" *Forum,* October, 1932.

HEDGES, M. H. "Mr. Dreiser," *Dial,* April 19, 1917.

HENNESSEY, JOSEPH, ed. *The Portable Woollcott.* New York, 1946.

HERRMANN, EVA. *On Parade,* ed. Erich Posselt. New York, 1929.

HICKS, GRANVILLE. "Dreiser to the Rescue," *SRL,* February 22, 1941. Review of *America Is Worth Saving.*

———. *The Great Tradition.* New York, 1933.

————. "The Gutter—and Then What," *Forum*, December, 1928.

————. "Literature and Revolution," *English Journal*, March, 1935.

————. "Theodore Dreiser," *American Mercury*, June, 1946.

————. "The Twenties in American Literature," *The Nation*, February 12, 1930.

HOFFMAN, FREDERICK J. *The Modern Novel in America*. Chicago, 1951.

HOFSTADTER, RICHARD. *Social Darwinism in American Thought, 1860-1915*. Philadelphia, 1944.

HOWE, IRVING. Review of Robert H. Elias's *Theodore Dreiser*, *The Nation*, February 5, 1949.

HOWELL, EILEEN. "Theodore Dreiser's Development as a Naturalist," Unpublished M.A. thesis, New York University, 1950.

HUMBOLDT, CHARLES. "The Novel of Action," *Mainstream*, Fall, 1947.

HUNT, E. L. "The Social Interpretation of Literature," *English Journal*, March, 1935.

HUTH, J. F., JR. "Dreiser and Success: An Additional Note," *Colophon*, Winter, 1938.

————. "Theodore Dreiser, Success Monger." *Colophon*, Winter, 1938.

————. "Theodore Dreiser: 'The Prophet'," *American Literature*, May, 1937.

JACKSON, CHARLES. "Theodore Dreiser and Style," *Book Find News*, March, 1946.

JOHNSON, A. T. "Realism in Contemporary Literature: Notes On Dreiser, Anderson, Lewis," *Southwestern Bulletin*, September, 1929.

JOHNSON, OAKLEY. "Great Dreiser," *Scribner's Magazine*, June, 1931.

JONES, ELIOT. "Dreiser vs. the United States," *SRL*, February 27, 1932. Review of *Tragic America*.

JONES, HOWARD MUMFORD. "Dreiser Reconsidered," *Atlantic Monthly*, May, 1946.

JONES, M. M. "Theodore Dreiser—A Pioneer Whose Fame Is Secure," N. Y. *Times Book Review*, January 13, 1946.

JOSEPHSON, MATTHEW. "Dreiser, Reluctant, In the Films," *NR*, August 19, 1931.

————. *Portrait of the Artist as American*. New York, 1930.

————. *Zola and His Time*. New York, 1928.

KARSNER, DAVID. Review of *Free*. N. Y. *Call*, October 27, 1918.

————. *Sixteen Authors To One*. New York, 1928.

KAUN, ALEXANDER S. "Choleric Comments," *Little Review*, November, 1915.

KAZIN, ALFRED. "Lady and the Tiger," *Virginia Quarterly Review*, January, 1941.

————. *On Native Grounds*. New York, 1942.

KELLY, C. "American Victory or Tragedy; Dreiser vs. Ulysses S. Grant," *National Republic*, March, 1930.

KERN, ALEXANDER. "Dreiser's Difficult Beauty," *Western Review*, Winter, 1952.

KIRK, C. M. "The Marxist Doctrine in Literature," *English Journal*, March, 1935.

KIRKWOOD, M. M. "Value in the Novel Today," *University of Toronto Quarterly*, April, 1943.

KNIGHT, GRANT C. *The Novel in English*. New York, 1931.

KRIKORIAN, YERVANT H., ed. *Naturalism and the Human Spirit*. New York, 1944.

KRIM, SEYMOUR. "Theodore Dreiser," *Hudson Review*, Winter, 1952. Review of F. O. Matthiessen's *Theodore Dreiser*.

KRIOG, L. W. "The Dreisers," *Commonweal*, July 23, 1933.

KRUTCH, JOSEPH WOOD. "Dreiser Simplified," *The Nation*, April 1, 1936.

——. "Literature and Propaganda," *English Journal*, December, 1933.

——. "Plain and Colored," *The Nation*, February 13, 1924. Review of *The Color of a Great City*.

KUNITZ, STANLEY J., ed. *Living Authors*. New York, 1931.

KWIAT, JOSEPH J. "Dreiser and the Graphic Artist," *American Quarterly*, Summer, 1951.

——. "The Newspaper Experience: Crane, Norris, and Dreiser," *19th Century Fiction*, September, 1953.

LANGE, W. W. "Theodore Dreiser, Bibliographical Checklist," *Publishers' Weekly*, December 22, 1922.

LAWSON, JOHN HOWARD. "Dreiser: 20th Century Titan," *Sunday Worker*, February 3, 1946.

——. "Tribute to Theodore Dreiser," *Book Find News*, March, 1946.

LEAVIS, F. R. "Arnold Bennett: American Version," *For Continuity*. Cambridge, England, 1933. Review of Dorothy Dudley's *Forgotten Frontiers: Dreiser and the Land of the Free*.

LECHLITNER, RUTH. Review of *Chains*. N. Y. *Evening Post Literary Review*, May 28, 1927.

LEISY, ERNEST E. *American Literature: An Interpretative Survey*. New York, 1929.

LENGEL, WILLIAM C. "The 'Genius' Himself," *Esquire*, September, 1938.

LERNER, MAX. "On Dreiser," N. Y. *PM*, December 31, 1945. Reprinted in *Actions and Passions*. New York, 1949.

LE VERRIER, CHARLES. "Un Grand Romancier américain: Theodore Dreiser," *Revue Hebdomadaire*, January 21, 1933.

LEVIN, HARRY. "What is Realism?" *Comparative Literature*, Summer, 1951.

LEVINE, RICHARD. "Characterization in Dreiser's Fiction," Unpublished M.A. thesis, New York University, 1951.

LEVINSON, ANDREI Y. *Figures Americains*. Paris, 1929.

LEWIS, SINCLAIR. "The Literary Zoo," *Life*, October 10, 1907.

——. "Nobel Prize Speech of 1930," *Appreciation of Lewis and Address by Lewis Before the Swedish Academy*. New York, 1930.

LEWIS, WYNDHAM. "The Propagandist in Fiction," *Current History*, August, 1934.

LEWISOHN, LUDWIG. *Cities and Men*. New York and London, 1927.

——. *Expression in America*. New York and London, 1932.

——. "Portrait of an Artist," *The Nation*, April 4, 1923.

LLONA, VICTOR, ed. *Les Romanciers Américains*. Paris, 1931.

LLOYD, JESSIE. "Two Americans Look at Russia," *The Nation*, March 13, 1929.

LOGGINS, VERNON. "Dominant Primordial," *I Hear America . . . Literature in the United States Since 1900*. New York, 1937.

LONG, WALTER. "Shots for Four," *Modern Quarterly*, October-December, 1925.

LORD, DAVID. "Dreiser Today," *Prairie Schooner*, Winter, 1941.

LUCCOCK, H. E. *Contemporary American Literature and Religion*. Chicago and New York, 1934.

LUDLOW, FRANCIS. "Plodding Crusader," *College English,* October, 1946.
LYDENBERG, JOHN. "The Anatomy of Exhaustion," *SRL,* December 6, 1947.
LYNN, KENNETH S. *The Dream of Success.* Boston, 1955.
LYONS, EUGENE. *The Red Decade.* Indianapolis and New York, 1941.

McAFEE, HELEN. "The Literature of Disillusion," *Atlantic Monthly,* August, 1923.
McCOLE, CAMILLE JOHN. *Lucifer at Large.* London and New York, 1937.
———. "The Tragedy of Theodore Dreiser," *Catholic World,* October, 1930.
MacCOLLOUGH, MARTIN (pseud. for Samuel W. Tait, Jr.). *Letters on Contemporary American Authors.* Boston, 1921.
McDONALD, EDWARD D. *A Bibliography of the Writings of Theodore Dreiser.* Philadelphia, 1928. An early listing of Dreiser's works with a foreword by Dreiser.
———. "Dreiser Before *Sister Carrie,*" *Bookman,* June, 1928.
McFEE, WILLIAM. "Americana," *NR,* June 15, 1927. Review of *Chains.*
McINTYRE, O. O. "Dinner With Dreiser," *Cosmopolitan,* December, 1933.
M. L. "Dreiser à la Carte," *Scribner's Magazine,* November, 1929.
MACY, J. A. *The Spirit of American Literature.* Garden City, N. Y., 1913.
MAILLARD, DENYSE. "L'Enfant américain dans le roman du Middlewest," Unpublished Ph.D. dissertation, University of Paris, 1935.
MALLORY, H. S., ed. *Backgrounds of Book Reviewing.* Ann Arbor, 1923.
MANCHESTER, WILLIAM. *Disturber of the Peace: The Life of H. L. Mencken.* New York, 1951.
MARBLE, ANNIE R. "Revolt and Escape," *A Study of the Modern Novel, British and American, Since 1900.* New York and London, 1928.
MARKEY, GENE. "Two Great Realists: Theodore Dreiser and E. Phillips Oppenheim," *Literary Lights: A Book of Caricatures.* New York, 1923.
MARQUIS, DON. "205 Words," *SRL,* October 15, 1932.
MASTERS, EDGAR LEE. *Across Spoon River.* New York, 1936.
———. "Dreiser at Spoon River," *Esquire,* May, 1939.
———. "Theodore Dreiser," *The Great Valley.* New York, 1916. Poem. An amplification of "Theodore the Poet," which appeared in Masters' *Spoon River Anthology.*
———. "Theodore Dreiser: A Portrait," *Reedy's Mirror,* November 12, 1915.
MATTHIESSEN, F. O. "Dreiser's Politics," *Tomorrow,* January, 1951.
———. "Of Crime and Punishment," *Monthly Review,* October, 1950.
———. *Theodore Dreiser.* New York, 1951.
MAURICE, ARTHUR B. "Makers of Modern American Fiction (Men)," *Mentor,* September 1, 1918.
MAURY, J. W. "In the Workshop of an American Artist," *International Book Review,* March, 1926.
MAYBERRY, GEORGE. "Dreiser: 1871-1945," *NR,* January 14, 1946.
———. "Dreiser: The Last Chapter," *NR,* April 1, 1946.
MENCKEN, H. L. "The American Novel," *Prejudices: Fourth Series.* New York, 1924.
———. "The Creed of a Novelist," *Smart Set,* October, 1916.

——. "Dithyrambs Against Learning," *Smart Set,* November, 1918. Contains a review of *Free, and Other Stories.*

——. "The Dreiser Bugaboo," *The Seven Arts,* August, 1917.

——. "Footnote on Criticism," *Prejudices: Third Series.* New York, 1922.

——. "The Human Face," *Prejudices: Second Series.* New York, 1920.

——. "The Life of an Artist," *New Yorker,* April 17, 1948.

——. *Mencken Chrestomathy.* New York, 1949. Contains a reprint of his *American Mercury* review of *An American Tragedy.*

——. "Theodore Dreiser," *A Book of Prefaces.* New York, 1917. Reprinted in *The Shock of Recognition,* ed. Edmund Wilson. Garden City, N.Y., 1943.

MEYER, GEORGE WILSON. "The Original Social Purpose of the Naturalistic Novel," *Sewanee Review,* October-December, 1942.

MICHAUD, REGIS. "Le Mouvement littéraire et social de Gauche aux États-Unis," *Grand Revue,* February, May, and June, 1936.

——. *Panorama de la littérature américaine contemporaine,* Paris, 1928.

——. *Le roman américain d'aujourd'hui.* Paris, 1926. Translated as *The American Novel of Today.* Boston, 1928.

MILLER, HENRY. *The Books in My Life.* London, 1952.

——. "Dreiser's Style," *NR,* April 28, 1926.

MILLER, RALPH N. *A Preliminary Checklist of Books and Articles On Theodore Dreiser.* Kalamazoo: Western Michigan College Library, 1947.

MILLETT, FRED B. *Contemporary American Authors.* New York, 1940.

MONROE, HARRIET. "Dorothy Dudley's Frontiers," *Poetry,* January, 1934.

MOORE, H. T. "The American Novel Today," *London Mercury,* March, 1935.

MORDELL, ALBERT. "My Relations with Theodore Dreiser," *Critic and Guide,* March, 1951.

MORE, PAUL ELMER. "Modern Currents in American Literature," *The Demon of the Absolute.* Princeton, 1928.

——. "A Revival of Humanism," *Bookman,* March, 1930.

——. "Theodore Dreiser, Philosopher," *Review,* April 17, 1920.

MORRIS, LLOYD R. *Postscript to Yesterday.* New York, 1947.

MOSES, MONTROSE J. and JOHN MASON BROWN. *The American Theatre as Seen By Its Critics, 1752-1934.* New York, 1934.

MULLER, HERBERT J. "Impressionism and Fiction," *American Scholar,* Summer, 1930.

——. "The New Psychology in Old Fiction," *SRL,* August 21, 1937.

MUMFORD, LEWIS. "The Shadow of the Muckrake," *The Golden Day.* New York, 1926.

MUNSON, GORHAM B. "Motivation of Theodore Dreiser," *Destinations.* New York, 1928.

——. "Odds and Ends," *SRL,* June 25, 1927. Review of *Chains.*

——. "Our Post-War Novel," *Bookman,* October, 1931.

MUTCH, F. J. "The Dreisers," *Commonweal,* August 18, 1933.

NATHAN, GEORGE JEAN, ET AL. *The American Spectator Yearbook.* New York, 1934.

——. *The Intimate Notebooks of George Jean Nathan.* New York, 1932.

——. *The Theatre, The Drama, The Girls.* New York, 1921.

————. "Three Friends: Lewis, O'Neill, Dreiser," *The Borzoi Reader,* ed. Carl Van Doren. New York, 1936.

NICHOLSON, MEREDITH. *The Hoosiers.* New York and London, 1900.

NORTH, STERLING. "Dreiser's Last Testament," N. Y. *Post,* March 21, 1946.

NOTMAN, OTIS. "Talks With Four Novelists," N. Y. *Times,* June 15, 1907.

OAK, V. V. "The Awful Dreiser," *The Nation,* June 2, 1926. A letter.

O'BRIEN, E. J. *The Advance of the American Short Story.* New York, 1923.

ORTON, VREST. *Dreiserana: A Book About His Books.* New York, 1929.

————. "Notes to Add to a Bibliography of Theodore Dreiser," *The American Collector,* 1928.

OVERTON, GRANT M. *An Hour of the American Novel.* New York, 1929.

PARRINGTON, VERNON L. "Theodore Dreiser: Chief of American Naturalists," *Main Currents of American Thought,* III. New York, 1930.

PATTEE, F. L. *The Development of the American Short Story.* New York and London, 1923.

————. *A History of American Literature Since 1870.* New York, 1915.

————. "Theodore Dreiser," *The New American Literature, 1890-1930.* New York and London, 1930.

PAVESE, CESARE. "Dreiser e la sua Battaglia Sociale," *La Culture,* April-June, 1941.

PERRY, RALPH BARTON. "The Anatomy of Democracy," *Virginia Quarterly Review,* Summer, 1941.

PORTERFIELD, ALLEN W. "An American Achievement," *Outlook and Independent,* December 18, 1929.

POSSELT, ERICH. "Statements of Belief," *Bookman,* September, 1928.

POWYS, JOHN COWPER. *Autobiography.* New York, 1934.

————. *One Hundred Best Books.* New York, 1916.

POWYS, LLEWELYN. "Good Friends," *The Verdict of Bridlegoose.* New York, 1926.

PREECE, HAROLD. "Proletarian Writers," *Modern Thinker,* December, 1935.

PRESTON, JOHN HYDE. "True Style," *SRL,* May 22, 1926.

QUINN, ARTHUR H. *American Fiction.* New York and London, 1936.

RAHV, PHILIP. "On the Decline of Naturalism," *Partisan Review,* November-December, 1942. Reprinted in *Image and Idea.* New York, 1949.

————. "Proletarian Literature: A Political Autopsy," *Sewanee Review,* January, 1939.

RANKIN, T. E. *American Writers of the Present Day, 1890-1920.* Ann Arbor, 1920.

———— and WILFORD AIKEN. *American Literature.* New York, 1922.

RASCOE, BURTON. "Does Dreiser's Final Novel Reveal Spiritual Creed?" Chicago *Tribune,* March 24, 1946.

————. *A Bookman's Daybook,* ed. C. Hartley Grattan. New York, 1929.

————. *Prometheans, Ancient and Modern.* New York and London, 1933.

————. *Theodore Dreiser.* New York, 1925.

————. *We Were Interrupted.* Garden City, N.Y., 1947.

REEDY, WILLIAM MARION. *Reedy's Mirror,* January 14 and May 29, 1914, July 14 and September 22, 1916, December 13, 1918. Short reviews.

RICE, DIANA. "Terrible Typewriter on Parnassus," N. Y. *Times Magazine,* April 27, 1924.

RIDDELL, JOHN. See Ford, Corey.

RILEY, LESTER LEAKE. "America Is Worth Saving," *Churchman,* April 1, 1941.

ROLFE, EDWIN. "Theodore Dreiser," *Poetry,* June, 1946.

ROLO, CHARLES J. "Dreiser's America," *Tomorrow,* February, 1948.

ROSS, WOODBURN O. "Concerning Dreiser's Mind," *American Literature,* November, 1946.

RUBENSTEIN, ANNETTE. "A Pillar of Society," *New Masses,* April 30, 1946.

RUOGG, A. "Theodore Dreiser's Abkher vom Katholizimus," *Schweizerische Rondschau,* 1932.

S. L. C. Review of *The Color of a Great City.* Boston *Evening Transcript,* January 9, 1924.

SAMPSON, ASHLEY. "Religion in Modern Literature," *Contemporary Review,* April, 1935.

"The Scavanger." "The Scavanger's Swan Song," *Little Review,* November, 1915.

SCHELLING, F. E. *Appraisements and Asperities As To Some Contemporary Writers.* Philadelphia and London, 1922.

SCHNEIDER, ISIDOR. "Dreiser . . . A Man of Integrity," *Book Find News,* March, 1946.

———. "Theodore Dreiser," *SRL,* March 10, 1934.

SCHRIFTGIESSEN, K. Review of *Chains.* Boston *Evening Transcript,* June 11, 1927.

———. "Boston Stays Pure," *NR,* May 8, 1929.

SCHWARTZ, JACOB. *110 Obscure Points: The Bibliographies of 25 English and 21 American Authors.* London, 1931.

SCHYBERG, FREDERIK. *Moderne Amerikansk Litteratur, 1900-1930.* Copenhagen, 1930.

SCULLY, FRANK. "Dreiser," *Rogues' Gallery.* Hollywood, 1943.

SEAVER, EDWIN. "Theodore Dreiser and the American Novel," *New Masses,* May, 1926.

SEBESTYEN, KARL. "Persons and Personages: Theodore Dreiser at Home," *Living Age,* December, 1930.

SHANKS, EDWARD. "Dreiser Looks at Russia," *Sewanee Review,* May, 1929.

SHAPIRO, CHARLES. "Dreiser and the American Dream," Unpublished M.A. thesis, Indiana School of Letters, Indiana University, 1953.

———. "The Role of Attitudes in the Novel," *Folio,* Fall, 1952.

SHERMAN, STUART P. "The Naturalism of Mr. Dreiser," *The Nation,* December 2, 1915. Reprinted in *On Contemporary Literature.* New York, 1917.

SHERWOOD, MARGARET. "Characters in Recent Fiction," *Atlantic Monthly,* May, 1912.

SIEGEL, ELI. "The Worst," *Scribner's Magazine,* March, 1932.

SILLEN, SAMUEL. "Dreiser's J'Accuse," *New Masses,* January 28, 1941.

SINCLAIR, UPTON. *Money Writes!* New York, 1927.

———, ET AL. "Tributes to Theodore Dreiser," *Book Find News,* March, 1946.

SMITH, BERNARD. *Forces in American Criticism.* New York, 1939.

SMITH, EDWARD H. "Dreiser—After 20 Years," *Bookman,* March, 1921.

SMITH, LEWIS W., ed. *Current Reviews.* New York, 1926.

SMITH, LORNA D. "Dreisers Leave for Hollywood . . . ," Glendale *News-Press,* May 8, 1939. Interview.

SMITH, R. W. "Portrait of an American: The National Character in Fiction," *Southwest Review,* April, 1936.

SMITH, WINFIELD. "The Worker as Hero," *American Bookman,* Fall, 1944.

SNELL, GEORGE. "Theodore Dreiser: Philosopher," *The Shapers of American Fiction, 1798-1947.* New York, 1947.

SPILLER, ROBERT E. "Dreiser as Master Craftsman," *SRL,* March 23, 1946.

———, ET AL. *Literary History of the United States.* New York, 1948.

SQUIRE, JOHN COLLINGS. *Contemporary American Authors.* New York, 1928.

STALNAKER, J. M. and FRED EGGAN. "American Novelists Ranked: A Psychological Study," *English Journal,* April, 1929.

STARK, HAROLD (Pseud. "Young Boswell"). *People You Know.* New York, 1924. Contains an interview, originally in N. Y. *Tribune,* April 7, 1923.

STEADMAN, R. W. "A Critique of Proletarian Literature," *North American Review,* Spring, 1939.

STEPANCHEV, STEPHEN. "Dreiser Among the Critics," Unpublished Ph.D. dissertation, New York University, 1950.

STEVENS, BENNETT. "The Gnats and Dreiser," *New Masses,* May, 1932.

STOVALL, FLOYD. "From Idealism to Naturalism," *American Idealism.* Norman, Okla., 1943.

STRAUSS, HAROLD. "Realism in the Proletarian Novel," *"Yale Review,* December, 1938.

STRUNSKY, SIMEON. "About Books, *More or Less:* Said Without Flowers," N. Y. *Times Book Review,* May 29, 1927.

STUART, HENRY LOGAN. "As Usual Mr. Dreiser Spares Us Nothing," N. Y. *Times Book Review,* May 15, 1927. Review of *Chains.*

SWINNERTON, FRANK. "A Tribute to Theodore Dreiser," N. Y. *Times,* December 15, 1926.

TAYLOR, G. R. S. "Theodore Dreiser," *London Outlook,* December 18, 1926.

———. "The United States as Seen by an American Writer," *The Nineteenth Century,* December, 1926.

TAYLOR, WALTER F. *A History of American Letters.* Boston, 1936.

THOMAS, NORMAN. "Dreiser as Economist," *The Nation,* April 6, 1932.

THOMPSON, ALAN R. "The Cult of Cruelty," *Bookman,* January-February, 1932.

———. "Farewell to Achilles," *Bookman,* January, 1930.

TITTLE, WALTER. "Glimpses of Interesting Americans: Theodore Dreiser," *Century,* August, 1925.

TJADER, MARGUERITE. "Theodore Dreiser: World Spirit," *Free World,* April, 1946.

———. "Dreiser's Last Visit to New York," *Twice A Year,* Fall-Winter, 1946-1947

TONER, W. M. "Theodore Dreiser: Indiana University's Only Literary Genius," *The Vagabond,* November, 1925.

TORWILL, HERBERT W. "London Discusses Mr. Dreiser," N. Y. *Times Book Review,* January 9, 1927.

TOWNE, CHARLES HANSON. "Behind the Scenes with Author and Editor," *International Book Review,* July, 1926.

TRILLING, LIONEL. "Dreiser, Anderson, Lewis, and the Riddle of Society," *Reporter,* November 13, 1951.

————. "Dreiser and the Liberal Mind," *The Nation,* April 20, 1946. Reprinted in revised and expanded form as "Reality in America," *The Liberal Imagination.* New York, 1950.

UNTERMEYER, LOUIS. "New Poetry," *SRL,* July 13, 1929.

VAN DOREN, CARL. *The American Novel.* New York, 1921. Revised and enlarged edition, 1940.

————. "American Realism," *NR,* March 21, 1923.

————. "Contemporary American Novelists: Theodore Dreiser," *The Nation,* March 16, 1921.

————. "Jurgen in Limbo," *The Nation,* December 16, 1922.

————. "The Nation and the American Novel," *The Nation,* February 10, 1940.

VAN GELDER, ROBERT. "Interview With Theodore Dreiser," N. Y. *Times,* March 16, 1941. Reprinted in *Writers and Writing.* New York, 1946.

VARIOUS WRITERS. *Theodore Dreiser: America's Foremost Novelist.* New York, 1916-1917. Includes: photograph by Ira L. Hill Studios; poem by Edgar Lee Masters; "What Manner of Man He Is," by Harris Merton Lyon; "To Theodore Dreiser on Reading *The Genius,*" by Arthur Davison Ficke; caricature by P. B. McCord; and "The Writer and His Writings," by John Cowper Powys.

VERNADSKY, GEORGE. "Russia Today," *Yale Review,* Spring, 1929.

VERNON, GRENVILLE. "Chains," *Commonweal,* September 28, 1927.

VIVAS, ELISEO. "Dreiser, an Inconsistent Mechanist," *Ethics,* July, 1938.

WAGENKNECHT, EDWARD. "Theodore Dreiser, The Mystic Naturalist," *Cavalcade of the American Novel.* New York, 1952.

WALCUTT, CHARLES C. "Naturalism in 1946: Dreiser and Farrell," *Accent,* Summer, 1946.

————. "The Three Stages of Theodore Dreiser's Naturalism," *PMLA,* March, 1940. Revised for this volume.

WALDMAN, M. "A German-American Insurgent," *Living Age,* October 1, 1926. Reprinted from *London Mercury,* July, 1926. Also in *Contemporary American Authors,* ed. John Collings Squire. New York, 1928.

————. "Tendencies of the Modern Novel: America," *Fortnightly Review,* December, 1933.

WALKER, CHARLES R. "Business in the American Novel," *Bookman,* December, 1927.

————. "How Big Is Dreiser?" *Bookman,* April, 1926.

WALLACE, MARGARET. "Books . . . The Legacy of Theodore Dreiser," *Independent Woman,* July, 1946.

WARD, A. C. *American Literature, 1880-1930.* New York, 1932.

WEEKS, EDWARD. "The Best Sellers Since 1875," *Publishers' Weekly,* February 21, 1934.
———. "A Modern Estimate of American Best Sellers, 1875-1933," *Publishers' Weekly,* April 21, 1934.
WENDT, LLOYD and MICHAEL KOGAN. *Lords of the Levee.* Indianapolis and New York, 1943.
WEST, RAY B. *The Short Story in America, 1900-1950.* Chicago, 1952.
WESTLAKE, NEDA. "Theodore Dreiser's *Notes on Life,*" *University of Pennsylvania Library Chronicle,* XX, 1954.
WHIPPLE, THOMAS K. *Spokesmen: Modern Writers and American Life.* New York and London, 1928.
WHITE, WILLIAM ALLEN, ET AL. *The Novel of Tomorrow.* Indianapolis, 1922.
WILSON, EDMUND. "Equity for Americans," *NR,* March 30, 1932.
———. "Tragic America," *NR,* March 30, 1933.
WILSON, J. S. "The Changing Novel," *Virginia Quarterly Review,* January, 1934.
WINTERICH, J. T. and DAVID RANDALL. *A Primer of Book-Collecting.* New York, 1946.
WITHAM, W. TASKER. *Panorama of American Literature.* New York, 1947.
WOLLSTEIN, R. H. "You Know Mr. Dreiser," *Musical America,* February 25, 1929.
WOOLBERT, ROBERT GALE. "America Is Worth Saving," *Foreign Affairs,* July, 1941.
WOOLLCOTT, ALEXANDER. *Going to Pieces.* New York and London, 1928.

YOUNG, STARK. *Immortal Shadows.* New York, 1948.

II BOOK REVIEWS AND NOTICES

A. SISTER CARRIE (*1900*)

Anon. *Bookman*, May, 1907; August, 1907; April 1, 1910.
———. *Churchman*, December 29, 1900.
———. *Current Literature*, January, 1901 and July, 1907.
———. *Dial*, December 16, 1900.
———. *Forum*, July, 1907.
———. *Interior*, February 21, 1901.
———. *Life*, November 24, 1906 and October 10, 1907.
———. *Musical Leader*, November 28, 1907.
———. *The Nation*, November 15, 1900.
———. *Newspaperdom*, October 24, 1907.
———. *Paris Modes*, September, 1907.
———. *Publishers' Weekly*, November 17, 1900; June 1, 1907; June 29, 1907.
———. *Recreation*, January, 1901.
———. *Style and American Dressmaker*, July, 1907.
ATHERTON, GERTRUDE. N. Y. *Times*, December 29, 1907.
CABELL, ISA CARRINGTON. *Bellman*, April 6, 1912.
CARROLL, LAWRENCE. St. Louis *Mirror*, April 25, 1912.
COATES, JOSEPH. *North American Review*, October, 1907.
COOPER, FREDERIC T. "The Fallacy of Tendencies in Fiction," *Forum*, July, 1907.
———. "The Fetish of Form and Some Recent Novels," *Bookman*, May, 1907.
COWLEY, MALCOLM. "Sister Carrie's Brother," *NR*, May 26, 1947.
———. "The Slow Rise of Sister Carrie," *NR*, June 23, 1947. The two articles are reprinted in this volume as "Sister Carrie: Her Fall and Rise."
FARRELL, JAMES T. "James T. Farrell Revalues Dreiser's *Sister Carrie*," N. Y. *Times Book Review*, July 4, 1943. Reprinted in *The League of Frightened Philistines*. New York, 1945.
GEISMAR, MAXWELL. *Sister Carrie*, ed. with an Introduction by Maxwell Geismar. New York (Pocket Books), 1949.
———. "Jezebel of the Loop," *SRL*, July 4, 1953.
HACKETT, FRANCIS. *NR*, February 23, 1918.
HARRIS, FRANK. "Twenty Favourite Books," *Academy*, May 27, 1911.
HORTON, GEORGE. Chicago *Record Herald*, March, 1901.
KERFOOT, J. B. *Life*, March 7, 1901.
KNIGHT, ARTHUR. "Dreiser, Sister Carrie and William Wyler," *SRL*, July 12, 1952.
LOCKE, W. J. N. Y. *Times*, November 21, 1908.
MACY, BALDWIN. Chicago *Evening Post*, August 4, 1911.

MENCKEN, H. L. *"Sister Carrie's* History," N. Y. *Evening Mail,* August 4, 1917.
NORRIS, CHARLES G. "My Favorite Character in Fiction: Hurstwood," *Bookman,* December, 1925.
RASCOE, BURTON. Introduction to *Sister Carrie.* New York: Limited Editions Club, 1939.
RHODES, HARRISON. "Mr. Dreiser's *Sister Carrie," Bookman,* May, 1907.
RICE, WALLACE. Chicago *American,* January 26, 1901.
STEINBRECHER, GEORGE JR. "Inaccurate Accounts of *Sister Carrie," American Literature,* January, 1952.
VAN WESTRUM, A. S. "The Decadence of Realism," *Book Buyer,* March, 1901.
WATTS-DUNTON, THEODORE. *Athenaeum,* September 7, 1901.

N. Y. *Tribune,* November 3, 1900.
Louisville *Times,* November 20, 1900.
Detroit *Free Press,* November 24, 1900.
Chicago *Daily News,* November 30, 1900.
Philadelphia *Literary Era,* c. 1900, University of Pennsylvania Dreiser Collection.
Hartford *Courant,* December 6, 1900.
Toledo *Blade,* December 8, 1900.
N. Y. *Commercial Advertiser,* December 19, 1900.
Albany *Journal,* December 22, 1900.
Omaha *Daily Bee,* December 22, 1900.
Pittsburgh *Commercial Gazette,* December 28, 1900.
San Francisco *Chronicle,* December 30, 1900.
St. Louis *Mirror,* January 3, 1901.
New Haven *Journal Courier,* January 12, 1901.
Indianapolis *Journal,* January 14, 1901.
Chicago *Chronicle,* January 14, 1901.
Chicago *Times Herald,* January 16, 1901.
Denver *Republican,* January 20, 1901.
Seattle *Post Intelligence,* January 20, 1901.
Minneapolis *Journal,* January 26, 1901.
Syracuse *Post-Standard,* c. February, 1901, University of Pennsylvania Dreiser Collection.
Louisville *Courier-Journal,* February 23, 1901.
Chicago *Tribune,* February 25, 1901.
Indianapolis *News,* March 9, 1901.
London *Daily Mail,* August 13, 1901.
Newark *Sunday News,* September 1, 1901.
N. Y. *Commercial Advertiser,* September 18, 1901.
St. Louis *Post Dispatch,* January 26, 1902.
Chicago *Tribune,* April 27, 1907.
N. Y. *Sun,* May 11, 1907.
N. Y. *Herald,* May 19, 1907.
N. Y. *Times,* May 25, 1907.
Syracuse *Post-Standard,* May 25, 1907.

N. Y. *Sun,* June 1, 1907.
N. Y. *World,* June 1, 1907.
Philadelphia *Public Ledger,* June 1, 1907.
Boston *Daily Advertiser,* June 5, 1907.
Boston *Transcript,* June 5, 1907.
St. Louis *Mirror,* June 6, 1907.
Buffalo *Times,* June 6 and 16, 1907.
Hartford *Courant,* June 7, 1907.
Buffalo *Courier,* June 8 and 9, 1907.
Kansas City (Mo.) *Star,* June 8, 1907.
Newark *Evening News,* June 8 and 15, 1907.
Houston *Post,* June 9, 1907.
N. Y. *Times,* June 15 (interview), 16, 22, and 29, 1907.
Cleveland *Plain Dealer,* June 16, 1907.
Baltimore *American,* June 17, 1907.
N. Y. *Sun,* June 18, 1907.
Louisville *Times,* June 19, 1907.
St. Louis *Republic,* June 22, 1907.
Chicago *Post,* June 25, 1907.
Baltimore *Sun,* June 26, 1907.
Boston *Globe,* June 27, 1907.
Chicago *Advance,* June 27, 1907.
Indianapolis *Star,* June 29, 1907.
Denver *Republican,* June 30, 1907.
Detroit *News-Tribune,* June 30, 1907.
New Orleans *Picayune,* July 1, 1907.
N. Y. *Press,* July 3, 1907.
Boston *Journal,* July 4, 1907.
Riverside (Calif.) *Enterprise,* July 4, 1907.
San Francisco *Bulletin,* July 5, 6, and 7, 1907.
N. Y. *Dramatic Mirror,* July 6, 1907.
New Orleans *Statesman,* July 7, 1907.
N. Y. *Herald,* July 7, 1907.
Hartford *Courant,* July 8, 1907.
Denver *News,* July 15, 1907.
Denver *Times,* July 15, 1907.
N. Y. *Times,* July 15 and 20, 1907.
Washington (D.C.) *Star,* July 20, 1907.
N. Y. *Tribune,* July 23, 1907.
Chicago *Evening Post,* July 27, 1907.
Indianapolis *Star,* July 27, 1907.
Lewiston (Me.) *Journal,* July 27, 1907.
Louisville *Journal,* July 27, 1907.
Washington (D.C.) *Post,* July 27, 1907.
Harrisburg *Star-Independent,* July 31, 1907.
N. Y. *Press,* July 31, 1907.

Los Angeles *Express,* August 3, 1907.
San Francisco *Argonaut,* August 3, 1907.
N. Y. *Globe,* August 7, 1907.
Syracuse *Herald,* August 7, 1907.
Detroit *Journal,* August 10, 1907.
San Francisco *Town Talk,* August 10, 1907.
New Orleans *Times-Democrat,* August 25, 1907.
Boston *Herald,* September 14, 1907.
Mobile *Register,* September 15, 1907.
Atlanta *Journal,* November 16, 1907.
Akron *Journal,* November 30, 1907.
N. Y. *Standard,* January 2, 1908.
Springfield *Republican,* August 21, 1908.
Philadelphia *Item,* August 22, 1908.
Cleveland *Plain Dealer,* August 23, 1908.
N. Y. *Evening Mail,* August 29, 1908.
Boston *Advertiser,* November 27, 1908.
Denver *Republican,* August 5, 1910.
Baltimore *Sun,* March 22 and August 13, 1911.
Boston *Transcript,* August 12, 1911.
Brooklyn *Eagle,* April 20, 1912.

B. JENNIE GERHARDT (*1911*)

Anon. "The Story of a Book," *Bookman,* November, 1911.
———. *Craftsman,* January, 1912.
———. *Current Literature,* January, 1912.
———. *Everybody's Magazine,* January, 1912.
———. *Independent,* December 7, 1911.
———. *Metropolitan,* January, 1912.
DELL, FLOYD. "Book of the Week," Chicago *Evening Post,* November 3, 1911.
GUITERMAN, ARTHUR. Poem. *Life,* December 14, 1911.
KERFOOT, J. B. *Life,* January 4, 1912.
LUBLIN, CURTIS. *Town and Country,* February 3, 1912.
MACY, BALDWIN. N. Y. *Post,* August 4, 1911.
MENCKEN, H. L. "A Novel of the First Rank," *Smart Set,* November, 1911.
PEATTIE, ELIA W. Chicago *Tribune,* November 11, 1911.
WARREN, FREDERIC BLOUNT. N. Y. *Telegraph,* November 5, 1911.
WINTER, CALVIN. *Bookman,* December, 1911.

N. Y. *Globe and Commercial Advertiser,* October 20, 1911.
N. Y. *Tribune,* October 21, 1911.
N. Y. *World,* October 21, 1911.
Kansas City (Mo.) *Journal,* October 22, 1911.
N. Y. *American,* October 25, 1911.
N. Y. *Herald,* October 28, 1911.

Chicago *Herald Record,* November 4, 1911.
Kansas City *Post,* November 9, 1911.
Birmingham *Herald,* November 12, 1911.
New Orleans *Picayune,* November 12, 1911.
Philadelphia *Telegraph,* November 15, 1911.
New Orleans *Times-Democrat,* November 19, 1911.
N. Y. *Daily People,* November 20, 1911. Interview.
Denver *Times,* November 23, 1911. Interview.
Brooklyn *Standard Union,* November 25, 1911.
New Haven *Courier,* November 25, 1911.
N. Y. *American,* November 25, 1911.
Washington (D.C.) *Evening Star,* November 25, 1911.
St. Paul *Pioneer Press,* November 26, 1911.
Baltimore *Evening Sun,* November 27, 1911.
Boston *Daily Advertiser,* December 2, 1911.
N. Y. *Sun,* December 2, 1911.
Philadelphia *Press,* December 2, 1911.
San Francisco *Chronicle,* December 3, 1911.
Philadelphia *Inquirer,* December 9, 1911.
Kansas City *Independent,* December 16, 1911.
Minneapolis *Bellman,* January 6, 1912.
London *Daily News,* March 26, 1912.
Columbus *Dispatch,* May 11, 1912.
Toronto *Globe,* July 13, 1912.
Indianapolis *News,* February 14, 1914.

C. THE FINANCIER (*1912*)

ANDERSON, M. "The Decadent in Literature," *Trend,* November, 1913.
Anon. "Arriving Giant in American Literature," *Current Literature,* December, 1912.
——. "The Bookshelf of a Workingman," *Weekly People,* October 28, 1922.
——. "Mr. Dreiser's Financier," *Independent,* February 27, 1913.
——. "The Financier," *Book News Monthly,* February, 1913.
——. "Frenzied Finance Through Theodore Dreiser's Eyes," *Current Literature,* December, 1912.
——. Humorous Poem. *Life,* February 13, 1913.
——. *Ainslee's,* April, 1913.
——. *Atlantic Monthly,* May, 1913.
——. *Building Management,* March, 1913.
——. *Dial,* February 1, 1913.
——. *Harper's Monthly Magazine,* December, 1912.
——. *The Nation,* December 19, 1912.
——. *Review of Reviews,* February, 1913.
——. *Town Topics,* December 19, 1912.

——. *Vogue,* April 1, 1913.

BASHFORD, HERBERT. San Francisco *Bulletin,* November 16, 1912.

CARY, LUCIAN. Chicago *Evening Post,* November 22, 1912.

COOPER, FREDERIC T. "The Theory of Endings and Some Recent Novels," *Bookman,* December, 1912.

DAWSON, CONINGSBY. "A Row of Books," *Everybody's Magazine,* April, 1913.

FORD, JAMES L. New York *Herald,* November 2, 1912.

HANSEN, HARRY. "Theodore Dreiser Revises," N. Y. *World,* April 18, 1927.

HAZARD, LUCY L. "Theodore Dreiser," *The Frontier in American Literature.* New York, 1927.

JARMUTH, EDITH DE LONG. Letter. N. Y. *Evening Globe,* April 11, 1913.

MENCKEN, H. L. "Against the Busy Fictioner," *Smart Set,* January, 1913.

——. N. Y. *Times Book Review,* November 10, 1912. Reprinted in Los Angeles *Times Magazine,* December 8, 1912.

REEDY, WILLIAM M. "Dreiser's Great Book," *Reedy's Magazine,* January 2, 1913.

ROBERTSON, CARL T. Cleveland *Plain Dealer,* November 16, 1912.

WOOD, GARDNER W. "Books of the Day," *McClure's Magazine,* February, 1913.

Baltimore *Evening Sun,* October 29, 1912.

Brooklyn *Eagle,* November 2, 1912.

Boston *Evening Transcript,* November 6, 1912.

Waco *Texas Times Herald,* November 14, 1912.

New Orleans *Picayune,* December 8, 1912.

Raleigh *News and Observer,* December 8, 1912.

Kansas City (Kan.) *Gazette Globe,* December 11, 1912.

Des Moines *Register Leader,* December 14, 1912.

Augusta (Ga.) *Chronicle,* December 15, 1912.

Mobile *Item,* December 15, 1912.

Kansas City (Mo.) *Journal,* December 17, 1912.

N. Y. *Evening Post,* December 21, 1912.

San Francisco *Argonaut,* January 25, 1913.

St. Joseph (Mo.) *Press,* January 31, 1913.

St. Louis *Star,* March 3, 1913.

Washington (D.C.) *Evening Star,* June 14, 1927.

Ashville *Times,* August 7, 1927.

D.   A TRAVELLER AT FORTY (*1913*)

Anon. *Bookseller,* November 15, 1913.

——. *Building Management,* February, 1914.

——. *Christian Intelligencer,* January 21, 1914.

——. *Real Estate Management,* March, 1914.

——. *Spur,* February 15, 1914.

——. *Travel,* February, 1914.

——. *Vogue,* February, 1914.

DELL, FLOYD. "Mr. Dreiser and the Dodo," *Masses,* February, 1914.

GILDER, JEANETTE. "Mr. Dreiser in His Travels," Source unknown, probable date, December 3, 1913, University of Pennsylvania Dreiser Collection.

HENRY, STUART. *Bookman,* February, 1914.

HESSELGRAVE, CHARLES E. "A Holiday Trip into the Land of Books," N. Y. *Independent,* December 11, 1913.

Lee, J. M. *Book News Monthly,* February, 1914.

MARKHAM, EDWIN. Atlanta *American,* January 4, 1914.

MENCKEN, H. L. "Anything But Novels," *Smart Set,* February, 1914.

SOLON, ISRAEL. Chicago *Evening Post,* December 5, 1913.

TOWNE, CHARLES HANSON. "'A Traveller—And Sporty,' by Theorore Dry, Sir," N. Y. *Tribune,* February, 1914.

Chicago *Evening Post,* September 12, 1913.

N. Y. *Post,* November 19, 1913.

Savannah *News,* November 22, 1913.

Boston *Traveller and Evening Herald,* November 29, 1913.

Buffalo *Commercial,* November 29, 1913.

St. Louis *Globe-Democrat,* November 29, 1913.

N. Y. *Times,* November 30, 1913. Interview.

Boston *Evening Transcript,* December 3, 1913.

N. Y. *Evening Globe,* December 6, 1913.

Portland (Ore.) *Telegram,* December 6, 1913.

San Francisco *Bulletin,* December 6, 1913.

N. Y. *Chronicle,* December 7, 1913.

N. Y. *American,* December 13, 1913.

N. Y. *Tribune,* December 13, 1913.

Brooklyn *Eagle,* December 20, 1913.

Chicago *Record Herald,* December 20, 1913.

N. Y. *Times,* December 23, 1913.

Baltimore *Evening Sun,* January 3, 1914.

San Francisco *Argonaut,* January 3, 1914.

N. Y. *Press,* January 11, 1914.

Boston *Times,* January 24, 1914.

Philadelphia *Public Ledger,* January 24, 1914.

Indianapolis *News,* January 31, 1914.

Minneapolis *Bellman,* March 21, 1914.

Kansas City (Mo.) *Star,* May 16, 1914.

London *Gazette,* January 5, 1915.

Indianapolis *Catholic,* March 17, 1916.

E.　THE TITAN (*1914*)

Anon. "Dreiser and His Titan," *Town Topics,* June 18, 1914.

———. "The Failure of Success," *Independent,* October 12, 1914.

———. "The Financier Gets Out of Jail," *Current Opinion,* July, 1914.

———. *Atlantic Monthly,* October, 1914.

———. *The Nation,* June 11, 1914.

CARY, LUCIAN. *Dial,* June 16, 1914.

COOPER, F. T. "Summer-Time Fiction," *Bookman,* June, 1914.

EDGETT, E. F. Boston *Evening Transcript,* May 23, 1914.

FORD, FORD MADDOX. London *Outlook,* Fall, 1914.

HAWTHORNE, HILDEGARDE. "Mr. Dreiser's Trilogy," N. Y. *Times,* May 24, 1914.

MENCKEN, H. L. "Adventures Among the New Novels," *Smart Set,* August, 1914.

SKIDELSKY, BERENICE C. *Book News Monthly,* August, 1914.

WING, DE WITT C. "An Unreeling Realist," *Little Review,* July, 1914.

F. THE "GENIUS" (*1915*)

(* indicates discussion of the suppression of the novel.)

Anon. "The New Massive Novel by Theodore Dreiser," *Current Opinion,* January, 1916.

———. "Too Much Genius," *Independent,* November 8, 1915.

———.* "Vice Society Assails Book," N. Y. *Times,* August 21, 1916. Also: March 19, 1917; March 22, 1917; May 2, 1917; July 12, 1918. Review appeared October 10, 1915.

———.* *Bang,* September 25, 1916. Entire issue devoted to discussion of the suppression of *The "Genius."*

———. *Bookseller, Newsdealer and Stationer,* October 1, 1915.

———.* *Christian Work,* September 16, 1916.

———. *Harper's Weekly,* January 1, 1916.

———.* *International,* October and December, 1916.

———.* *Literary Digest,* October 27, 1916.

———.* *NR,* August 26, 1916. Untitled editorial.

———.* *Out West,* March, 1917.

———. *Reedy's Mirror,* October 8, 1915.

———.* *Saturday Evening Post,* October 28, 1916.

———.* *Vogue,* November 15, 1916. Review appeared February 1, 1916.

AUERBACH, J. S.* "Authorship and Liberty," *North American Review,* June, 1918.

Author's League of America (Executive Committee).* "Theodore Dreiser's *The 'Genius,' "* *Reedy's Mirror,* September 22, 1916.

BIDDLE, FRANCIS P. Philadelphia *Public Ledger,* October 13, 1923.

BOURNE, RANDOLPH. "Desire as Hero," *NR,* November 20, 1915.

BOYNTON, H. W. "Varieties of Realism," *The Nation,* October 14, 1915.

COOPER, F. T. *Bookman,* November, 1915.

DELL, FLOYD. "The Genius and Mr. Dreiser," *New Review,* undated, University of Pennsylvania Dreiser Collection.

———. *Masses,* August, 1916.

EDGETT, E. F. Boston *Evening Transcript,* October 9, 1915.

FICKE, ARTHUR DAVISON. "Portrait of Theodore Dreiser," *Little Review,* November, 1915. Poem.

FORD, JAMES L. N. Y. *Herald,* November 20, 1915.

GILMAN, LAWRENCE. "The Biography of an Amorist," *North American Review,* February, 1916.

HALE, EDWARD E. *Dial,* November 11, 1915.

HARRIS, FRANK.* "Mr. Sumner Under the Microscope," *Pearson's Magazine,* August, 1917.

KWIAT, JOSEPH. "Dreiser's *The 'Genius'* and Everett Shinn, the 'Ash Can Painter'," *PMLA,* March, 1952.

LENGEL, WILLIAM C. *International,* December, 1915.

LEONARD, BAIRD. N. Y. *Morning Telegraph,* October 2, 1915. Humorous poem.

LEWIS, ADDISON. "Dreiser's *Genius,*" *Bellman,* November 6, 1915.

M. A. A. *The Nation,* December 16, 1915. Letter.

MASTERS, EDGAR LEE. Chicago *Evening Post,* October 22, 1915.

McCORD, P. B. Los Angeles *Sun Times,* April 7, 1918. Caricature.

MENCKEN, H. L. "A Literary Behemoth," *Smart Set,* November, 1915.

MORDELL, ALBERT. Philadelphia *Record,* November 13, 1915.

Numerous American Authors.* "A Protest Against the Suppression of Theodore Dreiser's *The 'Genius,'* " undated 4-page pamphlet. Reprinted in McDonald, Edward D. *A Bibliography of the Writings of Theodore Dreiser.* Philadelphia, 1928.

POUND, EZRA.* "Dreiser Protest," *The Egoist,* October, 1916.

POWYS, JOHN COWPER. "Theodore Dreiser," *Little Review,* November, 1915.

QUENTIN, JOSEPH M. Portland *Oregonian,* October 10, 1915.

ROSENBLUM, JOSEPH.* "Candor or Secrecy," *Tomorrow,* June, 1918.

SAUNDERS, CHAUNCEY ELWOOD. Austin *Statesman,* October 28, 1923.

"The Scavanger." "The Dionysian Dreiser," *Little Review,* October, 1915.

SKIDELSKY, BERENICE C. *Book News Monthly,* January, 1916.

YEWDALE, MERTON STARK.* "Is Dreiser's *The 'Genius'* Immoral?," N. Y. *Sun,* February 24, 1918.

———. Forward to *The "Genius."* New York, 1923.

Chicago *Herald,* October 2, 1915.

N. Y. *Tribune,* October 2, 1915.

St. Louis *Globe-Democrat,* October 2, 1915.

Brooklyn *Eagle,* October 9, 1915.

St. Louis *Republican,* October 9, 1915.

Providence *Journal,* October 10, 1915.

Louisville *Courier-Journal,* October 25, 1915.

San Francisco *Bulletin,* November 6, 1915.

San Francisco *Argonaut,* November 13, 1915.

Chicago *Tribune,* December 4, 1915.

Minneapolis *Journal,* December 19, 1915.

*Los Angeles *Sun Times,* August 27, 1916.

*Boston *Evening Transcript,* September 2, 1916.

*N. Y. *Sun,* September 9, 1916.

*N. Y. *Tribune,* September 9 and 10, 1916.

*N. Y. *Sun*, October 14, 1916.
*Kansas City (Mo.) *Star*, October 18, 1916.
*Philadelphia *Public Ledger*, November 4, 1916.
Chicago *Examiner*, January 8, 1917.
*N. Y. *Morning Telegraph*, May 2, 1918.
*N. Y. *Sun*, May 2, 1918.
*Brooklyn *Eagle*, June 9, 1918.
*Philadelphia *Press*, July 21, 1918.

G. PLAYS OF THE NATURAL AND SUPERNATURAL (*1916*)

Anon. "Fourth Dimensional Dramas," San Francisco *Chronicle*, March 23, 1916.
———. "A New Dramatic Form," *Spectator*, February 3, 1917.
———. "Printed Plays," *Smart Set*, June, 1916.
———. "The Understanding of Mr. Dreiser," *The Nation*, October 12, 1916.
———. *Athenaeum*, November, 1916.
———. *Independent*, June 26, 1916.
———. *New England Magazine*, August, 1916.
———. *Review of Reviews*, May, 1916.
———. *Theatre*, July, 1917.
———. *Vogue*, October 15, 1916.
COLSON, ETHEL M. Chicago *Herald*, February 26, 1916.
D. L. M. Boston *Evening Transcript*, March 18, 1916.
JONES, LLEWELLYN. Chicago *Evening Post*, March 24, 1916.
MOSES, MONTROSE J. "Plays by Theodore Dreiser," *Book News Monthly*, May, 1916.
WOODBRIDGE, HOMER E. "Some Experiments in American Drama," *Dial*, May 17, 1917.

N. Y. *Globe*, February 26, 1916.
San Francisco *Call*, March 4, 1916.
N. Y. *Sun*, March 12, 1916.
Brooklyn *Eagle*, March 18, 1916.
Los Angeles *Times*, March 19, 1916.
Buffalo *Express*, March 26, 1916.
New Orleans *Times-Picayune*, March 26, 1916.
Louisville *Courier-Journal*, May 8, 1916.
Providence *Journal*, December 24, 1916.

H. THE HAND OF THE POTTER (*1918*)

Anon. "A Pathological Play," N. Y. *Medical Journal*, March 6, 1920.
———. "Tragedy and Trifles," *The Nation*, September 6, 1919.
———. *Dial*, September 20, 1919.

——. N. Y. *Times Book Review,* October 26, 1919.
——. *Outlook,* October 1, 1919.
BECKER, M. L. N. Y. *Evening Post,* October 25, 1919.
BENNETT, JESSEE LEE. "The Incomplete Skeptic," *NR,* October 8, 1919.
FOREST, BELFORD. Albany *Knickerbocker Press,* September 21, 1919.
HOLMES, RALPH F. Springfield (Mo.) *Morning Union,* October 26, 1919.
KARSNER, DAVID. N. Y. *Call,* December 6, 1919.
LEWISOHN, LUDWIG. "Year's End," *The Nation,* December 28, 1921.
NATHAN, GEORGE JEAN. "Dreiser's Play and Some Others," *Smart Set,* October, 1919.
RASCOE, BURTON. "Dreiser Shakes the Potter's Hand," Chicago *Tribune,* October 11, 1919.

N. Y. *Tribune,* September 6, 1919.
St. Louis *Republican,* September 8, 1919.
N. Y. *Review,* September 13, 1919.
N. Y. *American,* September 14, 1919.
Boston *Evening Transcript,* September 17, 1919.
N. Y. *Globe and Commercial Advertiser,* September 20, 1919.
Washington (D.C.) *Star,* September 21, 1919.
Detroit *News,* October 12, 1919.
Indianapolis *Star,* October 19, 1919.
Springfield *Republican,* October 26, 1919.

Selected reviews of the performance of *The Hand of the Potter* (1921-22) by the Provincetown Players.

Anon. *Greenwich Villager,* no date, University of Pennsylvania Dreiser Collection.
DE FOE, LOUIS. Philadelphia *Record,* December 18, 1921.
G. D. E. *Michigan Daily Magazine,* January 22, 1922.
LEWIN, ALBERT P. "Play Things," *Jewish Tribune,* December 16, 1921.
SCHAUERMANN, KARL. "The Devil's Playground and Work Shop," Milwaukee *Leader,* December 11, 1921.

N. Y. *Globe,* December 6, 1921.
N. Y. *Herald,* December 6, 1921.
N. Y. *Call,* December 8, 1921.
N. Y. *Call,* December 11, 1921. Illustrations.

I. TWELVE MEN (*1919*)

Anon. "American Types," *The Nation,* May 24, 1919.
——. "A Baker's Dozen of Dreiser Portraits," *Current Opinion,* June, 1919.
——. "Groups of Short Stories," *Independent,* March 22, 1919.

———. *A.L.A. Booklist,* July, 1919.

———. *North American Review,* October, 1919.

BALLOU, ROBERT. Introduction to *Twelve Men.* New York, 1928.

BROUN, HEYWOOD. N. Y. *Tribune,* April 26, 1919.

EDGETT, E. F. Boston *Evening Transcript,* April 30, 1919.

HARRIS, FRANK. *Pearson's Magazine,* July, 1919.

KARSNER, DAVID. *Call,* April 27, 1919.

M. A. *NR,* May 3, 1919.

MENCKEN, H. L. Baltimore *Sun,* April 13, 1919.

———. "Novels, Chiefly Bad," *Smart Set,* August, 1919.

POWYS, JOHN COWPER. "Real American Book by Genius is Star in Literary Heavens," San Francisco *Bulletin,* August 23, 1919.

RASCOE, BURTON. "Dreiser Gives Us His Best Effort in *Twelve Men,*" Source unknown, undated, University of Pennsylvania Dreiser Collection.

RUNYON, DAMON. N. Y. *American,* October 25, 1920.

WEBB, DORIS. *Publishers' Weekly,* March 15, 1919.

Newark *Evening News,* April 26, 1919.

N. Y. *Globe,* April 26, 1919.

N. Y. *Times Book Review,* April 27, 1919.

Boston *Evening Transcript,* April 30, 1919.

Baltimore *Evening Sun,* May 3, 1919.

N. Y. *Morning Telegraph,* May 3, 1919.

N. Y. *Evening Sun,* May 10, 1919.

San Francisco *Chronicle,* May 14, 1919.

Philadelphia *Press,* May 17, 1919.

Los Angeles *Times,* May 18, 1919.

N. Y. *American,* May 18, 1919.

Toledo *Daily Blade,* June 7, 1919.

Chicago *Post,* June 13, 1919.

Philadelphia *Ledger,* February 25, 1920.

J. HEY RUB-A-DUB-DUB (*1920*)

Anon. *Catholic World,* May, 1920.

———. *Dial,* September, 1920.

———. Springfield *Republican,* May 2, 1920.

BROOKS, VAN WYCK. "According to Dreiser," *The Nation,* May 1, 1920.

DE CASSERES, BENJAMIN. "Mr. Dreiser Talks of Many Things," N. Y. *Times Book Review,* April 11, 1920.

HACKETT, FRANCIS. "Mystery, Terror, and Confusion," *NR,* May 26, 1920.

MENCKEN, H. L. "More Notes From a Diary," *Smart Set,* May, 1920.

MEYER, ANNIE NATHAN. "Mr. Dreiser's Battle for Truth," *Review,* May 8, 1920.

K. A BOOK ABOUT MYSELF (*1922*)

Anon. *Catholic Review*, March, 1923.
————. *Modern Review*, April, 1923.
————. N. Y. *Times Book Review*, December 24, 1922.
BOYNTON, H. W. "Der Arme Theodor," *Independent*, February 3, 1923.
EDGETT, E. F. Boston *Evening Transcript*, December 30, 1922.
KRUTCH, JOSEPH WOOD. "Dreiser's Wanderjahre," N. Y. *Evening Post Literary Review*, January 20, 1923.
LEGALLIENNE, RICHARD. "Literary Sins of Theodore Dreiser," *Literary Digest International Book Review*, February, 1923.
LEIGHTON, EDITH. Boston *Evening Transcript*, December 30, 1922.
————. "Literary Confessions," *Bookman*, December, 1922.
MADOWSKY, THEODORE. *Forum*, April, 1923.
MENCKEN, H. L. "Adventures Among Books," *Smart Set*, March, 1923.
PEARSON, EDMUND L. *Independent*, January 6, 1923.
RASCOE, BURTON. "The Interesting Dullness of Dreiser's Life," N. Y. *Tribune*, December 31, 1922.

L. AN AMERICAN TRAGEDY (*1925*)

ALPERT, HOLLIS. "Double Bounty From Hollywood," *SRL*, September 1, 1951. Review of the film, "A Place in the Sun."
ANDERSON, SHERWOOD. "Dreiser," *SRL*, January 9, 1926.
Anon. "American Victory or Tragedy," *National Republic*, no date, University of Pennsylvania Dreiser Collection.
————. *America*, March 6, 1926.
————. *Journal of Sexology and Humanity*, October, 1926.
————. London *Times Literary Supplement*, October 7, 1926.
————. *Review of Reviews*, June, 1926.
————. *SRL*, February 20, 1926.
————. *Spectator*, October 9, 1926.
BAKSHY, ALEXANDER. "Emasculating Dreiser," *The Nation*, September 2, 1931.
BENCHLEY, ROBERT. "Compiling an American Tragedy," *Benchley Roundup*, selected by Nathaniel Benchley. New York, 1954.
BLAIR, EMILY NEWELL. "Some Books Worth While," *Good Housekeeping*, October, 1926.
BODENHEIM, MAXWELL. "On Writing," *SRL*, February 13, 1926.
BRENNECKE, ERNEST, JR. *Commonweal*, April 28, 1926.
CAHAN, ABRAHAM. "Dreiser's New Novel and What the Critics Say About It," *Jewish Forward*, January 4, 1926.
CRAWFORD, J. W. N. Y. *World*, January 10, 1926.
DARROW, CLARENCE. N. Y. *Evening Post Literary Review*, January 16, 1926.

DONNELLY, TOM. "A Great Film That Might Have Been," Washington *Daily News*, July 2, 1946.

DUFFUS, R. L. "Undisciplined Power," N. Y. *Times Book Review*, January 10, 1926.

E. M. K. *Sewanee Review*, October-December, 1926.

EDGETT, E. F. Boston *Evening Transcript*, January 9, 1926.

FARRAR, JOHN. *Bookman*, February and April, 1926.

FARRELL, JAMES T. "An American Tragedy," N. Y. *Times Book Review*, March 6, 1945.

FRANZ, ELEANOR WATERBURY. "The Tragedy of the 'North Woods,'" *New York Folklore Quarterly*, Summer, 1948.

FREEMAN, JOHN. *London Mercury*, October, 1927.

HARLEY, L. P. *SRL*, October 30, 1926.

HORWILL, H. W. "English Opinions of *An American Tragedy*," N. Y. *Times Book Review*, January 9, 1927.

JAFFRAY, NORMAN R. "American Tragedies," *Saturday Evening Post*, January 4, 1936. Humorous poem.

JONES, L. "An American Tragedy," *Current Reviews*, ed. Lewis W. Smith. New York, 1926.

KAYDEN, E. M. *Sewanee Review*, October, 1926.

KRUTCH, JOSEPH WOOD. "Crime and Punishment," *The Nation*, February 10, 1926.

LAWSON, W. ELSWORTH. Foxboro (Mass.) *Reporter*, January 16, 1926.

LEWIS, SINCLAIR. Kansas City (Mo.) *Buzz Saw*, January 28, 1926. Text of a talk delivered before a local Rotary Club.

LINSCOTT, R. N. *Atlantic Monthly*, March, 1926.

MATTHIESSEN, F. O. "Of Crime and Punishment," *Monthly Review*, October, 1950.

MENCKEN, H. L. "Dreiser in 840 Pages," *American Mercury*, March, 1926.

——. Introduction to *An American Tragedy*. Cleveland, 1948.

MOUNT, GRETCHEN. "Theodore Dreiser Surpasses Even Himself," Detroit *Free Press*, February 21, 1926.

MUIR, EDWIN. *Nation and Athenaeum*, October 16, 1926.

PALMER, ERWIN GEORGE. "Symbolic Imagery in Theodore Dreiser's *An American Tragedy*," Unpublished Ph.D. dissertation, Syracuse University, 1952.

PEARSON, EDMUND. *Outlook*, February 10, 1926.

PHELPS, WILLIAM LYON. "As I Like It," *Scribner's Magazine*, April, 1926.

PICHEL, IRVING. "Revivals, Reissues, Remakes, and 'A Place in the Sun,'" *Quarterly of Film, Radio, and Television*, Summer, 1952.

POWYS, JOHN COWPER. *Dial*, April, 1926.

RASCOE, BURTON. N. Y. *Sun*, January 9, 1926.

ROBERTS, R. E. "Theodore Dreiser," *London Bookman*, December, 1926.

SHAFER, ROBERT. "An American Tragedy," *Humanism and America*, ed. Norman Foerster. New York, 1930.

SHERMAN, STUART P. "Mr. Dreiser in Tragic Realism," N. Y. *Herald Tribune Books*, January 3, 1926. Reprinted in *The Main Stream*. New York and London, 1927.

STONG, PHIL D. Denver *Post*, November 28, 1926. Interview.

STUART, HENRY LOGAN. N. Y. *Times Book Review*, June 27, 1926.

TULLY, JIM. "Mr. Dreiser Writes An American Tragedy," *Literary Digest,* February, 1926.

WALKER, CHARLES R. "Dreiser Moves Upward," *Independent,* February 6, 1926.

WHIPPLE, T. K. *NR,* March 17, 1926.

WELLS, H. G. N. Y. *Times Magazine,* May 15, 1927.

WOOLLCOTT, ALEXANDER. "American Tragedy," in *The American Theatre As Seen By Its Critics, 1752-1934,* ed. M. J. Moses and J. M. Brown. New York, 1934.

YOUNG, STARK. "An American Tragedy," *NR,* November 3, 1926. A review of the play.

M. A GALLERY OF WOMEN (*1929*)

Anon. "Fair Women," *SRL,* April 19, 1930.

————. *Book League Monthly,* c. 1930, University of Pennsylvania Dreiser Collection.

————. *Plain Talk,* April, 1930.

————. *Spectator,* April 12, 1930.

————. *Theatre Guild,* 1930.

BROWN, ROLLO WALTER. "Fifteen Women," *SRL,* February 8, 1930.

DIVINE, CHARLES. N. Y. *Telegram,* November 30, 1929.

HANSEN, HARRY. "The First Reader," N. Y. *World,* November 30, 1929.

HOBSON, THAYER. N. Y. *Herald Tribune Books,* December 1, 1929.

KNIGHT, GRANT C. "A Gallery of Women," *Bookman,* November, 1929.

LINTOTT, H. J. B. *Nation and Athenaeum,* April 12, 1930.

MENCKEN, H. L. "Ladies, Mainly Sad," *American Mercury,* February, 1930.

PATERSON, ISABEL. N. Y. *Herald Tribune,* November 29, 1929.

RIDDELL, JOHN. "A Gallery of Dreiser," *Vanity Fair,* February, 1930.

ROSS, MARY. "Women in Fiction," *Atlantic Monthly,* April, 1930.

SOSKIN, WILLIAM. N. Y. *Evening Post,* November 29, 1929.

STOKES, W. N. Dallas *Morning News,* April 27, 1930.

YUST, WALTER. Philadelphia *Public Ledger,* December 2, 1929.

N. Y. *Times Book Review,* December 1, 1929.

Albany *Press,* January 19, 1930.

Syracuse *Post Standard,* January 19, 1930.

N. Y. *Herald Tribune,* April 10, 1930.

Fort Wayne *Journal-Gazette,* c. 1930, University of Pennsylvania Dreiser Collection.

N. DAWN (*1931*)

Anon. "An Appreciation of Dreiser's *Dawn,*" *Constable's Quarterly,* Summer, 1931.

————. *New Statesman and Nation,* October 3, 1931.

ARVIN, NEWTON. "An American Case History," *NR,* August 5, 1931.

CHAMBERLAIN, JOHN. "An American Record," *Forum,* July, 1931.

CHURCH, RICHARD. "The American Balzac," *Spectator,* July 25, 1931.

D. W. "Dawn," *Outlook and Independent,* May 27, 1931.

HANSEN, HARRY. "The First Reader," N. Y. *World Telegram,* May 8, 1931.

HAZLITT, HENRY. "Another Book About Himself," *The Nation,* June 31, 1931.

HERRICK, ROBERT. "Dreiseriana," *SRL,* June 6, 1931.

HERRMANN, JOHN. "Honest Autobiography," *New Masses,* September, 1931.

MENCKEN, H. L. "Footprints on the Sands of Time," *American Mercury,* July, 1931.

PETERSON, ISABEL. N. Y. *Herald Tribune,* May 8, 1931.

RASCOE, BURTON. "Dreiser's Early Youth," N. Y. *Sun,* May 10, 1931.

SOSKIN, WILLIAM. "Books on Our Table," N. Y. *Evening Post,* May 8, 1931.

THOMPSON, ALAN REYNOLDS. *Bookman,* July, 1931.

WILDES, HARRY EMERSON. Philadelphia *Public Ledger,* May 7, 1931.

New York American, May 4, 1931.

Rochester *Times-Union,* June 4, 1931.

O. THE BULWARK (*1946*)

Anon. "Bulwark Has a History," *Publishers' Weekly,* March 2, 1946.

———. "Reading," *Town and Country,* August, 1946.

———. *Bulletin of the Virginia Kirkus Bookshop Service,* January 15, 1946.

———. *Promenade,* May, 1946.

———. *Religious Book Club Bulletin,* Summer, 1946.

———. *Virginia Quarterly Review,* Summer, 1946.

B. G. *Writers' Markets and Methods,* May, 1946.

BROWN, CARROLL T. "Dreiser's Bulwark and Philadelphia Quakerism," *Friends Historical Association Bulletin,* Autumn, 1946.

CAMPBELL, HARRY M. "A New Dreiser," *Western Review,* Winter, 1947.

GARDINER, HAROLD C. "Faith and Worldliness," *America,* April 6, 1946.

GREGORY, HORACE. "In the Large Stream . . ." N. Y. *Herald Tribune Book Review,* March 24, 1946.

KENNEDY, JOHN S. "Fiction in Focus: *The Bulwark,*" *Sign,* May, 1946.

M. J. C. "Religion Faces Life's Pressures," *Jewish Bookland,* September-October, 1946.

MATCH, RICHARD. *Tomorrow,* June, 1946.

POORE, CHARLES. "Books of the Times," N. Y. *Times,* March 21, 1946.

PRESCOTT, ORVILLE. "Outstanding Novels," *Yale Review,* June, 1946.

PUCCIANI, ORESTE. *World in Books,* June, 1946.

SEAVER, EDWIN. *Book Find News,* March, 1946.

STEINBACH, HERBERT. *Cresset,* July, 1946.

TJADER, MARGUERITE. "Dreiser's Last Year—*The Bulwark* in the Making," *Book Find News,* March, 1946.

WADE, MASON. *Commonweal,* June 14, 1946.

WILSON, EDMUND. "Theodore Dreiser's Quaker and Graham Greene's Priest," *New Yorker,* March 23, 1946.